Whole Bible Christianity

Blessings Pressed Down And Overflowing

An Adventure in Discovering How Following All of God's Word Will Change Your Life

Whole Bible Christianity
Blessings Pressed Down and Overflowing

Published by
The Word of God Ministries

© 2016 Bruce S. Bertram
All rights reserved

This book may not be reproduced in whole or in part without the express written consent of the author or his agent.

www.wholebible.com
Youtube channel The Whole Bible Christian

ISBN 978-0-9975014-1-4

Printed in the United States of America

Cover art ©2016 Bruce S. Bertram

Front cover art title: Proclaiming the Word

Table of Contents

Introduction 1

1 The Whole Picture 7
    Reintroducing Whole Bible Christianity 10
    The Original Four-Letter Word 14
    The Heart of the New Covenant 15
    The Believer's Daily Bread 18
    Which Law? 20
    Law AND Grace 22
    Law Under Grace 23
    Faith 24
    The Rejection of the New Covenant 27
    Who Put the Church in Charge? 30
    Street Theology 34
    Shadows and Copies 36
    One Continuous Promise 37
    What did Jesus do? 39
    Salvation by Love 41

2 A Whole God 45
    God is One 46
    Jesus is God 47
    The Seed of the Woman 49
    Jesus in the Old Testament 51
    Old, Jewish God? 52
    Sin 54
    Idolatry 56
    Mixing 59
    Fear 60
    Humility and Pride 63
    Salvation, Purgatory and Worms 65
    Love 71
    Grace 74
    Unconditional Love and Tolerance 76
    Repentance 78
    A Personal God 79

3 A Whole Body 83
    The Modern Church 85
    A New Old Thing 86
    Israel in Three 89

- The Mixed Multitude ... 91
- Strangers in the Mix ... 92
- I Will Build My Ecclesia ... 94
  - The Remnant or Elect ... 95
  - The Kingdom of God ... 97
  - The Olive Tree ... 97
- The Presence of the Holy Spirit ... 99
- The Jews? ... 100
  - Judaism ... 101
  - The Messianic Movement ... 103
  - Roots ... 103
- Growing pains ... 104
- The Nicolaitans ... 105
- Tradition ... 113
- The Other Anointing ... 114
- It's a God Thing ... 117

4 A Whole Faith ... 119
- A Continuous Message ... 119
- Continuous through generations ... 120
- Law before Law ... 123
- The Promise ... 127
- The Foundational Testament ... 131
- The Natural Man and Spiritual Relevance ... 133
- Six Assumptions about Bible Interpretation ... 136
  - One. It is the Highest Authority. ... 138
  - Two. It Reveals God's Will and Plans. ... 138
  - Three. It is Clear. ... 139
  - Four. It Means What He intends. ... 141
  - Five. It is Self Explaining. ... 144
  - Six. It Requires a Response. ... 144
- Can The Bible Be Trusted? ... 146

5 A Whole Heart ... 149
- The New Covenant ... 149
  - What It Is ... 150
  - What It Was ... 151
  - What It Shall Be ... 152
- Living in the New Testament Synagogue ... 153
- Commandment Math Made Easy ... 155
- Living with God as Our Center ... 158
- The Gospel ... 160
- Inherit Eternal Life ... 162
- Free Will ... 163
- What About the Temple? ... 165

God's Barbecue 168
The Order of Melchizedek 170
The Temple Rebuilt 172
Choose Life 174

6 A Whole Bible 175
The (Second) Sermon on the Mount and the Law 176
   Examples of Fulfilling the Law 177
The Testing of Jesus and the Law 179
   The Test on Signs 179
   The Test on Divorce 181
   The Test On Paying Taxes 182
   The Test On The Greatest Command 183
   The Test On Stoning the Adulteress 183
The Acts 15 Council and the Law 185
Paul Teaches the Law 188
   Paul Governs Stepmother Relations by the Law 188
   Paul Corrects Passover Observance 190
   Paul Teaches the Validity of Circumcision 190
   Paul Judges Romans 14 Opinions by the Law 191
   Paul Nails the Law in Colossians 2 194
   Paul Justifies the Law to the Galatians 196
   Paul Knocks Down the Wall with the Law 198
Spirit and Law 199

7 Whole Bible Objections 201
"All I Commanded You" (Not) 201
Only the Moral 203
Paul Tells Us It Is Okay 204
Can't Do the Law 205
It's a Curse 207
Nailed To The Cross 208
It's Legalism 210
Works of The Law Are Bad 211
Not Under the Law 213
No Punishment 215
No Pay 216
It's Judaizing 217
The Crucifixion 218
It's a Shadow 219
It's All Good (Genesis 9, Acts 10) 220
Freedom In Christ 223
Salvation Is Enough 224
I Don't Hear Jesus 225

    Lifting Jesus Up 225
    It's Not Restated 227

8 Whole Bible Blessings 230
    Connects 230
    Justice 232
    Protects 234
    Moves 234
    Straightens 235
    Perfect Practice 236
    Universal 236
    Life Abundant 237
    It Marks His Children 238
    Best Discipleship Method Ever 239
    Teaches Children 241
    Esteems God 242
    Draw near, Touch God 243
    Still a Tutor 244
    The Fruit of The Spirit 246
    He's in There 247
    An Effective Mirror 248
    The Key to Understanding 249
    It's Love 250
    It's Worship 251
    Trains Our Hearing 253
    Helps Prayer 254
    Putting On Christ 255
    Restores integrity 256
    What's The Big Deal? 256

9 Whole Bible Instruction 258
    1. Read the Word 259
    2. Do the Word 263
    3. Hold Still the Word 264
    4. Live on the Word 267
    5. Test God by the Word 268
    6. Worship with the Word 270
    7. Follow the Leaders of the Word 271
    8. Value the Word 273
    9. Weigh the Word 274
    10. Investigate the Word 275
    11. Judge with the Word 278
    12. Balance the Word 280
    Do What Jesus Did 282

10 Whole Bible Applications 284
A New Definition of Cult 284
The Feasts of Jesus 288
Sabbath 288
Passover 290
Pentecost 291
The Feast of Trumpets 291
Atonement 291
Tabernacles 292
The Calendar 292
Food 292
Tassels 293
Tithe and Money 294
Circumcision 295
Clean and Unclean 297
Sex 299
Vows 300
Stuff That Is Not Commanded 300
Head Coverings 301
Day of Meeting 301
Christmas and Easter 301
Two Sacraments 303
Meat and Dairy 303
Drinking Alcohol 304
Bad Things And Good People 305
Our True Identity 309
Represent 311
Torah Tyrants 313
Rest On The Rock 313

Acknowledgements 315

Scripture Index 316

Introduction

It's popular nowadays to try and help people connect with God and with each other in the body of Christ. Many books promise delivery of methods or keys for touching Jesus and making Him more real in a believer's life. Truck loads of self-help books say that if you'll just follow their simple steps you'll see more fruit of the Spirit or improve the quality of your walk with Jesus. Some of the books recognize that the world is going to pieces and that there is a need for repentance, a word that means "return," but authors are a little vague about where exactly we should return. Parts of the Bible are used in some of the books. Some of the advice works some of the time. A little of it works more often. Too much of it depends on sentiment which is as changeable as the weather. None of it is as complete or effective as God's whole and complete Word.

I didn't just want to write this book, I had to. I struggled for years, as a lot of people do, trying to connect with God in more intimate and personal ways and make changes in myself. I read the books, listened to the teachings claiming to help and tried to implement them, followed church tradition faithfully, and got advice from all sorts of church leaders. Over the years I've regularly attended more than 15 churches in 10 different denominations. But the Bible seemed hard to read and understand, and the fruit of the Spirit just didn't want to "fruit" in me like the Bible said (and I thought) it should. In spite of lengthy helpful explanations from pastors and other leaders, and the self help books, something was missing.

Then I discovered a way to connect with God that is so simple, and makes the Bible so clear, I got as excited as I did when I was saved. All I had to do was accept the terms of the New Covenant and follow the instructions of Jesus in John 6:53 through 58 (among others). Allow the Spirit to write His Law on my heart of flesh, then keep it going by eating His body and drinking His blood (hear and obey). Sounds easy, and it is. It only gets complicated if you pay attention to the self help books!

As this purpose to drive my life took root His words have come alive. Connections with God are increasing every day, the fruit of His Spirit is sprouting all over, and intimacy with Him is getting deeper all the time. So I just had to share it with others. This discovery I call whole Bible Christianity. I should say "rediscovery." It's been around for a long time. The first century church was all about the whole Bible for instance. The Reformation recovered some of it. I just didn't see it for two reasons: one was the human tendency to hide from God, and the other was that I was actually guided away from it by the self help books, church tradition and dogmatic teaching.

God has the best method and the keys to connect with Him and each other already laid out for us in His Word. It's the God-help book. He's got everything: love, life, light, forgiveness, blessing, love, truth, fruit of the Spirit, love and righteousness, all in concrete easy-to-follow steps connecting us and Him together. Did I mention love? Because God is all about love. Every word He speaks is packed full and overflowing with love. Sadly, many who wear the Name in the modern world are leaving His Word or parts of His Word behind in the quest for self-seeking.

We need the whole of His Word, every part, in order to touch Him fully and feel His touch everywhere in every corner of our lives. When we only take in part of His Word, we only get part of His love. It's like looking through a crack in the door to the light, life and love of His kingdom instead of walking in and bathing in all He has to offer. The measure we use with Him is the measure He uses when giving abundant life.

> "Judge not, and you will not be judged; condemn not, and you will not be condemned; forgive, and you will be forgiven; give, and it will be given to you. Good measure, pressed down, shaken together, running over, will be put into your lap. For with the measure you use it will be measured back to you." (Luke 6:37–38, ESV. See also Matthew 7:2 and Mark 4:24)

This book will help you realize that all of the Word and all of its blessings are for every believer, all the time, no matter what. I'm going to show you a different viewpoint than is typically offered in the church that connects His Words together and makes it easy to abide in those Words. You'll learn how to take in the whole of His Word and through it connect to God and other members of the Body of Christ more easily than you ever thought possible. Hold onto your hat and get ready for an influx of abundant life pressed down, shaken together, running over, suffused and overflowing with His love and truth. His Word works.

Believers do not have the information they need to take in all of His Words and act on them because much of the book advice or church teaching steers us away from large sections. Negative teaching on His Word abounds, especially on His Law. For instance, the Bible in some corners is thought to be from two different gods; a harsh and demanding god of blood in the Old Testament and a relevant permissive god of love in the New Testament. Or ignoring Paul's teaching that there is only one Father, one Savior, one faith, and one body (Ephesians 4:4-6), some of His Word is deemed to be for two different "bodies:" the old stuff is for Jews and new stuff for Christians. So most believers can't think of large parts of His Word without nervously shrinking back from "rules and regulations" or "religion" or "laws." This leads to practices such as watered down "seeker friendly" methods of holding our Sunday meetings. As if somehow God's Word alone is not seeker friendly.

On the contrary, His God-help book is the ultimate in seeker friendliness. It has a lot to do with how we view it. A heart of stone looks at His words as laws imposed from the outside and so resists them like stone is resistant to a chisel. But a heart of flesh, given to us through the New Covenant signed with His Word by the Spirit, sees His Word as life and love and longs to take it all in and act on it. Following it becomes a normal, loving response to the love given to us by Him in the first place. His Word converts our hearts from stone to flesh, if we submit to it in humility. To a heart of flesh, law is "living oracles."

God offers you many benefits in whole Bible Christianity. Freedom will come when you realize that all of the Word is yours. God's Word in your life will set boundaries which promote safety and security, while acting also as defenses against those who would make you give up His blessings. If you want to let more of His light in by resting on Saturday, changing your diet, or celebrating a holiday as He directs, you can do it and no one using church tradition or philosophies of men can take it from you. This is the true meaning of Colossians 2:16.

Your identity as a child in God's household will be plain and rock solid, whether you go to a church or not. No one will be able to tell you that if you don't go to church, or their church, you are not in the body of Christ. If you can't attend, because they won't let you due to your insistence on following the Word, or because of their hypocrisy, you can still enjoy intimacy with your Father and Messiah. Every time you choose not to eat pork or shellfish, you reinforce your identity as His son or daughter. Your identity is not tied up in a church or synagogue, but in Him.

As you weave each of His commands into the fabric of your life the threads of intimacy between you and your Father will increase and His presence will be real and ever stronger. Touching God, and God touching you, will be a daily occurrence. Fruit of the Spirit follows a whole Bible way of life, naturally popping out all over, because His Word resides in your new heart of flesh. The proof is in your pursuit of His ways. The end result of all this will be the peace of the presence of God. He is where His Word is; where people are worshiping Him in Spirit and truth.

Whole Bible Christianity simplifies walking with God and producing the fruit of the Spirit. It will strengthen faith with the best discipleship system ever devised. I'll show you how to easily connect with God in more intimate ways on a minute-by-minute basis, simply by trading all of your heart for all of His. It's not my program, it's His. It's all right there in your Bible. Whole Bible Christianity clears up what has become a cracked picture of God and His Word by showing the unity of the Bible message, with over 800 verses directly quoted in the book (and over 1,400 in the index) along with His keys to understanding and walking the Word as a whole.

Searching people will want this book because it is in contrast to unsatisfying modern church teachings. There are lots of people (George Barna of Barna Research www.barna.org estimated 20 million at one point) who are Christians but do not go to church. They're turned off by hypocritical soft-soaped seeker friendly social justice teachings contrary to the Bible. They're hungry and thirsty and wandering in a desert of ear-tickling messages. They are looking for the real thing. In whole Bible Christianity you will be reassured that the Bible is the real thing, and all you have to do is read it and do it.

In an age when the constant hammering on the authority and absolute truth of God's Word has become deafening, <u>Whole Bible Christianity</u> takes a stand against the 'spiritual but not religious' teachings current in the church, and we decry the false idea of 'social justice' that is replacing biblical truth for many. We advocate reading and heeding the whole of the Word as the body and blood of Jesus, including the Law with its feasts and helps for daily living.

There was a lot of thought and prayer that went into the name and concept of whole Bible Christianity. We were trying to tie a lot of biblical concepts into a complete package, with an instantly descriptive name. Some names that we used at first just didn't have quite the meaning we wanted them to have. The answer to prayer came when we realized one of the main difficulties in the church is that much of the Bible only gets lip service.

Some have used, or will use, "whole Bible" in a different way than we do. This is due to a limited definition of "belief." For many, belief is simply mental agreement with an idea, as in "I believe there's a God." But biblical belief, I discovered, has a deeper dimension. Read this book and you will figure out why.

Every thought I have was given to me by someone else. I don't claim any unique knowledge. It's all right there in the Bible already recorded. A part of this book comes from what I recognize as truth in the various church teachings (or self help books) to which I've been exposed. You might recognize some teaching from your own denomination or school of thought. I'm just clearing away some of the underbrush and assembling the pieces in a biblical way so you can get more of what you need. Many of the subjects I just touch on could have their own books, or even a shelf of books. I can't cover all of it in one. If I tried, you'd need a wheelbarrow to cart the book around. Even if it was electronic.

I believe the root of almost every controversy in the church right now is really about whether we should obey the Law or not, and if so how much of it applies. That's right where things seem to go fuzzy for everyone. It's been that way since the first command was given to Adam and Eve. In the first chapter, however, I point out how God clears up the fuzziness with the New Covenant. Rightly understood (um, just read it) it is the Law written on a new heart of flesh by the Spirit. Fuzziness clears right up when we read and follow His Word instead of the words of pastors or best-selling authors alone.

The second, third, and fourth chapters of this book have parts of Ephesians 4:4-6 (one God, one Lord, one Body, and one faith) as their starting point. Chapter 2 is about God and Jesus as one and the same. Chapter 3 speaks of the one Body of the Christ, and emphasizes the inherent unity of all believers throughout history. Chapter 4 concerns the single faith of the Body, which in this case is the Bible. Chapter 5 looks at the new covenant and what it really means. The last four chapters explain New Testament examples of Law, biblical answers to unbiblical objections against whole Bible Christianity, blessings from it, and applications of it.

There might be some strong statements that seem in-your-face or blunt to you, or you might detect some irritation here and there. It gets exasperating dealing with the bureaucracies of the churches. It's not so bad if people want to have a club; there has to be some club rules here and there. But I know firsthand what it feels like for religious leaders to slam doors.

> "But woe to you, scribes and Pharisees, hypocrites! For you shut the kingdom of heaven in people's faces. For you neither enter yourselves nor allow those who would enter to go in." (Matthew 23:13, ESV)

I write both as a warning and encouragement. The warning is that many have drifted from God and need to repent and come back to the whole of His Word. The encouragement is for those individuals who have repented or who would repent but cannot find guidance. Some might just need a helping hand and a little affirmation that they are headed in the right direction. So if I can heal the splits in our picture of God, and in His Word and His Body, and assist people in grabbing hold of what God is, then I will count my efforts successful. And who knows? Maybe the warning will be heeded, too. But if people will not listen to God's Words, why would they listen to mine?

> [10] To whom shall I speak and give warning That they may hear? Behold, their ears are closed And they cannot listen. Behold, the word of the LORD has become a reproach to them; They have no delight in it. (Jeremiah 6:10 NASB95)

Along the way, we are going to biblically refresh word definitions and revisit basic concepts, because many words have been redefined by part-bibleists wrongly. With the Spirit, we will unmask His riches and find the heart of the new covenant. When we have the foundation together, we will gain stability and blessings as we learn to make our stand on The Rock. Then we won't be blown about by stray winds of fads or feelings. The fruit of the Spirit that seems so hard to produce under standard church teachings will multiply to you 30, 60, or a hundred fold.

Crunch time is here. Things are heating up in the world, and it ain't global warming. Jesus is coming back in judgment soon. Lines are being drawn sharply between good and evil.

> [10] "Many will be purged, purified and refined, but the wicked will act wickedly; and none of the wicked will understand, but those who have insight will understand. (Daniel 12:10 NASB95)

The salvation of the church, the return to the first century model, is in re-embracing the whole, absolute truth of the Word of God. I hope we heed His encouragement to forsake our foolish ways, turn around, and partake fully of His life giving body and blood. Then maybe we can lead the way out of our culture rot and moral freefall. Thank you for taking the time to read, and may our Father bless your reading and doing of His Word. Nearly all puns are intended. As they say in the seventh Narnia book, "Further up and further in!"

1 The Whole Picture

"Behold, the days are coming, declares the Lord, when I will make a new covenant with the house of Israel and the house of Judah, not like the covenant that I made with their fathers on the day when I took them by the hand to bring them out of the land of Egypt, my covenant that they broke, though I was their husband, declares the Lord. For this is the covenant that I will make with the house of Israel after those days, declares the Lord: I will put my law within them, and I will write it on their hearts. And I will be their God, and they shall be my people. And no longer shall each one teach his neighbor and each his brother, saying, 'Know the Lord,' for they shall all know me, from the least of them to the greatest, declares the Lord. For I will forgive their iniquity, and I will remember their sin no more." (Jeremiah 31:31–34, ESV. See also Exodus 20:6; Deuteronomy 5:10; Ezekiel 11:19-21)

The Garden of Eden was a perfect place within a perfect creation. Birds, plants, trees, animals and people were healthy and growing at phenomenal rates. The sweetest, nutritionally perfect food grew all over and didn't need work to produce. It just waited to be plucked and eaten. The weather was exactly what you'd ask for in paradise. There was only one season having a blend of mist from the ground to water plants and a sun that was bright but didn't burn. Cloud and sun and temperature were so well balanced people didn't need houses. The oxygen content and the air pressure were high enough people could run all day and not get tired.[1] They played with lions or dinosaurs and there was no hurt. Bees didn't sting, mosquitoes didn't bite. There was no harm anywhere. No death or even the shadow of death, no disease, no worry and no stress.

We worked for the enjoyment of working in the Garden, and we didn't have to pay a mortgage or buy food. There was no need for insurance or utility payments. Pollution, decay, and filth did not exist. We didn't age, and we could live for a long time. Since there was no death (and no time), that meant a very, very long time.

Then Adam and Eve disobeyed God by eating the wrong piece of fruit. Through this simple act sin and death entered our perfect paradise and destroyed it. We now live short lives in a wrecked world full of toil, sweat, thorns, pain and sorrow. It didn't take much to go from perfection

---

[1] Some of this comes from a DVD series by Creation Science Seminars and Dr. Kent Hovind, specifically volume 2 'The Garden of Eden' and volume 6 'The Hovind Theory.'

to cursed existence. All it took was the breaking of one small dietary command.

It really was a simple Law that Adam and Eve disobeyed. But the deceiver explained in his theology that of course God didn't really mean what He said. The father of lies deftly twisted the plain meaning of God's word from "thou shall not" to "he's just afraid you'll become like him!" Eve bit on the reasoning and shared some with her husband. Ever since, God's Laws have been getting similar helpful explanation. Satan has had centuries to refine his twisted theology, and like bad scenes in a TV drama the church has repeatedly bitten on the arguments over and over. In recent years especially the church has taken great pains to explain large portions of God's unchangeable Word into non-existence with arguments straight from the mouth of the serpent. Arguments such as, "Jesus fulfilled and eliminated much of the Law with His death;" "it's shadows;" "Jesus made everything clean;" "we don't have to obey if it's only civil or ceremonial," and the ever popular "it's not a salvation issue." If you listen close you can sometimes even hear the hissing.

Those who see through the theology and won't bite on the false reasoning (again) instead accept the plain meaning of the New Covenant (see above). If you'll notice, it has two parts. One is a heart of flesh that is soft and responsive to God, and the other is His Law. That's right. The new covenant is The Law written on a soft heart. Not parts of the Law – all of it. Not helpful explanations – just His simple truth. No shadows – it's all substantial. No splits – it's a continuation. An identical application of Law in every heart baptized into one body. The fulfillment of the Law is when it is written on a new heart of flesh by God in love. Ezekiel, who lived around the same time as Jeremiah, added that God will give a new spirit, and the Holy Spirit will cause believers to walk in God's statutes and abide in His oracles.

> And I will give you a new heart, and a new spirit I will put within you. And I will remove the heart of stone from your flesh and give you a heart of flesh. And I will put my Spirit within you, and cause you to walk in my statutes and be careful to obey my rules. (Ezekiel 36:26–27, ESV)

Jeremiah and Ezekiel were written about 600 years before Christ, and everyone knew what "my statutes" meant. Just like Adam and Eve knew the one command in the Garden. It is none other than the living oracles, as Stephen called them in Acts 7:38, the ones given at Mt. Sinai by God through Moses. It is what Jesus called "my commandments" in John 14:15, 21 and 15:10.

Adam and Eve did not need a Law for salvation. They were already "saved." So why give them a Law? Everything was already perfect, and they were children of the King. They didn't need a "law" because it wasn't a "law." It was instruction for living. All they had to do was *abide in His Word* and things would've continued. That's what God is telling us to do even now – abide in His Word. In a way, paradise is provided again through Jesus, and all we have to do is accept and abide in His covenant like we should've in the Garden. The new covenant is a restoration of intimacy with God and a path back to His paradise.

Sounds easy, doesn't it? Except the modern church has lost sight of the New Covenant. We can see this in the fact that our church does not resemble the first century church very well. Many of the blessings of the new covenant that the first century church enjoyed have gone missing. The blessings are gone like those in the Garden of Eden because we don't abide in God's Law. We do not teach and live the entire Word of God as Adam and Eve wish they had or as the first century believers. If you don't believe me try getting answers to some questions like these next ones I've asked of many different teachers in my search for those missing blessings.

- Why does Hebrews 4:2 describe what was given at Mount Sinai as "the gospel?"
- Why is the New Covenant in the Old Testament?
- What is the existing olive tree believers are grafted into? (Romans 9-11)
- How come I need so much explanation from pastors to understand the Bible?
- Why rebuild the Temple (Ezekiel 40-47) and start up sacrifices during the millennium when Jesus is reigning on the earth?
- How can Paul say he is a model of a law-following Jew (Philippians 3:4-6) and at the same time a follower of Christ?
- If God and Jesus are one, didn't Jesus give the Law to Moses at Sinai?
- Why does Paul (1 Cor. 4:6) say not to go "beyond what is written" when the New Testament wasn't written at the time?
- How did Paul teach about Jesus from "the Law and the Prophets?" (Acts 28:23)
- What did first century believers use as a guide for living out their faith?
- Why is it the modern church does not look or act like the first century church?
- What does it mean to "believe" in Jesus and how can I increase my faith?

I don't know how you'll do, but I haven't been too successful getting answers to these questions. Well, I should say I get lots of answers.

Answers from men's knowledge I've got coming out my ears. Bible answers from men not so much.

Through years of reading the Word, studying systematic theologies, going to many different types of churches (like I said, 15 churches in 10 different denominations by the time I was 40) and searching every type of book that promised to connect me to the truth of God's Word, I discovered whole Bible Christianity. Right there in the Bible. It was present the entire time; I just couldn't see it because of wrong teaching, tradition, and some of my own hard-headedness. It answers all the questions and restores the missing blessings. I think first century believers lived a whole Bible life, which is why they were so successful. This book is a guide to reclaiming that spirit.

There's a general sense in many thoughtful people now of a need for repentance. Popular books like The Harbinger by Jonathan Cahn discuss it. Mega-Church pastors (current and former) are warning of it, such as Mark Driscoll in his book A Call To Resurgence: Will Christianity Have a Funeral or a Future? Even if you don't believe in God there's still an awareness that the world is going in the wrong direction. The preaching of repentance is a good thing, and I agree it's needed. Repentance means turning around, but those preaching it aren't very exact about where to turn. They'll say we should "go back to the Bible" or "back to God" but what does that look like? Whole Bible Christianity is a little more specific. We need to return to all of His Words. Every single one. Including the Law. After all, we are the ones who began the drift away from His Word in the first place. We are the ones with the "helpful explanations" explaining how many different ways we think God didn't really mean what He says. We are the ones who have led the way into the current moral decline.

Reintroducing Whole Bible Christianity

Whole Bible Christianity is moving back to living the entire Bible literally. It is the practical outworking of the new covenant. Though first century believers didn't use the term "whole Bible" I think it's obvious that they lived the whole Bible (1 Corinthians 7:19). They lived the new covenant; therefore they lived the whole Bible.

Many churches have tried to recapture that spirit with practices such as "baptisms" (as in baptism of the Holy Spirit), "cell groups," home Bible studies, or "new wine in new wineskins" (meaning split off and start a new church). Others try to get us interested in a "social Jesus" who apparently ditched all the rules from His Father and prefers a hipper image disconnected from anything old. In general, we haven't succeeded in the same way the first century church did. We've achieved some growth in numbers, new wineskins turn into mega-churches, and to some the picture of Jesus is much more relevant. But these are not the same as growth in the Spirit.

Too often the efforts just shift the furniture around, like rearranging the deck chairs on the Titanic. Recapturing the first century spirit doesn't come through gimmicks. There's more to a walk with Him than just rearranging the furniture or ripping out the carpet. Ditching church rules is fine. If you hate religion but love Jesus that's great. It's not a matter of "rules;" it's a matter of life. We need to repent of our own knowledge and recover our whole Bible belief. Embrace God's rules. Man's teachings have pushed out the Bible or at least parts of the Bible, taken over the church, and sidetracked our commission (Matthew 28:19, 20). A bold statement perhaps, but one I'm going to back up with almost 1,400 Scriptures in this book.

> "The Word of God well understood and religiously obeyed is the shortest route to spiritual perfection. And we must not select a few favorite passages to the exclusion of others. Nothing less than a whole Bible can make a whole Christian." A.W. Tozer

Whole Bible belief and practice makes a whole Christian. Whole Bible Christians accept the Bible as the highest authority. It is absolute truth which reveals God and His will in plain, easy to understand language, and it means what the Author intended. Whole Bible Christianity is sort of a do-it-yourself (or really, do-it-Himself) walk which doesn't need a charismatic leader, a nice building, a sinner's prayer, or permission from someone to pursue. All it takes is you and God. You just put one foot in front of the other and follow His footsteps. Read and heed His Word. He gives believers a new heart of flesh, His Word and the Spirit. What else do we need?

"What's the big deal, Bruce?" you ask. "I'm a Christian and I believe the whole Bible too. Doesn't every Christian?" Um, maybe not. You mightn't think a book like this was needed, until you take a hard look at what has happened in the church and realize what whole Bible Christianity really is. The Reformation (in the 1,400's) was fueled by people who compared the first century church in Acts from their freshly translated, common-language Bibles to the church of their times. They found their church to be sorely lacking. We need to do the same thing now. So hold up a minute and hear me out. We're going to do some translating and comparing too. You might think different after a look at the whole picture.

Whole Bible Christianity follows in the footsteps of the first century church and imitates Christ (and Paul, and Peter, and James and John...), so we include such things as God's feasts or holy days (Exodus 23:14;

Leviticus 23; 1 Corinthians 11; Luke 22) diet changes (Leviticus 11; Acts 15), and Sabbath (Genesis 1; Acts 13:14, 42, 44, 16:13, 17:2, 18:4). It's not about rules, though. It's about God's living oracles. Every instruction is taken seriously, and no opportunity to abide in His Word is overlooked. We don't re-explain it out of existence. We don't add helpful explanations effectively making God out to be a liar.

Some of His instructions we can't follow because we don't have a government that follows God's Law. Others we can't do because we don't have a Temple. Some laws are for males, some are for females, and some are just for priests. But we diligently search and try to apply all that we can. This is a different mentality than is commonly found in the church today.

If you read the New Testament carefully, this is what the first century believers were doing (including making offerings at the Temple Acts 8:27; 21:26). Those believers did not think the Law nullified the work of Jesus on the cross, but that the cross and His Law complement each other. He is the end or goal of the Law. His death paid the penalty for disobedience of the Law. He gives us the Spirit and a new heart of flesh with His Law or Word written on it. Freedom in Christ means that we don't labor under the death penalty if we make a mistake. It's His Word we're living, after all. This puts a much different light on the meaning of whole Bible.

We got kicked out of the Garden and were given a death sentence because we broke one command, eating fruit from the wrong tree. That was it. Seemingly minor, but apparently not so to God. We had it all there. A perfect place to live, perfect companionship, and a perfect walk with our loving Father. One apparently tiny act of disobedience to His Law wrought all the sin, pain and misery we experience today. Makes you think that perhaps a little disobedience is really not so "little" after all.

For many, following the entire Bible including the Law is not comfortable; scary even. It seems antiquated or too "Jewish." It's so last year. It ain't hip, it ain't happenin. To these people the Law is some old hard set of rules from a stern and unyielding God who forces us to do things that aren't reasonable or relevant anymore. Or that He didn't really mean what He said.

But actually His Law is wonderful, positive and loving, relevant, universal, love and life. It is health, a lamp and a light. Just like God. The Hebrew word for the Law is "torah" which means instruction, and every word He speaks is designed to instruct us in love. When we do what He says we love Him back. Whole Bible believers include The Law in our walk with a loving God because it's part of, well, the whole Bible. We call His instructions "law," but it isn't a negative thing unless we go against it. All the words God says are Law, and they are eternal.

The Law is a problem for many Christians partly because of our natural tendency to hide from God, and partly that we've been taught to avoid it. Spurgeon said[2] "law has a tendency to make man rebel." The fault lies in the heart, not the Law. We've been told the Law is not for the church, it's only for Jews, it's been done away with, or we can't do it. We're taught so many negative things about the Law that we just dismiss the subject every time it's brought up. But the Bible says the Law is for the church (His body, anyway) it's not just for Jews, it hasn't been eliminated, and we *can* do it. For instance, early on Israel is told that the Law is not out of their reach, and that it is life and blessings.

> "For this commandment that I command you today is not too hard for you, neither is it far off. It is not in heaven, that you should say, 'Who will ascend to heaven for us and bring it to us, that we may hear it and do it?' Neither is it beyond the sea, that you should say, 'Who will go over the sea for us and bring it to us, that we may hear it and do it?' But the word is very near you. It is in your mouth and in your heart, so that you can do it. (Deuteronomy 30:11–14, ESV)

Paul quotes from this text in Romans 10, especially that "the word is near you, in your mouth and in your heart." He also tells us in Romans 7 that the Law is "holy," "righteous," "good," and "spiritual." The problems are not due to the Law, but to hearts inclined to self-righteousness.

Church leaders have come up with all sorts of helpful explanations as to why we shouldn't follow all or even some of the Law. The reasons they give us are then used by others inside and outside of the church to void the entire Bible, like we void a check in our checkbooks. See, I told you that you might want to wait before you say this book isn't needed. Wait till you get a load of the rest of it.

There are those who say that since we can't gain salvation with the Law, then we don't have to do it. That's like saying I found a cavity in a tooth so I should stop brushing. Or it's like saying I don't have to because I'm not getting paid. But framing disobedience with "I don't get paid" is not a loving response to the love given by God. Everything He says is a salvation issue. His Law connects obedience with love. It's the heart of the new covenant. And it's our daily bread.

---

[2] C.H. Spurgeon, Sermon 37 'Law and Grace,' on Romans 5:20, August 26, 1855.

The Original Four-Letter Word

Among the many things given to their descendants by Adam and Eve was the first four-letter word. The word 'obey' quickly became a bitter epithet, used like a cuss word whenever God was talked about or even thought about. It is still in use today in all languages, and various forms of the word are getting more use as cuss words than ever before. Instead of linking obey with love as our Father does, we have filled it with hate. One pastor recently told us we were "all about rules and regulations." Apparently "obey" was among his four-letter words, as it has been for many people throughout the millennia. This was particularly evident when he told us we couldn't attend his church.

I don't blame him – he looks at God's Word through what's in his heart. Instead of obedience with love all he sees are hateful rules and regulations. He looks at God as if God is imposing rules from the outside. Like many, many church leaders he doesn't see obedience welling up from a loving, Spirit-filled heart of flesh from the inside, because that is not in *his* heart. Oddly, also like many, he didn't see that he has a rule or regulation about rules and regulations!

Many people give out similar invectives or cuss words when looking at God's Law. Humans really dislike the fact that God is in charge. But obey is to love as colors are to sunlight. Obey is part of love and inseparable. Whole Bible Christianity is all about love, and love is much more than sentiment. It's doing what's right. To obey is love, and loving is obeying. The starting point for what is right is given by God, in the whole of His Word. Wrong (or hate) is anything short of His Word. Paul gives us a pretty good definition of love in that famous passage of his first letter to the Corinthians.

> Love is patient and kind; love does not envy or boast; it is not arrogant or rude. It does not insist on its own way; it is not irritable or resentful; it does not rejoice at wrongdoing, but rejoices with the truth. Love bears all things, believes all things, hopes all things, endures all things. (1 Corinthians 13:4–7, ESV)

Notice that love "rejoices with the truth." The truth is all of God's Word, and of course that includes every word that proceeds out of His mouth. Including His Law. So love rejoices in the Law. *"If you love me you will keep my commandments."* (John 14:15). The Bible is filled with examples of God's love for people as He builds His kingdom. In the Garden of Eden God "birthed" mankind, sharing His love with us in the breath of His lives (Genesis 2:7). We (using the corporate we) spurned this love and chose knowledge with self-will (and rule Romans 2:6-8) instead. Kind of like a self-abortion, if you'll excuse the comparison. Mankind has been dodgy with the Law ever since.

God loved before the cross. Really, He did. Love has been associated with God since, well since forever. Genesis 24:27 mentions God's "steadfast love" to Abraham which is repeated in Exodus 34:6 by God when He passes before Moses on Mt. Sinai. Love is a key ingredient of the Law. Deuteronomy 6:5 is where God links loving Him with commands being "on your heart." In Deuteronomy 7:9 God says that He "keeps covenant" and "steadfast love with all those who love Him and keep His commandments." Obviously Law and love are intimately connected.

The phrase "For God so loved the world," from that famous verse we see on signs at football games on TV (John 3:16) shows that He has always been a God of love. The giving of the Law at Mt. Sinai was a loving act. It set boundaries on the self-will we chose in the Garden and prepared Israel as a place for people to take a shot at living together with God again. The Law has always been around. His Word is eternal. At Sinai He simply reintroduced the Law as the standard of right living.

God's love is revealed in His Law. "Love the Lord your God with all your heart and with all your soul, and with all your might" (Deuteronomy 6:5). "This is my commandment, that you love one another as I have loved you" (John 15:12). When we sow righteousness (do what God says) we read steadfast love.

> Sow for yourselves righteousness; reap steadfast love; break up your fallow ground, for it is the time to seek the LORD, that he may come and rain righteousness upon you. (Hosea 10:12, ESV)

The sacrifice of Jesus is the pinnacle of God's love. It was loving obedience that led Him to the cross. The message of the Christ is for people to repent; to turn back to the loving ways of God. The New Testament writers emphasize God's message of love, telling us over and over that repentance is interwoven with love, trust and obedience to His Law. The Law is not as much about rules and regulations as it is about love. Love and the Law are one, just as He is One. As distance from the Law grows, love waxes cold.

> [12] And because lawlessness will be increased, the love of many will grow cold. (Matthew 24:12 ESV)

As we can tell by observation, the love of many is growing cold now. I think it's obvious this is in direct proportion to our distance from His Law.

The Heart of the New Covenant

Many Christians say they follow the "new covenant" instead of the "old covenant." Yet they don't know what the new one is or where it is in the Word (let alone what a covenant is). Don't take my word for it, just ask around. Generally, the New Testament is mistaken for the New Covenant. It's a part, but is not by itself the new covenant.

As Jeremiah records (quoted at the beginning of this chapter) the heart of the new covenant is God's Law written on a new heart of flesh. But the new covenant goes all the way back to the beginning when you realize that loving God and doing what He says has been His goal since before Genesis. The Law was delivered by Moses, but it is not the word of Moses. It is the Word of God. It has been made into a scary thing by some, but when written on a heart of flesh it is anything but scary. Contrary to what you have probably heard, the Bible doesn't say the Law is scary. Or hard, old, outdated, a curse, or beyond our ability. Those are teachings of men. The teachings of His Word, or Law, are a reflection of God's character, and include mercy, justice, truth, instruction, love and life.

Every word from God's mouth is Law, and life giving. Even those words that have punishment in them are designed to encourage life. Death is what happens when we turn away from His words of life (or Law). He is the source of life, so when we ignore any part of His word, or His Law, by that much we separate ourselves from life. After all, Adam and Eve were booted out of the Garden for what, a dietary command violation? (Actually it was for self-seeking, but more on that later.) We have to be completely connected to life in order to get the full effect. The measure we use is the measure that is used on us (Matthew 7:2; Mark 4:24; Luke 6:38).

The new heart of flesh is a symbol of love, soft and responsive to its Creator and sustainer. Love is an action word marked by humility and a desire to do what God says. A heart of flesh is opposite of a heart of stone (Ezekiel 11:19). A heart of flesh is alive; a heart of stone is dead. A heart of flesh rejoices in every word coming from God. The heart of stone is marked by pride and resistance to God's commands, statutes, laws, and instruction. A heart of flesh is guided by God's eye. A heart of stone is like a horse or mule that needs bit, bridle and whip to hold it in check. Soft-hearted believers leap to go where God merely glances. Stone hearts need a hammer and chisel to get even the smallest response from them.

> [8]I will instruct you and teach you in the way which you should go; I will counsel you with My eye upon you. [9]Do not be as the horse or as the mule which have no understanding, Whose trappings include bit and bridle to hold them in check, Otherwise they will not come near to you. (Psalm 32:8-9 NASB95)

A heart of flesh is different than the old tablets of stone that the Law was once written on, because it's inside and more responsive to God's Word in love. Jesus followed the Law, Paul followed it, and all the apostles followed it. By nature there are those who do what the Law requires though perhaps unaware (Romans 2:14-16). There are also many more all over the world waking up to the ideas in this book.[3] It is not the Law that is difficult, or old, or irrelevant. It is all the stone-hearted opinions, traditions, and interpretations that make it seem that way.

The new part of the new covenant is the heart, not the Word. "New" is the heart, "covenant" is the Law. Through the sacrifice of the Christ, believers trade in old hearts of stone for new creations. Our new heart is soft and responsive to God's every thought. As the pagans move further away from the Word, believers need to move closer. We want to be heart to heart with God (1 John 5:1-12).

The truth is not often a real fun subject. But our holy and loving God insists that His children follow His truth because it is the only path of life. Living His Words requires humility and trust in Him, which goes against our pride and knowledge. The Law is a hot button because down deep, in our heart of hearts, in our very natures, we do not want to do what God says. It's like we have a hangover from losing the Garden. This is why most of the church has soft-soaped His truth so much. But in doing so they've scrubbed the life out of the Law. Much the same as the Pharisees and Sadducees did way back when. Truly, "obey" is the original four-letter word.

> [16] And it shall come to pass, if they will diligently learn the ways of my people, to swear by my name, 'As the LORD lives,' even as they taught my people to swear by Baal, then they shall be built up in the midst of my people. [17] But if any nation will not listen, then I will utterly pluck it up and destroy it, declares the LORD." (Jeremiah 12:16-17 ESV)

Some say the new covenant came with huge changes in the unchangeable Word when the Christ died. Or that the physical words of the Bible message have (allegedly) merged into spiritual thoughts. Either way, now we can eat a ham sandwich, as long as we think about God while we're doing it. We can live an alternate lifestyle, as long as we insist on "social justice" at the same time. Adultery is okay as long as we

---

[3] Park Street Church in Boston did a "30-Day Leviticus Challenge" in 2008 and participants learned a great deal of what I present in this book. They've since disabled the 'Living Levitically' section on their website, but you can read about it on the Christianity Today website at http://www.christianitytoday.com/ct/2008/august/13.30.html or you can buy the book with the same title by David Harrell.

shout out God's name in the middle of it. It's clear that these sorts of new covenants aren't all that new, and they aren't from a heart of flesh, either.

The Believer's Daily Bread

Jesus describes the new covenant in the gospel of John in a different way. He calls it "eating (His) flesh and drinking (His) blood," and equates it to bread.

> [53]Then Jesus said unto them, Verily, verily, I say unto you, Except ye eat the flesh of the Son of man, and drink his blood, ye have no life in you. [54]Whoso eateth my flesh, and drinketh my blood, hath eternal life; and I will raise him up at the last day. [55]For my flesh is meat indeed, and my blood is drink indeed. [56]He that eateth my flesh, and drinketh my blood, dwelleth in me, and I in him. [57]As the living Father hath sent me, and I live by the Father: so he that eateth me, even he shall live by me. [58]This is that bread which came down from heaven: not as your fathers did eat manna, and are dead: he that eateth of this bread shall live for ever. (John 6:53-58 KJV)

Remember, this was said at a time when there was no New Testament. You might think Jesus is talking about a so-called sacrament here. But the Protestant crackers and grape juice ceremony hadn't been created. Neither had the mystical wafer the Catholics favor. It isn't the feast of Passover or Unleavened Bread (1 Corinthians 10:16), and He's not saying we should nibble His fingers, or tap His main artery like a vampire. There is life in His flesh and blood, but He doesn't mean the tissue and corpuscles (although we could argue that point).

> [63]"It is the Spirit who gives life; the flesh profits nothing; the words that I have spoken to you are spirit and are life. (John 6:63 NASB95)

All Jesus is talking about is consuming God's Words for our souls like we do food for our bodies. Not such an odd concept. Jeremiah (Jeremiah 15:16) Ezekiel (Ezekiel 3) and John (Revelation 10:9) did it. Our new hearts of flesh are fed by the bread of life and it's pumped to our limbs for action. This "reading and doing" (hear or see and obey)[4] the whole of the Word is the basis of whole Bible Christianity. His Words – all of them – are His body and blood. It's not just the words in red that we colored in later. The word "obey" is pretty much the same as "abide" or "remain" and goes along with "hear and see," "eat and drink

---

[4] See for instance Exodus 24:7; Deuteronomy 4:6, 5:27; Jeremiah 5:21, 11:6; Ezekiel 12:2, 33:31, 32; Matthew 13:13; Mark 8:18; Luke 8:21, John 8:43, 12:47.

His body and blood," and our daily bread. Life comes with abiding in God's Word (John 6:35).

> And I know that his commandment is eternal life. What I say, therefore, I say as the Father has told me." (John 12:50, ESV)

The Law is part of His body and blood. Real communion is to hear and follow. Salvation is faith in action - to hear, obey, abide, and exchange our ways of death for God's Way of Life. To abide in His love through His Word. Jesus isn't talking about a picnic, or mystic wafers and wine. He is talking about obedience.

Life is in His Word, His body and blood or bread, and we eat and drink when we read and do (Matthew 5:6, 6:33). Literally, we are what we eat. To eat the flesh and drink the blood of the Christ is to hear everything God says, and do exactly and only what He says. We abide when we obey. Jesus emphasized the life in His words to the woman at the well in John chapter 4. She received living water (verse 15). A few minutes later, the disciples were told about real food.

> ³¹Meanwhile the disciples were urging Him, saying, "Rabbi, eat." ³²But He said to them, "I have food to eat that you do not know about." ³³So the disciples were saying to one another, "No one brought Him anything to eat, did he?" ³⁴Jesus said to them, "My food is to do the will of Him who sent Me and to accomplish His work. (John 4:31-34 NASB95)

Food for Jesus is to do the will of God the Father and accomplish His work. The Law gives believers a start point for eating and drinking the will of God. The will (and Word) of God and Jesus are identical.

> ⁹Jesus said to him, "Have I been so long with you, and yet you have not come to know Me, Philip? He who has seen Me has seen the Father; how can you say, 'Show us the Father'? ¹⁰"Do you not believe that I am in the Father, and the Father is in Me? The words that I say to you I do not speak on My own initiative, but the Father abiding in Me does His works. (John 14:9-10 NASB95)

The Word on the page is to the Spirit as flesh and blood is to the Messiah. Jesus the Bread of Life (John 6:35) is there in the Words of Life. This absolute true Word of His flesh and blood is the only thing that satisfies our hunger and thirst for righteousness (Matthew 5:6). We can speak of accepting Jesus as a person or even as God, but the proof is in eating and drinking His Word. It makes us as different from the world as the Garden of Eden is from a landfill.

God commands us to "test the spirits" (1 John 4:1-3) by confessing Jesus, but this does not just mean to go around saying "Jesus, Jesus, Jesus." Israel did this at times with the Temple (Jeremiah 7:4-11) and it didn't amount to a hill of beans then either. Anyone can say His name (even demons – Acts 19:15) or call Him Lord.[5] But to confess Him means to change our life. This is pure religion (related to "godliness" 1 Timothy 3:16[6]) – humbly receiving the whole Word; hearing and doing all that God says (James 1:22-27). We can't say we trust God if we won't do what He says.

Members of the one body eat and drink the one faith or truth of the Bible, which is the body and blood of the Messiah Jesus. We cannot fully function without it. If we have the Son we have life (1 John 5:10, 11), and if we have the Son we abide in His Words. Abiding means we do His Words. Believers live by every Word from the mouth of God.

If we found the Fountain of Youth we wouldn't just take a test tube and analyze some in a laboratory. We wouldn't stick a toe in and complain it was too cold or too warm. We wouldn't just stand there looking at it either. We would dive in and do the back stroke. We would splash around and drink large quantities until it was coming out our ears. And that's what we need to do with God's Word – drink it by the bucket full by reading large parts of it daily. Jump in and swim around. *"Labor to show yourself approved"* (2 Timothy 2:15) and search the Scriptures like Bereans (Acts 17:10-12). Take in His Word *and do it* as if it is life.

Many people already read the Bible and try to follow what it says. But when we get right down to it, most reading is sparse or casual, and our practice features a take-it-or-leave-it attitude. This "shallow root" is prone to destruction by sun, thorns and the cares of the world (Matthew 13).

Which Law?

One thing we have to decide about Law is to pick which Law we're going to follow. Different groups split up the Law into different chunks. Some people think The Law is just the first five books (the Pentateuch). They call it the "Law of Moses" though it is actually the Law of God. This is a reasonable start, but it doesn't go far enough, because God gave further instruction later. Other people (like Thomas Aquinas, Calvin, and C. H. Spurgeon) will divide the Law of Moses into three sections called civil, ceremonial, and moral. They like to say only the "moral laws" count and that the law was for a specific purpose other than as a lifestyle

---

[5] Matthew 7:21, 22; Isaiah 45:23 every knee bows and swears allegiance; Romans 14:11.
[6] Greek *threskeia* Strong's 2356 in James 1:26, 27 means worship; in 1 Timothy 3:16 'godliness' is the Greek *eusebeia* Strong's 2150 meaning reverence, respect or piety towards God. We don't have to be afraid of religion.

(such as "to increase the trespass" they'll quote from what Paul says in Romans 5:20). Some Christians think there are only ten Laws, and some prefer only two laws now (love the Lord your God and love your neighbors as yourself, Matthew 22:36-40).

There is generic "law" which could include natural law (like the law of gravity), Roman law, and the Jewish oral law (called Talmud). Oral law for sure would've been included when the apostles wrote about generic "law." Talmud is based on the Law of Moses but includes thousands of interpretations, traditions and rulings from rabbis which many times override the Word. The church does the same thing with many of their traditions today. Then we've got the "red letter" people telling us to pay attention only to the words colored red. Lastly, there are people who think the Law is imaginary, or merely spiritual, and as long as we *think* we are obeying then we must really be obeying.

The Law we pick should be effective everywhere; our heart as well as our actions. A Law that stays on the outside (the letter without the Spirit as Paul says in 2 Corinthians 3:6) won't produce satisfactory results either in spirituality, growth or maturity because it excludes love. We need a Law that resides inside, written on a heart of flesh by the Spirit that flows out to our feet and hands. What is inside will come out under pressure, so the Law we pick should be inside as well as outside (Matthew 23:25, 26).

God's whole Law is the only one that applies both inside and out. Like the Pharisees, too many stop the law at the outside and ignore the Spirit's efforts at bringing it inside (see Romans 7:4-6; 2 Corinthians 3:5-6). Whole Bible Christians, as the name implies, believe that every word from the mouth of God is Law (Deuteronomy 8:3, Matthew 4:4). It is plain to our heart of flesh that The Law is every word that He speaks from Genesis to Revelation. We believe "all of the above" when it comes to His Law. His Law is more than just three sections or five books or two commands. His words have ultimate authority, overriding any law of men. It's all moral. It's all Law, all love, and all grace. Red letters, black, purple or whatever, doesn't matter. Every word is read and followed inside and out as much as we can.

God is love and life. Jesus said, *"I am the way, the truth, and the life"* (John 14:6). The love, truth and life He shares with God are the Way to go. Truth is God's Word. God's Word includes the Law. All of the Laws. Every Word that proceeds from His mouth, not just the two commands we like or those that fit into our feelings. His kingdom comes into our lives (or we enter in to His Kingdom) as we follow Him in every way.

His Words (and Law) are intimately woven around history and God's dealings with men. There is no avoiding the Word, whether we call it Law or something else. Most of *this* book is about the Law, or rather objections to the Law, because most of *His* book is about the Law (and objections to it). The subject of His whole Law (commands, statutes, charge, ordinances, etc.) is mentioned thousands of times in the Word, as well as related subjects such as obeying His voice (Genesis 22:18, 26:5; Exodus 19:5), hearing His voice (John 10:16, 27, 18:37; Revelation 3:20), abiding or remaining in His Love (John 6:56, 8:31, 15:1-16) and ears that don't hear and eyes that don't see (Jeremiah 5:21, 6:10; Ezekiel 12:2; Mark 8:18). His Word and His Law is the same thing. Let me assure you – all of His Law applies to everyone, all the time, everywhere. One of the wisest men in history said it this way.

> The end of the matter; all has been heard. Fear God and keep his commandments, for this is the whole duty of man. For God will bring every deed into judgment, with every secret thing, whether good or evil. (Ecclesiastes 12:13–14, ESV)

Law AND Grace

I'll talk more about this later, but here I'll tell you – Law and grace go together like ice and snow. Like bones and tissue. Like bricks and mortar. Like mountains and valleys. Or pick your simile. Grace is in the Law, and Law comes from grace. Law is misused if we take grace out of the picture. Calvin quotes Augustine on this: "Thus Augustine says, "If the Spirit of grace be absent, the law is present only to convict and slay us."[7] Grace is misused if we take Law out of the picture. A gracious God gave the Law. We are saved by grace through faith in Jesus (or even better as we'll discuss later, by love through love) and then we live a life of love pleasing to God. Including the Law. Following the Law does not take away from the sacrifice of Jesus. The Law helps us follow Jesus after we are saved.

A related concern might be the unbiblical idea that we have to live the Law perfectly or not at all. Obviously, this idea is wrong on the face of it when we see the Law as part of His whole Word and apply it to, say, "thou shall not covet." If we find ourselves coveting, we don't erase the law on coveting. We repent of coveting. The "perfect or not" thought is missing the piece that we only have to do the Law perfectly if we are trying *to earn our own* salvation (an impossible task).

Jesus paid the penalty for sin, and all we need to do is confess and repent. Forgiveness is a part of the Law and through repentance and forgiveness a heart of flesh follows God's will naturally. Some try to buy salvation with works, which would mean they would "have" to follow

---

[7] Calvin, J. (1997). *Institutes of the Christian religion*. II, vii, 7. Bellingham, WA: Logos Bible Software quoting August. de Corrept. et Gratia. Ambros. Lib. 1 de Jac. et cap. 6 de Vita Beat.

the whole Law perfectly ("you who would be justified by the Law" as Paul says in Galatians 5:3-4). The two problems with this are that 1) people think the Law is only external, and 2) they don't include the Spirit. Works don't work if the Spirit in a heart of flesh is missing. We only think we are following the Law if it is only external. With Jesus paying the penalty, there is no reason not to abide. His blood covers us and makes any effort at abiding perfect. We just have to keep abiding.

Law Under Grace

If we are "not under the Law" as Paul says (Romans 6:14, 15; Galatians 5:18), but are under grace, then where is the Law? It is "under grace" also. It always has been. We are under grace, and so is the Law. According to the New Covenant it is right there with us in our new heart of flesh.

> But someone will say, "You have faith and I have works." Show me your faith apart from your works, and I will show you my faith by my works. (James 2:18, ESV)

There is a false split between grace and Law in many people's minds. But grace and Law are both parts of God's love, holiness and will. When Jesus gave the Law (which we will talk more about later) He didn't stop grace. When He grants grace, Law is not far away. There is abundant grace in the Law. Law is in a heart of flesh under grace and with the Spirit.

"Works" is not a bad thing. We are supposed to "work out our salvation with fear and trembling" (Philippians 2:12). The problem with "works" or "works of the Law" or "works of the flesh" is if we "work" without God or His Spirit. If we "work" to gain salvation, we are working without God. Salvation is a gift. Our "works" are to do what He says or abide in His Word with a heart of flesh. We *were* slaves to sin, working apart from Him. Now we are slaves to righteousness working *with* Him. We don't live by bread alone, but by every Word. We are redeemed from lawlessness, as Paul tells Titus.

> For the grace of God has appeared, bringing salvation for all people, training us to renounce ungodliness and worldly passions, and to live self-controlled, upright, and godly lives in the present age, waiting for our blessed hope, the appearing of the glory of our great God and Savior Jesus Christ, who gave himself for us to redeem us from all lawlessness and to purify for himself a people for his own possession who are zealous for good works. (Titus 2:11–14, ESV)

Our training tool for renouncing ungodliness and worldly passions is the Law. The only reason someone would be under Law alone (trying to be justified by works) is when they are out of whack in their relationship to God. There are those who use the law unlawfully in the flesh (1 Timothy 1:8). Others use it lawfully in the fullness of grace with the power of the Spirit. Believers shouldn't use the Law without grace or without the Spirit. It is one whole package to be followed as God intended. He lived in the midst of Israel in the desert in grace, and the Law was fully functional. It could not be otherwise.

Faith

You wouldn't think we would need to talk about faith, would you? After all, everyone knows what it is, right? However, it is my observation that most believers have lost the meaning, or at best have had it obscured by many good-sounding philosophies of men. Biblically, faith is much different than most of the current church teachings make it out to be.

During the Reformation, one doctrine among many that was re-delivered to the Body was called in Latin *sola fidei*, meaning "faith alone." Faith alone is how a person is justified (declared righteous for salvation) by God (Leviticus 18:5; Psalm 31:1-2; Habakkuk 2:4; Galatians 3:6-7). Protestants had to recover this doctrine because the church at the time had changed the meaning so that "faith" was a belief in the Catholic Church and its many traditions. If you weren't part of the church, you did not have "faith." We have to recover it again because church tradition has snuck up on us again, causing more confusion on the subject of faith.

Part of the current teaching on faith is that it is mental agreement only, as in "I believe the Bible is true," or "I believe in God." There are many who teach that if good things are not happening for you then you must not have enough "faith" or "belief." But faith is an illusion if there is no action in keeping with belief. Where there is faith, there are related actions. Paul calls it "the obedience of faith" in Romans 1:5. The illusion of faith without action is what some, such as Reformed (Presbyterian) Reverend Steve Schlissel, call "alone faith."[8] If a person believes that a train is coming, yet refuses to get off the track, there might be reason to doubt the faith is real. It certainly wouldn't be saving faith. If we believe God, we will do all that He tells us.

Faith is more than hearing the Word, more than seeing truth, and more than belief. It is not just raising your hand and going forward or

---

[8] 'True Confessions;' Reverend Steve Schlissel; Messiah's Covenant Community Church; www.messiahnyc.org, http://www.wholebible.com/PdfLibrary/true%20confessions1.pdf; September 21, 2002.

attending church weekly. It is trusting God by action in keeping with His Words. It is following God with all our heart, soul, mind and strength. Related words are "abide," "faithfulness" and "steadfast love." Opposite words are "deceit," "treacherous," and "offend." Good fruit is action in keeping with God's will and words. Bad fruit is actions that deny Him or His Word.

One of the big faith sections in the Word is Hebrews 11, and all those people acted on their belief. Enoch pleased God by "walking with Him" (without faith it is impossible to please God). Noah followed through on building a boat. Abraham kept God's charge, commandments, statutes and laws (Genesis 26:5). When God said pack up and move, Abraham moved. Rahab sheltered the Israeli spies. Abel made the right sacrifice. Jesus was led like a lamb to the slaughter. Peter walked on water and healed the crippled. Paul started many new synagogues and was beaten, shipwrecked, flogged and stoned in the process. These all trusted God and did something about it. The food and drink they got from God and His Word moved them to action.

Lack of action or wrong action means there is no faith. Israel refused to go into the Promised Land as God commanded (Numbers 14). Esau sold his birthright for a fast food dinner (Genesis 25). Nadab and Abihu offered strange fire (Leviticus 10). Achan kept back things devoted for destruction (Joshua 7). Korah decided he was in charge instead of God (Numbers 16). Jesus was crucified by leaders that had knowledge of the Word but no faith. Disciples left Jesus because of unbelief (John 6:66). Ananias and Sapphira lied to the Holy Spirit (Acts 5). There's no middle ground. *"For the one who is not against us is for us"* (Mark 9:40). Faith must have both trust in God, and action in keeping with His Word, in order to be genuine and productive.

Trust and obedience is why Jesus said that faith can be as small as a mustard seed yet move mountains (Matthew 17:20). If we trust God and abide in His Word then the mountain will move. Of course, knowing His will means we would know whether God wanted the mountain to move. Or maybe that we should get off the train track. In a hurry.

Everyone is given a measure of faith (Romans 12:3) though many don't grow in it and some deliberately burn it out resulting in a seared conscience (1 Timothy 4:2). The Word is scattered everywhere, and faith grows because trust and obedience to the Word grows. Faith is fed as we keep trusting and abiding in His Word. This is what it means to accept the kingdom like a child (Matthew 19:14; Mark 10:15; Luke 18:17). A child trusts mom and dad and responds to them without doubt. The more we trust and obey, the more faith we have.

A section of the church presents faith as a magic carpet to get wealth, healing, happiness, or success. We are told that if we "have enough faith" God will heal and bless with financial success. All we have to do is "believe" and we will get what we're after. But they are selling an illusion. Faith is walking after the Lord our God, fearing Him, keeping His commandments and obeying His voice. A payoff in the form of healing or financial success may or may not come, but we keep walking.

> "If a prophet or a dreamer of dreams arises among you and gives you a sign or a wonder, and the sign or wonder that he tells you comes to pass, and if he says, 'Let us go after other gods,' which you have not known, 'and let us serve them,' you shall not listen to the words of that prophet or that dreamer of dreams. For the LORD your God is testing you, to know whether you love the LORD your God with all your heart and with all your soul. You shall walk after the LORD your God and fear him and keep his commandments and obey his voice, and you shall serve him and hold fast to him." (Deuteronomy 13:1–4, ESV)

We walk with God by fearing Him and keeping His commands. If a sign or a wonder comes to pass (like a "faith healing"), but the connected message is to ignore His Word or parts of His Word, that is the equivalent of going after other gods. When we don't abide in God's Word it is idolatry. The missing ingredient in the illusory faith the false prophet or teacher speaks of is obedience to God. Strong faith is due to trusting God and doing what He says in every way. Weak faith comes from a lack of trust or obedience, and usually both.

This is why we can't just "believe more" and have magic things happen. If we really trust God, really have faith, we will do what He says whether we get paid (in blessings) or not. Start with small things and work our way up. If we are following with all our heart, mind, and strength, and if it is His will, then He will bless with wealth, children, long life, health or other blessings. Seek the kingdom of God and His righteousness first, and all these things will be added to you (Matthew 6:33).

Faith and belief are sometimes interchangeable words. But godly belief has to respond to God in the same way faith does. Demons believe in God, and tremble (James 2:19) yet they don't do what He says. At the end of this age, every knee will bow and every tongue confess that Jesus is Lord (Philippians 2:9-11) but not all will be saved because *they didn't do what He said* to do.

> [9]For this reason also, God highly exalted Him, and bestowed on Him the name which is above every name, [10]so that at the name

of Jesus every knee will bow, of those who are in heaven and on earth and under the earth, [11]and that every tongue will confess that Jesus Christ is Lord, to the glory of God the Father. (Philippians 2:9-11 NASB95)

God is in charge whether anyone admits it or not. So merely stating that "He is Lord" is obviously not saving faith. We have to act like He is Lord if our faith is going to save us.

The Rejection of the New Covenant

Church history shows a habit of rejecting God's Laws (which in effect is a rejection of the New Covenant) mostly because they were seen as Jewish. Not at first, because in the book of Acts believers were still following all of the Word. But later, as some of the Jews rebelled against Rome resulting in destruction of the temple and ultimately Jerusalem itself, the church was born and tried to distance itself from anything that looked "Jewish." I'll explain as we go why the church and the body of Christ are two different groups, and why I said that the church was born later (officially in 325 A. D.) than the events of the book of Acts.

Immediately after the resurrection, there was a split in churches between Jews who did not accept the Messiah (represented by those who handed Him over to be crucified) and those who accepted Him (represented by the apostles and other leaders). All of them, though, claimed to follow the Torah (the Old Testament or Law). Those Torah-followers who accepted Jesus as the Messiah promised in the Old Testament were expelled from existing synagogues and formed their own, because they stuck with the "whole" message of the Bible. Jesus and the Law. Both. In my view this accounts for the wonderful "kick starter" events of Acts chapter 2 when believers were "all together" (Acts 2:44).

Cornelius (Acts 10) was an example of Gentiles who also believed. He was a Roman centurion who was called a devout man and "God-fearer" because he followed the Torah but didn't convert to Judaism. He is a high-profile example of Gentiles included in God's kingdom. Gentiles always had the opportunity to be included (see for instance Ruth and Rahab); there was just a bottleneck at the time of the book of Acts because of the extra-biblical rulings of non-believing Jewish leaders. In Acts 10 Peter was shown that the Jewish leaders were not correct, and so the message got out more effectively to the Gentiles.

Over the years after the resurrection, more Gentiles were accepted by the new synagogues (or believing congregations). In general, they all looked and acted similar. Gradually the population in the congregations switched around to being mostly Gentile, but also became more anti-

Jewish and anti-Law, at least partly because the Jews got more and more rebellious towards the Roman government. As the rebellion reached its peak in the destruction of the Temple and eventually Jerusalem, believers reacted by defining themselves more and more as "not Jewish" to avoid as much of the Roman backlash as they could.

There were two parts to this reaction. One was in rejecting the Law (seen as "Jewish"), especially the visible parts that would mark the believer as a law-follower (or "Jew"). The other part of the reaction was creating a "new thing" called "the church." This time period is called the "parting of the ways" by historians and theologians. Later in the first century A.D., and on into the second and third centuries, the church developed a new priesthood or hierarchy. (See page 105 on The Nicolaitans.)

Around the year 325 A.D. the church got officially recognized when the Roman emperor Constantine accelerated the rejection of the New Covenant and all things regarded as Jewish, particularly the Torah or Law. He joined the church and made his version of Christianity the official religion of the empire, mixing part of the Bible (the "non-Jewish" part which doesn't really exist) with a whole lot of paganism. Everyone had to convert. Or else. Conversion was often nothing more than slapping Christian labels on pagan practices and being anti-Jewish. The slapping was literal in some cases because Constantine did things like chiseling off idol's names and chiseling "saints" names on the pagan statues. This mixing is called syncretism.

Constantine went further than simply being non-Jewish. He tried switching the real Sabbath from Saturday (last day of the week) to Sunday (check any calendar for the first day of the week and the last day of the week), forbade the observance of the holy days of Leviticus 23 (and other places) and "Christianized" pagan feasts that have come to be known as Christmas and Easter. If you wanted to get the empire off your back and do some business, you had to at least look like a Christian (again, not Jewish) on the surface (can you see a practice run for the anti-Christ of end times here?). Conversion was easy because all you had to do was look like a Christian and do what everyone else was doing. (Does this sound like the modern church to you too?)

About a thousand years later the Reformation kicked in which was an attempt to reform this Roman Catholic (catholic means universal) church. The church had formed practices that were bastardizations of Judaism but still not Jewish, and had loaded up God's Word with all sorts of non-biblical rulings and traditions. (If you can see how similar this is to the Judaism of the apostle's time then shout "Amen!") The reformers were not successful in reforming the Catholics. They had to leave and start their own churches, like in the book of Acts where the believers had to separate from the orthodox Jewish establishment. However, the reformers were still by and large against anything Jewish. Luther for instance ended up being very anti-Jewish. Church converts even at this time still had to give up their Jewish practices (centering on the Law). While recovering many good teachings the reformers continued to use only part of the Bible. They kept on with rejecting the Law as mostly Jewish and promoting the church as a separate entity, again effectively denying the New Covenant. This brings us to more modern times.

Constantine's part Bible approach to building churches is called pragmatism.[9] This is a word that means "practical." I call it the sacrifice of whole Bible truth so we can get more people in the door. It has been a plague in the church for a long time, and reared its head again in the emotional revivals of the 1820's and '30's (sometimes called the "second great awakening") and the 1850's to the early 1900's (the third great awakening).

Sort of like Constantine, preachers and evangelists during these awakenings thought they should reduce the Bible message to "whatever gets them in the door." The reasoning was that once people were attending they would learn over time. Either that or the unbeliever's tithe would help "reach the lost." So they further watered down the Bible message and changed the definition of the New Covenant, making it more palatable and comfortable. Perhaps we could even say "ear tickling" (2 Timothy 4:3). Modern false theories such as evolution were also mixed in (preached from the pulpit before accepted by scientists). But the watered down message is all people want to hear once they're inside. So now we've raised part Bible pragmatism to an art form and call it "seeker friendly."

Pragmatism is where the practice of raising hands and going forward comes from, as well as many other "seeker friendly" inventions. The result of being too practical is that we have a large population of church-goers that think watering down the Bible is okay. They keep the practices of raising hands going, for instance, as if it represents salvation. They think they follow the New Covenant when they don't even know what it is or where it's at in the Bible. The enemy continues to sow his tares of "seeker friendly, spiritual but not religious" teachings under the pragmatic (or syncretistic) cover of seeming to advance the Kingdom (more people does not equate to Kingdom growth). That's why some people can claim a status as homosexual Christians and other biblical

---

[9] Constantine is not the only one to blame. People have always been pragmatic with the Word of God. We do it on our own just fine. But he is one of the main and most visible figures in early 'church' history, so it's simpler here to use his brand to summarize.

impossibilities. When we sacrifice truth on the altar of expediency we might fill buildings, but not hearts.

You may recognize that Constantine's church still exists today. You might also recognize that the church has also pretty fully rejected the New Covenant, while trying to keep the illusion they haven't. The trouble with "getting them in the door" by watering down the Word is that after they are in you still can't teach anything harder than water (or milk – Hebrews 5:13). The Law is too scary and still perceived as "too Jewish." Church pragmatism is like bait and switch advertising without the switch. Whatever you tell people to get them in the door is all they want to hear once they're in. It's a large factor in the rejection of the New Covenant even today. People don't want an objective standard.

Pragmatism by itself is not necessarily bad. God is very pragmatic. Except His pragmatism works. Man's doesn't. We have to ask ourselves if our pragmatism featuring the near absence of His Law is working very well. It doesn't seem like it. The answer is to cling to the whole of God's Word, working it in to every corner of our lives. His Law creates many practical changes that produce life, health and blessing. Man's pragmatism might be great for buildings, paychecks and ego feeding but obviously doesn't work for the fruit of the Spirit.

Who Put the Church in Charge?

This might come as a shock, but God didn't make the church. Nor did He put it in charge. It has developed over time into something that looks like what Jesus warned about in the letters to the seven congregations in Revelation. He's not building a church; He makes new hearts and adopts individuals into the Body of Christ (also called a congregation or assembly). The church as we see it is created by men. Why is this an important difference to make? Because the church generally has not only led the way away from God's Laws, gutting the New Covenant in the process and contributing hugely to our cultural rot, it also (generally and historically) stands square in the way of repentance and a return to His Word. Just try mentioning that you think the Law is an excellent lifestyle and discipleship method for believers in a church gathering, and see for yourself what happens.

The church has had its ups and downs over the last 2,000 years. Depending on your measuring stick some think the church in modern times is up, though they might admit it has a few problems here and there. Tim Hawkins (a Christian comedian) likes to say that each church is like one of those clear boxes of strawberries from the grocery store, with the real nice ones on top and the moldy ones underneath. None are perfect because they're just made up of "folks." As funny as that is, others, including me, can clearly see that what we've got doesn't bear a lot of resemblance to the congregation in the book of Acts, top or bottom.

I've had folks tell me that they and their churches are functioning well without parts of the Bible (or Law). The tremendous evangelistic results in Africa and South America are held up as a sign that the church is not down for the count.[10] We were all excited that Jakarta, Indonesia starting around 2013 was experiencing a big jump in people professing Christianity. Fingers will point to Billy Graham and successors who have stadiums full of interested people and millions of "decisions for Christ" recorded. Mega-churches pop up all over with thousands of congregants so of course that means everything's okay. And the 1972 film *A Thief in the Night* (and sequels) along with books like The Late Great Planet Earth made huge inroads into popular culture that are still being felt today.

I agree that the church has had a positive impact in many ways. But divorce and suicide rates amongst church-goers are the same as the ones outside the church. The "part Bible," pragmatic approach isn't making us look like the first century church. Denominations are splitting over actions clearly forbidden to believers in the Word (whatever your view on the rest of the law). Drugs for anxiety are handed out like communion bread. Is it just me, or does anyone else see that the system we've got isn't working as well as many think? Could it be that by rejecting His Law we are not only rejecting the New Covenant but also missing out on His peace and fruit of the Spirit? The church would do well to heed the warning to the Sardis congregation (Revelation 3:1) or even Laodicea (Revelation 3:14-22).

It's funny, and I don't mean humorous, that whenever we start talking about the health of the church people point to numbers. We don't examine the health of individuals. It's like telling a guy with a fatal disease he's going to be okay because he has all his fingers and toes. How come the measuring stick for success is never the lack of divorce? Why don't we judge by the prevalence of drugs for anxiety? How about knowing and following God's Word? Are we making solid Bible disciples on purpose, or mostly by accident? Do you notice that these types of measurements are almost never considered when rating the health of the church or the success of its programs?

God cares nothing for numbers. He populated the world starting with two people. He made a nation of millions out of a family of 70 (Genesis 46:27; Exodus 1:5). He's got one (Son of) man building a Kingdom with

---

[10] However, according to John Phillip Jenkins in his book The Lost History of Christianity there used to be a huge population of Christians in Africa through about 1250 A.D. They were slaughtered by Muslims. He says that population would not recover its former numbers until the 1960's.

numbers greater than the sands of the sea or stars in heaven (even after He was murdered). God doesn't want or need numbers; He wants sons and daughters. It's disciples He's after who love and live like He does, and abide in His Word of life without question. I'm told any dysfunction I see (or that is measured by surveys and polls) in the church is a good thing due to welcoming all types with open arms. So of course the message of this book is off base to the numbers people; they don't see anything wrong with the church.

I don't agree. The mere fact that the whole of the Word is not taught or practiced by the church in general is by itself a huge indicator of building on sand. Something is not right when discipleship is hit or miss and the fruit of the Spirit is in short supply. We have lots of decisions, but little commitment. There is loyalty of a sort, but mostly to personalities. My friend Mike calls them "personality cults."

If the dysfunction was just from welcoming any sinner, you'd think after a while the longtime believers would not be as dysfunctional. They'd be getting better, not worse. The fruit of the Spirit would be popping out all over. We'd easily be able to make new Bible disciples, too (in contrast to disciples of personalities or a denomination). After all, the first century church also took in thousands of new converts all at once. The difference is that though they were "devout men" (Acts 2:5) they still felt the need to repent (Acts 2:38). Do we feel the same need?

Modern dysfunction affects long-time attendees the same as new ones. It affects old-line denominations just like newer ones. The longer people are in church it seems the worse things get. Based on observation, education, personal experience, other people's testimony and professional surveys, we need a lot of improvement. We might be pragmatically growing in numbers, but in maturity and fruit of the Spirit we are severely lacking. The modern church is flat, like soda pop without the bubbles. We need to repent and get back to the first century whole Bible practice.

How could anyone be happy with what we've got? The church in Acts was full of the fire of the Spirit, growing in love and power and community. The church of today is, um, not so much. Where are the prophets? (Locked out because they don't preach the party line.) Where is the (genuine) healing? (Pre-empted by the TV circus acts masquerading as healing.) Were these gifts just for the first century? (No.) Did God stop giving them, or did we stop receiving them?

In my opinion, the gifts are locked out because parts of the Word are locked out of the church. Part Bible belief and practice reigns supreme. We still have a little fire, and there are some good things being accomplished. Many churches do a good job of attracting people with a rock concert or stadium revival, but not so good keeping them going in the faith.[11] They're great at making decisions for Christ; not so great at making disciples.

Real evangelism is life to life, meaning we live the Word and it spills over to those we know. It's not supposed to be in an impersonal setting with people unknown to you using big screen TV's and professional musicians. The Law helps us publicize the whole Word, and as we live it we show that we really believe it. People can't help but be attracted to a person who is full of the love and peace of God and who has concrete answers to troubling questions. I find that using the Law in a lawful fashion makes me less judgmental, more open and interested in others, and more able to converse with those outside my faith. More law equals more loving (the inverse of Matthew 24:12). This is how we effectively shared the Bible message way back before there were modern films, stadiums, jet airplanes, and superstar evangelists. The Law is down to earth and for sharing the love of God minute by minute.

The people who think everything's okay in the church today are either not paying attention or are like the proverbial frog in a pot of water being slowly brought up to boil (it won't jump out and will die if you do it slowly enough). I'm sure the people before the flood thought everything was fine. Israel ignored or outright killed prophets for suggesting that all was not right in Jerusalem. The skies over Sodom and Gomorrah gave no indication the day it rained fire and brimstone too. Sandy foundations look fine right up until the storm hits.

Things made by people tend to fall apart. Fresh injections of God's Word (like at Mt. Sinai, the Reformation or in Acts 2) restore some life. His Spirit works to keep things going also (as far as reaching individuals). There are things the church is doing right, but some key things are wrong. The modern church, especially in the U. S. and Europe, is by many biblical measures actually in a downward swing. Instead of being a bulwark of morality and defense of the faith it's abandoning the principles of God's Word left and right. Mostly left.

We know God's message is still getting out. His Word will not return void (Isaiah 55:10-11). He can preach it with barnyard animals if He has to, like the sermon from the donkey in Numbers 22. Come to think of it, He must still be using donkeys since I hear a lot of braying. This, I think, is a reason God allows the church to continue. But a lot of times the bright spots are in spite of the people who claim His name and in spite of

---

[11] Ray Comfort says he found an 80% to 90% failure rate for decisions in one study. He cited a major denomination which in the early 90's racked up 294,000 "decisions" but later could find only 14,000 in fellowship (95% failure). From 'Hell's Best Kept Secret' http://www.livingwaters.com/learn/hellsbestkeptsecret.htm. Of course, "failure" depends on your perspective. I suppose you could look at the 14,000 as a success compared to zero.

the church appointing itself in charge. All too often God has to work around us instead of through us. "Hit or miss" Christianity is not God's intent.

Street Theology

Everyone, Christian or not, has a belief system. Street theology is my term for the belief system we make for ourselves out of what we hear from the pulpit and what we read (or see) or even learn in school. We use it, whether we know it or not, to make decisions daily.

The question is from where do church-goers get their system? They probably would say "the Bible," but is that really true? Do they get it from the Bible, or do they get it from professionals who tell us *about* the Bible? To answer my own question, they generally get it from professional opinions about the Bible. But if we depend on what we hear, and not very much on what we read, then it isn't the Word dwelling in our hearts richly (as in Colossians 3:16). It is the pastor's word (or priest's, or rabbi's).

You know the game Telephone, don't you? The first person in a group whispers a message to a second person. Then the second whispers it to the third person, and on around the group. By the time it gets to the last person, whatever the first person has said has changed so much it's not even the same message! This is the game we play when we depend only on what we hear. Especially when what we hear are the teachings of men, philosophy and empty deceit. It is like those seven sons of Sceva who didn't know the person behind the name they were using.

> Then some of the itinerant Jewish exorcists undertook to invoke the name of the Lord Jesus over those who had evil spirits, saying, "I adjure you by the Jesus whom Paul proclaims." Seven sons of a Jewish high priest named Sceva were doing this. But the evil spirit answered them, "Jesus I know, and Paul I recognize, but who are you?" And the man in whom was the evil spirit leaped on them, mastered all of them and overpowered them, so that they fled out of that house naked and wounded. (Acts 19:13–16, ESV)

Sceva's sons were trying to make their "telephone" street theology work in a real spiritual battle. But it didn't work. They were playing Telephone and simply repeating what they'd heard. They didn't do what I call "taking ownership" of the theology. Taking ownership means to thoroughly study and accept an idea as your own in your street theology. Taking ownership of Bible teachings means to accept and do them completely in such a way that they become yours, written on a heart of flesh.

Professors take years to learn things about the Bible. They teach pastors on a shorter timeline. Pastors in turn teach it to other pastors and their flocks in an even shorter timeframe (albeit with more repetition). The average person tries to understand it, live it and teach it to his friend. That's at least four "whispers" in the Telephone line (Bible to professor to pastor to you to a friend or what friends and neighbors see from us). Sometimes there are five or more whispers. I know of specific cases where the local pastor gets recordings from the top pastor of the denomination and simply repackages the top guy's sermons as his own on Sunday. His street theology has no Bible backup. Like the seven sons of Sceva.

If we depend only on what we hear from a teacher instead of reading (and doing) it ourselves, how do we know that what is taught is actually what is in the Bible? The answer is we don't. We have to go to the source. Stop playing Telephone and go straight to the First Guy in line (God). Modify your street level theology by getting to know Him and His ways first hand. Take ownership of the doctrine by knowing the source personally, reading and abiding directly in the whole of His Word.

Don't get me wrong. Some of the professionals are part of the gifts that the Spirit gives to the Body. We need the professionals to give us translations we can understand, for instance. A lot of professionals work on translations into common languages (over 100 on the English Standard version for instance) and we can also minimize translation errors (or prejudice) by comparing translations. However it is translated, we need to go direct to His Word if we are to stay on track.

Whole Bible Christianity is a street level theology that is self-contained and self-correcting. Read it and do it. No telephone, no whispers. It doesn't get much simpler than that. Point each person to the Bible, and show them how easy it is to understand and follow. Give them the Father's living oracles in such a way that they can dwell in a heart of flesh. Academics remain in their proper place, discovering and training. They deliver a translation or educate leaders; our job is to read the Word and do it.

Believers owe a lot to professionals such as archeologists, translators and theologians. It's a lot of hard work to go through the schooling necessary to understand the details of Hebrew and Greek, the writings of the church fathers, or the most effective ways to unearth and interpret old stuff. Academics help bridge the gap between our fathers in the faith and us with solid information to help explain and back up the message of the Bible. But sometimes these leaders get so caught up in academics and the pursuit of recognition from their peers (called the "publish or perish" syndrome) they make things too complicated.

The academics are not the last word on the Bible. The Bible itself is the last word. If we depend mostly on what we hear, then unscriptural teachings can easily slip in. The teaching that "we can't do the law" is a case in point. For years I believed it, defended it, and taught it. Right up until I started reading and doing the whole of the Word and realized that God says it is doable and not too hard (Deuteronomy 30:11-20).

> "For this commandment that I command you today is not too hard for you, neither is it far off. (Deuteronomy 30:11, ESV)

It is not far away or beyond our ability or He wouldn't have given it to us. We can do the Law just fine. What we "can't do" is earn salvation from God for doing it. In order for a non-biblical teaching such as "we can't do the law" to get traction at the street level we need lots of extra-biblical explanation from the academic (without resorting to the Word itself). The street level believer, depending on what they hear, has a hard time figuring out doctrines like this all by themselves. The doctrines don't match the Word, so the academic or pastor has to be around to explain such non-biblical teachings to us. Then we have to trust that the professional knows what he or she is talking about. Next thing you know, we trust the professional instead of God's Word.

Street level theology should match the theology in the Bible, which is one of the reasons for this book. We want to show how the whole Bible message is the best street level theology there is. No more games of Telephone. Just go direct to the source. Whole Bible theology is easy to implement, understand, and check against the Word because we are not doing it long distance. His Word is living and active. All we have to do is plug in to His energy source (the Bible) and it'll charge us up for whatever we need to do.

> "And to the angel of the church in Sardis write: 'The words of him who has the seven spirits of God and the seven stars. " 'I know your works. You have the reputation of being alive, but you are dead. Wake up, and strengthen what remains and is about to die, for I have not found your works complete in the sight of my God. Remember, then, what you received and heard. Keep it, and repent. If you will not wake up, I will come like a thief, and you will not know at what hour I will come against you. (Revelation 3:1–3, ESV)

Shadows and Copies

One of the many areas that professors and pastors overly complicate is in calling portions of the Law "shadows" (from Colossians 2:17 and

Hebrews 10:1) and "copies" (Hebrews 8:5) which were "fulfilled" and eliminated by Jesus. Therefore we don't have to do them anymore. While it's true that words like shadows and copies are used of the Law, the conclusion that therefore it is eliminated and we don't have to do it (or parts of it) is not. Two major flaws in the shadows and copies argument (besides that the conclusion is not biblical) is the fact that 1) There was an original when they were established, and 2) Shadows are effective.

All proponents of the shadows and copies position admit that when the shadows and copies were established they were patterns after the original. In other words, there was a Temple in heaven that was the pattern for the Tabernacle (and later Temple) and its so-called "temporary" ceremonies. Yet God directed the construction of the Tabernacle and instituted the ceremonies anyway. This does not make sense if God was just kidding around and later the Messiah would remove the shadows. It also doesn't make sense that the death penalty would be incurred for disobedience of shadows and copies. One of these days the Bible says that there will be major changes, and instead of a copy of a Temple we will have the real thing among us. In the meantime, however, even if we call parts of His Word a shadow they are still real.

The other major flaw in the shadows and copies position is that the shadows and copies are effective. Not only did the correct observing of them allow God to dwell in their midst, Israel couldn't subdue the Land or be victorious in battle if they weren't following all of the shadows exactly and correctly. The sin of Achan (Joshua 7) shows us this in stark relief. When Jericho was being destroyed, Achan took some of the devoted things that belonged to God, and God's anger burned. God, however, didn't just hold Achan responsible but the entire nation (Joshua 7:1). When they went up to battle the city of Ai, they were defeated by a much smaller army and 32 died, all because one Israeli man held out on everyone else. One man sinned, but God said it was the nation of Israel that sinned. Apparently shadows and copies are a whole lot more important than we have been led to believe.

One Continuous Promise

Whole Bible Christianity is based on an understanding of the Word that includes continuity and unity. Continuity means that the Bible is one continuous message from Genesis to Revelation without breaks in it like an "age of Law" and a separate "age of grace," a page with New Testament or Old Testament printed on it marking an imaginary boundary, or an "age of Israel" with a separate "age of the church." Unity has close to the same meaning in that we can see the Bible agrees with itself, it is one whole message and each part is needed to help understand the whole. It is not contradictory. The alleged contradictions are mostly in the minds of the people who read the Bible with no intention of doing what it says.

It's easy to say the Bible is written around the unifying theme of Jesus, but it might be a little difficult to see exactly where He is sometimes. He gets obscured by tradition, sentiment and funny ways of looking at and teaching His Word. And again I don't mean "funny ha ha." One way to spot Him is through words that are used to tie together His presence and teachings such as "promise" and "covenant." But sometimes even those key words are absent such as in Genesis 3:15 when God promises (without using that word) a descendant (Jesus) who will crush the head of the serpent. So we have to look sharp and use the whole Bible.

Abraham was "promised" (using the word "covenant" instead) that this descendant (the seed of the woman) would be from a child born to Sarah (Isaac - the "son of the promise" from Romans 9:9) and through this descendant (Jesus) Abraham would "bless the nations." This promise (the Messiah or God with us) is tied with the "seed of Eve" all through the Bible. David was included in bringing the promise to us. God said he would have a son who would sit on his throne in a kingdom that would last forever (2 Samuel 7).

This promised descendant or son and blessing was part of the gospel (good news or God with us) preached to Israel at Sinai (Hebrews 4:2 - see chapter 5). The Law was part of the promise (and the gospel) because it lays out behavior expected by God as He takes up residence with us according to the promise (remember - God with us). He took up residence in Israel (His children) and expected certain actions. As He takes up residence now in believers the expectations remain.

If the Bible really is "one faith" (chapter 4 of this book) delivered to "one body" (chapter 3) by "one God" and "one Lord" (chapter 2) as Paul says in Ephesians 4, then the next question is "Why isn't the church following it?" If the New Covenant is the Law written on a heart of flesh, then it seems some biblical practices are being ignored by those who are supposed to have this covenant as their operating document. If the Bible really is one continuous, unified message (and it is) with no breaks or stops and starts or churches created, then the next step is to grab hold and put it into every area of life. Not just as a novelty or for some inspiring stories once in a while, but hungering and thirsting for it as if His Word was a treasure hidden in a field or a pearl of great price. I know I'm mixing metaphors but you get my drift.

> "The kingdom of heaven is like treasure hidden in a field, which a man found and covered up. Then in his joy he goes and sells all

that he has and buys that field. "Again, the kingdom of heaven is like a merchant in search of fine pearls, who, on finding one pearl of great value, went and sold all that he had and bought it. (Matthew 13:44-46, ESV)

All the books of the Bible were written by people who understood the continuity of this promise from God and included continuous revelation from God as to how this promise would be realized. All the believers throughout the ages who accepted God's Word looked forward to the delivery of the promise and its full implementation. The first century church lived all of it. When we throw out parts of the Word, whether we dismiss them as merely "civil" or "ceremonial" shadows or "fulfill" them and terminate them, we destroy the unity and continuity of His living oracles. Like a guitar with a string missing or a violin without a bow, if we remove any part of His Word the gospel and the promises of God are reduced to a limited discordant series of feel-good proverbs, lacking the power to move us as they are intended. This is what I call "bumper sticker Christianity" and it just doesn't do the job to produce fruit.

What did Jesus do?

One of the responses a whole Bible Christian will get when sharing opinions like these with a group of standard Christians is, "We don't have to follow the Law. It's not a salvation issue." But the Bible makes no split between salvation issues and non-salvation issues. I usually respond to this with, "So let me get this straight. God is born into a human body, suffers in all ways as we do for around 30 years, and dodges people trying to kill Him. He preaches what He'd been preaching for thousands of years about salvation by love through love only to be arrested on trumped up charges and executed in the most horrible, torturous fashion available at the time. And He was completely blameless through all of it. My question is, was it a "salvation issue" for Jesus? What I mean is *He* didn't need saving; *we* did. He didn't "have to" submit to a torturous death. But He still did it.

What did Jesus do? Jesus talked a lot about the Law. He gave it, established it, and lived it perfectly. He did not abolish it but filled it up full of love and the Spirit as it was intended (Matthew 5:17-19). He lived by every word from the mouth of God (Matthew 4:4) including the Law. His food was to do the will of the Father (John 4:34). He said that all should do the weightier commands as well as the lighter (Matthew 23:23; Luke 11:42). His parting instruction was to teach disciples all He commanded (Matthew 28:20). He pointed people to the Law to inherent eternal life (Mark 10:17-19; Luke 10:25-28, 18:18-22). He said Moses wrote about Him, and to disbelieve the words of Moses is to disbelieve His words.

> [46]"For if you believed Moses, you would believe Me, for he wrote about Me. [47]"But if you do not believe his writings, how will you believe My words?" (John 5:46-47 NASB95)

The Law is part of the gospel (Hebrews 4:2; again, see chapter 5), and it is unequaled as a lifestyle and discipleship method. We don't *have* to follow the Law, we *get* to. The message of the Bible, from the Garden to Jesus to you and me, is do what God says. Charges of hypocrisy are leveled at the church because they simply do not do what they say they believe. Much of the church claims to "believe" the whole Bible but does not follow it. Not only do we skip out on "civil" and "ceremonial" laws (except for the tithe of course – got to have something with which to build those earthly kingdoms!) but the very rationalizing we use to avoid them is also used to skip out on many other laws. When we call parts of the Law a "shadow" or say that they were "fulfilled" and terminated, what's to keep others from using the same logic for homosexuality, adultery, theft, or other "moral" laws? And in fact the church is enabling others to do just that.

The other side of hypocrisy is integrity. It means wholeness, honesty, or holding to moral and ethical principles. Integrity or wholeness as applied to the Bible is related to faithfulness. God acts with integrity or faithfulness to His character all the time. He expects the same from us. Integrity and faithfulness in a Christian context means to be consistent in your thoughts and behaviors with the words that God speaks. We are not consistent when we start trimming the pieces we don't like from God's Word. Integrity is the first casualty of picking and choosing. Faithfulness suffers when we slice and dice the Word to suit our own understanding.

Hypocrisy is the result when we won't maintain our biblical integrity and stay faithful to God. Even simple things everyone agrees we are supposed to do go by the wayside. When was the last time you saw the church discipline described specifically by Jesus in Matthew 18:15-20 actually carried out in any church? Divorce and adultery are rampant, even though God hates divorce and says we are not to leave the wife of our youth (Malachi 2:15-17). Leaders don't have to be "husbands of one wife" because we reinterpret this to mean "one wife at a time." It doesn't really matter though, does it, because there are so many churches on so many street corners competing to see who can build the next mega-church. Right?

Some in the church say, "The shadows are just small things. They're not important." But the Bible has an answer for that, too. He who is faithful in little is faithful in much. The church who isn't faithful in little won't be faithful in much (Luke 16:10). Faith is not about size or quantity. It's about doing what God says in all things, whether we think they are big or little. The lack of respect for the (so-called) small things shows up too in our lack of obedience in big things like divorce and suicide, which are as common inside the church as out.

I submit that we cannot claim to be faithful in the big things while sitting in judgment on His Word for (alleged) small things. It's like trying to drive a car with a wheel missing. Jesus tells us not to ignore the lighter commands while placing proper emphasis on the weightier ones (Matthew 23:23). I can't find any biblical proof that some of the Law is not worthy of our attention. A loving relationship with God does not have room for judging what we are willing to do and what we are not. He gave us everything including the blood of His only begotten Son in boundless love and grace. Returning that gift with partial effort and picky sentiment doesn't reflect a new heart of flesh.

Jesus didn't "have to" save us. He died and was resurrected because He loves God and followed His loving will. He loves us. If it could've been done any other way He would have done it that way. *"My Father, if it be possible, let this cup pass from me; nevertheless not as I will, but as you will"* (Matthew 26:39). He laid down His life of His own accord (John 10:18). Whole Bible Christians echo our Messiah and say, "Not as I will, but as you will." In all things we lay down our life as He directs. He loved us so much that He left His glory in heaven shared with the Father and submitted to some miserable things in life. But He did it willingly, because of His gracious love.

So do you believe "we don't have to," or should we copy our Messiah, do what Jesus does, and do as our loving and gracious heavenly Father instructs?

Salvation by Love

Some of the pragmatism of church leaders can be seen in discussions over salvation by grace through faith (Ephesians 2:8) as opposed to salvation by faith plus works (Ephesians 2:10). The modern version of salvation by grace through faith focuses on man. People get into all kinds of debates about whether the will of man is "free" or whether it is too depraved to do anything. On the other side is an argument of salvation by faith plus works, which puts the focus on merit. Then you get into all kinds of other debates about which works are going to get the job done, or what is a work of the flesh, or legalism versus God's grace and the cross.

The whole Bible variation on both of these is salvation by love (Psalm 13:5, 31:16, 40:10, 85:7, 119:41; Zephaniah 3:17; 1

Thessalonians 5:8). Perhaps we can even say salvation by love through love. Salvation by love means that God loved us and acted on it, and we love Him and act on His Word. It's that simple. This puts an entirely different light on grace, faith and works. Debates ended. Well, the debates aren't ended, but it leaves a lot of people without a biblical basis for arguing. If we just read the Word (and do it) we would easily solve a lot of these types of theological issues.

This love is not a halfway, nitpicky type of love. It's a sold out, all in, nothing left kind of love. It isn't built on feelings or sentiment, though there are feelings or emotions that are involved. We move forward in His love by abiding in His Word. God put it all on the line in love, giving His only begotten Son. Jesus sold out to His Father's plans and programs. He didn't hold anything back either in life, death or resurrection. If we buy into His kingdom, it is with everything we have. God didn't go half way then stop. He went all in. He wants His children to do the same. Sell out to Him. Buy the field having great treasure or the pearl with everything we have (Matthew 13:44-46), give up body parts if we have to (Mark 9:33-48) don't look back (Luke 9:62) leave house, wife, brothers, parents, children (Luke 18:29-30), take up our cross daily (Luke 9:23) and lose our lives (Matthew 10:39, 16:25; Mark 8:35; Luke 9:24, 17:33; John 12:25).

In its pragmatism the church ignores the Law and so refuses to make a distinction between holy and common or clean and unclean (or at least parts of it). Jesus "made everything clean" (we preach) but poison is still poison. God's Law shows us what is clean and holy but when we surgically alter it to suit ourselves we open the door to all sorts of exceptions.

> Her priests have done violence to my law and have profaned my holy things. They have made no distinction between the holy and the common, neither have they taught the difference between the unclean and the clean, and they have disregarded my Sabbaths, so that I am profaned among them. (Ezekiel 22:26, ESV)

A little leaven leavens the whole lump. We are the ones who have done violence to His law and profaned His holy things (Ezekiel 22:23-31; Zephaniah 3:4). We consider ourselves "not under the Law" while the works of the flesh are evident in us – sexual immorality, impurity, sensuality, idolatry, sorcery (use of drugs), enmity, strife, jealousy, fits of anger, rivalries, dissensions, divisions, envy, drunkenness, orgies and things like these (Galatians 5:21; Ephesians 5:5). Jesus didn't come to bring peace, but a sword (Matthew 10:34). This sword is the Word of God, and divides true believers in God and His Son from unbelievers. Those who do His word are separated from those who won't.

You may be thinking this book is a little uncomfortable. I can't help it – I rewrote it a bunch of times trying to make things nice and comfy. I know what sells are books that focus on feelings, are soft and sweet, and allow us to do what we want. Nifty prayers, finding "purpose" in a driven life, meeting a (false) god in a shack, or helping the church "emerge" are the way to go for profit. I could make a lot of money writing about 10 Rules for Getting Everything You Want out of Life as long as they aren't an objective set of God's Ten Rules.

I would've liked to make this book feel more comfortable, but God wouldn't let me. I can only tell you what He says. You might think I'm being overly negative about the church, and feel like jumping to the defense of your own church. But negative is positive when the goal is God. Instead of judging His Word we should judge ourselves with right judgment (John 7:24) and judge ourselves first. God encourages us to constantly stay on guard and self-correct.

> But if we judged ourselves truly, we would not be judged. But when we are judged by the Lord, we are disciplined so that we may not be condemned along with the world. (1 Corinthians 11:31–32, ESV)

He is very clear about the cause and the treatment of sin. He's not confused, and He doesn't change His mind from one minute to the next. His loving Word can be uncomfortable at first, but if we claim His Name, we get disciplined the same as any son or daughter.[12]

> If we say we have no sin, we deceive ourselves, and the truth is not in us. If we confess our sins, he is faithful and just to forgive us our sins and to cleanse us from all unrighteousness. If we say we have not sinned, we make him a liar, and his word is not in us. (1 John 1:8–10, ESV)

Maybe you are one of those people who really want to feel God but just can't seem to reach. Like me, you've looked in a church; maybe even a number of different churches. While there are some good things, God seems to be just a bit beyond your fingertips still.

You've tried a home fellowship or two and learned to pray like that guy Jabez. Seminars to help you find purpose to drive your life are coming out your ears. You've tried all the latest church fads; bought the bestselling books. You've gone looking for shacks. You get excited for a while, but none of it really works to touch God or produce Spirit fruit.

---

[12] Judged first, as sons. 1 Corinthians 5:12, 6:2-3; Hebrews 12:5, 8, 10, 11; 1 Peter 4:4, 5; Revelation 3:19.

You can't get over the huge disconnect between what you see around you in the church and what's in the Word.

If we really want to start looking like the first century believers, we have to do it right. Love is not always comfortable. Deep cuts are sewn together with needle and thread. Bleeding has to be stopped; cauterized if necessary. Infection has to be killed. Failing hearts need a shock to get working again. Friends don't let friends drive drunk, or something like that. The truth is going to hurt a little, but we've got to have it. (Clear!)

You're not alone, even if it might be a little lonely at times. Jesus is in the same boat (when He wasn't walking on top the water) and so are the apostles. Paul found himself floating with us. Maybe you'll want to climb on in. Watch the first step though. It's a doozy.

Before you come aboard, close the book and set it aside for a few minutes. Ask yourself how bad you really want to touch Him. This is what Jesus calls "counting the cost."

> "Whoever does not carry his own cross and come after Me cannot be My disciple. "For which one of you, when he wants to build a tower, does not first sit down and calculate the cost to see if he has enough to complete it? (Luke 14:27-28 NASB95)

Can you ditch all you know if it doesn't measure up to the Word? Are you ready to set the broken legs, sew up the wounds, and defibrillate the hearts? Do you hunger and thirst for God, His kingdom, and His righteousness? Are you willing to trade the unsatisfying food and drink you have stockpiled for the only truly satisfying meal around? Are you interested in learning more about abiding in salvation by love? Will you give up your pride, humble yourself, and submit to His every command? If so, keep going.

2 A Whole God

⁴"Hear, O Israel! The LORD is our God, the LORD is one! ⁵"You shall love the LORD your God with all your heart and with all your soul and with all your might. (Deuteronomy 6:4-5 NASB95)

God is one. If you read the Bible this seems self-evident. But we have to talk about God being One because a main tool used to distract from, eliminate or severely prune the Law is to cast it as a different message from another God. To some people it's as if Jesus and the Father were two separate gods at loggerheads with each other. Splitting God helps a person who wants to dodge the Law pretend it came from someone who either changed His mind or didn't mean what He said in the first place. We also have to review this subject because there are people who advocate for the Law in a believer's life yet deny the deity of Jesus.

You may already accept that God and Jesus are one, but you may not realize exactly what it means. The church tends to skip over that part. For instance, if God and Jesus are one, then Jesus gave the Law at Sinai. So when He tells us in Matthew 28 to teach the disciples "all I commanded," it includes the Law that He "filled up full" or fulfilled.

A cubist painting looks like it has been cut up and put back together out of order. You know, the nose is where the ear is supposed to be, and the eyes are not lined up. Every part is out of place. The picture of God painted by the modern church now looks cubist.[13] God is variously described as a fierce, distant and unfriendly god, or a buddy from out of town who winks at sin. He's either a god of cloud and flame and lightening, or a pacifist hippie flower child who spouts one-liners about peace and love.[14]

The church uses artistic license sort of like cubism to interpret the patterns in the Word and make a picture that doesn't even resemble the original. One pattern is for Jews and another is for the church. This part is for me and that part is for you. There are "old" and "new" god models. The old god is supposed to be a severe, demanding god of bloody

---

[13] Pablo Picasso was a cubist painter.

[14] A guy named Marcion in about 140 A. D. advanced some of these ideas. He was thrown out of the church as a heretic, but the ideas linger still. He wasn't the first, or the last. Gnosticism (secret knowledge) had been floating around for a while, and mysticism is alive and well in modern times. False mysticism, that is.

sacrifices and death. The new god is a sweet guy who looks the other way when we sin. The old god beat us up with rules we couldn't obey and restricts what we eat. The new god came to change all the stuff the old god gave us, and died so we could eat a ham sandwich. We have created, as Dr. Michael Brown says, a "worldly, cultural Christianity" with a "Jesus who radically empowers us" rather that a "Jesus who radically changes us." I agree with him that "that's why we have 'Christian' lingerie models and 'Christian' rappers who frequent strip clubs."[15]

The picture of God is critical to faith. When we paint Him as capricious, powerful and judgmental, giving us laws we could never obey, we can't trust Him or do what He says. On the other hand when we paint Him with the color of sentiment (without justice or holiness) our false picture might let us do whatever we want even if it kills us. But that isn't love.

In addition to artistically rearranging pieces of the Word to make a picture of God we like better, we also change the picture according to our street theology and tradition. Ideas we've already got in our brains before we even start reading His Word can cause us to miss God's real message. One of these ideas is that we assume He's like us. Then we impose our own limitations on Him as if He is manic-depressive or bi-polar. One minute He's throwing laws around that we can't obey, the next He's telling us that He was just kidding. Ever since the deceiver told Adam and Eve they could be "like God" we've been cutting and pasting and cubing and splitting to make Him look like us.

In this chapter we will reinforce the simple biblical facts that Jesus is God and God is one. We will do this by matching the picture given to us by many in the church or synagogue with the one God gives us in the Word. One picture is genuine, one is a forgery. It's like they have two completely different painters. The graffiti of men's opinions (on both pictures) make it hard to tell which is which. And yes, I know this book is just another opinion. But my opinion is we should read and do the whole Bible to clear up the picture. So let's revisit some of the core Bible concepts of God here; see if we can't freshen up our viewpoint and recover some hijacked vocabulary. As we compare the Bible picture with the church picture we'll clean off some of the graffiti, as it were.

God is One

If I were to tell you, "I am one," and I wasn't talking about my birthdays, you might think I was a little odd. Of course I'm one person.

---

[15] Online article http://townhall.com/columnists/michaelbrown/2013/01/03/whats-right-and-wrong-with-american-christianity-n1478711/page/full by Dr. Michael Brown; http://askdrbrown.org/home.

Even if I had a twin, I'm still only one person. We don't have to tell others that we are "one" because it is self-evident. So why does God have to tell people that He is one?

There are at least three reasons bearing on whole Bible Christianity. One is that God's name can sometimes be plural. He refers to Himself often as "we" or "us" (Genesis 1:26 for instance). The second is the Angel of the Lord, who appears every so often in the biblical accounts and is called God. So we need to account for this angelic person who behaved differently than other angels and other men (He had to be Jesus). The third of course is Jesus, who is also an angel (the word means "messenger") of the Lord and is also God. I think God emphasized His oneness for centuries before the Incarnation because He knew Jesus would be rejected for equating Himself with, um, Himself.

Jesus is God[16]

Some names for God, such as *Elohim* (ell-oh-heem) are plural. In the verses at the chapter head for instance, *Elohim* is translated God (YHVH or The LORD is our *Elohim*). God is saying there is more to Him than meets the eye. He functions as three people that we know of, yet these three are One (Hebrew *echad*). It sounds odd to our ears, but He is plural and also one plurality. He has to say He is one because humans have the tendency to worship only parts of God. The parts they like. The Father says He is one package – that if you get part you get the whole thing. If we want to follow Him it's all or nothing.

We know from Scripture that there are at least three parts (or people) to God – Father, Son, and Holy Spirit. But that may not be all. Revelation 1:4, 3:1, and 4:5 for instance tell us that there are seven spirits of God. So there is more to this idea than we know at the moment. But there are at least three people (or nine) to YHVH our Elohim, they are all God, and God is one.

Jesus says that He is one with the Father (John 10:30, 17:11) and that if you've seen Him you've seen the Father (John 14:7, 14:9). For all intents and purposes, Jesus is the son of God, and is God. He is central to the Bible, which is one reason people attack the absolute truth picture of the Word all the time. Mess up the Word and you mess up God. Split God into two and anything you don't like from the old God (such as the Law) can be rejected in favor of a new message from a new God (such as Jesus).

---

[16] The Messiah is savior, yet only God can save; He did things only God can do; He literally fulfilled hundreds of OT prophecies; He accepted worship; He said He was God, He always existed, etc. See also Matthew 23:37-39.

It is fun to get the unbelievers upset, so I'll say it again just for grins: Jesus is God. People go nuts about this, mostly because they want to dictate to God what He can and cannot do. God is not human (though He is the source of human life) in their minds. The idea of Him inhabiting a human body just freaks them out. They can't figure out how He does it. It doesn't help their thinking that Jesus allowed Himself to be crucified, and that He didn't use a lot of flashy signs. It also doesn't help that humans are not just bodies, either. Meaning we have different parts (body, soul, spirit) and each of us is also "one."

When we were made (in Adam) it was in the image of God (Genesis 1:26 – another place He is plural). He breathed into us the "breath of lives" so why couldn't He also impart Himself into a man's body? A lot of people will tell you God is spirit and has no form. They'll spend a lot of time trying to say that "image" means anything other than an actual carbon copy. But since the Messiah (Jesus the Christ) has always existed, it is no stretch to see He is the pattern for humans, and we were made in His actual image (arms, eyes, legs, etc.).

Seems to me most of the "Jesus can't be God" arguments revolve around God "can't" do something like that. The God who made everything, who breathed the breath of lives into us, who made man in "our" (His) image, and with whom "all things are possible" somehow can't inhabit a human body. Jesus is called the "seed of the woman" because God used this seed to make Himself a body. We have the breath of His lives in us, but we can be separate and distinct from Him. Why not Jesus? I'm just not convinced by the types of extra-biblical arguments claiming God can't do something. Even when the Bible is used to sort-of bolster the arguments.

Many have a problem with God dying a miserable, torturous death on a chunk of wood. Why would the all powerful, all knowing, all present God allow this to happen to Himself? There is a lack of understanding here, because there is a lack of understanding love. God could indeed allow it, because it was the only way to reconcile us to Him in justice, holiness and love. It is a beautiful example, indeed the pinnacle of examples, of God's love for us. Our Father laid down His life (through Jesus the Messiah) for His brothers, sisters or friends. His death has bonded us together in a tighter and more permanent way than simple physical birth or marriage.

Another problem is failure to understand the concept of One (or echad). Why would God have to claim that He is One? Wouldn't that be self-evident? I don't have to tell you I'M one. So if God is solitary or singular, then He wouldn't have to tell us He is One. He is One, but He has seven spirits. How can that BE in the Jesus-isn't-God definition of One? It seems obvious that He has to reaffirm that He is one because in fact He appears in different ways or forms. Man and woman become "one flesh" in marriage, yet obviously are not sharing the same body. There are lots of ways that echad (one) is shown as a unity and not just singular.

If Jesus is not God, then worship of Jesus is idolatry. Yet He accepted worship, forgave sins (the ones against God, which only God can forgive) and claimed that He and God were the same in Word and deed (and in being around before Abraham). Jesus said "I AM" which can only be said of God. There is no other name under heaven by which men may be saved, but we are saved by Yeshua haMashiach? How can this happen? The answer is it cannot, unless Jesus is in fact God. Since He looks like God, acts like God, and does things only God can do, then He must be God! If He isn't God in the flesh, He is close enough to be indistinguishable from the Father anyway. So why quibble?

The Seed of the Woman

In Genesis 3:15, God promises that the seed of the woman (the Messiah) would crush the head of the serpent. This is an odd way to phrase the promise of the Messiah. Women don't have seeds – men have the seeds. Women have the eggs.

The seed of the man carries Adam's sin nature. We were all created at the same time in Adam.[17] When he fell, he affected all of us because we were right there with him. After Adam, whenever a man and a woman make a baby, the new life inherits the nature of his or her dad which is handed down from Adam.[18] But, if God didn't want the Messiah to share Adam's sin nature, He could (and did) take the seed of the woman and by His own Spirit create a body. Not so far out of the realm of possibility for the creator of everything (Genesis 1:2). And the God who made Adam out of dirt.

So we have a Savior who has the nature of God, yet dwells in a human body. We see pictures of this throughout the Word. For instance, there's the bush burning without being consumed (Exodus 3) and God dwelling with Israel in a tent and a temple. The Messiah's physical body is a reason that Jesus liked to call Himself "the Son of Man" so often.

Jesus shares the nature of God and the humanness of man, so He is qualified to be the Kinsman-Redeemer,[19] the mediator between God and man (Genesis 48:16; Leviticus 25:25; Isaiah 41:14, 35:1-10, 59:20-21.

---

[17] The word 'life' is plural in Genesis 2:7. It is actually "breath of lives" that God breathed in Adam's nostrils.
[18] This is called 'traducianism.' The belief that a new soul is created at conception is called 'creationism.'
[19] A kinsman-redeemer was the closest relative who could buy back the person or property of another relative.

See also 1 Samuel 2:25). He had to be related to both parties in order to buy us back from the power of the evil one (and for other reasons as well).

Jesus is the head of His Body (Colossians 1:18) the source of our life (Acts 17:24-28) the control center for creation (Romans 8:19-22). He is the will of God personified. No one, saved or *unsaved*, can do anything without Him (John 15:5). All creation was made and is maintained by Him (John 1:3); He upholds everything by the Word (and Law) of His power (Hebrews 1:3). Even people who do not acknowledge Him are dependent on Him and His Word for their life and breath.

Jesus is the virgin-born promise and son of God. In God's perfect timing He was incarnated to heal the breach between man and God and continue to restore creation to its clean, perfect, and joyful state. He is the "right hand" (Isaiah 41:10; Psalm 48:10; Matthew 16:19; Acts 2:33, 5:31; Romans 8:34) and the "glory" of God.[20] He is the Holy One of Israel (Isaiah 47:4, 54:5). He is the physical representation of God and is God (John 1:18, 6:46; 2 Corinthians 4:4; 1 John 4:12). He has always existed, and always will exist (John 1:2; Colossians 1:18; Hebrews 7:1-3).

He spent time on earth as a man. His works and teachings testified to His identity and purpose (see: the Bible). At the appointed time, He was killed through the efforts of all people acting together. He was not killed by "the Jews" but by the Romans, although the Jewish leaders were accessories and would've done it by themselves had they chosen.[21] God the Father would not allow Him to stay in the grave, so He was brought back and given a seat at the right hand of God (Colossians 3:1).

> [41]Now while the Pharisees were gathered together, Jesus asked them a question: [42]"What do you think about the Christ, whose son is He?" They said to Him, "The son of David." [43]He said to them, "Then how does David in the Spirit call Him 'Lord,' saying, [44]'THE LORD SAID TO MY LORD, "SIT AT MY RIGHT HAND, UNTIL I PUT YOUR ENEMIES BENEATH YOUR FEET" '? [45]"If David then calls Him 'Lord,' how is He his son?" [46]No one was able to answer Him a word, nor did anyone dare from that day on to ask Him another question. (Matthew 22:41-46 NASB95)

---

[20] Deuteronomy 5:24; 2 Chronicles 5:14; Isaiah 35:2; Ezekiel 9:3; Acts 7:55-56; 2 Corinthians 4:4; Titus 2:13; Revelation 21:23.

[21] Many times people were stoned in back alleys and the stoners weren't caught or punished. There's more to this than meets the eye.

Jesus in the Old Testament

Jesus is not just in the New Testament, He is all through the Old Testament (John 1:15). In type (like the Passover lamb) and prophecy for sure, but also right out there in front presenting God to man in visible form. How do I know this? I'm glad you asked. Besides the evidence I've already given, John quotes Jesus (see John 14:9) in his gospel *"No man has seen the Father, but the only begotten of God who is in the bosom of the Father, He has revealed Him"* (John 1:18). It is also written,

> [37] "And the Father who sent Me, He has testified of Me. You have neither heard His voice at any time nor seen His form. [38] "You do not have His word abiding in you, for you do not believe Him whom He sent. (John 5:37-38 NASB95)
>
> [7]"If you had known Me, you would have known My Father also; from now on you know Him, and have seen Him." (John 14:7 NASB95) (See also Luke 10:22; John 6:46, 14:9, 15:24; and 1 John 4:12).

On the one hand, Jesus says that no one has seen God, yet many people are recorded as saying they did. If no man has seen the Father, then any time people saw God it was Jesus the Son revealing the Father.[22] He was in the Garden, He is the seed of the woman, and He is the Promise.

In John 5:37-38 (above) Jesus is speaking with the religious leaders, and He means that their hearts were not soft flesh and did not have His Word written (or abiding) on them. God speaks all the time through the created order, and through His Words, and people don't see Him or hear Him then either. Jesus reveals the Father to us, and is the primary agent in that revelation. I think it is clear that Jesus has been around as long as the Father, and has been interacting with people for far longer than we sometimes realize.

Jesus was the torch and pot of Genesis 15; He was the Angel of the Lord who spoke with Abraham about Sodom and Gomorrah (and appeared in all other places that the Angel of the Lord is mentioned).[23] He was the burning bush (Exodus 3:2, 3) and is the person who wrote the Ten Commandments on the stone tablets (He spoke with Moses "face to face" in Exodus 33:11 and Deuteronomy 34:10).

---

[22] Three possible exceptions: Daniel 7, Matthew 3:16-17, and Matthew 17. But what is seen, I think, is a picture (not the actual Father). Both could be Jesus (probably not). These examples also do not take away from Jesus revealing the Father.

[23] Genesis 16:7-11, 22:11; Numbers 22; Judges 6 & 13; 1 Chronicles 21 and Psalm 34:7.

Jesus is the "glory of the Lord" and shows up "face to face" with Jacob (Genesis 32:30) and again on the mountain (Exodus 24:16, 33:20-23, 34:5-7). Joshua sees Him as captain of the Lord's hosts (Joshua 5:12-14). Amos sees Him standing with a plumb line (Amos 7:7, 8) and by the altar (Amos 9). Isaiah sees Him high and lifted up (Isaiah 6) and Daniel sees Him as the Son of Man (Daniel 7:13-14).

These and many others are all instances of the pre-incarnate Jesus revealing the Father to men. As near as I can tell, every physical representation of God in the Scriptures was Jesus. Anywhere in the Scriptures that people saw God, or spoke face to face with God, was Jesus. Jesus has revealed the Father to us in function *and* form. The Word of God, with the Law of God, is the same unified message whether coming from the Father or the Son.

> But as for you, continue in what you have learned and have firmly believed, knowing from whom you learned it and how from childhood you have been acquainted with the sacred writings, which are able to make you wise for salvation through faith in Christ Jesus. (2 Timothy 3:14–15, ESV)

Old, Jewish God?

I was once told by a woman that she was glad there was a New Testament. She said if Christianity only had the Old Testament she would not consider herself a believer. She might not be a believer at all then if she actually read the Bible.

> [39] You search the Scriptures because you think that in them you have eternal life; and it is they that bear witness about me, [40] yet you refuse to come to me that you may have life. [41] I do not receive glory from people. [42] But I know that you do not have the love of God within you. [43] I have come in my Father's name, and you do not receive me. If another comes in his own name, you will receive him. [44] How can you believe, when you receive glory from one another and do not seek the glory that comes from the only God? [45] Do not think that I will accuse you to the Father. There is one who accuses you: Moses, on whom you have set your hope. [46] For if you believed Moses, you would believe me; for he wrote of me. [47] But if you do not believe his writings, how will you believe my words?" (John 5:39-47 ESV)

Jesus says that a person who believes the writings of Moses (the Law) will believe Him. Obviously, then, if a person believes Jesus, he will believe the writings of Moses. Jesus is, in fact, the "old, Jewish God." People keep trying to sell two gods, but there is only one. Jesus is the same age as the Father.

I think people who "believe" the way that lady did have a deeper problem of anti-Jewishness, perhaps even a problem with abiding in God's Word. They want to reject the "Jewish" god and paint Jesus as a permissive Greek hero or something (in many cases literally!). They also want a subjective standard (instead of God's objective Law) so they can shape it as they wish. The puzzle for those who reject the Jews[24] is that the new covenant is Jewish, Jesus is Jewish, all the apostles are Jewish, the gospel goes first to the Jews, the initial "churches" were Jewish, salvation is from the Jews, and all writers of the Bible are Jewish.[25] Like it or not, God worked and is working through Israel.

God is the same always (Malachi 3:6 and Hebrews 13:8 for starters). Even though without the sacrifice of the Christ He certainly would be a God of blood and judgment, it was also He who sent His Son (Galatians 4:4-6; 1 John 4:9-14) to be the payment for our sins.

The Son submitted to God's will in this matter, but the Father did the offering. We see a picture of this in Genesis 21 and 22 when Abraham almost sacrificed his own son Isaac (the son of the promise), but God provided a ram instead. In a very real sense, God can be thought of as so identified with Jesus that they are identical.

God owns everything (Deuteronomy 10:14; Jeremiah 23:23-24, 27:5) and is everywhere. He is perfect, without sin or shadow of turning (James 1:17). He has all the power (omnipotent Jeremiah 10:12) and knows everything (omniscient Daniel 2:20-22). These are all traits shared by both God and Jesus (Matthew 28:18; Luke 4:6; John 17:2). They are not separate gods even if at times they seem to have slightly different identities or functions. *"I and the Father are One,"* as Jesus says (John 10:30). If God looked in a mirror, He would see Jesus staring back at Him. But this means more than just family resemblance.

Jesus was active in the Old Testament long before His Incarnation. It was He who walked in the Garden with Adam and Eve. Jude says that Jesus was the one who brought Israel out of Egypt and Paul says that they drank from the same spiritual rock which was Christ (1 Corinthians 10:4).

> Now I want to remind you, although you once fully knew it, that Jesus, who saved a people out of the land of Egypt, afterward destroyed those who did not believe. (Jude 5, ESV)

---

[24] I'm using the word here to describe physical kids of Jacob. Next chapter we will look at this more closely.

[25] Luke is the only slight question mark, and the only reason people think he was Gentile is because of his name and that he was a physician. But wait – lots of Jewish people have alternate Gentile names (see Paul) and are doctors! Nebuchadnezzar is another possibility (Daniel 4) but it is more likely that his testimony is recorded by Daniel.

Jesus expelled Adam and Eve from Paradise and placed a guard at the entrance so they couldn't get back in. But it was also Jesus who paid the price to allow believers to return to Him. The Scriptures do not support the view that God has a split personality.

Some try to defend their point of view that Jesus is not God by saying that there were stories of a son of a god born from a virgin who died and was resurrected which were told long before Jesus was incarnated. They use the presence of these stories in other cultures to discount the Scriptures telling of the virgin birth or the Incarnation as similar fabrications. They conclude that Jesus is not God and was not born of a virgin, and is just another fable in a long line of such fables. In this they are correct: there were stories around for a long time of a virgin-born messiah who was the son of a god and who would die and be resurrected. The problem is that the Messiah promised by God in Genesis 3:15 predates all fables, and is the source for them. The Promise came first. The Old Testament writings came first. The stories of other messiahs were not the originals. They were copies of the promise, manufactured by Satan who heard the first Promise himself. He merely tried to poison the well in order to dilute God's own story.

Many of God's words have been hijacked in a similar fashion by false teachers in order to obscure His Law and steal authority. God is one – complete and unchanging. He is a righteous judge and a loving God at the same time. When He gives a Law He doesn't stop being gracious. The Law does not detract from His Promises, it was added (Galatians 3:19). The creation of two gods or the denial of Jesus as God is just the start of the hijacking. Words have been hijacked in order to split His Word and hence our relationship to God and each other. So let's take a whole Bible look at some of what goes into the character of God and how we relate to Him. We shall reclaim the words and terms that have been stolen or split up that keep us from life more abundant with our Father and Messiah.

Sin

Also called iniquity[26] or lawlessness, sin is anything less than perfection. It splits us apart from God. It is an inclination (sin nature) as well as actions (sins). If given a choice (and we do have a choice), we naturally lean towards sinning. Without the influence of God's Word we sin. The Hebrew word *chet* and the Greek word *hamartia*, translated into English as "sin," are both archery terms and mean "miss the mark." The Hebrew word for the Law (*torah* or instruction) also comes from archery and is literally "the mark."

---

[26] Greek *anomia* meaning literally 'no law' Enhanced Strong's Lexicon G458.

Missing the mark of God's Word is sin, and there is no gray area. Either we hit the target or we miss it. We can miss by a little or miss by a lot, and it's the same – we whiz by the target as we fly off to something that is not God. Sometimes we think getting close to the target should count. But as you've probably heard, close only counts in hand grenades and horseshoes.

> Behold, the LORD's hand is not shortened, that it cannot save, or his ear dull, that it cannot hear; but your iniquities have made a separation between you and your God, and your sins have hidden his face from you so that he does not hear. (Isaiah 59:1–2, ESV)

We'd like to think there are two targets – a hard, old one and a new easy one (or even "who cares about a target?"). But the biblical evidence is that there is only one mark or target, one standard of right behavior. God and Jesus speak the same word, not two different words to two (or more) different people groups.

God's Word is not some complicated, impossible task master that constantly keeps us guessing as to where the trip line is for a hidden trap. It is clear and plain and easy to understand and practice. The Law draws sin out of us because it challenges our pride on every level. Each command is a call to forsake our own knowledge of good and evil, gained in the Garden, and humbly choose the tree of life – the body and blood of His life in His word.

Sin is natural. We are born with sin natures. We get better at it as we get older. Some try to use genetics to excuse sins such as homosexuality. Of course. The argument is sound, because all sin is genetic or "natural." Duh. God's way out is the blood of Jesus. He tells us to leave what is only natural (the flesh) and do what is spiritual instead. All of God's words help us with this.

The Law includes forgiveness for sin. There are sacrifices and restitution included, and forgiveness is mentioned dozens of times. As it is written.

> The Lord passed before him and proclaimed, "The Lord, the Lord, a God merciful and gracious, slow to anger, and abounding in steadfast love and faithfulness, keeping steadfast love for thousands, forgiving iniquity and transgression and sin, but who will by no means clear the guilty, visiting the iniquity of the fathers on the children and the children's children, to the third and the fourth generation." (Exodus 34:6–7, ESV. See also Numbers 14:18.)

So we can say that if the requirements of the Law are answered, we must be forgiven. There are no ifs, ands, or maybes about it. And so it is. Jesus paid the price of not meeting the requirements of God's Law. He is the High priest that made atonement for us with His own blood, so forgiveness is granted when we confess and repent. We should be grateful that the Law is so firm and permanent, because that means forgiveness is also permanent. We get closure for sins forgiven because the Law is so firm in all its requirements. Including the requirement to grant forgiveness because the debt has been paid. A wishy-washy Law would mean we get a wishy-washy forgiveness.

Paul tells us that the Law "was added because of transgressions" (Galatians 3:19). In other words, transgression (sin) exists and the Law simply brings it out. The Law is not sin, and it does not cause sin. It is a catalyst – something that changes people without itself being changed. As His Word approaches we either repent or run. It reveals the will of God and gives us a choice: love Him or don't. His Word is love and life. Anything short of it is sin and death.

Idolatry

Idolatry is a major sin. In modern times, we think of it only as bowing down to a statue or other image. This is part of it, but there is much more to idolatry than statues.

> [1]God says, "If a husband divorces his wife And she goes from him And belongs to another man, Will he still return to her? Will not that land be completely polluted? But you are a harlot with many lovers; Yet you turn to Me," declares the Lord. [2]"Lift up your eyes to the bare heights and see; Where have you not been violated? By the roads you have sat for them Like an Arab in the desert, And you have polluted a land With your harlotry and with your wickedness. [3]"Therefore the showers have been withheld, And there has been no spring rain. Yet you had a harlot's forehead; You refused to be ashamed. [4]"Have you not just now called to Me, 'My Father, You are the friend of my youth? [5]'Will He be angry forever? Will He be indignant to the end?' Behold, you have spoken And have done evil things, And you have had your way." [6]Then the Lord said to me in the days of Josiah the king, "Have you seen what faithless Israel did? She went up on every high hill and under every green tree, and she was a harlot there. [7]"I thought, 'After she has done all these things she will return to Me'; but she did not return, and her treacherous sister Judah saw it. [8]"And I saw that for all the adulteries of faithless Israel, I had sent her away and given her a writ of divorce, yet her treacherous sister Judah did not fear; but she went and was a

harlot also. ⁹"Because of the lightness of her harlotry, she
polluted the land and committed adultery with stones and trees.
¹⁰"Yet in spite of all this her treacherous sister Judah did not
return to Me with all her heart, but rather in deception," declares
the Lord. (Jeremiah 3:1-10 NASB95)

Idolatry is "cheating" on God. We cheat Him with less than whole-hearted commitment. In public, we might claim to be like loyal spouses and do what God says. But when we ignore His Word it's just like cheating on a spouse. Any thought or action that doesn't match His Word is idolatry. Or adultery.

We might comfort ourselves that we are not idolaters because we don't have a statue in the living room (let's overlook the crucifix, Christmas tree, Easter eggs and bunnies for now). But idolatry is not limited to actual images. Paul says that covetousness is idolatry (Ephesians 5:5). God says the Chaldeans worship their own might, Jesus says that Mammon is a god, and Paul says that some people have their belly as their god (Philippians 3:19). And don't even get me started on American Idol. If we reject His ways and go our own way, even in the smallest thing, it's idolatry.

¹¹ Then they sweep by like the wind and go on, guilty men,
whose own might is their god!" (Habakkuk 1:11 ESV)

¹³ No servant can serve two masters, for either he will hate the
one and love the other, or he will be devoted to the one and
despise the other. You cannot serve God and money." (Luke
16:13 ESV)

The statue in the center of disobedience is the self-image. A 3-D statue is really self-will personified. Idolatry comes from inside, from the heart. The statue just gives it a physical shape. Adam and Eve were booted out of paradise, not because they bowed to an image, but because they bowed to self-will and knowledge. Obedience is worship. Their obedience to their own understanding was just the same as worshipping a statue of themselves.

We get all uptight when we read about people in the Old Testament who sacrificed their children to pagan gods. "Thank God that doesn't happen anymore" we think. But abortion is a pagan god practice. Babies are just sacrificed to the god of self-interest, rather than some statue. Yes, idolatry in its many forms is alive and well in modern times.

Sometimes we try to excuse our self-centered behavior, saying that motives count more than actions. If we are doing a wrong action, but we say it's for the "right" reasons, we think we're okay with God. So let me ask you something. Let's say your spouse is cheating on you. Yet he or she claims to be faithful because they "thought of you" while with the other person. Would you agree that the cheating spouse was faithful? I'm guessing, um, no. We cannot "think of God" while we are disobeying Him, and then try to convince Him we were actually being faithful. We wouldn't buy it from a spouse, and He sure isn't going to buy it from us, either.

> Beware lest there be among you a man or woman or clan or tribe whose heart is turning away today from the LORD our God to go and serve the gods of those nations. Beware lest there be among you a root bearing poisonous and bitter fruit, one who, when he hears the words of this sworn covenant, blesses himself in his heart, saying, 'I shall be safe, though I walk in the stubbornness of my heart.' This will lead to the sweeping away of moist and dry alike. (Deuteronomy 29:18–19, ESV)

Idolatry is bitter, and bears poisonous fruit like wormwood. It is "a root of bitterness" we get when we turn away from the covenant and "walk in the stubbornness of my heart." When we turn away from His Law, we turn from justice or the fruit of righteousness to bitter wormwood and cast down righteousness to the earth (Amos 5:7, 6:12).

Worshipping Jesus is not idolatry because God and Jesus are the same. If you've seen Jesus, you've seen the Father. Their wills are the same, their words are the same, and their Spirit is the same Holy One. They don't do things separately, except for the brief period of separation when Jesus was hanging on the cross (which must have been terrible to go through).

The Bible doesn't show a "father's section" or a "son's section." All the words should be red (or better yet, none of them). The Law belongs just as much to Jesus as it does to God, so when Jesus says "my commandments" He is grouping all the commandments together. When He says "it is written" He is talking about words that He spoke at Mt. Sinai or were recorded by the prophets. Scripture is as whole and complete as Jesus and God together could make it.

If, however, we isolate Jesus from God; if we repaint Him as a Greek god and forget the Father; if we claim Jesus teaches different things than the Father does, then we are indeed at risk of idolatry. Though He accepts worship (John 20:28) Jesus always directs us to the Father (Matthew 6:9, 12:50; Luke 10:22, 23:46; John 5:43). All power and authority are given to Jesus (Ephesians 1:21) but He will hand the kingdom over to the Father in the end (Obadiah 21; 1 Corinthians 15:24). Just because the Son is submissive to the Father on some occasions does not mean they are any less equal with each other. The Son and the Father are one and inseparable, and should be given their proper place in our teaching and practice of their Law.

Mixing

When Israel was judged by God in the golden calf incident, it was not only because they made an idol, but that they also called the idol "God."

> ³Then all the people tore off the gold rings which were in their ears and brought them to Aaron. ⁴He took this from their hand, and fashioned it with a graving tool and made it into a molten calf; and they said, "This is your god, O Israel, who brought you up from the land of Egypt." (Exodus 32:3-4 NASB95)

All sin makes God angry, but this sin of mixing really seems to set Him off. When God's things are mixed with anything that is not God's, it gives the glory rightfully due Him to something else. When we mix God's things and our things, such as when we dilute His Word with our own knowledge or tradition, we turn lukewarm.

> ¹⁵'I know your deeds, that you are neither cold nor hot; I wish that you were cold or hot. ¹⁶'So because you are lukewarm, and neither hot nor cold, I will spit you out of My mouth. (Revelation 3:15-16 NASB95)

Lukewarm water is hot and cold mixed together. Notice in these verses that deeds are equated to the quality of the individual. If deeds are lukewarm, the person is lukewarm. Idolatry is mixing hot things (God's) with cold things (idols). God does not want to share His glory with another. He doesn't want something that is not Himself getting credit for His own actions. Mixing is misleading; it's truth and lies combined. It blesses bad things and corrupts good things. It confuses people and makes it difficult to find the narrow path leading to life. We rob God of glory when we mix His works with idols, including the idol of self-will.

> ⁸"I am the Lord, that is My name; I will not give My glory to another, Nor My praise to graven images. (Isaiah 42:8 NASB95)

Mixing God's things with things that are not God's has always been popular, but especially so in modern times. People are mixing teachings from the Bible with teachings of men all the time. Like Seventh Day Adventism, Mormonism, or Christmas and Easter. Mixing (also called syncretism) is a sure fire method of trying to hide or make the Mark bigger, so we can convince ourselves we are hitting it even if we aren't.

One of the reasons I don't like vampire stories is because they are real. Oh, not the Hollywood version with theatrical makeup and long teeth. Vampires are demons, and the life they take is our life in the Word. They bleed us by mixing a little truth with a lot of lying, siphoning off our lifeblood with tiny pinpricks of doubt and distrust. If we rely on their mixed truth, they've got us. Just because someone doesn't have long teeth doesn't mean they aren't sucking the life out of us in other ways.

It's just silly to think demons are stopped by silver crosses or garlic flavored holy water. What really frightens them is the pure, whole, absolute truth from God's mouth. We boost our immunities to demons as we live the body and blood of Jesus. They wouldn't dare bite a believer because we literally taste terrible. We even smell bad to them (2 Corinthians 2:15-16).

Mixing is a seductive, pervasive sin. It is easy to compromise the Word for the sake of something we think is important, especially since it's in our nature to wander away from God anyway. We mix evolution with creation. The emerging church uses mixing to force the world's version of social justice on the flock in the name of Jesus. Mixing is in music and prayer which uses practices from eastern religious mysticism such as vain repetition.

How do we know if teachings are mixed? Fruit. Islam claims to worship Abraham's God, but actions are not consistent with His Law. Churches claim the name of Jesus but reject the Law. Synagogues say that God is One, but reject Yeshua (Jesus) the Messiah. The sin of Balaam (Revelation 2:14) and Jezebel (Revelation 2:20) was in mixing sexual immorality with some of God's practices. This sin continues to the present day in most organized religion with the acceptance of adultery, divorce, and homosexuality. And most every group mixes man-made tradition with parts of God's Word.

There is nothing good in mixing. We have to maintain the purity of God's things apart from all of the polluting effects of what is not God. The problem is that a little mixing is a slippery slope leading to a lot of mixing. Like a "white lie" leads to "black lies," so a little mixing leads to so much mixing we can't see the plain meaning of His Word.

Fear

Speaking of God getting upset, our one God has a scary side that we don't talk much about anymore.

> [20]Moses said to the people, "Do not be afraid; for God has come in order to test you, and in order that the fear of Him may remain with you, so that you may not sin." (Exodus 20:20 NASB95)

The Scriptures have many admonitions for His people everywhere to "fear" Him. The Law was written down so that His people would learn the fear of Him (Deuteronomy 4:10, 14:23, 17:19, 31:13). "Don't be afraid" here means believers don't have to fear destruction at His approach, but we should keep a little of it so "that the fear of Him remain(s) with you" (basically the same Hebrew word). Fear motivates even the most reluctant.[27]

Jesus is not a pacifist. He was meek at His incarnation because that was what the Father wanted from Him at that time. When He comes back, it will not be with roses and chocolates. He will bring a sharp sword and a rod of iron (Revelation 19:14-16, 21). Jesus will come back with His army, speaking God's Word (the sword) and crushing resistance (rod of iron – Psalm 2:9). His rod and staff (the Word of God) will comfort His people (Psalm 23:4) and He will destroy iniquity (lawlessness). The Law will again go forth from Zion.

Lots of teachers try to soft-soap this concept. They tone down the terror part of fear and play up the "reverence" and "respect" aspects. All of these are part of the fear of God, but especially the terror part. Not a blind, unreasoning terror that overwhelms us. Just a healthy terror of knowing exactly what God can and will do to evildoers. *"Fear Him who is able to destroy both soul and body in hell"* (Matthew 10:28).

There is nothing wrong with being a little terrified of God. Usually it's only people with faith who are capable of being terrified anyway. People with seared consciences aren't generally afraid enough. A part of His being can and does terrify creation. If you've ever been in a fierce thunderstorm or an earthquake, the kind where you have to change your shorts afterwards, you know what I mean. It would behoove us to pay more attention to fearing Him in addition to expressing the reverence and respect He deserves.

If you're going to worship a god, make sure He's the God who can destroy all other gods. Don't choose those wimpy gods who cannot see or hear and don't even have the power to blow their own noses. If more people feared God, we might see more gentle treatment of each other. We might also see a greater interest in what He says.

> "The rest will hear and be afraid, and will never again do such an evil thing among you." (Deuteronomy 19:20 NASB95)

My son tells me that there were a number of things he didn't do when he was younger. He avoided them because he was genuinely afraid of what I'd do to him if he misbehaved. "My dad would kill me" was not such a bad motivation for avoiding certain behavior. Especially when there is a lack of understanding in the child, and the big issue is just to

---

[27] Of course, there is the fear exhibited in places such as Revelation 6:15-17 where it is combined with refusal to repent. One of those instances of too little, too late.

avoid harmful behavior. Of course I wasn't ever going to actually kill (or even injure) him (shhhh!) but it didn't hurt to be afraid of me at least a little. Enough for him to avoid straying into destructive actions.

I love my kids and do not want them to learn the hard way. I want them to avoid natural consequences. So I develop other, perhaps more immediate and painful, artificial consequences to help them learn how to make good choices. A swat on the butt as a reminder to obey Dad is much better than getting run over by a car. The getting run over thing tends to be a one-time only learning experience. God does the same for us.

> [7]I form the light, and create darkness: I make peace, and create evil: I the LORD do all these things. (Isaiah 45:7 KJV)

> Who has spoken and it came to pass, unless the Lord has commanded it? Is it not from the mouth of the Most High that good and bad come? Why should a living man complain, a man, about the punishment of his sins? (Lamentations 3:37–39, ESV)

God creates evil in the sense that there are bad things that happen if we don't listen to Him. He does it because He loves us, and wants us to see the cost of moving away from Him before it's too late. If a little bit of true terror will help me choose correctly, it is much better than learning too late that my choice was wrong. He wants us to fear Him above any person, teaching, or situation that might tempt us to abandon trust and obedience. It is not a blind fear that He wants, but it is still a fear that is tinged partly with terror as well as respect and reverence.

> [14]I know that, whatsoever God doeth, it shall be for ever: nothing can be put to it, nor any thing taken from it: and God doeth it, that men should fear before him. (Ecclesiastes 3:14 KJV)

> [12]"You are not to say, 'It is a conspiracy!' In regard to all that this people call a conspiracy, And you are not to fear what they fear or be in dread of it. [13]"It is the Lord of hosts whom you should regard as holy. And He shall be your fear, And He shall be your dread. (Isaiah 8:12-13 NASB95)

Fear of Him should override fear of anything else. If we are His kids, we do not fear destruction or rejection. But it's good to be afraid of what He can and will do if we are not on His good side. If you are not His kid, you have every right to be terrified when He comes for you in judgment. One way or the other, sooner or later, fear of Him will impress itself on everyone. Better to feel it now and move closer to Him than to feel it when it's too late.

Humility and Pride

The proper fear of God leads us to humility. Humility is one of those terms that has either fallen out of favor or been redefined to mean something it is not. Fearing God and humility go together like air and breathing. Not enough fear and we suffocate in pride. It is unfortunate that much of our interaction with each other and with our God is laced with a great deal of pride.

Pride is the single biggest obstacle to grabbing hold of the whole of the Word. A prideful person does not want to be a humble servant of God. Most objections to His law are centered in pride (see chapter 7). We tend to swing from thinking too much of ourselves, to being proud that we are so humble. It's a struggle to find a balance between extremes.

C. S. Lewis, writing as the fictional demon Screwtape, describes humility to the junior demon Wormwood as "self-forgetfulness" in his book The Screwtape Letters.

> "You must therefore conceal from the patient the true end of Humility. Let him think of it, not as self-forgetfulness, but as a certain kind of opinion (namely, a low opinion) of his own talents and character. Some talents, I gather, he really has. Fix in his mind the idea that humility consists in trying to believe those talents to be less valuable than he believes them to be. No doubt they are in fact less valuable than he believes, but that is not the point. The great thing is to make him value an opinion for some quality other than truth, thus introducing an element of dishonesty and make-believe into the heart of what otherwise threatens to become a virtue. By this method thousands of humans have been brought to think that humility means pretty women trying to believe they are ugly and clever men trying to believe they are fools. And since what they are trying to believe may, in some cases, be manifest nonsense, they cannot succeed in believing it, and we have the chance of keeping their minds endlessly revolving on themselves in an effort to achieve the impossible. The enemy wants to bring the man to a state of mind in which he could design the best cathedral in the world, and know it to be the best, and rejoice in the fact, without being any more (or less) or otherwise glad at having done it than he would be if it had been done by another." The Screwtape Letters, C. S. Lewis, Macmillan Publishing, 1977, pp. 62-66.

Humility does not consist of the value of what we are or have; it is recognizing that what we have has been given to us by God. It is taking equal pleasure in all good actions whether they are by us or by others. It is learning to be content and at the same time moving further up and further in to His kingdom through His Word. Some have said that humility isn't thinking less of yourself; it's thinking of yourself less. Jesus describes this as just doing what should be done.

> [10]"So you too, when you do all the things which are commanded you, say, 'We are unworthy slaves; we have done only that which we ought to have done.' " (Luke 17:10 NASB95)

Eating and drinking His body and blood, living by every word from His mouth, is only what unworthy slaves should do anyway. There's no pride in humbly submitting to the King of kings. Humility is fear tinged with love and respect, which leads us to respond rightly to His Word. It is seeing God and ourselves with clear vision, as Isaiah did, and having a desire for Him to make us clean so we can be part of His household.

> [1] In the year that King Uzziah died I saw the Lord sitting upon a throne, high and lifted up; and the train of his robe filled the temple. [2] Above him stood the seraphim. Each had six wings: with two he covered his face, and with two he covered his feet, and with two he flew. [3] And one called to another and said: "Holy, holy, holy is the LORD of hosts; the whole earth is full of his glory!" [4] And the foundations of the thresholds shook at the voice of him who called, and the house was filled with smoke. [5] And I said: "Woe is me! For I am lost; for I am a man of unclean lips, and I dwell in the midst of a people of unclean lips; for my eyes have seen the King, the LORD of hosts!" (Isaiah 6:1-5 ESV)

The Roman centurion (Matthew 8 and Luke 7) was a man in authority, but also a humble man. He recognized in Jesus a man of authority also, able to heal his servant if Jesus just said the word. He didn't think he was worthy for Jesus to come into his house, probably because of the stigma attached to Gentiles by Jews (John 18:28). Jesus marveled at the man's faith, which was unlike any in Israel. The centurion shows us at least two things: that a man of power can still be humble, and that even at a distance a humble man can recognize the Lord and submit to His power.

Another example of humble submission is the Canaanite or Syrophoenecian woman of Matthew 15 and Mark 7. She does not argue about being outside Israel, or whether she was worth less than a child of the household, or that she wasn't worthy at all. She was too humble for that. She recognized her position, but begged for mercy on behalf of her daughter. This woman had to have traveled a distance to get there. She must have been moved by recognition of the position and power of Jesus.

She probably knew she might not get her request granted because of her Gentile status. Yet in humility she made the trip, and gave such a good answer to Jesus that He marveled at her faith too. Her answer showed both obedience and humility.

If God is who He says He is, and we recognize it, there are two reactions. One is to defy Him and do our own prideful thing anyway. The other is to throw ourselves down in humble submission to His majesty and glorious holiness. Pride says God's Word means nothing. Humility says I will do anything you ask. Pride will get humbled one day anyway, but the humble will be lifted up.

Salvation, Purgatory and Worms

We have to talk about these terms because of the claims that following God's Law is not a "salvation issue." In other words, if it doesn't save me I don't have to do it. Not a lot of humility in that kind of response to the King of kings, is there? Salvation is the result of humble fearing and obedience. We become servants of the most High God. It is a restoration of the intimate relationship shattered in the Garden.

We started out with God creating man using the "breath of lives." He animated dirt by breathing out a part of Himself. We had a bond with Him that went to our core. Then we decided (and still daily decide), like spoiled rotten little kids, to take off on our own and do things ourselves. We broke the connection to life and chose death, ruining everything. Salvation is God's gift allowing us to reverse those choices, returning us to life with Him.

To be saved means to be rescued *from* the effects or penalties of sin. It also means we are restored *to* an intimate relationship with Jesus and God the Father. We usually only teach the first half of this: the "escape clause." We can be saved from our enemies, or a life-threatening circumstance. We can also be saved from hopelessness and despair. Believers will be saved from the coming destruction. All of these are included in the idea of salvation.

But the main penalty of sin is being cut off from the life of God. Sin separates us from life now and forever. It creates a debt that has to be paid. If we don't pay the debt, we will remain separate from God for all eternity in a place of fire, torment and darkness. And worms.

> [16]The face of the Lord is against evildoers, To cut off the memory of them from the earth. (Psalm 34:16 NASB95)

> [47]"If your eye causes you to stumble, throw it out; it is better for you to enter the kingdom of God with one eye, than, having two eyes, to be cast into hell, [48]where their worm does not die, and

> the fire is not quenched. (Mark 9:47-48 NASB95)

> [23]"And it shall be from new moon to new moon And from sabbath to sabbath, All mankind will come to bow down before Me," says the Lord. [24]"Then they will go forth and look On the corpses of the men Who have transgressed against Me. For their worm will not die And their fire will not be quenched; And they will be an abhorrence to all mankind." (Isaiah 66:23-24 NASB95)

This place where "the worm does not die and the fire isn't quenched" was probably created just for the Satan (Matthew 25:41). But all beings that followed him into rebellion against God are going to also end up in that place.

> [8] "But for the cowardly and unbelieving and abominable and murderers and immoral persons and sorcerers and idolaters and all liars, their part *will be* in the lake that burns with fire and brimstone, which is the second death." (Revelation 21:8 NASB95)

> [6] For after all it is *only* just for God to repay with affliction those who afflict you, [7] and *to give* relief to you who are afflicted and to us as well when the Lord Jesus will be revealed from heaven with His mighty angels in flaming fire, [8] dealing out retribution to those who do not know God and to those who do not obey the gospel of our Lord Jesus. [9] These will pay the penalty of eternal destruction, away from the presence of the Lord and from the glory of His power, [10] when He comes to be glorified in His saints on that day, and to be marveled at among all who have believed—for our testimony to you was believed. (2 Thessalonians 1:6-10 NASB95)

Another way of describing salvation is from Zacharias's prophecy in Luke chapter one, speaking of John's message and the mission of Jesus.

> [71] Salvation FROM OUR ENEMIES, And FROM THE HAND OF ALL WHO HATE US; [72] To show mercy toward our fathers, And to remember His holy covenant, [73] The oath which He swore to Abraham our father, [74] To grant us that we, being rescued from the hand of our enemies, Might serve Him without fear, [75] In holiness and righteousness before Him all our days. [76] "And you, child, will be called the prophet of the Most High; For you will go ON BEFORE THE LORD TO PREPARE HIS WAYS; [77] To give to His people *the* knowledge of salvation By the forgiveness of their sins, [78] Because of the tender mercy of our God, With which

the Sunrise from on high will visit us, [79] TO SHINE UPON THOSE WHO SIT IN DARKNESS AND THE SHADOW OF DEATH, To guide our feet into the way of peace." (Luke 1:71-79 NASB95)

We are rescued *from* the hand of our enemies *to* serving Him without fear (of destruction) in holiness and righteousness. He saves us *from* a future date with hell or eternal separation from God. He also saves us *to* a present abundant life through a relationship with our Father and His Son the Christ Jesus. We are sons, adopted into His family.

> [15] For you have not received a spirit of slavery leading to fear again, but you have received a spirit of adoption as sons by which we cry out, "Abba! Father!" [16] The Spirit Himself testifies with our spirit that we are children of God, [17] and if children, heirs also, heirs of God and fellow heirs with Christ, if indeed we suffer with *Him* so that we may also be glorified with *Him*. (Romans 8:15-17 NASB95)

The earth and everything in it belongs to God (Deuteronomy 10:14) and in a way all people are children of God, but natural children must become spiritual children also (John 3). We have to reverse that first choice to eat of the tree of knowledge and choose Him. Physical descent is not enough to gain entrance into His Kingdom.

He has given us space to "choose this day whom we will serve" as Joshua says (Joshua 24:15). Those who are born naturally also have to be adopted into God's family no matter their family tree. As Jesus says in John chapter 3, everyone must be "born again" to enter God's kingdom. This spiritual birth or adoption is much more binding than natural birth.

I was adopted at 14 by my own request. I asked my natural parents to relinquish their parental rights and signed my own adoption papers with my new family. So I understand the concept very well. Adoption means that the former family is not yours anymore. You have a new one. Even your birth certificate is changed to reflect the change in families.

I don't agree with people who were adopted young and later search for their birth parents. Birth parents that let go of their offspring are just egg donors and sperm donors to me. They have nothing to do with the blood, sweat and tears of raising a child. So in my view they are not really the parents. Adoption is permanent, and at the age I was adopted I had the privilege of choosing a new family. They are more than merely genetic influences for me.

When we are adopted into God's family, it is the same. We make the choice, and it's permanent. God takes us as His children, with all of our faults and failures. He chooses us even if we are not the model child. Like my adoptive parents, He sticks with us through our teenage years when we know everything but are still dumber than rocks. He is patient, loving, and kind, and requires that we live by the rules of His household. We are treated just like any other son or daughter, protected and nourished and disciplined to stay on the right path.

Some people object to this kind of teaching, because it seems to require the faculties to make a decision. They wonder about babies that die or people without the ability to comprehend God's Word. I understand the objections because I have an autistic nephew and friends whose babies have died. I have no answer for this except to say that our Father is wonderfully just, righteous, and good and He has the answer. What each individual has to be concerned with is his or her own salvation. Dad will take care of those who don't seem to be given the chance to make a commitment to Him.

I will not ignore or try to change the Word to accommodate my perception (or someone else's) of what is right or wrong – I will just try to live it and teach it as I can. I suspect that innocents who die without a full life will be part of His eternal kingdom by default.[28] If there is any sorting that is going to happen with them (like sheep and goats – Ezekiel 34:17; Matthew 25:32-33) it is beyond my knowledge and wisdom to fathom it.

I cannot back this thought up with a specific Scripture, and so it remains just a thought. My faith in God's goodness, however, is based on His loving, holy and just character. He will make it right one way or the other. It is not my call. But when all is said and done, no one will have any grounds whatsoever to accuse Him of any unrighteousness.

Some object to the permanency of the second death. They worry about the demise of a loved one who did not seem to live life for God or "accept Jesus as Lord and savior." They prefer a Catholic-like "purgatory" which will hopefully end someday, or that everyone is ultimately saved. But I cannot find these concepts in the Word. There are two verses that seem to imply all are saved, but they are misunderstood.

> [11]For the grace of God has appeared, bringing salvation to all men, [12]instructing us to deny ungodliness and worldly desires and to live sensibly, righteously and godly in the present age, [13]looking for the blessed hope and the appearing of the glory of our great God and Savior, Christ Jesus, [14]who gave Himself for us to redeem us from every lawless deed, and to purify for Himself a people for His own possession, zealous for good

---

[28] I think the reason we don't know for sure is it keeps men from killing babies thinking they will go to heaven. That would be an abhorrent behavior, but certainly within men's grasp, judging from history.

deeds. ¹⁵These things speak and exhort and reprove with all authority. Let no one disregard you. (Titus 2:11-15 NASB95)

¹⁰For it is for this we labor and strive, because we have fixed our hope on the living God, who is the Savior of all men, especially of believers. (1 Timothy 4:10 NASB95)

Titus 2:11 says, "*...bringing salvation to all men*" and 1 Timothy 4:10 says, "*...the Savior of all men.*" The tragedy is that while salvation is provided, and Jesus is the only one who can save, not everyone will take Him up on it. Consequently they will have no payment for their sin except their own merit, which isn't enough.

²⁸"Truly I say to you, all sins shall be forgiven the sons of men, and whatever blasphemies they utter; ²⁹but whoever blasphemes against the Holy Spirit never has forgiveness, but is guilty of an eternal sin"— ³⁰because they were saying, "He has an unclean spirit." (Mark 3:28-30 NASB95)

¹⁰"And everyone who speaks a word against the Son of Man, it will be forgiven him; but he who blasphemes against the Holy Spirit, it will not be forgiven him. (Luke 12:10 NASB95)

Many of the words used to describe eternal life are also used to describe eternal death. So if death isn't eternal, why would we need eternal life? Will eternal life come to an end in the same way that eternal death can (as some think) come to an end? Not according to Scripture.

¹ "Now at that time Michael, the great prince who stands *guard* over the sons of your people, will arise. And there will be a time of distress such as never occurred since there was a nation until that time; and at that time your people, everyone who is found written in the book, will be rescued. ² "Many of those who sleep in the dust of the ground will awake, these to everlasting life, but the others to disgrace *and* everlasting contempt. ³ "Those who have insight will shine brightly like the brightness of the expanse of heaven, and those who lead the many to righteousness, like the stars forever and ever. (Daniel 12:1-3 NASB95)

I'll let you in on a little secret. This life *is* purgatory. We are between heaven and hell, working out our salvation with fear and trembling. We have to decide *now* whom we will serve, and where we will end up living forever. Even if we don't choose, we still have made a decision.

It is very easy in this life to accept Jesus and live like God wants us to live. So if people won't accept Him when things are easy, what makes us think they will do it after a swim in the lake of fire? If they are forced into the second death by their own will and a sovereign God, why would they be any more amenable to what God wants? Wouldn't it just stimulate the pride and anger that surely fill them?[29]

> ³ O LORD, do not Your eyes *look* for truth? You have smitten them, *But* they did not weaken; You have consumed them, But they refused to take correction. They have made their faces harder than rock; They have refused to repent. (Jeremiah 5:3 NASB95)

> ²⁰The rest of mankind, who were not killed by these plagues, did not repent of the works of their hands, so as not to worship demons, and the idols of gold and of silver and of brass and of stone and of wood, which can neither see nor hear nor walk; ²¹and they did not repent of their murders nor of their sorceries nor of their immorality nor of their thefts. (Revelation 9:20-21 NASB95)

Everyone exists forever, but I would not call the second death "living." Those who end up in hell are said to weep and wail and gnash teeth.[30] Gnashing teeth is a sure sign of anger (Job 16:9; Psalm 35:16, 37:12, 112:10). My guess is they are angry at being cut off from the blessings of God by that same King of kings they refused to obey during their stay on earth. They want what God *has* but they do not want what God *is*. He's an absolute King, totally in control.

But it should come as a relief to realize that we don't know who will insist on dying a second time. Some live in complete obedience to God but do not take on external labels of Christian or Jew. They just do what they know to be God's will. Others have the name but not the actions. It's a good thing that God is the one who sorts it out.

The idea, of course, is to live as much like God wants as possible. We don't try to see how much we can get away with and still gain eternal life. This is our chance, right here and right now (Psalm 95:7-11; Hebrews 3:14-19).

There's a story about the queen of England interviewing three guys for a job driving her car. The first guy tells her he could drive so well he could come within ten feet of a nearby cliff without going over. The second guy says he's so good he could come within five feet. The third guy says, "I'm not going anywhere near that cliff."

Guess who got the job? Right. The guy who wasn't going to fool around and come anywhere close to the edge of the cliff. The point is that we should try very hard to stay completely away from hell, not see

---

[29] In addition to the verses shown, see also Hebrews 6:4-8; Revelation 16:9, 11.
[30] Matthew 8:12, 13:42, 13:50, 22:13, 24:51, 25:30; Luke 13:28.

how close we can come without falling in. We want a full and complete connection to life. We don't even want to flirt with death.

We can argue salvation by faith or salvation by works or some combination or separation of the two, but I think God's version is salvation by Love. He loved us first and made a way back, and we walk forward loving Him by doing whatever He says.

Salvation is both immediate and a process. When God makes a believer into a new creation, it will stick. The change will show itself in actions over time, which is part of the process. He doesn't translate us to heaven right away (John 13:33); He leaves us here to work out our salvation with fear and trembling (Philippians 2:12).

We don't suddenly become flawless in our actions; we learn righteousness from Him on a daily basis through all of His instructions. We are indeed fortunate to have such a loving God, one who continues working to bring the inside changes to the outside.

Not all who say "Lord, Lord" allow their lips to move their limbs (or are saved). We can't tell who is saved just by hearing what they say. We only judge actions as they relate to His Word. God does not assign any person the job of salvation cop except Jesus. Even in judging, we strive for repentance and restoration (rather than condemnation).

A person cannot be more saved or less saved, but he or she can be more/less mature (1 Corinthians 14:20; Hebrews 5:14, 6:1) more/less filled with the Word (Ephesians 5:15-21) more/less blessed (Job 42:12) more or less rich in Him (Romans 10:12; James 2:5) and so on. We can "have life" and that more abundantly (John 10:10) if the Word dwells in us abundantly. And if we abide in the Word abundantly.

All of God's Words are life. Doing more of God's Word means more life. Doing fewer of His words means less life. Eating more of His body and drinking more of His blood means having more energy and vigor and blessing. Jesus says that His words are the Father's (read John 14-16) and that they are life. When I hear what He says and do it, the foundation of my house is strong and can withstand storms (Matthew 7:24-29). The fruit of the Spirit just pops out all over. Those who do not hear and do end up treading water and spitting out sand.

Love

In modern culture love is defined as sex or really strong feelings. It is neither one, though these can be part of the expression of love. Love is a verb; an action word (look it up in a concordance). Biblically, it is not a noun like "sentiment" or "a profoundly tender, passionate affection for another person" as a secular dictionary puts it. Jesus did not go to the cross for affection. He went because it was the only way to restore creation and reunite God with men (and women). Love does not exist without God or God's Word. We cannot love outside of His will and ways. We can feel affection without God, but there is no love if there is no God. If we say we love God, but don't do what He says, we do not love.

The fact that God gave the entire Law is not seen by very many as a loving act. Nor is the fact acknowledged that the "two commands" summarize what God had already given and demonstrated with His own actions. Love is a motivating factor with God and always has been.

It is love that caused Him to create us, and love that keeps us functioning. Salvation is offered through the loving sacrifice of Jesus on the cross. He waits for us to return that love by molding our lives to fit His Word. Salvation by love transcends all the nitpicky details of many theological arguments. We refused to abide in His love long ago, and continue to refuse every time we go our own way. The overriding Law from God is love; love for the Father and love for our neighbor. Always has been and always will be.

How has Jesus loved us? Well, let me count the ways. We know that He "lay down His life" (John 10:11, 1 John 3:16) and that "greater love has no one than this" (John 15:13). We know that "while we were yet sinners" He died for us (Romans 5:8). "For our sake he made him to be sin who knew no sin that we might become the righteousness of God" (2 Corinthians 5:21). We know that He is the source of life, light, love, and all the blessings associated with those things (John 14:6).

"No man has seen the father but the son and He has revealed Him." So we also know that Jesus loved us from the beginning, when He created Adam and Eve and placed them in a perfect world. We know that He loved them (us) so much He promised that even after they chose to reject His Word (or Law) He would provide a way back to intimacy with Him.

We know that Jesus loves individuals such as our father Abraham (Romans 4:12, 16; James 2:21) as well as Isaac and Jacob. We know that He loves Israel, rescuing them from slavery and bringing them into a land flowing with milk and honey. We know that Jesus loved His people so much that He gave them wonderful Laws for pleasing behavior so He could live among them after He delivered them. He did all of this without anyone asking Him. These are some examples we have of how Jesus has loved us from the beginning. He has always rescued us from our own perversity, and is always willing to forgive anyone, if we are willing to repent. He gives us His Word to regenerate, restore, and revitalize.

We use these types of love examples from Jesus to love one another. We act as He has acted (John 15:12). The Words He gave us are the starting point and framework of those actions, which we will talk more about in the upcoming sections.

The Scriptures tell us that the Law is God's love, beauty, and mercy in action. Look at the example of Israel. First, they were rescued by God (saved by grace through faithful obedience to the Passover) were baptized (through the sea) then went to the desert to find out how God wanted them to live. All this He did without them earning even a small part of it.

In a similar way, God saves people now (born again); we are baptized, and then are given the Word of God to teach us how to live. It never happens in reverse order, where people live righteous lives then tell God they "deserve" life because they lived perfectly.

Love is one of those funny words that's used all the time but doesn't only have one definition. We think we understand it, but maybe we don't as well as we should. In the Bible, the meaning depends a lot on the context of how it is used. The Hebrew version is more context-dependant than the Greek, which has three different words for three different types of love (brotherly, romantic or sexual, and godly). We all know that "I love ice cream" is a lot different than "for God so loved the world," but we still use the same English word.

The highest and most pure form of love is the one which is between God and people. It is not an emotion, although it gives rise to many emotions. The Greeks call this love "agape" love, and it is primarily an action word (remember, a verb, not a noun). It is based on and defined by God's character and all the good things about Him.

He is the source of love, and is the one who first loved. We learn love from Him by how He treats us, and how we see Him treat others. As I said before, mercy, beauty, favor, preciousness, patience, long suffering, and forgiveness are some of the aspects of love. So are justice, order, correction, discipline, consequences, meekness and humility.

God showed His love through the giving of His only Son in a sacrifice for our sins. He also loves us by revealing Himself through His creation and His Word. Every one of His Laws is a beautiful example of love. They are perfect for teaching us how to love each other; that is, if they are not robbed of the love in them. This happens when we remove the Spirit and reduce them to a series of arbitrary legislative decrees. Or when we abuse them by trying to trade merit for salvation. We'll always be a few steps short when "buying a stairway to heaven."

Salvation by love means He loves us so much that "He gave" His Son. His Son loves us so much He laid down His life. In return, we lay our lives down through His Law. As we submit ourselves willingly to every word we return as much as we can of the love He has for us. Love is the basis of the Law. It permeates all of His Word, including the Law, and fills it up with the essence of His presence. As we perform each action He asks, it's as if the love flows in ever increasing proportion until it turns into a river of life.

Please excuse me if I wax a little poetic here, because as I'm writing I can see it and feel it, but it's hard to describe completely unless you've experienced it. Sexual love gives us a little bit of an idea (Song of Solomon), and brotherly love kind of helps us understand it in a small way. We can even get a taste of it when we eat ice cream. But as Paul said in that famous chapter he wrote, we are empty and useless and nothing without love.

> ^{12}For now we see in a mirror dimly, but then face to face; now I know in part, but then I will know fully just as I also have been fully known. ^{13}But now faith, hope, love, abide these three; but the greatest of these is love. (1 Corinthians 13:12-13 NASB95)

The thing about love, though, is it isn't static. We can't store it and expect it to last. It has to be shared to keep it moving, flowing, and filling. We share it with God as we respond with actions to the love He gave us. We share love with others when we share in His Laws.

Love is doing what is the best for someone else, even at the expense of short-term gain now. God's Word (or Law) provides the framework for learning love, and for teaching it to other people. We cannot follow the Law properly without love, for love and Law are as inseparable as the Father and the Son.

Grace

Grace will work its way into any discussion of Law and salvation, sometimes legitimately and sometimes with great misunderstanding. Some have defined grace as unmerited favor, but that is a partial definition according to the Bible. Happily, there is more to grace than is generally taught. Like God Himself, His grace has a plural meaning.

One aspect of grace is beauty. Another is mercy. The English word grace is defined[31] as charm, beauty, loveliness, favor and preciousness. The related word mercy is unmerited favor, kindness, pity, loving kindness (Exodus 20:6, 34:7, etc.) and compassion.[32] Part of the truth is that grace is found more often in the New Testament (233 times) than the Old (70 times).

However, the whole rich truth is that the word mercy is found more often in the Old Testament (248 times) than the New Testament (50

---

[31] Enhanced Strong's Lexicon H2580 and G5485
[32] Enhanced Strong's Lexicon H2617 and G1653

times).[33] This really shouldn't be a surprise. God extended a great deal of mercy to people we read about in the Old Testament and a great deal of beauty or grace through the incarnate ministry of Jesus. He has always given people love, grace, and mercy. The Law is jammed full of grace and mercy, if one has eyes to see.

Jesus graciously paid the penalty for our disobedience, but that did not change the terms of His Word or Promise. We still live in the same physical conditions. We still have to make His Word our priority if He is to take up residence in our midst, like He did in the wilderness with Israel. We cannot live right merely doing what is right in our own eyes. A positive response to His grace is required.

Whole-Bible Christians are aware that God, in all of His gracious dealings with man throughout history, has granted mercy to anyone who asked. Frequently even to people who didn't ask. Noah "found grace" (Genesis 6:8) in the eyes of God, Abraham was favored (chosen or known, Genesis 18:19) Moses was sought out when he wasn't even looking for God.

Everyone experiences some measure of God's grace. It can be seen in rain for crops or sunshine for a day at the beach (Acts 14:16, 17). It's there when He doesn't immediately destroy us because of sin. Sometimes He graciously grants a request from an unbeliever. Whole-Bible believers know that Jesus is the agent of God's mercy and beauty, and has always been so. Past, present and future, He is the eternally existent Word of God. He combines all aspects of mercy, beauty, grace and truth.

Grace and mercy are like two sides of the same coin, spinning in the air. Grace is a Righteous and Perfect God reconciling the world to Himself by sending His Son to die for us while we were yet sinners (Romans 5:8). Grace is God's love in action, opening the way back to perfection and life with Him. God in His grace desires and allows for repentance and restoration. But one thing grace is *not* is permission to sin.

Cheap grace is assuming we can live any way we want as long as we "believe in Jesus." It has no place in salvation by love through love. Thinking our "fire insurance" is paid up by visits to a congregation on holidays, or doing a good deed here and there, is no way to repay such a precious gift as His death. His grace doesn't require merit (no one can earn it) but there's still a cost – we owe Him our lives. Dietrich

---

[33] Although I don't agree with everything in his books, I am indebted to Avi ben Mordechai for showing me this truth in his book, 'Signs In The Heavens.' The book is out of print but I think that you can contact Avi at www.m7000.com or get used copies online.

Bonheoffer, a Lutheran pastor who resisted the Nazis till he was hanged, says it this way.

> "Cheap grace is the preaching of forgiveness without requiring repentance, baptism without church discipline. Communion without confession. Cheap grace is grace without discipleship, grace without the cross, grace without Jesus Christ."

Cheap grace is spoken of with correct disapproval most of the time in public. Yet many cheapen His grace privately without a second thought. The whole-Bible approach to living involves a greater devotion than merely attending a multi-media presentation once in a while or throwing a few bucks in the plate. Godly living is much more than hugs and holy kisses.

Unconditional Love and Tolerance

Speaking of cheap grace, it is fashionable nowadays to talk about "unconditional love" and its companion idea "tolerance." They are so overused I've even seen a shampoo called "unconditional love." Lots of people push these ideas by grabbing a stamp of approval from the Bible. They'd like to think that their version of unconditional love and tolerance comes right from God. But what might have started out as Bible motivated teachings have become teachings that are not biblical at all.

One current definition of unconditional love (frequently lumped together with tolerance) is to leave someone alone so they can sin all they want, yet still participate in God's kingdom. Another definition I heard from a friend is that it is "unmerited, undeserved, un-worked for, it is a free gift to be simply received." It's not hard to hear in these definitions a desire to be "saved" without stopping sinful behavior. It's odd how many separate concepts end up giving people permission to sin and still be accepted by God. Could it be that we have issues with being a servant?

His love does have an unconditional aspect to it. God loves because He IS love. He will accept any person on the sole basis of the sacrifice of His Son Jesus the Christ. His tolerance or forbearance, which we can think of as kindness in waiting, is meant to lead us to repentance (Romans 2:4). Whoever wants adoption may ask for it and it will be granted by grace through faith. We don't become perfect first, then seek acceptance. We don't follow the Law then demand salvation as wages. He has provided a way back to Him by the cleansing blood of Jesus. It's freely available to anyone. His kindness is just waiting for us to commit our lives to Him. This is why we call His love unconditional, and why we can call God "tolerant."

He tolerates us (grace) and waits with unconditional love for us to adjust ourselves to Him. But we cannot stretch the unconditional part of His love to cover any and every behavior. Many times He warns us that a relationship with Him is a two-way street (see the many references about Israel). One condition of our relationship to God is to repent of lawlessness (iniquity, in Greek literally "no law" Strong's G458).

> I am speaking in human terms, because of your natural limitations. For just as you once presented your members as slaves to impurity and to lawlessness leading to more lawlessness, so now present your members as slaves to righteousness leading to sanctification. (Romans 6:19, ESV)

Another condition is to continue on His path with repentance, forgiveness (Matthew 6:15) and obedience. If we love Him we abide in His Word. John 3:16 says "that whosoever believes might have eternal life" which means that belief is a condition. Those who don't believe don't get eternal life.

True love cannot be otherwise. One of the conditions of my marriage is to stay faithful to my wife. I must confine any intimacy (physical or otherwise) to her. She does not "tolerate" (and I wouldn't either) a situation where she is not the only one. This is one of the ways I "work out" my love for her. God is faithful to us, and He expects us to be faithful in return.

Love is expressed in actions, specifically actions that are good and right and light and life. You know – God. Hate opposes God. It means to do what is evil or wrong or darkened or death. When Jesus says we must love Him more than our close relatives (Luke 14:26) He means nothing should get between us and Him. Of course, true love includes any others who want to be with God also. If everyone loved as He loves, no one would have to worry about hating each other. It just wouldn't happen.

As it is taught by the compromised church, or the world (how frequently we can't tell the difference between the world and the church!) love is the false idea that you can do whatever you want and still partake of God's blessings (sort of like cheap grace). There are those who, for instance, teach that a person can be an unrepentant homosexual and still be part of God's household. The idea that God so loves that He allows people to persist in deadly behavior[34] is, I'm relieved to say, absolutely false.

---

[34] Everyone who persists in sin, especially in view of the sacrifice of Jesus, will die twice (1 Corinthians 6:9-10; Revelation 21:8, 22:15). Hebrews 9:27 says we "die once" and after that the judgment, which is the second.

In fact, He loves us so much that He refuses to let us continue to destroy ourselves. He accepts us just as we are in our sinful state (with repentance from lawless actions) but there is no way He will allow us to stay in sin. If He did, that would not be love.

He gives us a start by washing away our sins with the blood of the Lamb. But He expects us to continue in that cleanliness and new life by changing our behavior. He gives us all the power to do so by His Holy Spirit (2 Corinthians 1:22; Ephesians 1:13, 4:30) and the strength of our Savior. *I can do all things through Him who strengthens me.* (Philippians 4:13 NASB95)

Repentance

Repentance and love for God go hand in hand. We can't have one without the other. If we repent, we stop going our own way and start going His (1 Kings 8:47; 2 Chronicles 6:37; Job 42:6; Jeremiah 8:4-13; Ezekiel 14:6; Matthew 11:20, 21). The first recorded word out of the mouths of John the Baptist (Matthew 3:2) and Jesus (Matthew 4:17) for their public ministries was "repent."

Every revival in the Bible is a return to doing what God says. We repent of going our own way and come back to God's ways. This pattern is repeated many times. First we drift away (or run) from God's Word. Then we get into all kinds of trouble. All the while God is calling us back to His Word. Finally we return, are rewarded with increased blessings and reduced trouble, only to get fat dumb and happy and take off again. From the Garden to the book of Revelation the cycle never varies until God calls a halt finally (such as in booting Israel out of the land). We can see this pattern especially in the cycle of the kings of Israel.

The ministry of Jesus is a call to repent or return to God's Word, marked especially by His Law. Acts chapter 2 is likewise a call to return. It is not a call to take off and form another (church) group that goes through the same monotonous sin and repentance cycle like Israel did for centuries, all while claiming to be doing something different.

"Feeling sorry" for what we have done or are doing still, yet continuing to go the wrong way is not repentance. It is certainly not love. Joel says "rend your hearts, not your garments" (Joel 2:13). A lot of times, "sorry" feelings are very strong, to the point of weeping or other expressions of anguish. Herod was "exceedingly sorry" to behead John the Baptist, and did it anyway (Mark 6:26). Sorry feelings are not true repentance if they don't produce a change in behavior (Jonah 3:8, 9; 2 Corinthians 7:9-10). True repentance is when we stop the sin that we are doing (Matthew 3:8; Luke 3:8). We go from ignoring His Law to following it.

Biblically, repentance also means restitution. According to the Word, when a thief repents, not only must he stop stealing, but repay what he stole plus a penalty amount (Exodus 22:2, 7). Zacchaeus (Luke 19) restored four-fold what he might have defrauded, and gave half his goods to the poor.[35] Paul sent Onesimus back to Philemon (Philemon 18) to make things right. We do not follow through with this in modern times. A lot of times "feeling sorry" is the limit of repentance. But feelings of sorrow, by themselves, are not enough by God's Laws. If we repent, we make things right as much as we can.

> [10]For the sorrow that is according to the will of God produces a repentance without regret, leading to salvation, but the sorrow of the world produces death. (2 Corinthians 7:10 NASB95)

A Personal God

Modern teachers struggle to make God personal. They try to encourage intimacy with Him but fall short because they base this intimacy on feelings or sentiment alone. This is where things like "God loves you and has a wonderful plan for your life" or "If you were the only person on earth He still would've died for you" comes from. Statements like these are plainly self-centered and made to puff up our pride rather than humble our souls. Some want a personal god like they want a personal pan pizza. Pick your favorite stuff from the menu and have it served piping hot to your table. "I'd like to order a personal pan pizza with ham and sausage on a hand-tossed crust please." But He doesn't conform very well to our pans, or to our taste buds and lunch preferences. He wants us to conform to His Spirit, not He to ours.

He IS a very personal God. We access a personal relationship with Him by abiding in His Word. Moses asked God, "please show me your glory" (Exodus 33:18) just after he asked God to "show me now your ways that I may know you."

> Now therefore, if I have found favor in your sight, please show me now your ways, that I may know you in order to find favor in your sight. Consider too that this nation is your people." (Exodus 33:13, ESV)

God responds to the "ways and glory" request by saying He will have to hide Moses in a cleft of a rock and cover him with His hand (Exodus 33:19-23), AFTER God wrote up a couple new tablets (Exodus 34:1). First comes His Word, then we see His glory. If we want to see

---

[35] Remember, Zacchaeus was a tax collector. This occupation not only left a bad taste in almost everyone's mouth, but the office holders were usually corrupt, collecting more than they should for their own use.

Jesus, if we want intimacy with Him, if we want to experience His glory, if we really want a personal God, then we do what He says. He will make His glory known to us as we follow His commands. As the worldly rock band Rush says, "Show me don't tell me."[36] The world is waiting for us to show them a personal God of love. They are waiting for the visible church to drop the hypocrisy and walk in truth.

Having Jesus, or salvation, is about regaining the intimacy with God that we lost in the Garden. It is not just about mouthing some words, or "going forward," or attending a meeting at least twice a year on Christmas and Easter. We simply need to *do what He says* in love. Fruit (all kinds) will come if we really have Him. It's like, if we were to grab hold of a live electrical wire, we would certainly act differently than we would otherwise! (Disclaimer: do not try this at home.)

He is like a live electrical wire, and when we really get a hold of Him (or He gets hold of us) we are certain to act differently. If He gets a hold of us that means His life flows through us causing actions in line with His Word. Salvation and sanctification are not separate processes. We might show His life slowly, or more rapidly sometimes (see: the Parable of the Seed in Matthew 13), but as we abide in Him as a branch to His vine we WILL grow. The thief on the cross showed by repentance he had this life when he humbly asked Jesus to remember him. Repentance was all he was recorded as showing, but whatever life from Jesus he had after repenting it was enough. Like a video game character, we don't exist without His electric life. When Jesus tells us to act different, it doesn't mean wearing the name Christian, going to church meetings, or being "emergent." It's not "speaking in tongues" or healing services (read Jeremiah 7, 8). Holy-looking actions, without obedience to His Word, are like empty songs.

> [32]"Behold, you are to them like a sensual song by one who has a beautiful voice and plays well on an instrument; for they hear your words but they do not practice them. (Ezekiel 33:32 NASB95)

If we want true sensual and spiritual satisfaction, if we want to be truly Spirit filled, we need actions in keeping with His Law. We know Him because we keep all His commandments.

> [3]By this we know that we have come to know Him, if we keep His commandments. [4]The one who says, "I have come to know Him," and does not keep His commandments, is a liar, and the truth is not in him; [5]but whoever keeps His word, in him the love of God has truly been perfected. By this we know that we are in

---

[36] Song Title "Show Don't Tell," from the 1989 album *Presto* by the Canadian music group Rush.

Him: ⁶the one who says he abides in Him ought himself to walk in the same manner as He walked. (1 John 2:3-6 NASB95; Deuteronomy 10:12-13.)

The way to become saved is to repent of going our own way and go His way instead. We don't need "four spiritual laws" or a "sinner's prayer" (neither of which is biblical). We don't need membership in a club (church, synagogue). We don't need to be accepted by any group for that matter.[37] We don't need approval from modern-day Pharisees and Sadducees.

We have assurance of salvation because we trust ourselves to the One God. Our salvation depends on Him, not ourselves.[38] Many would rather there was some ceremony or guaranteed rite of passage or something. It feeds our pride. That's why we like the "raising hand and going forward" thing. If pastors ask it, they get to keep score. The individual gets a badge of honor, and everyone thinks of it as a righteous action.

The "mark" or badge of honor for a believer has more to do with a lifetime of humility and abiding in God's will than with a one-time heroic action. Raising the hand and going forward isn't backed by the authority of God (He didn't tell us to do this). So it doesn't work very well to produce the fruit of the Spirit. But the actions in His Law (Word) work perfectly because they have His authority and Spirit behind them.

God is one, but has a plural existence we can't fully comprehend. He is not split into two gods, nor is His glory shared with another. For all intents and purposes, Jesus and God are indistinguishable from each other. They are so linked that Jesus represents God in physical forms, and has done so since the beginning. The Words of Jesus and God are identical and cannot be parceled out as if coming from different gods to different people at different times.

Sin is turning from His Word. Disobedience. Not abiding. It separates us from Him because it is opposite of His holiness and love. Every time we choose self-will over His will we cheat on God, whether we have a statue in the living room or pick the fruit of our own knowledge tree. We may make the cheating more palatable by mixing it with some of His truth, but lukewarm action is rejected by God. His grace is meant to lead us to repentance, not give space for us to cheapen it with more disobedience. His unconditional love does not allow sin.

---

[37] Although getting together with other believers is always a good idea if it is possible on the basis of the Word.
[38] Calvinism and Arminianism mostly confuse the biblical issues by ignoring simple obedience.

At this point in history the whole truth is that we ought to fear and submit to Him who has shown His absolute power, and who can destroy body and soul in hell. Believers worship Him by obedience to all of His commands, in spirit and in truth, humbly thankful for the riches of His grace and mercy in providing for our salvation. We can split hairs all we want about His nature and position or names and titles, but the plain meaning of the Word is clear, if we choose to read it and follow it.

3 A Whole Body

²⁴"My servant David will be king over them, and they will all have one shepherd; and they will walk in My ordinances and keep My statutes and observe them. (Ezekiel 37:24 NASB95)

¹⁶"I have other sheep, which are not of this fold; I must bring them also, and they will hear My voice; and they will become one flock with one shepherd. (John 10:16 NASB95)

Now that we've put God back together, in our thinking at least, we have to tackle splits in the church. Like splitting God into two, the apparent splitting of the Body of Christ is another tool for diminishing the Word. I say apparent splitting, because the Body is really not split. It is one, it has always been one, and has never been in danger of going out of existence. Churches split all the time, but Paul says in Ephesians 4 that there is only one body. Jesus said the gates of hell would not prevail against His congregation (Matthew 16:18). What we see appears split because we forget the church is not the Body, and the Body is not the church. Keep this firmly in mind as we go through the rest of the book and as you read through the Bible. It'll help.

Splits have been happening since Adam and Eve split from God, and their sons split from each other. Splitting occurs all the time in the world, but the notable splits are between believers and unbelievers. We can see these splits all the way through the Word. God split Noah's family from the rest of humanity. Abraham and Lot went their separate ways. Israel was split off from Egypt. The ten northern tribes of Israel and the two southern tribes of Judah split over golden calf worship. Prophets who advocated repentance and a return to God were isolated and killed, Jesus was crucified, and apostles were chased away from the synagogue. The book of Acts is really about the splits between believing Jews and Gentiles and unbelieving Jews and Gentiles. Protestants split from the Catholics, Catholics are split into factions, and Protestants also continued to split into factions. There are splits between believers-in-name-only and real believers all the time, because unbelievers can't abide those who stick with God.

Many splits are due to an ego fight (pride) between leaders. Each wants to be "right" and maintain the power and unity of their respective (and separate) bureaucracies. Every organized group claims to be the "right" one, or the "true church," or something like that, because they need the authority in order to draw others and fill the offering plates. One of the main reasons for the crucifixion of Jesus was that religious leaders thought they would lose authority and power (John 11:48). God didn't split Israel and Judah. He doesn't split the Body of Christ either. Splits in some ways are a natural result of the tension between people who want to follow God and people who don't. In other ways splitting means we get to give to the other guys what we don't want from the Bible. For instance, the church gives the Law to the Jews. Or the Jews give the Greek Jesus to the church.

After we got kicked out of the Garden of Eden, people still had the choice between two trees – God's Word of life or the tree of self-will and knowledge. Though cursed (and by cursed I mean that God partially withdrew His presence and blessing) we were supposed to abide in His love and His will. The earth is His church, but the congregants are not very cooperative. There is a remnant that eats of the tree of life such as Abel, Enoch, Noah, Samuel, David, prophets, and the 7,000 mentioned to Elijah but are severely outnumbered by those who eat from the tree of knowledge. God's people are marked by love for Him and the following of His commands.

Abraham's congregation or church was at least 318 or so people (Genesis 14:14), perhaps double or triple that with wives and kids, and they were all marked by abiding in God's Word (Genesis 17:23, 26:5). Abraham celebrated the Passover (Genesis 21 & 22). He was a "sojourner" or traveler so he daily lived God's feast of Tabernacles or Tents (not exactly the specific feast, but he lived in tents all the time and didn't inherit land). He was a "friend of God (Isaiah 41:8) "believed God" and it was credited to him as righteousness (Genesis 15:6). Isaac and Jacob inherited their father's estates and had their own household churches. All made the choice to follow where God led and abide in His Word. That is real church.

For a while after the flood God's evangelism was focused on individuals. Later, He took a family church of 70 people (Jacob and his household Exodus 1:5) and created a nation of millions called Israel, gave them His living oracles in writing, and set up residence in their midst. The first mega-church (after the whole earth, I guess). He made a covenant with them that He would be their God and they would be His people. God promised to bless them, and they promised to abide in His Word. The fortunes and blessings of the church of Israel rose and fell depending on whether they continued to abide in those living oracles or not.

The book of Acts tells of the renewal of God's plans for His kingdom or Body, not the start. The church as we know it today grew out of Jewish leaders' fear of authority loss and rejection of Jesus.

> If we let him go on like this, everyone will believe in him, and the Romans will come and take away both our place and our nation." (John 11:48, ESV)

But the church has split from God just as Israel split from Him. The new (modern) Pharisees are the same as the old ones.

The Acts of the apostles are in response to the command of God to preach and teach the (existing) Word of God as the unbelievers tried to shut down the renewal. It is the story of the Body acting as God intended starting way back in the Garden, against great odds and the hatred of unbelievers. The body of Christ is composed of all individual believers who have faith in God. The story of the body of Christ (some of which are in the church) starts way before Pentecost. It goes back to the beginning of creation. Everyone who believes God and does what is right is welcomed by Him (Acts 10:34-35). His congregation has always been building, right from the start.

The Modern Church

There really is no church in the Bible. Yep, I know, I'm going to get some heat for this, but it's true. Not a single one of the denominations, organizations, or clubs, Catholic or Protestant, that exist now, are mentioned anywhere. Every group called a church (or synagogue) uses the name trying to get biblical recognition and authority. This is fine if they actually abide in His Word. The problem is many of them eventually end up using that authority to block entry into the kingdom of God unless you go through their gate. That's assuming, of course, that their gate actually goes to His kingdom.

In a country club (or any kind of exclusive group) you have to look and act like they do in order to be a member. They have a written code or rulebook you must follow to be a member. This code will tell you such things as how to act and how to dress. Churches and synagogues are similar. The rulebooks most of them use however are not the Bible. Rather it is their interpretation of the Bible, their traditions and philosophy. Many Jewish leaders thought (and still think) that one had to become Jewish (using circumcision as a ceremony) in order to be in God's kingdom. They had (and have) dress codes such as yarmulke (the hats), talits (prayer shawls) and phylacteries (the boxes strapped to the wrist and forehead). The church in like manner has thought for centuries that one has to stop being "Jewish" to be a Christian. Communion must be taken. Baptism (for some) is required for salvation. Pastors have to wear a suit and tie (everyone has to dress a certain way). Some rules are more subtle. For instance some people think you are only a true believer if you are poor. Others think the opposite because a person of "faith" must be healthy and wealthy. When extra-biblical laws are promoted and God's Laws rejected (or given lip service) (Matthew 23) we know we have wandered into something that is less like the Body and more like a country club.

The truth is that any group of people doing what God says is part of His One Body. The church and the synagogue have no say in membership at all. In Revelation 3:9, Jesus tells of "those of the synagogue of Satan who say they are Jews and are not, but lie." We can also say there are those of the *church* of Satan who say they are *Christians* and are not, but lie. It's important to get your mind around this idea, because many religious leaders have usurped God's authority, and have led people down a primrose path to a destination different than that of God. Just because a group calls itself a church does not mean they are part of the Body of Christ.

There are those that make you think that if you don't act like they do you must not be saved. But most churches/synagogues are not living the new covenant in the first place, even if they say they are. Their written code is called the Articles of Incorporation and the By-laws. So if you don't do what they do it might actually be a good thing. Much good has been done by people who stepped outside of the box of their churches or synagogues. Some have put their lives on the line. The struggle illuminated in the book of Acts has been going on for a long time.

Understand, I am not speaking of the many individuals in the church/synagogue (churchagogue?) who manage to find and teach God, who behave in many ways as He would want. But when people get together in a group, frequently the focus changes from the Bible to "the church" (or synagogue). We have to decide – are we going to defend our club, or cling to God and His Word?

A New Old Thing

One of the standard, visible church teachings is that a "new thing" called the "church" was created by God at Pentecost. It is taught that God got fed up with Israel and decided to start fresh. They say He didn't really mean any of the previous dealings with Israel. His goal all along was the "new thing." Two versions of this story have the church either 1) Inserted as an added parenthesis between the old and new physical Israel, or 2) Merging with and replacing "spiritual" Israel.

Both the "inserted" and "merging" versions are really just trying to replace Israel. The "inserted" theory says that after the "new church" is complete, it will be removed (at the "rapture") and Israel's program will resume. The "merging" theory is close to the truth but it's not the "church" doing the merging. The merging is between believers and the olive tree. Believers are grafted into (or merged with) the existing Israel olive tree as Paul reveals (more on this in a moment). Supposedly, the separate and brand new church entity for all "replacement theories" got started in Acts chapter 2. Replacement. Is. Not. From. The. Bible.

Replacement is not even close to what is in there. That is, if the Bible is allowed to speak for itself. At the root, teachings like these are developed to chip away the absolute truth of God's Word, and steal some authority. The Bible has only one Body of Christ, which has existed since the beginning. See for yourself. Look at the Greek or Hebrew words and you won't see the church anywhere. There are only believers and unbelievers, obedient and disobedient, law abiding and law breaking. Roles or jobs might be different,[39] but there is only one body.

> [12]For even as the body is one and yet has many members, and all the members of the body, though they are many, are one body, so also is Christ. [13]For by one Spirit we were all baptized into one body, whether Jews or Greeks, whether slaves or free, and we were all made to drink of one Spirit. [14]For the body is not one member, but many. (1 Corinthians 12:12-14 NASB95)

The English word "church" itself has a murky origin.[40] It is used to translate the New Testament Greek word[41] *ekklesia* (or *ecclesia*, pronounced a-klays-see-ah and means "assembly" or "congregation") but not all the time. For instance in Stephen's speech (Acts 7) he uses the word *ekklesia* to describe Israel, but the translators use the word "congregation" instead.[42]

> [38]"This is the one who was in the congregation (*ekklesia*) in the wilderness together with the angel who was speaking to him on Mount Sinai, and who was with our fathers; and he received living oracles to pass on to you. (Acts 7:38 NASB95 italics mine. See also Hebrews 2:12)

There are times when it's okay to translate a single Greek or Hebrew word into two or more different English words, or the other way around. For instance several Greek words for love (*eros*, erotic or sexual love, *phileo*, brotherly love, and *agape*, godly love) are all translated by the

---

[39] For instance, martyrs (Revelation 6:9-11) seem to have a different role and a different reward or perhaps even different position. The 144,000 (Revelation 7) could be part of this group or have still another member role to fill.

[40] Perhaps coming from the Greek *kuriakon* meaning 'of the Lord,' but more probably coming from the Greek word *kirkos* (ring or circle) by way of the Latin word *circus* (a round arena) or Germanic *kirche*.

[41] The same Greek word is used in the Septuagint but is not translated "church." Funny how that works.

[42] See also Acts 13:42-43 where congregation and synagogue are used interchangeably in the KJV.

one English word love. But *ecclesia* is not one of those words. There's no good reason to pick the word 'church' to translate it as opposed to assembly or congregation.

To be accurate, we should use the word church in all places where the Body of Christ is spoken of (as in "the church in the wilderness" of the King James Version Acts 7:38) or all uses of the word *ekklesia* should be translated as congregation[43] or even assembly. The reason they are not is simple preference, or a deliberate attempt to hijack Bible authority and transfer it to the church. Many extra-biblical doctrines don't allow the Body (confused with the church) to exist before the resurrection. The Catholic Church illustrates this with some hijacking of words when translating the King James Version (now called the Authorized Version). With the KJV they used the word "church" instead of assembly or congregation. At the time it came out the KJV was very controversial, and caused many Christians to reject using it for quite a while (mostly because of the word "church").[44]

The church is visible and is known for its organizational structures and belief systems (creeds, etc.). The Body of Christ, on the other hand, is organized around the Word (the Christ is the head), and is known for its fruit or actions. The church (and synagogue) has people who claim to follow Him, but do not. The Body consists of those who actually follow Him. The churchagogue is simply a congregation or assembly (or a series of congregations or assemblies) just like Israel was (and is) a congregation. The churchagogue (and Israel) have part of The Body in them, but they are not 100% filled with believers. The modern day church tends to think it is special, separate and somehow more acceptable, so it promotes a different name for itself (The Church as opposed to, say, 'assembly' or 'congregation.').

It's funny how a Baptist church never plants a Presbyterian church, or a Catholic church never starts an Assembly of God. Isn't it funny that Calvary Chapel always starts other Calvary Chapels, and never a Vineyard? How about a synagogue starting a Baptist church? If reaching the lost is the goal, why is it that churches always reproduce after their own kind? Are they really reaching the lost or building up their club? It makes you wonder.

One of the Satan's biggest successes, besides convincing people he doesn't exist, is the idea of the church. What I mean is, generally people

---

[43] See also Acts 15:30 where the word *plethos* is translated 'congregation' but is applied to the 'church.'

[44] Erasmus, the guy who worked on the KJV, didn't have all the Greek manuscripts he needed, so he translated some from Latin into Greek and then into the King's English. This caused a few errors to creep in. Most of the 'KJV positive' crowd wants to reinforce the authority of the church rather than try to keep the translations error-free.

think the "church" is God's, and anyone outside of "church" must be an unbeliever. Believers are supposed to be members of the church in whatever form. The church must be the good guys and the "not-church" must be the bad guys. But this setup is as fake as professional wrestling. This is not how the Word does it. The Bible says that the good guys do what God says (sheep); bad guys don't (goats). The "mother," "brother" and "sister" of Jesus is the one who does God's will (Matthew 12:48-50). Just look at mom and dad in the Garden, or Cain and Able, or Saul and David, or believing and unbelieving Israel, or (well, you get my drift).

The words "assembly" (Hebrew *qahal* ka-hall) and "congregation" (*edah* eh-dah) are used for Israel,[45] especially when they were camped out at Mount Sinai. So the word assembly = congregation = *ekklesia* = *qahal* = *edah* = church = synagogue = multitude.[46] They all mean pretty much the same thing. An ekklesia can be any group of people. Believers, on the other hand, are called names like saints or elect or the remnant or the olive tree or Israel or the body of Christ. There are small congregations and big assemblies, but there is only one called-out Body.

The name "Christian" (Acts 11:26, 26:28; 1 Peter 4:16) was bestowed on those who were "partisans of the Christ" early on, sort of like a political term. But there are lots of unbelievers that would call themselves a partisan yet refuse to actually do what the Christ says. Like the Roman emperor Constantine. So this is where the overlap comes in. People can call themselves partisans; maybe even believers (and sometimes they are believers), then form a club and call it a church. However, like Keith Green used to say, standing in a garage doesn't make you a Porsche.

Israel in Three

There are a few different names in the Bible for the body of Christ that we need to clarify. For instance, I see in the Word three groups called Israel. The first is the group of people physically descended from Jacob's (who got the new name of Israel from God) twelve sons (or those who were adopted). This was the group called out of captivity in Egypt by God through Moses. The second Israel, also called Ephraim (later Samaria), was the group of ten tribes living in the north part of the Land after the 12 tribes split into two nations.[47] The southern nation consisted of Judah and Benjamin but was called Judah.

---

[45] In the Septuagint, *ecclesia* is used quite a bit for the Hebrew words 'congregation' (*edah*) and 'assembly' (*qahal*).
[46] Compare also Matthew 4:23 where synagogue is used for G4864 *sunagoge* but in James 2:2 it's 'assembly.'
[47] Actually, the split between Israel and Judah goes as far back as the reign of King David and possibly even further.

The children of Jacob are now known in general as Jews, a name which comes from "people of Judea" or Judah. The word Jew can mean a physical child of Jacob, someone who dwells in the land of Judah, or someone who has converted to Judaism (someone who lives or acts like a Jew).

The third Israel is not as obvious in the text as the first two. It includes all people since the beginning who have believed and obeyed God no matter who their parents are. Paul highlights this fact in Romans.

> ⁶But it is not as though the word of God has failed. For they are not all Israel who are descended from Israel; ⁷nor are they all children because they are Abraham's descendants, but: "through Isaac your descendants will be named." ⁸That is, it is not the children of the flesh who are children of God, but the children of the promise are regarded as descendants. (Romans 9:6-8 NASB95)

Members of the third Israel[48] (otherwise known as children of the promise) are not determined by genetics but by obedience to God the Father and "the Promise" which is Jesus His Son.[49] All who accept the Promise (Jesus) are part of this third Israel. These people who join with the Messiah are also called the Bride (Isaiah 61:10; Revelation 19:17), the Body (Romans 12:5), the remnant (Isaiah 11:16-12:6, 28:5, 6; Acts 15:17; Romans 9:27, 11:5), an olive tree (Psalm 52:8; Romans 11), saints (called out ones), elect (chosen, Isaiah 65:9; Matthew 24:22; Romans 11:7), and a temple (1 Corinthians 3:16).

Joining with the Messiah is not limited to people who lived after the resurrection. Any person who trusts and obeys or abides in God is part of Israel (1 Peter 1:10-13; Hebrews 11:39, 40). Hebrews 11 contains a nice picture of those who will join all believers in the city God is building (Hebrews 11:13-16). This is the believer's family tree.

> ¹A Psalm of Asaph. Surely God is good to Israel, To those who are pure in heart! (Psalm 73:1 NASB95)

We know "all Israel" (all Jews) are not pure in heart. But the psalmist is equating those who are pure in heart with Israel. It is not the natural father or mother that proves membership in the family of Israel. It is the actions. A person shows they are a "chip off the old block" by behaving the same way as their parent. If we do what God says, He is our Father. If we don't, we are illegitimate.

---

[48] There is no numbering system nor are the numbers meant to imply primacy or lack of it.
[49] Search for the word 'obey' in the Bible. I found over 150 uses in the ESV that connect it with God's voice.

Jesus (or Paul) did not start a new thing called the church. He (they) promoted God's kingdom which He has been building since the beginning. Membership in the body (or Bride) is by the gracious choosing of God through trusting obedience (faith) to His call. Everyone must be "born again" in this process (even Jews) to be part of the body.

Believers are God's congregation, the sheep of His pasture, a nation of kings and priests (Exodus 19:5,[50] 6; Isaiah 61; 1 Peter 2:5, 9; Revelation 1:6, 5:10). At the present time, we are scattered like salt in the world. God has merged the first two Israels back together (Ezekiel 37:15-28) and will soon winnow the chaff from His kingdom and bring us all back to His home.

The Mixed Multitude

The Scriptures say that when God through Moses delivered the first Israel from Egypt, they came out a "mixed multitude," meaning there were lots of people that were not physical children of Jacob.

> [38]A mixed multitude also went up with them, along with flocks and herds, a very large number of livestock. (Exodus 12:38 NASB95)

This mixed multitude probably included Egyptians who learned to fear God through watching or experiencing the plagues. To support my conclusion the Bible mentions an Egyptian as the father of an Israelite man (Leviticus 24:10). Or perhaps there were slaves from other countries that had decided to join with Israel while they were still in Goshen.

> [20]The one among the servants of Pharaoh who feared the word of the Lord made his servants and his livestock flee into the houses; [21]but he who paid no regard to the word of the Lord left his servants and his livestock in the field. (Exodus 9:20-21 NASB95)

This is important for our study of names because the division of people in Egypt into Israel and not-Israel was not by genetics; it was by fear of the Lord. Fear of the Lord has always been the dividing line between groups and the Body of Christ. There were (and are) those who "feared the word of the Lord" and those who didn't. Just like now.

When the 12 spies returned from taking inventory of the Land, Caleb the Kenizzite (a non-native or non-physical descendant of Jacob) for instance advocated for God's plan along with Joshua (Numbers 32:11-12). Later, we see the mixed multitude in the Land mentioned in the

---

[50] Yes I know this verse applies to the first Israel, but it can apply to whoever acts like God's people Israel.

book of Joshua at 8:33-35. Another example of the mixed multitude of the third Israel is in Ezra (6:21) where he speaks of people who had separated themselves from the impurity of the nations joining Israel to seek God. Lots of people were (and are) part of Israel without having Jacob as a genetic father.[51] Like Ruth, we have taken refuge under the wings of the Lord, the God of Israel (Ruth 2:12; Nahum 1:7).

The founder of physical Israel was a Gentile. Abraham is part of Israel, but of course not descended from Jacob. Jesus has a reformed Gentile harlot (Rahab, Matthew 1:5) and a Moabite woman (Ruth, same verse) in His human lineage. Those believers who lived before Abraham are also, without a doubt, part of the third Israel. The kingdom of God has always been mixed in the genetic sense. Genetics have nothing to do with membership in God's household.

> [11]"Many nations will join themselves to the LORD in that day and will become My people. Then I will dwell in your midst, and you will know that the LORD of hosts has sent Me to you. (Zechariah 2:11 NASB95)

Strangers in the Mix

Some people limit the meaning of "stranger" to a person who is not a Jew. They will also apply the words "foreigner" and "sojourner" only to Gentiles. They've made it into a genetic thing when it's really not. It's true that at times the term "foreigner" or stranger can be applied to anyone outside of the community of Israel. But it seems from the text that the application of all these words depended on whether someone was following God correctly. In other words, if Israel was practicing God's instructions the right way, then a stranger was one who didn't. However, if Israel wasn't following Torah, then they were just as strange as the pagans. Perhaps even more so because they were supposed to know better.

When Adam and Eve sinned, they became strangers to God; not in the sense of lack of familiarity, but in nature. Perhaps "estranged" gives a better understanding. This is opposite of "knowing" God. The word "stranger" can be applied to any person or nation estranged from God. The Bible sometimes calls Israel strangers, and also people groups who are not physically children of Jacob. Gentiles[52] (a.k.a. the nations) are called strangers because they have not agreed to live by God's Word as

---

[51] 2 Chronicles 2:13-14 shows intermarriage in a good way. Numbers 25:1-3 shows a bad way. Ezra 9 and 10 speak of mixed marriages being bad but obviously because of idolatry (Ezra 9:13-14) rather than simple genetics.

[52] The English word 'Gentile' comes from the Hebrew word goy or goyim (plural) which is sometimes translated 'nation' (nations) and simply means a people group. The Hebrew word ger (gayr) means stranger and is applied to Israel (Exodus 22:21) and non-native residents in Israel, as well as those outside of Israel (Gentiles).

did the first Israel (Ephesians 2:12). The people of Israel were strangers in Egypt because it was not their land (Genesis 15:13; Exodus 19:34, 23:9). But when they wandered away from God they got stranger.

> ^{17}Then he said to me, "Have you seen this, O son of man? Is it too light a thing for the house of Judah to commit the abominations that they commit here, that they should fill the land with violence and provoke me still further to anger? Behold, they put the branch to their nose. (Ezekiel 8:17 ESV)

It is obvious in Scripture that the main division is between believers and non-believers (strangers or foreigners). The designation of stranger really applies to whoever acts like a stranger with God. People try to make a false division between Jews and Gentiles on the basis of genetics. God makes the division between sheep (believers) and goats (non-believers).

Paul describes the inclusion of Gentiles as "fellow heirs" in the body of Christ as a "mystery" (Ephesians 3:4-7). Not because it didn't exist until Acts chapter 2, it is because few were paying attention or in the case of Israel just weren't interested. If we study the Word, we can see that His congregation has always included anyone who wants to follow Him, regardless of parents. Like Caleb, Ruth and Rahab.

Instead of being a "house of prayer for all nations" (Isaiah 56:7; Matthew 21:13) the first Israel chose to disobey God. By the time of the Incarnation, it had developed into an exclusive club rather than a home for all followers of God. Gentiles have always been included in God's family if they choose to repent and follow the ways of God instead of their own. Heck, Noah and Abraham were Gentiles. The body of Christ does not have boundaries, nor is it limited by family or tradition. It is made up of all believers everywhere who fear God and do what He says.

> ^{3}Let not the foreigner who has joined himself to the Lord say, "The Lord will surely separate me from His people." Nor let the eunuch say, "Behold, I am a dry tree." ^{4}For thus says the Lord, "To the eunuchs who keep My sabbaths, And choose what pleases Me, And hold fast My covenant, ^{5}To them I will give in My house and within My walls a memorial, And a name better than that of sons and daughters; I will give them an everlasting name which will not be cut off. ^{6}"Also the foreigners who join themselves to the Lord, To minister to Him, and to love the name of the Lord, To be His servants, every one who keeps from profaning the sabbath And holds fast My covenant; ^{7}Even those I will bring to My holy mountain And make them joyful in My house of prayer. Their burnt offerings and their sacrifices will be

> acceptable on My altar; For My house will be called a house of prayer for all the peoples." ⁸The Lord God, who gathers the dispersed of Israel, declares, "Yet others I will gather to them, to those already gathered." (Isaiah 56:3-8 NASB95)

> ²³And He did so to make known the riches of His glory upon vessels of mercy, which He prepared beforehand for glory, ²⁴even us, whom He also called, not from among Jews only, but also from among Gentiles. (Romans 9:23-24 NASB95)

The first Israel is a real hard project for God (in more ways than one). But it is also a picture of God's efforts to form the third Israel or Body of Christ out of man in general. Some in both groups cooperate fully, others pretend to cooperate but just give Him lip service, and some reject Him utterly.

There is nothing special about the first Israel that would attract God (Ezekiel 16). God's plan for His Body was never halted by the fact that the first Israel didn't live or help share the Word as they should. The mixed multitude of the first Israel gives us a picture of the mixed multitude of the third Israel. There is no split in the Body between Jew and Gentile, male or female.

> There is neither Jew nor Greek, there is neither slave nor free man, there is neither male nor female; for you are all one in Christ Jesus. (Galatians 3:28 NASB95)

There is also no Catholic, Presbyterian, Baptist, Methodist, Anglican, Seventh-Day, non-Denominational, Mormon, Messianic, Church of Christ, Assembly of God, Muslim or whatever, either. Of course, we know that Jew and Gentile still exist. We know that male and female still exist. What a dull world we would have if there weren't such variety as God has created! "One body" doesn't mean everyone is identical, it just means that all believers are united through our Messiah Jesus. God does not treat a person born a Jew any differently than a person born a non-Jew, if each of them is adopted into His family, by grace through faith.

The Body goes by some other names in the Bible. These other names, combined with the church's general drift away from the Word, have caused some confusion as to how many groups there are and what parts of the Law apply to whom. Let's go over some and see if we can't get a more biblical understanding of God's plan.

I Will Build My Ecclesia

As we can see from Scripture, something called "the church" has not replaced Israel at all. Rather, Gentiles have been "grafted in" to an existing body of believers, as they have always been.

To object, some will quote Matthew 16:18, where Jesus says to Peter, "...*upon this rock I will build my ekklesia, and the gates of Hades will not overpower it.*" They say that "will build" means that the assembly had not been built. Jesus was going to build it later. The problem is, "will build" is not connected with time. It could just as easily mean the building blocks (believers) will be gathered together at some future time and used for building. After all, believers are still being added to the Body aren't they? And wouldn't you wait till you had all the material together to build something? Right now He's growing a temple (Ephesians 2:19-22) but it's not finished yet. So He was, and is, and will be, building His assembly then and now.

Paul cautions us to beware of arrogance, and replacement theologies are arrogant. What is grafted onto the tree can be broken off again, just as some of the natural branches were broken off. We must look to our own fruit, and abide in the vine. We don't want to end up as some of the natural branches. There is no room in the Body of Christ for pride of place.

The idea that a split God created a split Body is just not biblical. The one Father has been adding to one body through one faith by one Spirit and one baptism for a very long time. There are giants of the faith such as Abraham and Sarah, Noah, and Moses. There are also the humble of station such as Ruth and Rahab. Queens like Esther, and mighty kings like David and Solomon are included, as well as judges such as Samson, Deborah and Gideon. Believers in the Body share a wonderful family tree.

The Remnant or Elect

All through history, there has been a remnant for God (people who followed His Word) that He has preserved for Himself. Abel and Enoch were part of the remnant. Noah and his family were a remnant. God tells Elijah of 7,000 that hadn't bowed the knee to Ba'al (which were probably Jewish), and most of the prophets speak of the remnant.[53]

> [25]As He says also in Hosea, "I will call those who were not My people, 'My people,' And her who was not beloved, 'beloved.' " [26]"And it shall be that in the place where it was said to them, 'you are not My people,' There they shall be called sons of the living God." [27]Isaiah cries out concerning Israel, "Though the number of the sons of Israel be like the sand of the sea, it is the *remnant* that will be saved; [28]for the Lord will execute His word

---

[53] Isaiah 10:20, 22, 28:5; Jeremiah 31:7, 50:20; Ezekiel 6:8, 11:13; Amos 5:15; Micah 2:12, 5:7, 8; Zephaniah 2:9, 3:13; Zechariah 9:7; see also Romans 9:27 quoting Isaiah

on the earth, thoroughly and quickly." ²⁹And just as Isaiah foretold, "Unless the Lord of Sabaoth had left to us a posterity, We would have become like Sodom, and would have resembled Gomorrah." (Romans 9:25-29 NASB95, italics added)

¹⁸"Yet I will leave 7,000 in Israel, all the knees that have not bowed to Baal and every mouth that has not kissed him." (1 Kings 19:18 NASB95)

¹⁸Who is a God like You, who pardons iniquity And passes over the rebellious act of the *remnant* of His possession? He does not retain His anger forever, Because He delights in unchanging love. ¹⁹He will again have compassion on us; He will tread our iniquities under foot. Yes, You will cast all their sins Into the depths of the sea. (Micah 7:18-19 NASB95 italics added)

²God has not rejected His people whom He foreknew. Or do you not know what the Scripture says in the passage about Elijah, how he pleads with God against Israel? ³"Lord, they have killed Your prophets, they have torn down Your altars, and I alone am left, and they are seeking my life." ⁴But what is the divine response to him? "I have kept for Myself seven thousand men who have not bowed the knee to Baal." ⁵In the same way then, there has also come to be at the present time a *remnant* according to God's gracious choice. (Romans 11:2-5 NASB95 italics added)

    The "remnant" includes people who were not physical descendants of Jacob (Acts 15:16-17 ESV). Remnant is another one of those words that can have different meanings depending on context. It doesn't necessarily mean "saved" in the sense of eternal life. It mostly means a leftover group. Noah and family were saved from the flood, but we really don't know their "saved" status as far as being adopted into God's family. From later behavior, it seems that maybe some weren't. But most of the time remnant is another word for the *ecclesia*.

    The word "elect" is another term that is used for the Body or *ecclesia*. It is also used for other people or groups. Mostly "elect" is used in the NT and "remnant" in the OT. "Elect" is just a different way of saying "chosen" or "chosen for a purpose." Someone who is elect can be chosen for a purpose, like Pharaoh (Exodus 9:16-17; Romans 9:17). The word elect is not specifically applied to him, but "raised you up" is. The elect can also refer to Israel, as in "chosen nation." The remnant is also the elect, because they are chosen by God to be His own.

    The important thing about the words "elect" and "remnant" is that regarding eternal life (salvation) or God's household, they are all One

Body. There might be other remnants that are elected for a purpose, but there is only one remnant that is both elect and His one Body.

The Kingdom of God

In the broadest sense of the term, the kingdom is all creation. God rules everything all the time (Revelation 19:15, among many others) including Hell. But in the narrowest sense of the term, the Kingdom is anywhere that God rules the heart.

God doesn't rule in all hearts, so that is why the kingdom can be both "here" ("the kingdom is upon you" in places such as Luke 11:20) and "future." The here part is when God rules the heart. The future part is when Jesus returns to earth and sets up a nation starting with Israel and covering the whole earth. Then He will reign over many nations with a rod of iron, meaning that some still will not willingly participate. After a while of this (about 1,000 years it looks like) He will sweep all unwilling people into the dustbin outside of His kingdom (Revelation 22:15). Then His kingdom will continue to expand in a new heaven and new earth.

Many Jewish people think that the Kingdom is the same as physical Israel. To get into the Kingdom they say people must convert to Judaism and follow all those traditions and laws. Many church people think that to get into the Kingdom you must convert to Christianity and follow all the church traditions (and laws). But there's no Scriptural warrant for these beliefs. It's obvious that there are Jewish people in the Kingdom (Moses, Ezekiel, Nehemiah, etc.) and Jewish people who are not in the Kingdom (Korah (Numbers 16), Ahab, Jeroboam, etc.). There are Gentiles in the Kingdom and Gentiles who are not. Since when does the Kingdom have anything to do with genetics, or with a political term such as Christian? In the resurrection, righteous people will be in "the Kingdom" while unrighteous unrepentant people, whether Jew or Gentile, will not (Revelation 21:8).

Some people may look like they are part of the Kingdom, but they will not continue to follow God. The important thing to realize is that all creation belongs to God, and He will do with it what He chooses. He is in charge and everything is going according to His plan, though we may not understand it all. Our part is to accept His ways, His Word, and let them get past our lips, through our hearts, and into our limbs.

The Olive Tree

The new covenant is between God, Judah, and Israel (northern 10 tribes after the split). Gentiles are part, but they are grafted in to an existing body (see Romans 9 – 11 for Paul's view of this). Paul gives us another picture of the Body of Christ when he discusses the nature of the olive tree in Romans 11. He says that branches are broken off due to lack of faith, and other branches are grafted in by faith.

> [17]But if some of the branches were broken off, and you, being a wild olive, were grafted in among them and became partaker with them of the rich root of the olive tree, [18]do not be arrogant toward the branches; but if you are arrogant, remember that it is not you who supports the root, but the root supports you. (Romans 11:17-18 NASB95)

The olive tree is also a picture of the third Israel. Paul in Romans 9:6 says "they are not all Israel who are from Israel" and in 11:26 Paul says "all Israel will be saved." In other words, Israel is everyone who is truly following God. Natural branches have to produce fruit or they don't make the cut to stay part of the tree. Branches that are grafted in have to show they are part of the kingdom by also producing fruit. It they don't, they aren't really a part of the tree and can be broken off again.

Don't confuse the illustration Paul is using by inserting the argument of "once saved always saved," though true, because it doesn't belong here. It's not a stand-alone doctrine anyway. We're not tasked with trying to determine who is and isn't saved. Believers are tasked with living His Words. We correct, encourage and discipline each other as we go. Just because someone looks saved now doesn't mean they actually are saved. Those who persevere to the end are the ones who are saved, and we aren't at the end yet. The illustration of the olive tree is limited to fruit and grafting. Looking at the olive tree from outside, you can only tell a branch by its fruit.

Salvation cannot be lost in my opinion, but we do not really know who is saved and who isn't. We are not tasked with determining salvation, but making disciples. Someone can look like they are part of the tree for a while, or naturally grow from it. But if they have no fruit then they were not really part (dead branches). If we are saved we keep doing what God says. If we are not, we fall by the wayside. Maybe a saved person goes up and down, but they still move towards God. The parable of the sower in Matthew 13 tells us that of the four different kinds of people, three show growth. But only one of the three actually shows fruit.

It is more consistent with the Word to see the olive tree as the third Israel, planted and husbanded by God through the centuries. He has been grafting people on who come to trust Him, and pruning off branches that bear no fruit. So all believers are at least a little fruity. John the Immerser says this fruit is in keeping with repentance (Matthew 3:7-12).

The Presence of the Holy Spirit

Okay. So far in our quest for a biblical view of the Body of Christ, we've established that the Body is one, that it has been around since the Garden, that there are three Israels but only one is the Body of Christ, that God has never used genetics (or politics or doctrine) as a membership requirement for the Body, there are different names for the Body, and that the church is not the Body and has not replaced Israel.

But one other argument people use to bolster the idea of a separate church that is somehow special is that the Spirit didn't "fill" or "dwell in" believers until the first Pentecost (Hebrew *Shavuot*) after the resurrection of the Messiah. Part of this argument in some circles makes a big deal about the difference between being led by the Spirit and being filled by the Spirit. The filling of the Holy Spirit is supposed to set the "church" off as different and never before seen, because in the OT people were just "led" by the Spirit. The argument says no one was "filled" until Acts chapter 2. But even a quick look at the Word proves this to be false. The list of people in the OT directly said to be filled with and/or led by the Spirit is long and distinguished. It is also clear in the plain meaning of the text that there is very little difference, if any at all, between leading and filling.

- Bezalel (Exodus 31:3 and 35:31)
- Moses and the 70 Elders (Numbers 11:17, 25, 26, 29)
- Balaam (Numbers 24:2)
- Joshua (Numbers 27:18 and Deuteronomy 34:9)
- Othniel son of Joshua (Judges 3:10)
- Gideon (Judges 6:34)
- Jephthah (pronounced Yayftah - Judges 11:29)
- Samson (Judges 13:25, 14:6, 19, 15:14)
- King Saul (1 Samuel 10:6, 10, 11:6)
- King David (1 Samuel 16:13)
- Messengers of Saul (1 Samuel 19:20)
- Amasai, chief of the 30 (1 Chronicles 12:18)
- Azariah son of Obed (2 Chronicles 15:1)
- Jahaziel (2 Chronicles 20:14)
- The Branch (Isaiah 11:2); My Servant (Isaiah 42:1); the Anointed (Isaiah 61:1)
- The people of Israel (Isaiah 63:11)
- Ezekiel (Ezekiel. 2:2, 3:12, 14, 24, 11:5)
- Micah (Micah 3:8)
- Zerubbabel, Joshua, and the people of the land (Haggai 2:5)
- The former prophets (Zechariah 7:12)

There are also a number of Scriptures that explicitly state that Old Testament saints had the Spirit (such as Isaiah 63:10-14; 1 Peter 1:11). The presence of the Spirit is not marked only by speaking in other languages or with miraculous actions, or even by prophetic signs and utterances. His primary mark is on a heart that responds to God in trusting and loving obedience. God's Spirit is all around and works to varying degrees depending on the willingness of people to work with Him.

He may sometimes work in spectacular ways, but that is not the only way He works. For instance, He can be present without salvation, as He is in creation. He makes seeds grow and keeps air on our planet with gravity. The planets revolve and orbit the sun by His hand. The only place He has trouble getting His way is in the human heart.

The Jews?

It's probably good at this point to define the Jews too. But even Jews aren't sure who is a Jew. A Jew can be either a physical descendant of Abraham, or a convert to Judaism. Some think at least dad has to be a Jew; others think mom has to be a Jew. Throw in the different brands of Judaism (orthodox, ultra-orthodox, reformed, etc.), and there is a real problem figuring out who is Jewish. A person can be physically Jewish and still not practice Judaism, while a physically non-Jewish person can convert to most forms of Judaism.

A whole-Bible Christian holds a special place for the Jewish people in his or her heart. We bless the Jews in every way we can, from prayers to pocketbooks, because God asks us to bless them (Genesis 12:3). We "pray for the peace of Jerusalem" for "the sake of the house of the Lord our God" (Psalm 122). In fact, it is my firm belief that people who love Israel, and the Jewish people, love God. People who hate Israel hate God. The Satan hates Israel and keeps trying to destroy them because they are the physical representation of God's kingdom on earth. People who behave the same way are Satan's children. So one of the ways we can tell believers from unbelievers is by the love, or hatred, of Israel.

To our shame, the church (and our country) has not done what they should in defending the first Israel. The Jews are God's chosen nation on earth, whether they embrace the job or not. They are the "the apple of His eye."

> [8] For thus says the Lord of hosts, "After glory He has sent Me against the nations which plunder you, for he who touches you, touches the apple of His eye. (Zechariah 2:8 NASB95)
>
> [4] They are Israelites, and to them belong the adoption, the glory, the covenants, the giving of the law, the worship, and the

promises. ⁵ To them belong the patriarchs, and from their race, according to the flesh, is the Christ who is God over all, blessed forever. Amen. (Romans 9:4-5 ESV)

We don't bless them for their sakes, or because they deserve it, as much as we do it for God's sake (Obadiah 12-14). They are the elder brothers and sisters of the faith. In many ways if they are not moving forward in leadership pointing to God, then nobody else is moving forward either. God has selected them as His people. As long as they lead people to God, they do a wonderful job.

Judaism

Judaism, on the other hand, is a different subject than Israel or the Jewish people. Judaism is the collection of religious practices and traditions that Jewish people have gathered over a long history. It comes from rabbis, and its main point is to preserve Jewish identity.

Judaism includes the "oral law" in two different versions, both called Talmud (to learn). Both versions are merely collections of rabbinical rulings and teachings. The oral law was likely included in the term "whole law" spoken of in the New Testament. Much of the struggle with the law in the NT was over customs and traditions rather than with God's Word. It was definitely a big sore spot between Jesus and leaders of Judaism (Matthew 15:2-6; Mark 7:5-9).

Not all Jewish people are practicing the religious things of Judaism. It is difficult to estimate the number of non-practicing (secular) and practicing Jews,[54] because Judaism has so many sects. But about 30% to 40% are uninvolved and 60% to 70% are involved at least a little.

Religious Jews are split into all sorts of factions, from ultra orthodox (the smallest division) to barely practicing (perhaps the largest division) and even some anti-God humanists.[55] Like the Protestants, Judaism has many forms practiced by many different groups of people. It is not all one religion. Even at the time of the incarnation, it was like this. And like Christianity, Judaism has a core of godly beliefs. But they have not always been true to them either.

There is a tendency in some circles to think that being Jewish or practicing Judaism is the same as following God. The idea seems to be that a Jewish person, or a person who practices Judaism(s), is either automatically doing what God requires or is somehow practicing biblical

---

[54] According to Wikipedia (http://en.wikipedia.org/wiki/Jewish_population) the Jewish People Policy Planning Institute calculated in 2007 that there were 13.2 million Jews worldwide with 4.5 million as secular. Other estimates range from 12 to 18 million.

[55] For instance, Greg Epstein of Cambridge, the 'humanist rabbi.' Search online, you'll find him. Unfortunately.

faith in a way superior to non-Jewish people or practices. This comes from thinking that Jews have historically followed God. Therefore, they must have a sort of "inside track" that should be followed if we want to practice what we preach.

Sadly, the Scriptures tell a different story. In the pages of God's Word, Judaism is generally known for stiff-necked, belligerent and hard-hearted idolatry (see for instance Nehemiah 9). They got booted out of the Land because they refused to do what God said.[56] Happily for us, there is also a remnant of Jewish people, such as the writers of the Word and people like Jesus or Nicodemus or Joseph of Arimathea, who really do follow their (our) God.

But to say that Judaism, or any other group of religious practices, is automatically better in God's eyes is missing the point entirely. Judaism and Christianity both have seen success in God pleasing behavior, but both have also seen miserable failure. Neither is holier than the other.

It is not genetic or cultural or traditional people groups that define God's family; it is the response to what God says. "My sheep hear my voice" as Jesus says in John 10:27. Jewish people are like any other people. They have been known for both the highest and lowest behavior that is possible from human beings. So being Jewish, or practicing Judaism, does not mean the same thing as being Godly or doing godly things. It is the actions of the person as they match or stray from the Word that shows who is in the Body or not.

> [28]For he is not a Jew who is one outwardly, nor is circumcision that which is outward in the flesh. [29]But he is a Jew who is one inwardly; and circumcision is that which is of the heart, by the Spirit, not by the letter; and his praise is not from men, but from God. (Romans 2:28-29 NASB95)

> [19]Circumcision is nothing, and uncircumcision is nothing, but what matters is the keeping of the commandments of God. (1 Corinthians 7:19 NASB95)

> [6]For in Christ Jesus neither circumcision nor uncircumcision means anything, but faith working through love. (Galatians 5:6 NASB95)

The whole-Bible Christian realizes that there is a large difference between Jews and Judaism. We bless the Jewish people but don't have to copy every tradition. We do not embrace Judaism, nor do we reject it out

---

[56] Exodus 32:9, 33:3-5; Deuteronomy 9:6, 31:27; Judges 2:19; Nehemiah 9:16-29; Psalm 78:8; Ezekiel 3:7; Zechariah 7:8-14; Matthew 15:7-9; Acts 7:51-53

of hand. We just see the need to match up whatever we do with the Word. Keep what is good and avoid the bad.

The Messianic Movement

A sect we should include in our study of the Body is called the Messianic movement. In a way, most practicing Jews have always been "messianic" in that they look for God's Messiah. Some found Him when a group of Jews realized that the long-awaited Messiah was in fact Jesus (people like Peter, James, and Paul). The modern Messianic movement is an extension of this group that accepts Jesus as the Messiah, but also tries to maintain Jewish heritage and practice.

There are factions within this group just as there are in Judaism. It had grown a lot since the '70's, but seems to be shrinking in the last few years. This might be due to an emphasis on practicing Jewish extra-biblical traditions and trying to be as "Jewish" as possible. It might also be the confusion that's coming from a refusal to focus on the whole of His Law and getting caught up in unimportant side doctrines. It's clear to me, in view of the large number of non-practicing Jews, that even Jews are not all that interested in Judaism. Messianic or otherwise.

The Messianic movement had such great potential. Through some of the individuals and a couple of good organizations such as First Fruits of Zion, I learned much that is missing from the church about the unity of God and the Word. Tim Hegg of Torah Resource is an excellent teacher, who taught me some of what is in this book. Messianics had a chance to unite everyone in a type of whole Bible belief. But like the Pharisees in Judaism they traded their birthright for unbiblical doctrine pursued for the sake of tradition, power and influence.

Instead of a return to Bible traditions, now they've got a race to see who can be more Jewish orthodox. Instead of one faith for one body they hand out "divine invitations" to two houses.[57] Instead of a God and Messiah who are one, some want a God and a human messiah. The Messianic movement has become like the church in a talit (prayer shawl). They too have drifted away from where they had such a bright future in terms of bringing back believers to the Law. They still have a lot to offer if they would just focus on the whole Bible.

Roots

Some teach that Gentile believers have been "grafted in to a Jewish

---

[57] The two house doctrine is the belief that there are still two houses of Israel – Judah and Ephraim. Judah is supposed to be the Jews, and Ephraim in their opinion is descendants of the supposed lost ten tribes. Anyone who wants to follow the Law is considered one of those "lost" tribes, taken into captivity by Assyria long ago and dispersed into the nations. I know it's a little confusing. But that's part of my point.

(or Hebrew) root," or that the church has "Jewish roots." They do this to promote unity between Jews and Christians. The goal is worthy, but scripturally all believers are grafted into the root of the Messiah,[58] not the root of Judaism. Yes, Jesus is Jewish, from the tribe of Judah. But the Scriptures don't make a point of it except in respect to the Promise (Genesis 3:15).[59]

I agree that the roots of the church are in Judaism. Note how stubborn both groups are, and steeped in idolatry. Notice too how much they promote their dogma, and resist any changes that might correct their drift away from the Word.

But the roots of believers (the Remnant, body, bride, etc.) are in Jesus, and His body has been around for a much longer time.

The first Israel was supposed to be a holy nation of priests and kings (Exodus 19:6) but so far has failed to completely live up to the billing. The church in general has also poorly represented Him. Meanwhile God has kept a remnant for Himself in spite of the seeming wholesale departure of people from His rule.

The Body is grafted onto the root of the eternally existent Messiah. Judaism (or Christianity) is not and never has been the "root." Whole Bible Christians want to follow all of God's Word and realize that Judaism isn't the point. We also think that the church is not the point either, especially in the area of extra-biblical and worldly traditions. What counts is following all of God's Word including the commandments of God (1 Corinthians 7:19).

Growing pains

The book of Acts is not the beginning of the Body of Christ; it is another chapter in the story. It is also a picture of what the first Israel should have been from their beginning. This is why Jesus, the apostles and Paul (Acts 18:6) go to the Jews first. Since Israel is supposed to be God's point men, they are given a number of chances to get it right.

The book of Acts describes growing pains, not labor pains. The Body was already there. It just needed a kick in the pants and some direction again. The principles that God had been trying to get across for centuries (love, obedience, whole-hearted devotion) were dusted off and given a new push. The entrenched Jewish leaders resisted the move back to the purity of God's ways. So there were a series of "synagogue splits" between believers and non-believers (both Jew and Gentile). These early splits were over Jesus, the oral law, and rabbinical authority.

---

[58] Who is actually called the root, see for instance Isaiah 11:10, 53:2; Romans 11:16, 15:12.
[59] I have to make a note here also about the two-house teachings. I don't have space to cover it all here, but it is a false teaching that contains very little truth. There are articles on the whole Bible Christian website www.wholebible.com.

Paul makes it a habit to go into a synagogue in every new town he visits and attempt to unmask the riches of the Word. He mostly succeeds in getting himself booted out and needing to start a new synagogue. One of the main sticking points, besides Jesus, is his focus on Gentile inclusion in the Body. At the root this was a matter of rabbinical authority, because it was the rabbis who declared (outside of God's Word) that Gentiles were unclean and not fit to be included in Israel. Unless they converted to Judaism. In Acts 22:1-22, Paul is making a defense of himself to the Jews. They are fine with almost every statement (even the ones about Jesus) until he mentions including the Gentiles in verse 22. Then the fireworks really go off.

As time goes on, more and more believing Gentiles become a part of the new synagogues with believing Jews. Hardened non-believers (Jews and Gentiles) fight, kick and scream about it. After the time frame of the book of Acts, as the apostles depart this life for the next, the new congregations get more and more anti-Jewish. The Jewish leader's rejection of Jesus was part of the reason. There were also differences of opinion between believers and unbelievers about how to handle Roman occupation and the various high-handed actions against the Jews.

Two key events caused further separation. First was the destruction of the Temple in 70 A.D. Second was the destruction of Jerusalem itself in 135 A.D. But by the later part of the first century, the Christians were already starting to see themselves as a separate "church."

Over more time (several hundred years more), the roots of conflict in Acts show fruit in church teachings developed to either replace or merge Israel with the Church. This time is called "the parting of the ways" by scholars. All of these teachings on "church" have, sadly, a great deal of anti-Jewishness in them. In fact we could say that Christians defined (and continue to define) themselves more and more sharply in opposition to anything Jewish. This is the main thinking behind the modern rejection of His Law. Jesus took great pains to tear down the dividing wall between us, and we couldn't wait to build it back up.

The Nicolaitans

A lot of the impetus for "growing pains" and dividing walls is due to leadership that goes in a wrong direction from God's ways. In the letters to the seven congregations, Jesus speaks of Nicolaitans twice.

> 'But I have a few things against you, because you have there some who hold the teaching of Balaam, who kept teaching Balak to put a stumbling block before the sons of Israel, to eat things sacrificed to idols and to commit acts of immorality. 'So you also have some who in the same way hold the teaching of the

Nicolaitans. 'Therefore repent; or else I am coming to you quickly, and I will make war against them with the sword of My mouth. (Revelation 2:14-16 NASB95)

This is the only place in the Bible that uses this word. We do not know for certain what Nicolaitan means. Strong's Lexicon gives it the number G3531 and tells us that *nikolaites* are followers of Nicolaus. *Nico* we know is Greek for conquer and *laites* is Greek for laity or lay people (as opposed to priests). But we also know it has something to do with the methods of Balaam[60] and a hierarchy. A hierarchy has two groups – one of rulers and one of "lay" people. Balaam (and a case could be made for Jezebel too) introduced immorality and idolatry into Israel by methods that looked good, such as enticement with beautiful (pagan) women, but drew men away from God. So Nicolaitan is probably a name for leaders who maintain a division between a ruling class and the average believer, but at the same time allows behavior that leads away from God using sexual immorality as a tool. Balaam (and Jezebel) made disobedience look good. The ruling part of the Nicolaitan structure (the "conquer lay people" part) gives support to wrong, unbiblical teachings (from Jezebel and Balaam) and keeps them going by turning them into traditions.

Jesus tells us that wolves dressed in sheep's clothing will come to us (Matthew 7:15). We are to recognize them by their fruits and be wise as serpents and gentle as doves (Matthew 10:16) in dealing with them. The Nicolaitans I think can certainly be classed as wolves with sheep's clothing. In modern times we can identify them by their fruit in ruling over the average believer and engaging in or allowing sexual immorality.

> When anguish comes, they will seek peace, but there shall be none. Disaster comes upon disaster; rumor follows rumor. They seek a vision from the prophet, while the law perishes from the priest and counsel from the elders. (Ezekiel 7:25–26, ESV)

The Nicolaitans of yesterday are church leaders of today; wolves in Pharisee clothing. The fruit can be seen in tolerating sexual immorality such as adultery, divorce, and homosexuality (from Balaam and Jezebel) while denying the Law of Christ (Galatians 6:2) and the Law of the Spirit of Life (Romans 8:2). And yes, I just made the connection that the Law of Christ and the Law of the Spirit of Life are the same as the Law of God (or Moses). If the Law is spiritual (Romans 7:14) and was given by Jesus and God (both), then what Paul is calling the Law of the Spirit of Life (or the Law of Christ) are one and the same also.

---

[60] Balaam gets about three chapters in Numbers (22-24) and was noted as killed in Joshua 13:22. Revelation 2:14 summarizes his sin as teaching Israel to depart from God through immorality.

The followers of Nicolaus have a new name. We now call them a bureaucracy. Literally this means "rule by desk." Sometimes we can call it a "machine," or for you former hippies out there "the establishment" or a "corporation." Most churches or synagogues today are run by bureaucracy. In all my experience with churches, from Assemblies of God to Wesleyan, Baptist to Calvary Chapels or Evangelical Free to Vineyard and Messianic, every single one of them are "ruled by desk."

Not all leaders are Nicolaitans, and not all bureaucracies are all bad. There are many leaders throughout history, Jewish and Christian, even working within a bureaucracy, who have genuinely pursued God with all their heart (what we might call a "remnant"). To tell the difference we have to look at the fruit. It doesn't take much to introduce or allow sexual immorality. The first step away from God's Word will begin the process. As soon as it is decided that His Word is "old" or "Jewish" or "shadows" and doesn't apply anymore, that's the first fruit proving a wolf.

Wolves wear sheep's clothing because if they came in looking like a wolf it would be too scary and the sheep would run. They don't immediately teach obvious wrong things because they would be identified too quickly. They sneak up on believers, camouflaging their teachings with parts of the Word like the deceiver did with Jesus in the desert temptations. They have to mix their lies with some truth in order to tempt the sheep to follow. But their fruit is obvious. Sexual immorality can start with something as simple as forbidding marriage (1 Timothy 4:3). Adding and subtracting things God never commanded to His Word is a good way to obscure the path and get sheep going in the wrong direction.

Machines or corporations resist change because they take on a life of their own (if you can call it life). They get this way because the number one rule for all of them (church or not) is "survival of the bureaucracy." Nicolaitan machines rule the laity with tradition and the tree of knowledge and are concerned first with continuing the bureaucracy rather than God's Law.

Why am I talking about this? Because Jesus collided with such a machine, a hardened system run by Pharisees, Sadducees, priests and scribes (Matthew 23). This machine bears a striking resemblance to the church machine today. Jesus warned us of the problems involved, and His whole ministry might be characterized in part as a rebellion against them. In modern times we are still fighting the same machine with a different name.

The machines/bureaucracies/corporations have set themselves up as the "orthodox" and tell everyone that if we don't believe like they command then we are lost. Trying to follow the Bible by itself as whole Bible Christians do threatens their power structure and they name us their enemies. Just like they did with Elijah (1 Kings 19:1-2). Just like they did with the prophets and apostles. Just like they did with Jesus, and Stephen, Peter and Paul. Part of our whole Bible walk is to examine their fruit, reject it if it is bad, and continue to follow Him even if we are rejected by the "orthodox."

Jesus wasn't fond of machines. In fact every disagreement He had with the Nicolaitans in His day was over their wrong tradition and teachings. Nine times tradition is specifically mentioned in Matthew and Mark. The Jewish machine (represented by the leaders who crucified Him) had hardened over the previous centuries and would not listen to what Jesus had to say. They judged Him by their doctrine rather than the Word. They had "resisted the Holy Spirit" for such a long time that resisting Him became a habit. Jesus' fight with the machine was continued by the apostles. The Nicolaitans of the Jewish machine weren't content with crucifying Jesus. They had to stone Stephen, jail believers, and follow Paul around trying to cause trouble for him on a regular basis (flogging him 5 times and even getting him stoned to death).

You will run into this machine too when you try to follow the whole of the Word. It's not just a Jewish thing. Nicolaitans will tell you that you can't follow the Law and instead you have to follow their interpretations of the Word if you want to stay in the church. They will tell you that God's Law is many negative things rather than a beautiful lifestyle. Bureaucracies or machines are not what God intended for His Body. With God it's always His Word that rules.

> "You stiff-necked people, uncircumcised in heart and ears, you always resist the Holy Spirit. As your fathers did, so do you. Which of the prophets did your fathers not persecute? And they killed those who announced beforehand the coming of the Righteous One, whom you have now betrayed and murdered, you who received the law as delivered by angels and did not keep it." (Acts 7:51–53, ESV)

Modern machines or Nicolaitans claim they are not like the Pharisees, yet the fruit is identical. They all "receive the law as delivered by angels" but "do not keep it." Their "fathers" are those who did the same thing (the Pharisees). "Stiff necked people uncircumcised in heart and ears" always resist the Holy Spirit, even to persecuting and killing those who minister according to God's Spirit. They "shut the kingdom of heaven in people's faces" (Matthew 23:13); blocking the entrance while refusing to go in themselves. All the while they build tombs for prophets and decorate the monuments of the righteous, claiming that if they had lived in the days of their fathers they would not have shed the blood of the prophets (Matthew 23:29-36).

The letters to the seven congregations in Revelation 2 and 3 seem to be speaking of what we would call a machine today. Jesus just calls it by different names, such as the Nicolaitans or "the synagogue of Satan" in Revelation 2:9 and 3:9. Jesus tells John to speak to the congregations as a group, and I think what He says applies to any congregation whenever the same fruit is present. There were some individuals at the time who were "hold[ing] fast to what you have" (2:25, 3:3) and "who have not soiled their garments" (3:4). Others were "learning the deep things of Satan" (2:24) "tolerat[ing] that woman Jezebel" (2:20) or holding to the teachings of Balaam (2:14) and the Nicolaitans (2:6, 15). This is behavior that we see today all the time. Hey, it's not me saying this stuff. Everyone wants to be the congregation of Philadelphia. No one wants to be the synagogue or church of Satan. No one (least of all the wolves) wants to be identified as a Nicolaitan. But healthy trees produce good fruit. Bad trees produce bad fruit. If bad fruit is present, it speaks for itself. I'm just shining the light of the Word on what is happening.

As the centuries have progressed, the congregations have continued to split as described in Revelation and the book of Acts and divide and split again, mostly due to wolves that behave like Jezebel, Balaam, Nicolaus, or the church of Satan as they mingle with the flock. Some splits are from sheep running from the wolves. Some are from wolves leading sheep away. Every modern day church calling itself Christian (or some form of it) was formed by splits from other congregations. Some of these splits had good intentions trying to correct errors (as in the Reformation). Many were just splits for the sake of splitting, or control and power. Some came from a personal inability to get along. A handful came from revivals such as Pentecost. Some flocks split from the wolves only to find wolves sneaking in later.

So splitting is not necessarily bad. It is the reason for the split that has to be examined. If the split is for power, such as the split between Ephraim and Judah, that's bad. If it is over the Word, such as the many splits caused by Paul or the splits we see between "orthodox" church people and whole Bible believers, then it is good. In 1 Corinthians 1:10 Paul says "there should be no divisions" and in 1 Corinthians 11:19 he says there must be factions so that "those who are approved may become evident among you." Splits are not to be desired perhaps and painful when they happen, but generally good and needful if sheep are trying to follow their Shepherd's voice. Jesus did not come to bring peace, but a sword (Matthew 10:34). So if you are accused of being a "divisive person" (and you will be) because you are sticking to the Word, you are probably in the faction of "those who are approved" by God.

> ⁴Those who forsake the law praise the wicked, But those who keep the law strive with them. (Proverbs 28:4 NASB95)

Some people who have split think of themselves as "new wine" which can't fit into the "old wineskin" (Matthew 9:14 -17; Mark 2:22; Luke 5:37). So they think they have to make a new wineskin (organization). But a split by itself doesn't mean it's a good split. The fruit will let us know one way or the other. A wolf leads away from the Word, plain and simple. Just because he says something about "new wine" that isn't enough. Some groups might have started out as an attempt at a new wineskin, but over time they too get old. The wine spoils as the group drifts away from the Word and wooly looking wolves slink in. Say that last part ten times fast.

We are reaping fruit now from the pragmatic drifting in the 1800's inherited from Constantine which accelerated in the '60's and '70's.[61] Knowledge and practice of the whole of the Word has decreased, while splitting has increased. Do you suppose there's a connection? I think so. As Jesus says, a little leaven leavens the whole lump. Many church groups have rejected absolute truth and are polarized into fundamental and liberal camps. That doesn't mean one is correct and one isn't. Both could be built on sandy foundations. Why? **Look at the fruit**. The split by itself isn't important. It's the reason for the split (or the results of the split) that is critical. Those of us who are whole Bible Christians haven't split from the church; the church is splitting from the Word. The sheep will always follow the voice of the Shepherd (John 10:27).

In addition to the country club analogy another comparison that occurred to me a few years ago is that many churches have become like fast food franchises. They only serve certain food a certain way, they replicate only after themselves, and they have a rigid, top-down management structure. If you get tired of the same old food at one franchise, you have to go to another. A burger place doesn't serve pizza, and a taco stand doesn't serve burgers. If you want to change something, you can't. It doesn't matter how many complaint cards you fill out. The number of outlets is the most important thing to a franchise. The real concern for a franchise is making money (even if it's to "reach the lost). Yep, the more I think about it the more the current crop of churches looks a whole lot like a bunch of fast food stands.

---

[61] See for instance "A Patriot's History of the United States," Larry Schweikart and Michael Allen, published by Sentinel, a member of the Penguin Group, 2004. Especially pages 731 through 736 titled 'Sex, the Church, and the Collapse of Marriage.'

It's a safe bet that Nicolaitans included the unbelieving Jewish leaders at the time. It might have included Gentiles too by the time John wrote it. Either way we need to remember that there are only two types of people – believers and unbelievers. Even in leadership positions. Jesus routinely called the Jewish leaders hypocrites (see for instance Matthew 23). The word hypocrite is defined variously as men of falsehood (Psalm 26:4 ESV), ungodly, vain persons, deceitful men, profane, dissemblers (Psalm 26:4 AV) and pretenders. They were called hypocrites because they taught the law as if it was delivered by angels but personally did not follow it (Acts 7:53). Hypocrites make disobedience look good. Modern hypocrites in the church machines use the same tried and true methods handed down for thousands of years. Like Balaam, Jezebel or Constantine they make pragmatic disobedience look good. People are destroyed for lack of knowledge; knowledge of God that is replaced by "spiritual but not religious" teachings.

Bureaucracies or hierarchies certainly destroy people as the Nicolaitan name implies. The rigid, top down franchise management structure resists change by squashing almost every form of independent thought. Whatever doesn't conform to the Nicolaitan way is rejected like tacos at a burger stand. Graduates of colleges or seminaries get diplomas and doctorates and stay in line because they agree with the people who hand them out. Rather than teaching "how to think" based on reading and doing the Word, they teach "what to think." It has to be this way for Nicolaitans to survive.

> "Of all tyrannies a tyranny sincerely exercised for the good of its victims may be the most oppressive." C. S. Lewis

I have collided with many bureaucracies myself. It's bound to happen when a Bible reader asks questions, earnestly seeking God. Many theological systems and creeds are not biblical, or are part Bible, and biblical questions (like those in the first chapter) ruffle a lot of feathers. I wondered a lot whether the professed love of Christ was really present after I was told, sometimes politely, sometimes directly, to hit the road. There are quite a few loving people in the machines. But taken together the churches tend more toward self-preservation than preaching and practicing the Word.

Nicolaitans grab power and hold onto it at the expense of individuals. Often this is by preaching a message of unity. By unity, however, they mean the unity of the machine, not the Word of God. You have to think like they do. "That's not the way we do things here" (we make pizza not burgers) is the rallying cry of bureaucracies everywhere. This is why I think many of the gifts of the Spirit such as prophecy (either the "forth telling" or "foretelling" kind) are not to be found in the church very much anymore.

If people knew how to think for themselves while studying the Bible, they wouldn't need the bureaucrat. Then the paycheck for the priest, pastor, reverend and rabbi disappears (and maybe even the bureaucracy would disappear). The type of unity where dissenting thinking is eliminated is why pastors boast of everybody being of one mind in a congregation. It's because everybody either agrees with him or gets booted out (or chilled out or ignored).

So why does God allow the Nicolaitans to keep going? Well, it seems for the same reasons He doesn't just roll up the whole creation and start over. In His kindness He is waiting for people to repent and come to Him. Paul also says that *"whether pretense or in truth, Christ is proclaimed, and in that I rejoice"* (Philippians 1:15-18). So the word about Jesus is being spread, however watered down or masked. And Matthew quotes Jesus telling us to leave the weeds, sown by the enemy. He'll take care of them later (Matthew 13:24-30). However, that doesn't mean we have to eat the chaff they pass off as wheat. Nor does it mean we have to put up with wolves no matter how nicely they are dressed.

I hope I'm getting across to you the principle of Nicolaitans putting themselves in charge then blocking access to God's Word (Matthew 23:13). Believers are frequently placed in a position of trying to believe the Bible, yet being told by Nicolaitans that parts of it don't apply or are not true. These "leaders," from priests (even Levitical ones) to rabbis to Pharisees and Sadducees to pastors to scribes and Bible translators have been leading away from the Word for centuries. They all "sit themselves in Moses' seat" (Matthew 23:2) but we are not to do what they do. It is extremely important to state that we need to fixate on God's Words and avoid the path that the Nicolaitans show us. Nicolaitans are like tollbooths on a bridge to nowhere.

Jesus did not come to establish a bureaucracy or a hierarchy. Just because you don't belong to a machine doesn't mean you don't belong to God. Following God is an individual effort. We each answer for our own words and actions (Romans 14:10). We won't be able to blame a leader for leading astray, though they will have to answer for their actions. The Temple veil torn in two (Matthew 27:51; Mark 15:38; Luke 23:45) means Jesus restored direct access to God for everyone who wants it. A balanced meal is available directly from Him. We don't have to be satisfied with Nicolaitan burgers (or just tacos, or just pizza) only. The buffet in His Word is waiting and free for anyone who wants life and that more abundantly.

Tradition

The word "tradition" means something "handed down." It can be simple, such as baptism, or more complex such as the Christmas holiday. God's Law is "handed down," and in a way, almost any teaching we get handed down to us is a tradition. Tradition is accumulated knowledge or practical experience that works to hold society together.

Tradition by itself isn't bad, but bad traditions are bad. Bad traditions are those that interfere with following what God says, specifically because they accumulate wisdom from men. The Talmud (Jewish oral law) is an excellent example of the accumulated wisdom from man cluttering up the Bible message. The Talmud wasn't written down at the time of Jesus, but it was definitely in effect. Jesus and the apostles spent a lot of time fighting the traditions of men such as those that get in the way of The Way (the Bible).

We have many, many such traditions dear to the hearts of millions now. Christmas and Easter, for instance, are not in the Bible and have many pagan practices associated with them. The church has hijacked pagan holidays by mixing in some Bible stories, but mixing like this is never approved by God. Now the pagans want Christmas and Easter back, and I say let 'em have 'em.

One of the main tools used by the Nicolaitan machine to enforce their will is tradition. In their hands, tradition is a powerful weapon. It plays on our sentiments and conditions us to think a certain way. It's also full of practices that we want to do while ignoring the stuff that God wants us to do. It's street level theology run amuck. Tradition makes it easy to lead people in a way of the leader's own choosing. Many appeals to "orthodoxy" are actually appeals to tradition. One family I know instructed my son to return to "mainstream Protestant doctrine." They weren't happy with his desire to avoid paganism (like a Christmas tree) in his home. In their minds rejecting Christmas is the same as rejecting Jesus, which is not even close to the truth. My son wants to stay biblically true, but those people appealed to tradition rather than the Bible.

I remember a Catholic co-worker in the late '70's complaining of the switch in the Mass from Latin to English. I asked him if he spoke Latin and he said no. So I asked why the switch bothered him. The only thing he could come up with was that it was tradition. He couldn't understand what was said in Latin, but switching to English was wrong somehow. People have very powerful feelings about their traditions, and it makes us resist change.

Abby Johnson is a Christian lady who used to manage a Planned Parenthood clinic. She repented after she was asked to assist in an abortion, and now has an organization helping people to escape. Apparently the "abortion tradition" is very hard to quit. How could a Christian keep working there, you might ask? One of the reasons is that she regularly attended an Episcopalian church which had a "tradition" of defending abortion rights. Her parents disapproved, but I'm sure the church's "tolerance" and "unconditional love" made it easier to keep going in the baby murder industry.

Catholic theologians laugh privately at the Protestants, because though they "protest" the Catholics, they're still following many Catholic traditions. It is the Catholic Church that bought Christmas and Easter from Constantine and sustains those and other such traditions. They changed (or tried to change) the Sabbath from the biblically correct day of Saturday to Sunday. Protestants still follow these extra-biblical decrees, as well as many others, in lockstep.

Catholics also set up their priestly hierarchy (copied from Judaism). The Protestants in turn copy it with their own version of pastors and lay people. Protestants may not have a single pope, but all they did was trade one pope for many. Nicolaitan popes (or pastors or rabbis) are one reason why you'll get so much resistance as soon as you start asking about extra- or non-biblical rules or traditions.

Unguided sentiment, which goes hand in glove with tradition a lot, will get us off-track with God every time. When feelings become more important than His Word, they confuse us and get us lost. Unrestrained sentiment or hardened traditions have caused a lot of damage in history. We need the genuine tradition built on the rock of God's whole Word to guide us away from the sandy foundation traditions of men.

The Other Anointing

This brings us to the topic of anointing. Often, whenever a "lay" person such as myself questions the Nicolaitan rulers, the argument of "touch not mine anointed" is used as a defense (1 Chronicles 16:22). In other words, the religious bureaucrat thinks of himself as "anointed by God." He wants authority, and uses a supposed anointing to grab it and hang on to it. Therefore, according to them, if you question them you are questioning God (or His Word).[62] Kind of interesting, isn't it, in view of what Jesus said about another anointing? Remember the word "Christ" means "anointed."

---

[62] Mark Driscoll, for instance, in a video on 2/25/08 titled "Putting Preachers in Their Place" no longer available since his fall from grace said, "The Spirit of God anoints a preacher to open God's Word and preach God's Word." Really? Where's the reference? He assumed that the pulpit is needed for preaching, ignored the anointing of all believers, and implied that to question the preacher you are questioning God. He had no Scripture back-up for many of his positions.

> [24]"For false Christs and false prophets will arise and will show great signs and wonders, so as to mislead, if possible, even the elect. (Matthew 24:24 NASB95)

> [12] And what I do I will continue to do, in order to undermine the claim of those who would like to claim that in their boasted mission they work on the same terms as we do. [13] For such men are false apostles, deceitful workmen, disguising themselves as apostles of Christ. [14] And no wonder, for even Satan disguises himself as an angel of light. [15] So it is no surprise if his servants, also, disguise themselves as servants of righteousness. Their end will correspond to their deeds. (2 Corinthians 11:12-15 ESV)

Anointing, however, is proved by actions. Look what happened, for instance, with Saul and David. Both were anointed kings of Israel by God, yet Saul fell into pride and self-service. His actions were not consistent with his anointing and he had the kingdom torn out of his hands (1 Samuel 15:27-29). David, on the other hand, ended up being the most recognized and blessed of Israel's rulers next to Solomon. The reason was that he had a heart after God's own (1 Samuel 13:14) and acted *according to* his anointing.

In Matthew 16:13-20, Jesus asks the disciples if they know who He is. After Peter tells Jesus that "you are the Christ" Jesus responds with "on this rock I will build my church." This has been hotly debated for a long time. Some think Peter was the rock, and the first pope. Others think the confession of "Jesus is Christ" is the rock. Read carefully though. Just before this, Jesus warns the disciples to beware of the leaven of the Pharisees and Sadducees, right after that group had wrongly asked for a sign (so they could approve His authority). The issue was authority (or anointing). The leaders wanted to assert their authority by demanding to see a sign of Jesus' authority. The Jewish leader's grasped for authority, but it wasn't anchored with God's Word. The disciples were given authority consistent with the confession of Jesus as the Christ. By extension all believers have the same authority, if they teach in the same confession.

The disciples didn't have to worry about whether their authority (anointing) was recognized by the other Jewish leaders or not. This is very important to note. As long as they preached Christ as The Anointed and did what He said, their authority was on the rock. We are all like Peter in the sense of being a "rock" or stone if we confess Jesus is the Christ (and do what He says). And all of us living stones are being built into a spiritual house as the Rock says.

> [4] As you come to him, a living stone rejected by men but in the sight of God chosen and precious, [5] you yourselves like living stones are being built up as a spiritual house, to be a holy priesthood, to offer spiritual sacrifices acceptable to God through Jesus Christ. (1 Peter 2:4-5 ESV)

If a person says he is anointed, yet teaches or behaves in a way that contradicts the Word (not just mistakes) there is no way possible that he retains an anointing from God. Even if he had one to start with. We will, after all is said and done, know them by their fruits. And biblical fruit, proving anointing, has nothing to do with the number of followers or the size of the paycheck. It has to do with sticking with what God says.

Jesus never testified about Himself (except perhaps for quotes such as Luke 4:18) as many of the false teachers do, because His identity was obvious from His actions. He never used the "touch not" verse even though He really was The Anointed. A number of people sure did touch Him, some in a murderous fashion.

> [27] As for you, the anointing which you received from Him abides in you, and you have no need for anyone to teach you; but as His anointing teaches you about all things, and is true and is not a lie, and just as it has taught you, you abide in Him. (1 John 2:27 NASB95)

All believers are anointed. So if we follow the "touch not my anointed" dogma then no believer can be touched. Godly anointing is always, and I mean always, in line with His Word and the teachings in it. A truly God-anointed person does not flinch from godly, Bible-centered questions. He will always be glad to give an answer for the hope that is in him (1 Peter 3:15). He does not have to use the "touch not" verse because his life is "on the rock" in the first place.

The truly anointed will also not hesitate to spend time helping people understand the Word. Far too often the false anointed are quick to send a person away who asks too many questions. They prefer the wide-eyed, trusting and loyal proselyte (Matthew 23:15) over the Berean (Acts 17:10, 11). They don't teach the whole of the Word, they just teach their church's take on the Word. There may be an anointing on the bureaucrats, but more likely, it is a self-anointing by a spirit other than God's. We can see this in the fruit as Jesus teaches us (Matthew 7:15-23).

I have to spend time on this because a lot of these "anointed" guys will fight much of what I am relaying to you from the Bible in this book. The "educated" religious leaders of the time fought Jesus and Paul too.

But if leaders don't stick with scriptures, then all they've got is empty teachings lacking in nutrition.

Real authority comes from the Word. The anointing for many leaders comes from the self or from a club full of groupies, neither of which could be mistaken for the Holy Spirit. Maybe the (false) anointed was called into the ministry...by his mom. When the self-anointed chop the Word into little pieces and tell us to ignore some of them, authority goes right out the window. If teaching doesn't match the Word, don't follow. There is no reason to listen to such a person or be afraid of them.

It's a God Thing

Every once in a while, God decides to shake the bureaucracies, machines, systems and programs that man creates and remind us that He is the One who's in charge. He refreshes people with His Word. It's His Word, not ours, and it is living and active and sharper than any two-edged sword (Hebrews 4:12). He re-injects this Word in our machines through sermons on mounts, judges, prophets, apostles and events such as those in Acts chapter 2. He rescues believers, and provides ways around those who try to block access to Him.

We can see from history that after the Word refreshes, it doesn't take long for man to take over and pervert God's changes, innovations, and fresh starts. The systems of men hinder instead of help the work of the Spirit. Now He is repeating His message again, calling people to repent and return to the whole of His Word in thought and deed.

We do not need a bureaucracy to get to God. We don't need self-anointed leadership terrified of biblical questions that threaten the paycheck. God has taken great pains to make His Kingdom and His Word available to anyone who wants it. All we have to do is read and heed.

You may find yourself rejected by a bureaucracy. The church or synagogue may remind you more of a snooty country club than a family dedicated to God's Word. But don't think you are outside of the Body. The Body and the church are not the same by any stretch of the imagination. It is no surprise that truth seekers have trouble finding a place in the country clubs. Take comfort in the Word your Father provides, and hold onto it above all else.

The one Body goes back much further than just the first century; it goes all the way back to the Garden. It is as old as man's relationship with God. There is no split and no separation, except between believers and unbelievers. We need to return to God's roots, not the roots of Judaism, Hebrews, Christianity or the first century church. The one Body is built on the foundation of the whole of the Word which we eat and drink as if it was life itself. The gates of hell will not stand against it, and neither will the bureaucracies of men.

Believers are an anointed kingdom of kings and priests (Exodus 19:6; Revelation 1:6, 5:10) after the order of Melchizedek (Genesis 14:8; Hebrews 7). We take in the body and blood of His Word while offering sacrifices of lips and limbs, and share it with any who ask.

His kingdom is not a martial kingdom with bloodshed and forced rule (yet). It is a kingdom made up of obedient people born again by the Spirit. This kingdom, or body, is united by the common root of the Messiah Jesus according to the Scriptures. So we don't have to create unity (there is no Jew or Gentile) we just need to maintain it (Ephesians 4:3; Philippians 2:2). Our job is to take in His Word and apply it to ourselves, and then share it with those who want it. It isn't a Jewish thing or a Christian thing, it's a God thing.

4 A Whole Faith

⁴Then Jeremiah the prophet said to them, "I have heard you. Behold, I am going to pray to the LORD your God in accordance with your words; and I will tell you the whole message which the LORD will answer you. I will not keep back a word from you." (Jeremiah 42:4 NASB95)

P.S. – Before we start on this subject, I know I'm using the Bible to prove doctrines from the Bible. This is a logical problem for those who don't take the Bible as the accurate, error-free Word from God. But there's a literal mountain of evidence that proves the Bible is what it says it is. I can't cover all of it here. If you are in doubt, get some of the evidence and see for yourself. Or you could just open your eyes and look around. The Bible has never been disproved, ever. It has only been torn down, chopped up, and obscured with opinion. That fact in itself proves to most people, having a shred of real smarts, that there is something special about God's book.

A Continuous Message

We've seen biblically how Jesus has always been around, is the same as God, and has been directly involved with man since the beginning. We've seen that He has been building His one Body or Bride (remnant, olive tree, elect) for a long time. Now we need a shift in perspective concerning the unity, age, and relevance of the Word of God.

There have been discussions for a long time on the continuity or discontinuity of the Bible. Continuity means that the Bible is a continuous, unified message (one faith) directed to a single group of believers (one body). Whole Bible Christianity grows from the acceptance of the continuity of the Bible. Those who believe in discontinuity assert that there are different messages directed at different groups of people at different times, marked by imaginary dispensations or covenants, and the messages do not relate to each other except in a few very general ways.

I'm going to show you that His whole Word, including the Law, has been around since the beginning and its unified message applies to everyone. All of it was written to all believers throughout time. The translations we have now, the way they are worded, printed and formatted have not. But the principles of His Word, the ideas of right and wrong and the Promise to make things right again have been. The Bible is one faith. His Word comes from His holiness, perfection, and all around innate goodness, which has always been a part of His eternal being. He revealed these directly to man at the start, and continues that revelation through creation, the Son, the Spirit, and His written Word.

Dozens of writers over many centuries contributed to the Bible, but there is amazing unity, consistency and agreement between the writings. In contrast, nowadays we can't get three writers to agree even if they're the same age and gender, and write for the same newspaper at the same time. But the Bible message is clear, easy to understand, and in complete agreement. It does not contradict. We only think it does because of ideas we have before we start reading it.

Continuous through generations

One reason for the continuity and agreement in the Bible, especially the foundational part (before Joshua), is that the first generations were a lot closer to each other than many realize. People lived a lot longer, and as many as eight or ten generations were living at the same time. That's also one reason I think not as much was written right away (that we know of, anyway).

Image 1 is a table that shows dates of birth and death, After the Garden, to the Exodus. We don't know for sure if the dates are meant to be exact or not, but from it you can see that in the beginning lots of generations lived together. It was easy to hand down what God said. Seth and his father Adam were old men together. Noah's father, Lamech, was around at the same time all of his forefathers were. Noah and his sons knew Methuselah (Noah actually had the chance to know everyone from Enosh on down).

Noah ties 18 of the first 20 generations together (he knew Enosh through Abraham) and didn't die until about 53 years after Abraham was born. Noah's son Shem was born 100 years before the flood, outlived Abraham, and was around for at least four or five decades after Jacob was born. He was maybe present at the tower of Babel, and would have read about Sodom and Gomorrah in his morning newspaper. Abraham had ten forefathers living at the same time (Noah, Shem, Arpachshad, Shelah, Eber, Peleg, Reu, Serug, Nahor, and Terah). His cousins had long-lived relatives around too. Imagine having grandparents or parents around to tell you what it was like to walk with Adam or Methusaleh, ride Noah's Ark, or live through Babel.

> [11]The counsel of the Lord stands forever, The plans of His heart from generation to generation. (Psalm 33:11 NASB95)

Name	Born	Died	Age
Adam		930AG	930
Seth	130	1042	912
Enosh	235	1140	905
Kenan	325	1235	910
Mahalalel	395	1290	895
Jared	460	1422	962
Enoch	622	987	365
Methusaleh	687	1656	969
Lamech	874	1651	777
Noah	1056	2006	950
FLOOD		1656	
Shem	1556	2158	602
Arpachshad	1658	2096	438
Shelah	1693	2196	433
@ Babel – Nimrod[1]			
Eber	1728	2192	464
Peleg	1762	2001	239
Reu	1792	2031	239
Serug	1824	2054	230
Nahor	1854	2002	148
Terah	1883	2088	205
Abraham[2]	1953	2128	175
Destruction of Sodom and Gomorrah @ 2053[3]			
Isaac	2053	2233	180
Jacob	2113	2260	147
EGYPT	2243		2673
Moses	2593	2713	120
EXODUS		2673	

Image 1

[1] This is an approximation based on Nimrod being second from Ham as Shelah is second from Shem.
[2] Genesis 11:26 Terah begat Abram, Nahor, and Haran, perhaps not all at once or from the same wife.
[3] Based on a comparison of Genesis 17:24, 19:28, and 21:5.

This pattern continues with the New Testament. As long as there were eye-witnesses to the events and people surrounding the advent of the Messiah, there was no need for written records. You could just walk down to the corner synagogue and find out the latest news or get accurate teaching straight from the source. But within a few decades, as disciples were executed or died of old age, there was more of a need for letters and histories and such. So God made sure that important things were written down for succeeding generations.

People know God's charge, commandments, statutes or laws very well. Their consciences inform them even if they don't have the written Word (Romans 2:12-15). The expulsion from the Garden, and the curses, were the penalty for *ignoring* what God said, not for ignorance of it. The flood was also unleashed as a penalty for *ignoring* what God said, not for ignorance. For 1,656 years until the flood, people knew what God required, either by relay from the first parents or directly from God. They were without excuse, just like we are.

> [18]For the wrath of God is revealed from heaven against all ungodliness and unrighteousness of men who suppress the truth in unrighteousness, [19]because that which is known about God is evident within them; for God made it evident to them. [20]For since the creation of the world His invisible attributes, His eternal power and divine nature, have been clearly seen, being understood through what has been made, so that they are without excuse. (Romans 1:18-20 NASB95)

There are inadvertent sins, but sin at its core is willful defiance of God's Word. Adam and Eve did not just blindly fall into sin or trip over some tiny little regulation they didn't know about. They knew full well exactly what God required (which wasn't much) and they refused to give it to Him. They chose their own way over God's. History in a nutshell.

Adam and Eve, and of course many others, were married as they should've been. Cain and Able knew the right way to sacrifice, but Cain refused. Cain was guilty of manslaughter. Enoch behaved himself so well that he went straight to Heaven, bypassing death. Noah took clean animals on the Ark and had a God-pleasing barbecue after the flood.

As life spans got shorter, there was less contact between generations. By the time of Arpachshad (twelfth from Adam) life spans were cut in half. Only two more generations and they were halved again. It seems that it was partly for this reason that the Law was written down and Israel was set up as a light to the nations. People now do not know great-great-great-grandpa as people did around the time of the flood. So the written Word helps to bridge generations and maintains God's influence. Even if we can't speak directly with our nine-time (or many more) removed grandpa there's still no excuse for not knowing God's will.

The first Sermon on the Mount – Sinai that is – was not kicking off a new age as the discontinuity people teach. It was the same message given since the beginning. The main difference was that God's universal, simple, and easy to understand Word was written on a couple of stone tablets and in the Pentateuch. Also, for the first time His Word was adopted as the "constitution" of a nation in contrast, for instance, to Babylon which wouldn't give two figs for God's Word. Jesus, incarnated about 4,000 years after the Garden, also points us to God's Law. Still a constitution, and still for His kingdom. Jesus likewise didn't kick off some new project, but continued God's. His message was right in line with all the Words spoken by God to then.

> [1]God, after He spoke long ago to the fathers in the prophets in many portions and in many ways, [2]in these last days has spoken to us in His Son, whom He appointed heir of all things, through whom also He made the world. (Hebrews 1:1-2 NASB95)

If we are thinking biblically, this is obvious. Jesus was right there giving the Law at Sinai. It's the same Law He lived and taught when He walked among us as a man. It hasn't changed, yet. Century upon century, for 6,000 years, the message from God is plain and consistent – "Do what I say and live. Ignore it and die." The problem is not with the Word. The problem is with people.

Law before Law

I disagree with Spurgeon (yes, it's okay to disagree with spiritual giants; just make sure you're biblical) who said that "There was sin in the world long before God sent the Law."[63] His idea of Law is too narrow. He's right that sin was around for a long time before Sinai, but the Law was around long before the Garden. It is eternal. Sin is lawlessness, and Adam and Eve broke the Law (God's Word) bringing with it sin and death. To illustrate the continuity of God's Word or Law, I've put together a list of Law before Law (at Sinai). It's of some of the many places in the Bible that directly state people were following (or violating) God given Laws before the first Sermon on the Mount.

- Genesis 2:2-3 – Sabbath.
- Genesis 2:17 – Choose life not knowledge Deut. 30:19.
- Genesis 2:23-25 – One man, one woman for marriage.
- Genesis 3 – Redemption, blood sacrifice, and atonement.
- Genesis 4:3-7 – Offering first born of flock and fat Deut. 12:6, 15:19
- Genesis 4:4 – acceptable and unacceptable sacrifices.
- Genesis 4:10 – manslaughter penalties; avenger of blood; see Num. 35.
- Genesis 6:5, 11-13, 17 – Flood destroys innocent people?
- Genesis 7:2, 8 – clean and unclean animals on the ark.
- Genesis 8 – Noah's burnt offerings, uses clean animals.
- Genesis 9:4 – Don't eat blood Lev. 3:17, 7:26; Acts 15:20.
- Genesis 9:6 – Don't murder; equal justice; compare to Numbers 35:33.
- Genesis 9:20-27 – Uncovering father's nakedness Lev. 18:7, 20:11.

---

[63] 'Law and Grace,' Sermon 37, delivered on August 26 1855 by the Reverend C.H. Spurgeon among other places.

- Genesis 14:20, 28:22 – Tithing or giving.
- Genesis 17:13-14 – Circumcision given as sign of covenant made in chapter 15.
- Genesis 19:4-7 – Sodom and Gomorrah destroyed for homosexual sins.
- Genesis 20:3 – Adultery wrong.
- Genesis 22 – No sacrificing children.
- Genesis 22:13 – Abraham makes a burnt offering.
- Genesis 24:3, 28:1 – Don't marry Canaanites Deut. 7:3.
- Genesis 26:4, 5 – Abraham obeys God's charges, commandments, statutes, laws.
- Genesis 27; 29:26 – Firstborn inherits Deut. 21:15-17; Gen. 48:18.
- Genesis 30 – wrong to cheat a worker of his wages Lev. 19:13.
- Genesis 31:35 – Rachel prevents finding idols while in the "manner of women." Compare to Lev. 15.
- Genesis 31:54 – Jacob sacrifices.
- Genesis 35:2 – Jacob has the family put away gods, purify themselves and change garments. Compare to Exodus 19:10, 14; Lev. 14:9, 15:3; Numbers 8:7; John 13:12; Heb. 10:22.
- Genesis 35:14 – Jacob and drink offering with an altar and oil.
- Genesis 35:22 – Reuben wrong sex with Jacob's wife (see Genesis 49:3, 4)
- Genesis 38:6-26 – Er & Onan and an heir for a brother Deut. 25:5.
- Genesis 46:1 – Jacob sacrifices again.
- Exodus 4:26 – Circumcision again.
- Exodus 11 – Passover.
- Exodus 12 – additional mentions of circumcision.
- Exodus 13:2 – The firstborn belong to Adonai, compare to Exodus 22:29, 27:26; Numbers 3:12, 13, 16-18.
- Exodus 13:16 – "It shall be for you a token upon thy hand…"
- Exodus 16:4 – Manna, "that I may prove them, whether they walk in my law or no."
- Exodus 16:26-28 - "How long will you refuse to keep my commandments & laws?"
- Exodus 18:16 – Moses uses and teaches God's laws before Sinai.

I count over 40 occurrences of Law that were in place before the Law was given at Sinai. Most of these were codified at the first Sermon on the Mount, so obviously the Law did not just blink into existence after Israel left Egypt. This makes sense if we think about it. His Word is eternal, and what is holy is always holy. What is not holy is always not holy.

Think about this too: why, if there was no law, were the people before the flood condemned to die? And why were the people of Sodom and Gomorrah wiped out, since they also lived before the time of the

Exodus? Why does everyone die, even if they never heard of the Law? Paul says in two places that if there is no law, then there is no violation.

> ¹⁵for the Law brings about wrath, but where there is no law, there also is no violation. (Romans 4:15 NASB95)

> ¹³for until the Law sin was in the world, but sin is not imputed when there is no law. (Romans 5:13 NASB95)

There were violations, obviously, deserving of death, before Sinai, so there was Law. Wrong and right were known before the flood and in the cities of Sodom or Gomorrah. People's every thought were (and are) "only evil continually" (Genesis 6:5) "the men of Sodom were wicked, great sinners against the Lord," and "their sin [was] very grave (Genesis 13:13, 18:20). Departure from God, no matter how slight, always results in death. God is life, so going away from Him (even a little bit) is going away from life.

Everyone knows the will of God. God's law has always been around, because His Word is eternal. It permeates and upholds all of creation. Everyone was (and is) accountable because everyone knew it (knows it). This explains the flood and the destruction of city states. Murder and homosexuality are never right; God joins male and female together in marriage; He has always hated divorce; and the Sabbath was instituted before the fall. Anything different is a perversion of God's Word, His stated purpose and order. Partly we die because of Adam's sin, but partly we die because of sins acted out from our nature. Enoch (Genesis 5:24) and Elijah are exceptions, but I think they too will die.[64]

Hosea tells us that Adam disobeyed the same covenant as Israel (or vice versa).

> ⁶ For I desire steadfast love and not sacrifice, the knowledge of God rather than burnt offerings. ⁷ But like Adam they transgressed the covenant; there they dealt faithlessly with me. (Hosea 6:6-7 ESV)

The word "covenant" has a broader meaning than a specific agreement such as the one at Sinai. There is a built in covenant between God and any created being that assumes a continued reliance on the Creator. He gives life and we continue in that life by abiding in His Word. The normal condition is to be in God's Word. Perversity is to be outside of it. A person is created by the Word of God and it is implied

---

[64] I think Enoch and Elijah will be the 'two witnesses' mentioned in Revelation 11, and then they will finally experience death. Some might appear to bypass death in the rapture, but that could be considered like death. No one can enter the kingdom with this physical body. See Hebrews 9:27 and 1 Corinthians 15, especially verse 36.

that we will stay in that Word because it is life. When we get right down to it there is no sense in departing from the Author of Life. Israel and Adam dealt faithlessly with that Word. Neither was showing steadfast love because neither obeyed the living oracles. That is why Hosea says that they are the same covenant – a covenant of life.

In my opinion the "knowledge of God" mentioned by Hosea is a direct poke at the choice of Adam, because he chose the tree of knowledge of good and evil over the tree of life (God's Word). It seems obvious that God's Word, whether we want to call it a covenant, or promise, or Ten Suggestions, has always been around. Whatever Word He gives us, from "don't eat that fruit" to "love others as yourself" and everything in between, is part of "the covenant," because it is all His Word. And all of His Word is binding on His creation all the time, no matter what. To ignore His Word is to be faithless.

When the Law was delivered at Mount Sinai, contrary to standard church teaching, existing Law was written down. It was a condition of His residing with Israel. There were some additions and clarifications, probably due to changing physical circumstance. But by and large, it was the same Law that has always been around.[65] In the midst of the flood of evil threatening to engulf the world, God placed His Ark of the Covenant with the "living oracles" in Israel. Then He set up shop in Israel Himself, as a beacon of life for all men.

The reason Israel is treated a little different is that Israel agreed to live by God's Laws. They are like a bride (or priest) who was (and is) supposed to run God's household by His ways, and bear children of righteousness throughout the world. All the other nations of the world, though they are always subject to His Word, had (and have) not agreed to make it the center of their government as Israel did.

We've got to get out of the unbiblical habit of thinking the Word is chopped up by different ages or different programs. Or that it only applies to certain people groups at certain times and only under certain conditions. The Word is universal and unending, applies to everyone everywhere at anytime, and will be the center of His kingdom again.

His Spirit is still living among men, and still directing people to His Law. In the future, Jesus will come as a conquering King of kings (let it be soon, oh Lord). When He does, He will set up His kingdom (household). There righteousness will flourish and Law will go forth again.

---

[65] For instance, before Sinai we could marry sisters and other close relatives. I'm guessing that the collapse of the water canopy (2 Peter 3:5-6) during the flood maybe caused some genetic problems. Or there might've been other reasons God put a stop to it. The web site www.drdino.com has science videos with information on the flood.

> [1] The word which Isaiah the son of Amoz saw concerning Judah and Jerusalem. [2] Now it will come about that In the last days The mountain of the house of the Lord Will be established as the chief of the mountains, And will be raised above the hills; And all the nations will stream to it. [3] And many peoples will come and say, "Come, let us go up to the mountain of the Lord, To the house of the God of Jacob; That He may teach us concerning His ways And that we may walk in His paths." For the law will go forth from Zion And the word of the Lord from Jerusalem. [4] And He will judge between the nations, And will render decisions for many peoples; And they will hammer their swords into plowshares and their spears into pruning hooks. Nation will not lift up sword against nation, And never again will they learn war. (Isaiah 2:1-4 NASB95)

You should be starting to get the picture that God's Word is a whole, continuous message. People change, circumstances change, but God's Word doesn't.

God's list of commands is a test of the perverse will of man. Our will often runs counter to God's. He brings out what only seems to be a new instruction after we think of new ways to depart from His will. The Father constantly brings out of the treasure of His Law "things new and old" (Matthew 13:52). He's like a parent who gives endless instruction and correction to an unknowing or deliberately straying child. Anyone who has tried to corral a two year-old (or any child really) knows what this is like. "Stop throwing toys." "Don't eat that!" "Get down from there this instant!"

The Promise

Another theme helping the unity and consistency of the Bible, and which goes right along with the Law, is the Promise.

> [15] And I will put enmity Between you and the woman, And between your seed and her seed; He shall bruise you on the head, And you shall bruise him on the heel." (Genesis 3:15 NASB95)

Adam and Eve got expelled from God's presence, but He said it wouldn't last forever. God made a promise not to leave us hanging, cut off from Him. This promise was that the seed of the woman was going to come and destroy the Satan's authority and kingdom. God was saying that His kingdom will ultimately triumph through the birth of a man who would also be God. Everything in the Word relates to this promise in some way. Every event, every covenant, every law, every blessing, every genealogy, every king and every war has, as its backdrop, the promise.

Another word for promise is "covenant." A covenant between people is a legal agreement where each one "promises" to behave in a certain way or face a penalty. But when God is part of a covenant there is no one to force His obedience. So His part of a covenant is the same as a promise. God always holds up His end, no matter what we do. If I don't follow through on my promise, God still follows through on His. His promises (or covenants) never fail (1 Kings 8:56).

God gives a promise to Noah (and to us, Genesis 6:18, 9:9, 9:25-27) but calls it a covenant. It's one-sided, so we can easily see it's both a covenant and a promise. The covenant of Genesis 3:15 is still in effect. Noah's covenant fits right in with it, and is part of what is called progressive revelation. God is going to reveal over time exactly how He will deliver the Promise.

The promise shows up again with Abraham (Genesis 12:1-3). It is just given more detail, and fulfillment is connected with a specific person now. God says He will bless Abraham; that Abraham would also be a blessing, and "in you all the families of the earth will be blessed." The word "bless" or "blessing" is intimately connected with the presence (and promise) of God. To be blessed is to have God, the source of all blessings. It is impossible to be blessed without God. One cannot bless something God curses, and cannot curse something God blesses.[66]

So when God tells Abraham that through him all the nations of the earth would be blessed, it is an extension of the Promise. It means that God will literally be given to the nations. God tells Abraham that the seed of the woman, spoken of before, will come from his loins.

After Abraham, God chose Isaac, then Jacob (Genesis 13, 15, 17, 22, 24, 26, and 28) to inherit the promise of the Messiah's birth. Dr. Walter Kaiser Jr. calls it "the accumulating divine blessings."[67] Isaac was chosen to show God's promise isn't going to be sidetracked, and that it is not the children of the flesh who are children of God.[68] Jacob was chosen to show that it is God's choosing that counts, not who is born first (among other reasons). When Israel was delivered from Egypt, it was because of this promise of God.

> [24]So God heard their groaning; and God remembered His covenant with Abraham, Isaac, and Jacob. (Exodus 2:24 NASB95)

---

[66] Balaam tried to curse Israel, for instance, but God wouldn't allow it. See Numbers 21 and 22.
[67] The Promise Plan of God: A Biblical Theology of the Old and New Testaments, Zondervan, 2008, page 52.
[68] See Romans 9 and Galatians 4 for a discussion of this.

> [25]"When you enter the land which the Lord will give you, as He has promised, you shall observe this rite. (Exodus 12:25 NASB95, italics added. See also Exodus 6:8).

The giving of the Law at Mt. Sinai was more of the promise (Exodus 19:5). It was "God with us." He established His Word in writing and set up His tent in the desert to advance His eternal kingdom. Way after Sinai, David was given even more detail about the promise (2 Samuel 7:11-16). He was told by God that his son, who we now know is Jesus (the seed of the woman again) would be God's agent for taking God's Kingdom into eternity.

David summarizes the promise in a psalm of thanksgiving, after he brought the Ark back to Jerusalem and set it up in a tent.

> [14]He is the LORD our God; His judgments are in all the earth.
> [15]Remember His covenant forever, The word which He commanded to a thousand generations, [16]The covenant which He made with Abraham, And His oath to Isaac. [17]He also confirmed it to Jacob for a statute, To Israel as an everlasting covenant, [18]Saying, "To you I will give the land of Canaan, As the portion of your inheritance." (1 Chronicles 16:14-18 NASB95)

The "covenant forever" or "the word which He commanded to a thousand generations" is not limited to the Land. The land of Israel was (is) just the focal point for God's kingdom (and promise) on earth (remember, the kingdom has no end, both in time and space, Psalm 45:6; Daniel 6:26; Luke 1:33). David combines all of the parts of the promise together (Adam, Abraham, Isaac, Jacob, Israel).[69] The written Law was simply "added" according to Paul (Galatians 3:19) which makes the Law part of the promise. The Law is not contrary to the promises of God, but complementary. Notice in Galatians 3 verse 22 that Law is equated to Scripture (and Scripture cannot be broken says Jesus in John 10:35).

> [15] Brethren, I speak in terms of human relations: even though it is only a man's covenant, yet when it has been ratified, no one sets it aside or adds conditions to it. [16] Now the promises were spoken to Abraham and to his seed. He does not say, "And to seeds," as referring to many, but rather to one, "And to your seed," that is, Christ. [17] What I am saying is this: the Law, which came four hundred and thirty years later, does not invalidate a covenant previously ratified by God, so as to nullify the promise. [18] For if the inheritance is based on law, it is no longer based on a

---

[69] Exodus 20:6, 34:7; 1 Chronicles 16:15; Psalm 105:8.

> promise; but God has granted it to Abraham by means of a promise. ¹⁹ Why the Law then? It was added because of transgressions, having been ordained through angels by the agency of a mediator, until the seed would come to whom the promise had been made. ²⁰ Now a mediator is not for one party only; whereas God is only one. ²¹ Is the Law then contrary to the promises of God? May it never be! For if a law had been given which was able to impart life, then righteousness would indeed have been based on law. ²² But the Scripture has shut up everyone under sin, so that the promise by faith in Jesus Christ might be given to those who believe. (Galatians 3:15-22 NASB95)

The promise of blessing is the focus of the written Word. It is the glue that binds it. The apostles spoke about it a lot. They were able to teach about Jesus from the Old Testament because the promise was there from the beginning. Jesus is the promise and the goal.

> ³⁸Peter said to them, "Repent, and each of you be baptized in the name of Jesus Christ for the forgiveness of your sins; and you will receive the gift of the Holy Spirit. ³⁹"For the *promise* is for you and your children and for all who are far off, as many as the Lord our God will call to Himself." (Acts 2:38-39 NASB95 italics added.)

> ²³"From the descendants of this man, according to *promise*, God has brought to Israel a Savior, Jesus, ²⁴after John had proclaimed before His coming a baptism of repentance to all the people of Israel. (Acts 13:23-24 NASB95 italics added)

> ¹Paul, a bond-servant of Christ Jesus, called as an apostle, set apart for the gospel of God, ²which He *promised* beforehand through His prophets in the holy Scriptures, ³concerning His Son, who was born of a descendant of David according to the flesh, ⁴who was declared the Son of God with power by the resurrection from the dead, according to the Spirit of holiness, Jesus Christ our Lord, (Romans 1:1-4 NASB95 italics added)

> ¹⁶For this reason it is by faith, in order that it may be in accordance with grace, so that the *promise* will be guaranteed to all the descendants, not only to those who are of the Law, but also to those who are of the faith of Abraham, who is the father of us all, (Romans 4:16 NASB95 italics added)

> ²⁹And if you belong to Christ, then you are Abraham's descendants, heirs according to *promise*. (Galatians 3:29 NASB95 italics added)
>
> ¹²remember that you were at that time separate from Christ, excluded from the commonwealth of Israel, and strangers to the covenants of *promise*, having no hope and without God in the world. (Ephesians 2:12 NASB95 italics added)
>
> ⁹The Lord is not slow about His *promise*, as some count slowness, but is patient toward you, not wishing for any to perish but for all to come to repentance. (2 Peter 3:9 NASB95 italics added)
>
> ²⁵This is the *promise* which He Himself made to us: eternal life. (1 John 2:25 NASB95 italics added)

The point is, God's plan is continuous, not a series of stops and starts. As writings were added to the Bible they all revolved around God's Law and unified message of promise. The wisdom literature (Job, Proverbs, Psalms, Ecclesiastes, Song of Songs) extols the virtues and benefits of living according to God's promise (a.k.a. the covenant). The prophets continued telling the people of God's promise and filled in many details of the coming King, His kingdom, and ultimate victory. They called people to repent and turn back to a relationship with Him through His promise (or Law, or covenant).

The New Testament records the incarnation of the promise (Jesus) and realization of His benefits (and there's a lot more to come). Jesus is the fulfillment of all parts of the promise. God in the flesh, Immanuel, the blessing for all, arrived in a human body, and began crushing the authority and kingdom of the serpent. Only a little longer and the crushing will be complete.

This is another doctrine that needs a whole book to properly explore, and cannot be covered completely here. However, enough is given that you should be able to get a handle on the general drift of the whole Bible and the unifying Promise of Scripture.[70]

The Foundational Testament

You might be wondering still why I'm making such a big deal about the Law and the Promise. Especially the Law. It's because the Law, like the Promise, is so central to God's Word. In reading the Bible, you can't

---

[70] For more on the promise try The Prophets and the Promise by Willis Judson Beecher or The Promise-Plan of God: A Biblical Theology of the Old and New Testaments by Walter C. Kaiser Jr.

go two or three verses without running smack dab into one aspect or another of the Law. Obedience to God (or you could call it a response to God) is at the heart of every issue in the Bible, and indeed, every issue in life. It doesn't matter if it's a single command, like "don't eat from that tree" or is more involved like the Sinai instructions.

Grace came first, then Law, then the Promise (at least in the written record). But they are all part of the same God. God put Adam and Eve, by grace, in a beautiful world overflowing with every advantage and blessing. His Word, or Law, was present in the form of gracious commands such as "go forth and multiply" and "reproduce after their (your) own kinds."

The Torah (first five books) is so important we can call it, as my friend Mike says, the "foundational testament." God reveals Himself throughout the Word (He is ever full of fun surprises) and all of it is equally important. But Torah stands as the first and most central building block. Other words from God are added after, but they are all part of Torah (Law).

He upholds everything by the Word of His power (Hebrews 1:3; John 1:3). So it has to be perfect and unshakable for it to be the foundation of the cosmos. It is also the foundation of our own hope in Him. Happily, for us, the timeless, absolute and complete truth of His Word simply cannot be shaken. We might fall for the masks, tricks and deceptions that hide it, but the foundation of His Word will always remain unchanged.

> [8]The grass withers, the flower fades, But the word of our God stands forever. (Isaiah 40:8 NASB95)

The word "canon" means "rule" or "standard" and is related to "foundation." Technically, The Canon is those words first written on the stone tablets. Everything else in the Bible is measured by those ten words. But the five books Moses wrote were based on those tablets, with direct testimony from the Guy who was there (Jesus) and doesn't lie. Down through the centuries any other writing claiming to be from God has had to conform to this original "measuring stick." Every new book has gone through a complete review process based on the standard of the Pentateuch. This is how we ended up with the current 66 books.

There are those who say that the Bible contains the Word of God, and that not all the words are God's. In a way, this is true. Some of the words spoken or actions taken are not God's. Many of the words and actions were by men, and we only need to obey those of the Father. But God made sure that a true account of words and actions was written down, even if they weren't directly His. All of it is included so that His people may learn, change and grow as needed (2 Timothy 3:16-17).

Even though God may not have spoken some of the words of the Bible, or performed all of the actions, He has given us His testimony that what is recorded was real and actual (Jeremiah 30:2, 36:2; 2 Peter 1:16; Revelation 21:5). Ever since the first five books were written down successive messengers from God always assumed them to be true and from the Father. Jesus and the apostles taught the OT as 100% God's absolute truth. Saying that some words are God's and some are not is only partly true, and causes doubt instead of building faith. The whole of the Word is His testimony. It is as true and unchangeable as He is.

> [20]But know this first of all, that no prophecy of Scripture is a matter of one's own interpretation, [21]for no prophecy was ever made by an act of human will, but men moved by the Holy Spirit spoke from God. (2 Peter 1:20-21 NASB95)

This explains why there are so many attacks against it. There is a titanic battle that has been going on since the beginning to discredit, mix, and dilute His Word with philosophies or theologies of men. Shatter the Word and shatter the foundation. Frequently these start as whispers from Satan, but we come up with stuff on our own too.

Daniel gives us a peek into the magnitude of the battle. An angel tells him that God's Word in response to his prayer was delayed 21 days by the prince (another angel) of Persia (Daniel 10:12-13). The part of the battle we can see is just a reflection of the spiritual battle happening outside of our viewing range (although we can see a lot of the side effects).

The Natural Man and Spiritual Relevance

Some struggle to see the foundational testament or other parts of the Word as relevant in their lives. There's a reason for this. The center of the struggle is not the Word. The center of the struggle is the self or the natural man. The natural man doesn't like the Word. He recoils from spiritual things. As it is written:

> The natural person does not accept the things of the Spirit of God, for they are folly to him, and he is not able to understand them because they are spiritually discerned. (1 Corinthians 2:14, ESV)

The person who refuses God's Word is the natural man. When the natural man refuses to obey, confusion is generated. We read something, don't want to do it, and that's when the Word loses relevance. It doesn't appeal to the natural man so he turns away from God's wisdom.

His word does not age or fade away; it does not change or fall apart. People, on the other hand, easily change and harden. We move away from the Word but the Word, like bedrock, never moves. Circumstances change; people die, but the Word of the Lord and its relevance lives forever (Matthew 24:35).

The Word is one complete book of living oracles (one faith) given to all people by our one God and Savior Jesus the Christ. It is not "old" and "new" in the sense of outdated and updated, nor is any part of it irrelevant. It contains a great deal of wisdom, but it is not a book of disconnected wise sayings. It is full of many practical life instructions, but it is not a book of suggestions. To the lawless it is a puzzle book (1 Corinthians 1:18); to the humble and obedient heart it is plain and easy to understand.

> ^{25}With the kind You show Yourself kind; With the blameless You show Yourself blameless; ^{26}With the pure You show Yourself pure, And with the crooked You show Yourself astute. ^{27}For You save an afflicted people, But haughty eyes You abase. (Psalm 18:25-27 NASB95; see also 2 Samuel 22:26-28)

The Bible is given to all people, but some grab hold while others let it slip away. To believers every word from God is love, light, life, a lamp, instruction, law, commands, judgments, teaching, ways, wisdom and truth.

- **Love**—John 12, 13, 14, 15:10.
- **Light and lamp**—Proverbs 6:23; Psalm 119:105; Isaiah 8:20; Revelation 21:23, 22:5.
- **Life**—Deuteronomy 4:1, 32:46-47; Proverbs 8:32-36; Matthew 19:16, 17.
- **Instructions**—Isaiah 1:10; Exodus 16:4, 24:12; Jeremiah 35:13; Job 22:22, 36:10; Psalm 78:1; Zephaniah 3:1-7; Malachi 2:1-9; Proverbs 1:2,3,7,8; 4:1,2; Romans 15:4; Ephesians 6:4; 1 Timothy 1:5; 2 Timothy 4:2; 1 Thessalonians 4:1, 5:12.
- **Law**—Jeremiah 6:18-19; Zechariah 7:12; Deut 5:5, 17:11, 27:1-3, 26, 30:10,14, 32:46,47; John 15:25; Acts 6:2-4,7, 13:44, 48, 49, 28:23; Romans 9:28, 31, 32; 1 Corinthians 15:2; Galatians 5:14.
- **Commands, judgments, teachings & ways**—Isaiah 2:3; Proverbs 1:8, 3:1, 4:2, 5:12, 6:20-23; 7:2, 8:10, Jeremiah 32:33; Deuteronomy 4:1; 2 Chronicles 15:1-7; Matthew 4:23, 7:28, 29, 9:35, 13:54, 15:9, 28:20; Acts 2:42, 4:2, 18:11; Romans 12:7; 1 Corinthians 14:26.
- **Wisdom and truth**—Psalm 33:4, 119:43, 44, 142, 160, 138:2; Proverbs 23:23; Malachi 2:6; 1 Kings 2:3-4 (AV); John 17:17, 18:37-38, 8:31-32; James 1:18.

Everything God says could be described by any of these terms. "Law" is "instruction" and also a "lamp" and "light." "Wisdom" and "truth" is also "love" and "life." Some people separate His Words into cubbyholes. They think that somehow a word from Him that is "Law" is not "love," or that a word that is a "lamp" is not "Law." Obviously the Bible disagrees.

> For who knows a person's thoughts except the spirit of that person, which is in him? So also no one comprehends the thoughts of God except the Spirit of God. Now we have received not the spirit of the world, but the Spirit who is from God, that we might understand the things freely given us by God. And we impart this in words not taught by human wisdom but taught by the Spirit, interpreting spiritual truths to those who are spiritual. The natural person does not accept the things of the Spirit of God, for they are folly to him, and he is not able to understand them because they are spiritually discerned. The spiritual person judges all things, but is himself to be judged by no one. "For who has understood the mind of the Lord so as to instruct him?" But we have the mind of Christ. (1 Corinthians 2:11–16, ESV)

The "natural person" does not accept the things of the Spirit of God, for they are folly to him. The Word (the Law) looks foolish, so he refuses to do anything God says. God's Law is spiritual (Romans 7:14) so a natural man does not think it is relevant. It is as if a starving man were at a lavish banquet refusing to eat because it isn't served on china. All he has to do is reach out his hand and partake of God's blessings, but he won't because to his prideful mind it's not appealing. Only when we humbly submit to God do we see that His knowledge is not foolish. When we reject the knowledge of God given in the Law, it shows that we are not spiritual. A new heart of flesh written with the Law by the Spirit recognizes the blessings in the Law freely given us by God.

It doesn't matter how we label what God says as far as validity and truth. Different words just serve to highlight different aspects of the same living truth. For emphasis, we (or He) may use different words, but they are all relatively the same. Whether we call it Law or lamp, instruction, wisdom or truth, it is in all ways relevant and spiritual. His Laws, commands, judgments and teachings are life, love, wisdom, and truth.

> [16] All Scripture is inspired by God and profitable for teaching, for reproof, for correction, for training in righteousness; [17] so that the man of God may be adequate, equipped for every good work. (2 Timothy 3:16-17 NASB95)

The Bible is also relevant because it is the history of the believer's people, it is our heritage. Though I am not a physical descendant of Abraham I am his adopted son (Romans 4:16; Galatians 3:29). I don't have an inheritance in the land, but my inheritance is Jesus. I am a child of the promise, just like Isaac. When a genealogy is given, God is filling in details of my family tree. A promise is given to Abraham and his children; it is my promise too. The history of Abraham's people is the history of my people. The Law in which Abraham abided (Genesis 26:5) is the same Word of God that abides in me and me in it.

Six Assumptions about Bible Interpretation

An assumption we make before we read the Bible is also called a pre-conceived notion or presupposition. We accept our presuppositions as truth, but they may not be the truth. Taken together, pre-conceived notions are part of what I called "street level theology" in chapter one. Reverend Steve Schlissel says this about that.

> "Many times we use the word presuppositions without knowing what presuppositions are. Tricky but important things, they determine what facts and how facts are entertained by us. Presuppositions function like preferences or tastes. To illustrate, just as we never go near some foods, regardless of how well they may be prepared, so presuppositional biases can steer us away from certain approaches. We can actually find ourselves filtering out truths as we read the Bible. We don't see certain truths because they don't conform to our presuppositions. As another illustration, presuppositions function like teeth and like a mouth, since all potential nourishment must first pass through our presuppositions to be made fit for personal consumption. They function like a digestion system in which a nearly miraculous function occurs out of sight— detecting, sorting, and cataloguing the ingredients while we go about our business. Presuppositions also function like a "tusshy"—they are behind and under everything we do, and we do our life-long best to keep them hidden and protected. Generally, we never talk about them in polite company (though occasionally we must)."[71]

Everyone has a street level theology with many pre-conceived ideas or assumptions. They're impossible to avoid when reading and applying Scripture. Some presuppositions are so ingrained we are surprised when they are revealed to us. But even the "stealth" assumptions we have

---

[71] Covenant Hearing article by Reverend Steve Schlissel; Messiah's Covenant Community Church; messiahnyc.org or wholebible.com under All Articles; page 4; presented at the 2002 Auburn Pastor's conference.

affect how we behave and how we interpret information coming from any source.

Assumptions or presuppositions are not necessarily bad. We just have to recognize that we have them. Then we have to work hard at cross checking them with (in this case, biblical) evidence, and adjust them if they don't match up to Bible facts. All we know is not all there is.

What we think we know needs continuous overhaul from the Bible because we have a tendency to drift away from God. As often as possible we need a fresh look at His Word so we can cross-check our assumptions and keep from getting stale. Whole Bible belief and practice is the way to keep our street level theology fresh and vibrant. As we read the Bible we will come across ideas or teachings that don't seem to fit our present assumptions, and we'll need to decide if a change is in order. Changes like this led to the changes in my family's lives and the eventual writing of this book.

Be on guard for other people's assumptions as well as your own. Many theologies are stuffed with ideas which were developed hundreds of years ago, apart from the Scriptures, and are frequently assumed to be true now. For instance, dispensationalism imagines that there are different ages where God dealt differently with different people. So according to them the Law is "old" and we have two Bodies with two different sets of rules to go by. Covenant theology is another example that assumes God merged physical Israel into the church. For them the Law is not objective and real but merely spiritual.

Whether you know it or not this type of assumption stuffing is in every teaching you get from the church. Pastors and rabbis have been (willingly) drilled, hammered and cemented into one or more old theological systems, and they serve up the teachings like the system tells them to. In order to graduate from school or become a member in good standing of any related church group (or stay that way); they have to teach the system they've bought into. They learn to teach just as they are taught, and they don't deviate from the recipe one bit. I'll make the bold statement that they don't teach the Bible. They teach their chosen system, which might include some Bible but is definitely not the simple, plain teaching of the Word.

There are dozens of good rules for interpreting the Bible, and many books written. We will cover some more of the practical ones for daily living in chapter 9. But if you want a good book on interpretation try <u>Introduction to Biblical Hermeneutics: The Search for Meaning</u> by Walter C. Kaiser Jr. and Moises Silva. Here I'm going to give you a few general rules that both show you where I'm coming from and will also help keep a focus on what is important. The six whole Bible beliefs about the Bible we are going to talk about next may look like they have no foundation, but only because we could write books on each concept and we don't have the space to give them more than an introduction here. They are 1) that God's Word is the highest authority; 2) that the Bible reveals God, it doesn't conceal Him; 3) it is clear and plain; 4) it means what God intends; 5) the Word explains the Word, and 6) the Word requires a response.

One. It is the Highest Authority.

During the Reformation, in addition to "faith alone," another of the mostly forgotten truths that were brought up is in Latin called *sola scriptura*. This means "Scripture alone," and reinforces the point that Scripture, by itself, is the first and final authority in a believer's life (Matthew 4:4). Scripture overrides and transcends a priest's word, or a pastor's commentary, a rabbinic ruling and even a pope's bull.[72] One reason this truth (among others) had to be recovered, and now repeated, was that many teachings of men (then and now) obscure the plain meaning of God's Word for everyday people. Another reason is that church (or Jewish) traditions drift into overriding the Bible after a while.

There are good writings from many good teachers that help us understand more about the Bible. Talmud (the oral law) for instance, has a great deal of good commentary. The Apocrypha[73] has some interesting insights. But they are not the Word, and do not carry the same authority. No extra-biblical writing measures up to the Bible. Even the good ones just repeat what is already in the Word. As Solomon says, there is no new thing under the sun.

Many times the extra writings just lead away from the Bible. Papal bulls, the efforts of so-called "prophets" (Edgar Cayce, Ellen White, Charles Russell, John Smith, etc.) and almost all other extra-biblical writings just obscure or lead away from the plain meaning of His ancient message. People keep trying to trump God's Word with other writings. The Nicolaitans keep trying and trying to distract or cover over what God clearly tells us. They fool some of the people some of the time, but they can't fool all of us. Whole Bible Christians understand that there are many sources for learning, but only one with Authority.

Two. It Reveals God's Will and Plans.

God's Word is intended by Him to reveal His character, His will, plan and purpose to us. It was not written to conceal Him or what He intends for man.

---

[72] A papal bull is a message from the pope trying to clarify a teaching of the church or the Bible.

[73] The apocrypha (means 'hidden') is a group of books commonly found in Catholic Bibles. They are not accepted into the Protestant canon because they tend to contradict the Bible as well as themselves.

> ²⁹"The secret things belong to the Lord our God, but the things revealed belong to us and to our sons forever, that we may observe all the words of this law. (Deuteronomy 29:29 NASB95)

> ¹³For behold, He who forms mountains and creates the wind And declares to man what are His thoughts, He who makes dawn into darkness And treads on the high places of the earth, The Lord God of hosts is His name. (Amos 4:13 NASB95)

It would be somewhat nonsensical for Him to cause His words to be recorded, and then no one could figure them out. God lets us in on what He is doing and will do, and what He expects from man. We have no excuse to be ignorant of what God requires. The Bible is preserved for us so that we can read it and learn about God. He made sure the words were written down so other generations would have information they could use to find Him.

> ¹⁶"Come near to Me, listen to this: From the first I have not spoken in secret, From the time it took place, I was there. And now the Lord God has sent Me, and His Spirit." ¹⁷Thus says the Lord, your Redeemer, the Holy One of Israel, "I am the Lord your God, who teaches you to profit, Who leads you in the way you should go. ¹⁸"If only you had paid attention to My commandments! Then your well-being would have been like a river, And your righteousness like the waves of the sea. (Isaiah 48:16-18 NASB95)

> ⁷Surely the Lord God does nothing Unless He reveals His secret counsel To His servants the prophets. (Amos 3:7 NASB95)

One of the big reasons that the Reformation was so effective is that the Bible was translated into common languages. Everyone could compare the existing church with the one in the book of Acts. It didn't match up too well, and reform was demanded. God meant the Bible to be understood, and to reveal His works and character and power to all generations, at least to those of the generations searching for Him.

Three. It is Clear.

At the time of the Reformation, the average person did not read the Scriptures (sound like today?). But back then it was because they were in languages no one used and translations into common languages were forbidden so the church could hold onto its power. The synod of Toulouse in 1229 for instance specifically forbade people to have the Bible in their own language. It wasn't until 1962-64 at Vatican II that Catholics were encouraged to read their Bibles (after people were already doing it). Reading and interpreting for many even today is the special province of the clergy, and they insist that priests (pastors, rabbis) are the only people qualified to determine meaning and application. They allege the Bible is too difficult for the average person to understand. Of course, they used to think the earth was flat, too.

But God made sure the Word was well within the ability of anyone to understand it. Some of the people during the Reformation called this "perspicuity."[74] They were saying we don't have to be scholars to grasp most of the Word. We need to be reminded of this today because there are those who want to complicate the Word and keep it out of our hands.

It seems clear to me that the main issue that causes Scripture to be unclear is a refusal to do what is read (Jeremiah 7:28; Hosea 6:6). We have a nature, inherited from Adam, which tends to walk away from God. Many times, it wants to sprint. We hide from Him because in ourselves we don't measure up to His perfection, holiness and power. Like Adam and Eve in the bushes.

Obedience to the smallest word helps to clear up the meaning of more of the Word – more abiding means more understanding (Deuteronomy 4:6). Sometimes we don't understand, and sometimes we just don't know, but the bottom line is abiding.

Obedience requires humility. Humility allows the light of the Spirit unhindered access to the darkest corners of our hearts. Disobedience comes from pride, and pride causes confusion. Pride hardens the heart and actively resists the Spirit. I know I'm repeating myself, but this concept needs a lot of repetition.

Scripture itself tells us that many of the things that are written are for our understanding. Luke 1:4 says *"so that you may know the exact truth about the things you have been taught."* Paul says something similar.

> [14]I am writing these things to you, hoping to come to you before long; [15]but in case I am delayed, I write so that you will know how one ought to conduct himself in the household of God, which is the church of the living God, the pillar and support of the truth. (1 Timothy 3:14-15 NASB95)

The truth of the Word is plainly evident to everyone. But prepared hearts (looking for truth) who "study to show (themselves) approved" will get more out of it as we read it and do it. A hard hearted person understands, it's just that they profess ignorance or confusion because they don't want to follow under any circumstances (Acts 7:51-53; Ephesians 4:17-19).

---

[74] Some think the doctrine of perspicuity or clarity of Scripture applies only to those things related to salvation. I think it applies to all of the Word.

The Spirit is able to teach the redeemed, obedient soul, not because he or she has had a lot of schooling, but because the word of God is so structured as to speak to the heart. The biggest barrier to understanding the Word is not language, the age of the copies, grammar, or the culture. It is the refusal to accept the plain meaning and change our thinking and living patterns to conform to it.

> [2]"For My hand made all these things, Thus all these things came into being," declares the LORD. "But to this one I will look, To him who is humble and contrite of spirit, and who trembles at My word. (Isaiah 66:2 NASB95)

Four. It Means What He intends.

The clarity of Scripture includes the idea of a literal interpretation. What you read is what you get. When a writer sets down words to convey his thoughts to others, he tries to pick those which most accurately represent what he is thinking. When we read what he writes, we are supposed to use the words he chose to understand what he is trying to say. As I write this book, I have a purpose in mind, a thought to give, and I want you to get what I'm thinking. Even if you don't necessarily agree. So there is only one literal meaning to what I write (except for puns).

You don't pick up this book, or any other, including the Bible, and try to make it say what you want. You don't try to find a spiritual meaning because you think that I really didn't mean just what I said. You don't take apart my grammar, syntax, or look up the history of how the words that I chose were used centuries ago. Instead, you try to find my literal intent. The Bible authors are understood the same. Each one has a purpose for their word choices, sentence structure, order of narrative, or whatever. There is only one meaning. It has to be this way or words mean nothing at all.

Jesus and the apostles used the literal meaning of the Old Testament text, quoted it a lot, and reinforced instruction that had already been given by God (such as love). They relied on and supported the literal intent of the Old Testament authors, explaining some of the forgotten parts. None of them spiritualized the texts. They all avoided allegorizing (another word for spiritualizing) except for a couple of well-defined instances.

Interpretation can be something of a cross between science and art. Even when we try to understand what a close friend is saying in a conversation, we don't always get it right the first time. There are gestures, expressions, and tones that we don't always pick up on. There can also be inside jokes or figures of speech and the like. Happily, God's message is plainly and simply repeated. For good measure, it is repeated in many time frames, in many different cultures, through many different people. We can compare all of these together and get an exact understanding with confidence.

God very purposefully communicates His meaning so that there is no misunderstanding. Many people foolishly speak in a bad way about literal interpretation. They like to come up with their own fantasy spiritual meanings. Then they can steal authority from the Word and rule over others. They don't like a literal meaning because it restricts them from the flights of fancy they use to lead people away from the Word.

There is only one *meaning* to the Bible, but many *applications* I can draw from the author's meaning. Meaning includes dictionary definitions of words, sentence structure, subjects, predicates and grammar. Application can be thought of as "how the text applies to your life" or even "what does it mean to me."

When Matthew writes in his gospel chapter two verses 13 through 15 about Joseph and Mary fleeing to Egypt with Jesus, this is exactly what happened. It is not a metaphor. It does not mean anything mystical, nor point to some lost part of the ministry of Jesus. There is no "deeply spiritual" meaning other than what the author intended. Matthew tells us the reason he includes those facts in his gospel in verse 15 is it fulfilled a prophecy from Hosea 11:1.

We might draw some nifty comparisons based on these facts, but the words mean what Matthew meant them to, no more and no less. An application for me is reassurance that even when things look bad, God is in control. But my application is not the same as what the author's words mean. The meaning, or author's intent, might be very different from any application I might find.

Paul gives us an example of the difference between meaning and application in 1 Corinthians 9:9. He quotes Deuteronomy 25:4 where we are told not to muzzle the ox that treads the grain. He applies it to receiving financial help for his teaching efforts. The meaning of the text is clear: don't put a muzzle on the ox – let him eat. The application is also clear – if God cares for an ox, He also would want us to care for workers in His Body. Paul supports his teaching with practical references to vineyard workers, soldiers, shepherds, crop harvesters and priests who share in the sacrifices. His application is valid, but the meaning of the text doesn't change.

Too often, a person will discover a nifty application, then turn around and teach that his or her application is the meaning of the text. Mostly that is not the case, and we have to guard against turning applications into meaning.

Frequently there is more meaning in a group of words than simply the sum of the word definitions. For instance, we might say a guy has "egg on his face." But we do not mean that he has an actual bird egg on his face. We mean he was embarrassed in some way. Just because we use a literal interpretation does not mean we have to be inflexible when it comes to the meaning. Yet if words are to have any meaning when sharing ideas, they must have some consistency and uniformity. Otherwise, we would still be babbling as we did at the Tower of Babel. Come to think of it, we still are doing a lot more babbling than we should.

The interpretation method called allegorical or "spiritualizing" is used by many teachers to squeeze extra meaning from every letter of the Bible.[75] Even if the meaning is clear enough with plain reading. Spiritualizing treats the Bible like Aesop's Fables with a "hidden" and "more important" truth buried under what is plainly read. There is much in the Bible that is spiritually discerned. But that does not mean there is a deep spiritual meaning behind every word. Or that the supposed spiritual meaning is the only one that counts. Spiritualizing opposes the literal method of interpreting.

Spiritualizers have said that the fruit eaten by Adam and Eve wasn't a real fruit, or that the tree of knowledge wasn't a real tree. They were symbolic of something else. I've heard that the four rivers running out of Eden weren't real rivers but stood for four virtues.

This is one of the places that people who want to destroy the absolute truth of the Word start. The effect of this type of interpretation is to destroy the integrity of God's Word and so destroy our trust in it. Spiritualizing destroys the plain meaning of God's Word and removes objectivity. There are no language rules. Meanings or applications exist only in the mind of the person doing the spiritualizing. They can't be verified with objective methods by the average person reading the plain text. Spiritualizing promotes pride, because one who is "more spiritual" can allegedly see the assumed meaning. The alleged inferior "less spiritual" person cannot.

The person who spiritualizes then becomes the only authority on Meaning. The "less spiritual" person cannot read the text for himself, but must go back to the spiritualizer to get the "true" meaning. These "holier than thou" people just shift authority from the Scriptures to themselves, nullify various unpopular sections, and become kings of their own little kingdom. Allegory is present in the Word, and there are spiritual

---

[75] An example of this is the PaRDeS (p'shat, remez, drash, sod) system of rabbinical interpretation that is popular.

meanings too, but these are dependent on the literal meanings of words and the author's intent.[76]

Five. It is Self Explaining.

Okay, so we've figured out that the Word is the highest authority, it reveals God, is clear and easy to understand by the average person, it means what He intends, and so is to be taken literally. In addition to these we use God's Word to interpret God's Word. When we have questions on a text, there's a good chance there's a bunch of other texts that will help clear it up. We just have to make sure we compare apples to apples.

Comparing apples to apples works by comparing sections that have similar language or similar subjects that are closely related. What is important is to keep going through the whole of the Word to make all the comparisons we can find. It also means we need to do what we read. Terms might look the same, but that doesn't mean they are the same.

The challenge is to see the Bible as a whole and all of the parts fitting together in a complete picture. There are very clear teachings and some that are not so clear. But we can use the clear teachings to help clarify teachings that might not be as clear. For instance, God says He doesn't change and that His Word won't change. So if a section of the Bible appears to change His Word then our understanding must be out of whack. God is very consistent and His Word is very consistent too.

Providentially, God has not left us with only a few questionable fragments of His Word. He has given us such a wealth of revelation in a format that is so easy to understand there is no doubt what He intends for His people. A great American statesman, Daniel Webster, said it well.

> I believe that the Bible is to be understood and received in the plain and obvious meaning of its passages; for I cannot persuade myself that a book intended for the instruction and conversion of the whole world should cover its true meaning in any such mystery and doubt that none but critics and philosophers can discover it.[77]

Six. It Requires a Response.

Not only does His Word have the highest authority, revealing His will and plans very clearly, with a meaning He intends that is self-

---

[76] Paul makes an allegory for teaching purposes in Galatians 4:24, but it is clearly noted. He also explains his allegory thoroughly and does not leave it to the reader to guess his meaning. Jesus sort of uses an allegory in John 3 when He speaks of being 'born again.' Again, He clearly explains Himself. Parables are a form of allegory; most are explained or the tools for determining meaning are present in the Word.

[77] Daniel Webster, January 18, 1782 – October 24, 1852,
http://quotationpark.com/authors/WEBSTER, Daniel.htm

explaining, it also commands a response from men based on what He has revealed. It's not a request. He's not begging. Just because He delays judgment does not mean we get to delay a response. We are to turn from our own ways and follow His ways (choose life) or die, and He doesn't want us to die. He isn't kidding around in causing His Words to be written down and preserved through the centuries.

The key actions in repentance are reading and doing. If we only read part, then we only understand partly, and if we don't obey, why keep reading? The body and blood of the Christ will not help us if we don't open our hearts and respond. If we don't do what we read, our faith is suspect, and faith is a critical ingredient to understanding the Word. It all works together to get us where we want to go. History, grammar, culture and other tools are all important in finding the meaning, but these will only help in a small way until we respond.

> [21]Therefore, putting aside all filthiness and all that remains of wickedness, in humility receive the word implanted, which is able to save your souls. [22]But prove yourselves doers of the word, and not merely hearers who delude themselves. [23]For if anyone is a hearer of the word and not a doer, he is like a man who looks at his natural face in a mirror; [24]for once he has looked at himself and gone away, he has immediately forgotten what kind of person he was. [25]But one who looks intently at the perfect law, the law of liberty, and abides by it, not having become a forgetful hearer but an effectual doer, this man will be blessed in what he does. (James 1:21-25 NASB95)

"*In humility receive the Word implanted.*" This means to abide by the "law of liberty" in every action. This law is none other than the Law of Moses, the only perfect law. It's really very easy to understand and implement. There's so much freedom in the Law that it can be called the law of liberty. This is not "freedom in Christ" to ignore the Word of Christ, as many teachers have tried to get us to swallow.

In contrast to the simple clarity of the Word, men have come up with untold numbers of ways to reinterpret and confuse it. In fact, it's because of doubting and questioning the Word of God that so much time has to be spent on answers. Complications are added by men when they doubt what God said. This book is a little complicated because of the complicated teachings of men we are dismantling. It is not because the Word is all that complicated. When men don't want to act on what He says, objections are made up. This is where we get all those "philosophies of men" that Paul talks about (Colossians 2:8). This leads us to talk about trust.

Can The Bible Be Trusted?

I'm sure you've heard teachings that cast doubt on the authenticity of the Word. For instance, some claim that "translational bias" has corrupted the translations.[78] What they mean is that no one can translate well enough to get God's message across because our own brains get in the way. Too many of those presuppositions. Others claim that we have to use the original languages. Some go so far as to reject the New Testament because there isn't a Hebrew original.

It is true that when it comes to translating the Bible, even the most well trained scholar's bias can color his or her translating. Even scholars have assumptions. We all have a bias of some sort even when casually reading the Word. It's been a problem since the beginning.

> [1]Now the serpent was more crafty than any beast of the field which the Lord God had made. And he said to the woman, "Indeed, has God said, 'You shall not eat from any tree of the garden'?" [2]The woman said to the serpent, "From the fruit of the trees of the garden we may eat; [3]but from the fruit of the tree which is in the middle of the garden, God has said, 'You shall not eat from it or touch it, or you will die.' " (Genesis 3:1-3 NASB95)

The serpent was obviously against what God originally instructed the first man and woman to do. "Has God said" is a common refrain among those who seek to destroy the authority of the Father throughout history. Eve had a bias too, as shown by her "don't touch" twist on what God said (He only said "don't eat"). Created beings play fast and loose with God's Words, and we need to watch ourselves. Bernard Ramm puts it this way.

> "…we all need a new sense of respect for the Holy Scripture. Believing it to be the veritable word of God, we must exercise all the human pains possible to keep from overlaying it with a gossamer pattern of our own spinning. In each of those cases where human error enters, divine truth is obscured. Let us then steer a straight course through the Holy Bible, neither turning to the left side of heresy nor to the right side of unbridled imagination."[79]

---

[78] Translational bias means that translators can't help but put their own ideas into the text. One example of this is what we talked about earlier with the word 'church.' See also Acts 12:4 in the KJV where 'Easter,' obviously not invented at the time, translates the Greek word for 'Passover' (*pascha*, G3957).

[79] Bernard Ramm, *Protestant Biblical Interpretation*, Third Revised Edition, (Grand Rapids, Michigan: Baker Book House 1979), p. 290.

But in my opinion the weightiest truth against the claim of bias, or any other teaching casting doubt on the Bible, is that the foundation for 61 of the books is the first five. The Torah was the first canon by which any additional writing, or any prophet or preacher, is measured.

> To the law and to the testimony! If they do not speak according to this word, it is because they have no dawn. (Isaiah 8:20 NASB95)

This foundation is itself built on the bedrock of God's direct Word, spoken to Moses and inscribed on stone. All the prophet's messages point to it (His Word). The Wisdom Books contemplate some aspect or aspects of understanding from it. Jesus reiterates it in the gospels and the apostles carried a refreshed version of it to the world. John the Baptist and Jesus called the nation of Israel to repent and return to it. All of the Apostolic Writings (NT) extol the virtues and blessings of following it, and expect the child of God to live by it. The Revelation describes those who hold to the testimony of both the Messiah and His commands (Revelation 12:11; etc.). If we use the same foundation for our own reading and doing, then the unity and inerrancy of the whole is evident.

The copying and translation of the Word of God has been filtered through human understanding since Moses wrote the Pentateuch. In fact, it could be said that the translational bias goes all the way back to the first conversation and comes all the way down to the current reader. But it is a stone heart that will look for any excuse to avoid obedience to God. Even rock tablets written by the finger of God will not help such a one.

Understanding Hebrew and Greek first hand is very valuable. If we know them ourselves then we don't have to depend on translations to tell us the meaning. But it is not as though a person who has mastered these languages is the exclusive judge of meaning. The languages themselves aren't any more meaningful than any other language.

Granted, translators are people and can fail to see as clearly as they should, even in a group. Then again, people have been killed because they dared to translate the Bible into common languages. That puts a kink in the job description if you know what I mean. If you had to bet with your life you would want to make sure it was for something important.

The Torah also remains as the rule and guide for interpretation. All we need to do is remove bias such as the discontinuity introduced by extra-biblical theologies of dispensationalism or covenant theology. Then whatever shadow of spiritual damage that might be present in a translation is dissolved in the pure light of the Source.

The Law is an ancient message, when we see it as it really is. It has been around as long as God, and there are many instances of Laws being lived before Sinai. At first it was handed down directly from father to son; and along with nature and conscience informed us of God's will. It still functions to keep us safely in God's love.

The Promise of Genesis 3:15 is that we would one day go back to having "God with us" again. The Law was added to the promise because of transgression, and also to prepare a kingdom of kings and priests for spreading His "good news" throughout the world. The Law is always relevant in His kingdom if we allow it to guide us as He intended. It is one Word, one faith, ageless and fresh, always sharp and full of life. The believing heart relies on it as the sole authority for living. It reveals God clearly and says exactly what He means with no guesswork required. No other writings come close for power and peace. If freed from the weight of stone-hearted disobedience, it is the easiest of books to trust, understand and live by.

5 A Whole Heart

> [13]"Go, inquire of the LORD for me and the people and all Judah concerning the words of this book that has been found, for great is the wrath of the LORD that burns against us, because our fathers have not listened to the words of this book, to do according to all that is written concerning us." (2 Kings 22:13 NASB95)

One God, one Lord, one Body, and one Faith. I hope God has been able to remove the masks man has given you, and heal the fractures so you can see the Oneness and continuity for yourself. I also hope that your heart is filling with joy over the fact that what much of what you may have been told so far in the church, and what you instinctively suspected was not true, is not in the Bible. This is critical if you are going to make it the rest of the way, too. Your whole heart has to be in it with Him. It's all or nothing. All of your heart for all of His.

> [6] For to set the mind on the flesh is death, but to set the mind on the Spirit is life and peace. [7] For the mind that is set on the flesh is hostile to God, for it does not submit to God's law; indeed, it cannot. [8] Those who are in the flesh cannot please God. (Romans 8:6-8 ESV)

The New Covenant

Josiah became king of Israel when he was only eight years old and reigned 31 years (2 Kings 22 and 23). He was a good king and one of the best Israel (Judah) ever had (2 Kings 22:2). He did right and would not turn aside to the right or left. When he was a teenager, he started cleaning the land of idolatry. Then at 26, it was time to clean up the house of God.

In the process, the book of the Law was found and read to the young king. Josiah was greatly saddened and horrified because the people had ignored this book for a long time. He knew that the Lord must be very angry with Israel, so he sent some people to the prophetess Huldah to ask what should be done.

The bad news from God, through Huldah, was that the evil of all the words of the book of the law would be dropped on the people. The good news was that it would skip Josiah's lifetime. God was pleased that he had responded to the Word with humility and a "tender heart."

Josiah assembled all the people at the temple and read the book to them. Then they each made a covenant to "walk after the Lord, and to keep His commandments and His testimonies and His statutes, with all (his) heart and soul" (2 Kings 23:3 parenthesis added).

This is the attitude that God desires of His people. We might not have read the Law and we might not be aware that it is for all of His people everywhere. But what do we do when we hear that it is current and applies to us? That it is in the heart of the new covenant and all about love? That abiding and obedience are the same thing? Do we come up with dozens of excuses to continue to disobey? Or do we tear our clothes, hit the floor, and beseech the Lord for mercy?

Is our heart soft and tender flesh, like Josiah's, or hard like stone towards God's commandments, testimonies and statutes? Does His Law drive us to our knees in humility and obedience? Or do we raise our heads in proud defiance saying, "You have to give me grace 'cause I have Jesus?"

What It Is

The New Covenant is all about having a heart just like Josiah's, or more specifically just like God's. Oddly, the term "new covenant" is mentioned in only six verses in the New Testament.[80] None of them explains what the covenant is, except for a couple of partial quotes. The reason is that everyone knew what it was, and it didn't have to be repeated. All of the New Testament verses refer back to "old" Jeremiah 31 (and to places such as Ezekiel 11:19-20 and 36:22-37).

The new covenant is 1) Between God, Judah (southern kingdom) and Israel (northern kingdom). Gentiles can be included, but the emphasis is on inclusion not replacement. 2) It is not like the covenant at Sinai after the Exodus because 3) The Law (instruction, torah) is written on the heart, He will be God, and Israel His people. 4) All will know Him; no one will need to teach. 5) He will forgive iniquity and remember sin no more. It's obvious that not all of this has been fulfilled, but that's because He's patiently waiting for us.

> [4] Or do you presume on the riches of his kindness and forbearance and patience, not knowing that God's kindness is meant to lead you to repentance? (Romans 2:4 ESV)

The new covenant was written down by Jeremiah about 600 years before any book of the New Testament. But is has always been in the heart of God. Believe it or not, He wanted Adam and Eve to live by it (Hosea 6:7). Israel was not supposed to just give it lip service. There were individuals here and there, such as King Josiah, who lived it. Jesus

---

[80] Luke 22:20; 1 Corinthians 11:25; 2 Corinthians 3:6; Hebrews 8:8, 9:15 and 12:24

presented it again, but it wasn't accepted with open arms or open heart by the leaders. Even now we give it lip service, but we do not make the whole of it a part of our living. God has always desired that we would respond to Him with a heart of flesh and live His Word. The new thing about the new covenant is not the Word but the heart.

Jesus certified (sealed, ratified, notarized, made possible, fulfilled, filled it up full of the love it had always had) the new covenant (Luke 22:19; 1 Corinthians 11:25; 2 Corinthians 3:6) with His death and resurrection at God's perfect time. But since He is eternal, anything that happens to Him has eternal effects. In other words, believers were living in the new covenant before the cross and even going back to the Garden, because the sacrifice of Jesus resonates through time.

> [20]For He was foreknown before the foundation of the world, but has appeared in these last times for the sake of you [21]who through Him are believers in God, who raised Him from the dead and gave Him glory, so that your faith and hope are in God. (1 Peter 1:20-21 NASB95)

What It Was

The old covenant was written on stone tablets, which were not only hard like our natural hearts but also external. The tablets are a picture of our relationship with God before conversion – hearts hard as stone. After conversion, our soft heart of flesh responds to God in every way.

> [19]"And I will give them one heart, and put a new spirit within them. And I will take the heart of stone out of their flesh and give them a heart of flesh, [20]that they may walk in My statutes and keep My ordinances and do them. Then they will be My people, and I shall be their God. (Ezekiel 11:19-20 NASB95)

> [26]"Moreover, I will give you a new heart and put a new spirit within you; and I will remove the heart of stone from your flesh and give you a heart of flesh. [27]"I will put My Spirit within you and cause you to walk in My statutes, and you will be careful to observe My ordinances. (Ezekiel 36:26-27 NASB95)

Old and new do not apply to God's Word, but to our hearts. The old covenant is old not because His Word is old, but because it was imposed from outside. People's hearts just weren't in it. Our old hearts were made of stone, but the new ones are flesh. Our old hearts didn't know God intimately, but our new hearts are closer to Him than our own blood is to us. God's blood (His Word) has in truth become our blood.

Old hearts have to be coerced with penalties to do what God wants, but hearts of flesh obey with gladness and without fear of death. The old heart has to be told every detail of how to behave as He behaves ("be holy for I am holy"). We don't just know, or naturally want to do, what God wants, "by heart." The new heart may not know everything, but intently and earnestly looks for God's will and responds positively when it finds Him.

To the old heart, the Law is like a carrot and stick. It tries to get a carrot without getting whacked by the stick. The new heart on the other hand seeks out every one of His instructions, and acts on even the glance of His eye. Reward and punishment don't really enter into our actions too much. We love (God); therefore we do (His Word). No, old and new don't have anything to do with our ageless God or His Living Oracles; they have to do with our condition. Either God is outside beating on a stone heart, or He is inside and our hearts beat together as one.

What It Shall Be

The new heart of flesh we get, in exchange for a heart of stone, is the beginning of a new life which wants to abide in God's Word. Rather than the Law being eliminated, which is normally taught in many Christian circles, the New Covenant is The Law written on the heart, so all will obey. Eventually it will be written by the Spirit on all believing hearts; at least to the extent that no one will have to be taught about Him.

One reason the new covenant is not like the old is that eventually no one will have to be taught who He is and what He requires. Everyone will know Him. But this doesn't mean everyone will be saved. Not everyone willingly submits to Him in love. On the most basic level, there will be no doubt in anyone's mind that He exists and He orders everything according to His will. There will be those who reject Him, and those who accept Him, but no one will have to be taught what He expects. Some won't want to submit (see: the lake of fire) but they will know.

Another future aspect of the new covenant is that His people will be one. According to the text, the new covenant is only between God, Judah (the southern part of the kingdom after the split), and Israel (the northern kingdom). Gentiles are not mentioned anywhere. So are non-Jews locked out of the new covenant? Do we make up a new thing called the "church" and just butt our way in, pushing out Israel? This text doesn't say anything about Gentiles, so do we have to become Jews? Does it say anywhere in the Word that God has changed His mind and Jews are replaced by Gentiles? The answer to all these questions is a resounding NO. Hints like the following verse are sprinkled all through the Old Testament.

> ⁸The Lord God, who gathers the dispersed of Israel, declares, "Yet others I will gather to them, to those already gathered." (Isaiah 56:8 NASB95)

> ¹⁶"I have other sheep, which are not of this fold; I must bring them also, and they will hear My voice; and they will become one flock with one shepherd. (John 10:16 NASB95)

God tells people repeatedly that He isn't done with Israel; that He will gather them again, discipline them and bless them, and other sheep will be added. Paul describes this last process when he speaks in Romans 9 through 11 about being "grafted in to the olive tree." Israel is still the focus of God's plans and programs, and will always be that way. Non-Jews are included in the new covenant just as they are included in the One Body.

There is no place in any part of the Word where God says something called "the church" takes over for Israel. Israel is still a main part of God's plan for everyone on the planet and will always be so. For a while, God was angry with them because of their disobedience, and disciplined them by sending them out of His presence and out of the Land. Some who are descended from Jacob are not part of the Body. But never, ever does He say that He is done with them and now is setting up a separate body called "the church."

Much of the wrong attitudes about a separate church body come from simple anti-Jewishness. But even though as a group the Jews haven't always done what they should, true believers cannot write them off. Our Father tells us not to do so (remember the Zechariah 2:7-8 passage, among others). The new covenant stipulates that we will eventually be one as Jesus and God are one. It doesn't make much sense to attack your own body members. There's a word for that – cancer.

Living in the New Testament Synagogue

After Jesus ascended into heaven His followers started preaching His Words to everyone (the Jew first, then Gentiles). As they went, they created assemblies of people who wanted to follow what Jesus taught. These assemblies were made up of Jews and Gentiles in various proportions (mostly Jews at first, mostly Gentiles later), but they were still called synagogues.

In the first few decades or so after the resurrection, we have the "New Testament Synagogue," with one seemingly big problem: there is no New Testament. It will be written over the 30 or 40 years or so immediately after the resurrection (most of it before the destruction of the Temple in 70 C. E.).

Back then, a believer could check with apostles, or even the disciples of the apostles (like Timothy and Titus) if they needed some help. But as time went on there was less and less of a direct connection with them or Jesus, and more need for written books. As more time passed the new congregations could use letters written by eyewitnesses. Gospel accounts and many letters or scrolls floated around that were of dubious authenticity. It took a long time to write all the books of the New Testament, collect them and publish them as Scripture. This didn't happen until about 200 A.D.

In the meantime what did the New Testament Synagogue use as a guide for living? How did the believers compare new writings and decide which ones were Scripture until 200 A.D.? Where did the first century church get their direction for living?[81] How could they "test the spirits" (1 John 4:1) and authenticate the new writings? What did following God with a whole heart look like? Some of the letters from the apostles were generally addressed, such as Revelation, and some addressed to specific people, such as the Corinthians. How did the church in Galatia know that the book of Romans was legitimate, and that it applied to their congregations also?

Obviously, they all had in common the same book that Jesus and the apostles used. It wasn't called the Old Testament at the time. It was called the Torah or Law, or "Law, Prophets, and Writings." Sometimes they just said "the Law and the Prophets" and other times they said "it is written," "the Scriptures" or "the Word," and they may have even used the term Tanakh.[82]

So it is important to understand that all mentions of the "Scriptures" or "it is written" and such in the New Testament are referring to the Old Testament. One early reference to Paul's writings as Scripture was written by Peter in 2 Peter 3:16, but this is the only place where any of the New Testament writings are perhaps called Scripture. This is not to say the New Testament isn't Scripture, just that most of the references, and all of the quotes of Scripture, are from the Old Testament.

The focus on the New Testament in the modern church has caused a general rejection of the Old Testament as a guide for daily living. But what was good for believers in apostolic times and earlier should be good for us to live now. Loving God with all our heart, soul, mind, and strength takes us through both testaments. Both of them work together to give us a complete understanding of God's revealed plans and purposes.

---

[81] Many people want to return to the 'ideal of the first century church,' but have no idea what that really is. I'll give you a hint – look in your 'old' Testament.

[82] Comes from the first letters of the Hebrew words Torah (Law), Nevi'im (prophets), and Ketuvim (writings).

If the Old Testament was good enough for the "New Testament synagogues," it should be good enough for us too.

Most every Christian will tell you that they think the Word is whole and complete. However, most Christians also divide it up into old and new sections. They don't stop to realize that the Bible doesn't use those labels for itself—they were applied by men.

We mask the riches that God provides us in this area when we assume old is outdated, while new is updated and improved. But when a whole-Bible Christian says that the Word is complete, we mean that The Word itself doesn't recognize labels such as these. We do not accept the outdated and updated concepts. We may use the labels to help those who don't know any better, but we do not believe they are accurate. Because of hard hearts, they have been used to split up the unity of God's Word.

We label parts of God's Word law, but as I've said before all of His Words are law. Torah means "instruction" and is usually limited to the first five books of the Bible. Looked at properly, His Law is gentle instruction. Just because (for now) He allows people to make choices, and allows a wrong choice in many instances, does not mean that He finds the wrong choice acceptable.

> [30]"Therefore having overlooked the times of ignorance, God is now declaring to men that all people everywhere should repent, [31]because He has fixed a day in which He will judge the world in righteousness through a Man whom He has appointed, having furnished proof to all men by raising Him from the dead." (Acts 17:30-31 NASB95)

Everything in the New Testament is found in the Old, even if only hinted at in some instances. The New Testament is also Scripture, but it was certainly not written in a vacuum. All that Jesus and the apostles taught came from the Old Testament, rightly divided and properly understood and taught.

Commandment Math Made Easy

Rabbis have counted 613 distinct commandments in the Law. Interestingly, the late pastor Finnis Jennings Dake identified a list of 1,050 separate commands in the New Testament.[83] The Ten are a summary of the 613 (or even the 1,050) sort of like "don't eat from that tree" was really a summary of all of God's Word in the Garden. Jesus mentions two commands, "love the Lord your God with all your heart,

---

[83] To find these lists search the web. Or you can look on our site www.wholebible.com under Study Helps. Another way to find the lists is to buy The Dake Annotated Reference Bible and The 613 Mitzvot: A Contemporary Guide to the Commandments of Judaism by Ronald L. Eisenberg.

soul, and mind," and "love your neighbor as yourself." But Jesus makes the Bible math even easier with one command – "Love others as I have loved you" (John 15:12).

All of the 613 OT commands (and the 1,050) fit into one or another of the Ten. Notice that the first four of the Ten have God as a focus ("love Me"), and the next six have our fellow man as the focus ("love your neighbor").

> ¹Then God spoke all these words, saying, ²"I am the Lord your God, who brought you out of the land of Egypt, out of the house of slavery. ³"You shall have no other gods before Me. ⁴"You shall not make for yourself an idol, or any likeness of what is in heaven above or on the earth beneath or in the water under the earth. ⁵"You shall not worship them or serve them; for I, the Lord your God, am a jealous God, visiting the iniquity of the fathers on the children, on the third and the fourth generations of those who hate Me, ⁶but showing lovingkindness to thousands, to those who love Me and keep My commandments. ⁷"You shall not take the name of the Lord your God in vain, for the Lord will not leave him unpunished who takes His name in vain. ⁸"Remember the sabbath day, to keep it holy. ⁹"Six days you shall labor and do all your work, ¹⁰but the seventh day is a sabbath of the Lord your God; in it you shall not do any work, you or your son or your daughter, your male or your female servant or your cattle or your sojourner who stays with you. ¹¹"For in six days the Lord made the heavens and the earth, the sea and all that is in them, and rested on the seventh day; therefore the Lord blessed the sabbath day and made it holy. ¹²"Honor your father and your mother, that your days may be prolonged in the land which the Lord your God gives you. ¹³"You shall not murder. ¹⁴"You shall not commit adultery. ¹⁵"You shall not steal. ¹⁶"You shall not bear false witness against your neighbor. ¹⁷"You shall not covet your neighbor's house; you shall not covet your neighbor's wife or his male servant or his female servant or his ox or his donkey or anything that belongs to your neighbor." (Exodus 20:1-17 NASB95 with a similar list in Deuteronomy 5:6-21)

In summary list form, here they are again.[84]

1. No other Gods.
2. No images.
3. No taking His name in vain
4. No work on Sabbath: six days work, one day rest.
5. Honor father and mother
6. No murdering

---

[84] There are slightly different ways to number these depending on which sect is doing the numbering.

7. No adultery
8. No stealing
9. No false witness
10. No coveting

We might say that the Ten Commandments are a slight expansion of the twin ideas of loving God (first four) and loving neighbors (the other six). I think this is the reason Jesus stated that the greatest command is to love God, and the second is like it, love your neighbor.

> [28]One of the scribes came and heard them arguing, and recognizing that He had answered them well, asked Him, "What commandment is the foremost of all?" [29]Jesus answered, "The foremost is, 'Hear, O Israel! The Lord our God is one Lord; [30]and you shall love the Lord your God with all your heart, and with all your soul, and with all your mind, and with all your strength.' [31]"The second is this, 'You shall love your neighbor as yourself.' There is no other commandment greater than these." [32]The scribe said to Him, "Right, Teacher; You have truly stated that He is One, and there is no one else besides Him; [33]and to love Him with all the heart and with all the understanding and with all the strength, and to love one's neighbor as himself, is much more than all burnt offerings and sacrifices." (Mark 12:28-33 NASB95)

Neither of the two commands shows up as such in the 10 Commandments (Exodus 20:1-17). In other words, there are no commands to love God or love your neighbor as specific commands among the Ten. But they do show up as part of the Law a number of times, especially when speaking of motivation.[85] There are also other summaries of the Law, such as Psalm 15, 24:3-4, 101, and Ezekiel 18:4-9.[86] I'm sure God would be happy to just give us a couple of laws and let it go at that, like He did with Adam and Eve. But we all know how that turned out.

Looking at the two commands a little more closely, Jesus is said by some teachers to teach *only* two commandments—"love God" and "love each other." Those who insist that Jesus did away with the Law and

---

[85] See Leviticus 19:18; Deuteronomy 7:9, 10:19 for neighbor, and Exodus 20:5-6; Deuteronomy 5:10, 6:5, 10:12, 11:1, 13, 22, 13:3, 19:9, 30:6, 16, 20 (Deuteronomy 30:6 presages the New Covenant by the way) for loving God, as well as places like Deuteronomy 4:37, 7:7-8, 13 10:15, 18, 23:5, 33:3 for God loving us (His people Israel).

[86] There are many others too. Jeremiah 7:5-11, 22:3; Zechariah 7:8-13; Malachi 3:5 (really the whole book); Isaiah 1:16-17; Micah 6:8. Almost anywhere that God speaks of justice, the poor and widows, the stranger, and so on.

replaced it with these Two Commandments don't take into account that Jesus really boiled everything down to one.

> [12] "This is My commandment, that you love one another, just as I have loved you. (John 15:12 NASB95)

This command is at the heart of the first single command (don't eat the fruit) isn't it? And isn't it pretty much at the heart of anything God tells us to do? If we love God as He has loved us, then do we really need any other Law? We shouldn't, except humans do not perfectly love God or each other. Our natures still seek out selfish ways to do our own thing. So the Law was added to help define what it means to love God and each other, and train us to walk accordingly.

Way back in the Garden, there was only one command. Well, actually there were several positive commands such as "go forth, multiply, and subdue the earth," and "reproduce after your own kinds." But there was only one recorded negative command, which was "don't eat of the tree of knowledge of good and evil."

When God told Adam and Eve not to eat of this tree, He also told them they could eat of any other tree, presumably including the tree of life. They chose the wrong tree, and we've all been suffering ever since. Now we've got lots and lots of man-made laws, and a few from God. But iniquity still abounds and is getting worse. This is the fruit of the tree of knowledge, the fruit of not loving God.

The number of commands is not the point. God could write laws till His fingers cramped (assuming they could) and as long as we practice sin they would just be weird to us.

> [12] Were I to write for him my laws by the ten thousands, they would be regarded as a strange thing. (Hosea 8:12 ESV)

But just as Adam and Eve could've chosen the tree of life, we can choose it now. The Tree of Life is God and His Son Jesus, and they are revealed through the Word. We eat from this tree by following what God says, eating and drinking the body and blood of Jesus. In essence, what Adam and Eve did was turn from God's Word, represented by the "do not eat the fruit" command (or any other command) and went their own way. To follow God now, to eat of the Bread of Life or the Tree of Life, is to repent of our own ways and follow His: simply do what God says.

Living with God as Our Center

The Bible teaches that all of God's Word is for everyone. For one thing, everyone who wanted to live in Israel was supposed to be treated the same as the natives. When the promise of deliverance from Egypt was realized, and laws set up for governing the new kingdom, those laws were to apply uniformly to the whole Body.

> ⁴⁹"The same law shall apply to the native as to the stranger who sojourns among you." (Exodus 12:49 NASB95)

> ³⁴'The stranger who resides with you shall be to you as the native among you, and you shall love him as yourself, for you were aliens in the land of Egypt; I am the Lord your God. (Leviticus 19:34 NASB95)

> ²²'There shall be one standard for you; it shall be for the stranger as well as the native, for I am the Lord your God.' " (Leviticus 24:22 NASB95)

> ¹⁵'As for the assembly, there shall be one statute for you and for the alien who sojourns with you, a perpetual statute throughout your generations; as you are, so shall the alien be before the Lord. ¹⁶'There is to be one law and one ordinance for you and for the alien who sojourns with you.' " (Numbers 15:15-16 NASB95)

Our one body has one set of living oracles to live by, not two sets for two different groups. Perhaps Peter said it best.

> ³⁴Opening his mouth, Peter said: "I most certainly understand now that God is not one to show partiality, ³⁵but in every nation the man who fears Him and does what is right is welcome to Him. (Acts 10:34-35 NASB95)

"What is right" is God's Word. Everyone who does God's Word lives in His kingdom.

A casual reading through some of the prophet's writings also shows another thing: God judges all of the nations of the earth according to His Word. It is obvious He is in control, and all people are accountable to Him.[87] Even those nations who were used by Him to chastise Israel and other countries, such as Babylon, were in turn chastised because of their motivations and over-enthusiasm. Make no mistake, everyone is subject to the will of God whether they like it or not. Everyone will be judged accordingly.

The new covenant is a merging of grace and Law in a heart of flesh. Israel received the Law along with the presence of God. Grace and Law lived together in the wilderness just as they live in the heart of the

---

[87] Browse through the prophets to find prophecies concerning all sorts of godless nations. They aren't listening to Him, but He sure is paying attention to them!

believer. We wander through a figurative desert too. The Law is God's grace in action (note that the tablets are under the "mercy seat" in Exodus 40:20). Like Israel, we are learning to live with God as our center.

God did not have to give Israel instructions on how to prepare for Him to take up residence, as He did when beginning to inhabit the Tabernacle. He could've just erased everything and started over.[88] Instead He re-instructs His people in loving and holy living, acceptable to Him.

When the Law is written on the heart, it is also a gracious act. Following a few rules is not the point. The point is to learn to live with Him as our center.

> [16]For of His fullness we have all received, and grace upon grace.
> [17]For the Law was given through Moses; grace and truth were realized through Jesus Christ. (John 1:16-17 NASB95)

Verse 17 is not saying that the law stopped and grace started. It's not saying that Law doesn't have grace, or that Jesus doesn't have the Law. John says we have all received from the fullness of Jesus, grace (the Law) upon grace (the Incarnation).

Through Moses, Jesus from His fullness and grace gave the Law. Grace and truth were also "realized" or literally came to be (were born) in the Incarnation. My paraphrase: "For of (Jesus') fullness we have all received, grace upon grace. In His fullness we received grace in the Law given through Moses; (in the Incarnation) grace and truth came to be through Jesus in human form."

The Gospel

Like the New Covenant, most New Testament or part-Bible Christians cannot tell you what the gospel is either. We tend to think of it as a feel-good message about Jesus being our buddy and saving us from bad stuff. Then He allows us to do whatever we want.

The gospel, which means good news, might really make us feel good, and it should, but the message is not about feelings. It is about "God with us," which is the meaning of one of the names of Jesus (Immanuel, Isaiah 7:14 and Matthew 1:23).

Did you know that the gospel was preached to Israel at Mount Sinai by God through Moses? So says the writer of Hebrews.

> [2]For indeed we have had good news preached to us, just as they also; but the word they heard did not profit them, because it was not united by faith in those who heard. (Hebrews 4:2 NASB95)

---

[88] And He almost did after the golden calf incident Exodus 32:10.

Stephen calls the group at Sinai the "congregation in the wilderness" (Acts 7:38) and that they received "living oracles" to pass on to their kids. These living oracles were none other than the Law. This is another way of saying the gospel was preached to the church at Mount Sinai.

But why is the Law called the gospel in Hebrews? Easy. The good news at Sinai was that God was going to live with His people, and the Law was part of it. In other words, the church at Sinai had the good news of "God with us" preached to them just as we have.

The Law was to facilitate God with us, a.k.a. the gospel. God, in His grace, was taking up residence. Following the Law was (and is) a loving response (faith) to His presence. Jesus is the good news or gospel because He is God with us. But it's not as though He's a statue on the dashboard or a stained glass picture. He is with us, and speaks to us of life. The Law, His Word, facilitates His dwelling amongst us. His sacrifice makes it possible for God to dwell within us forever, and we in Him, and the Law helps us learn to live accordingly. So the living oracles are part and parcel of the gospel.

> ⁶Therefore, since it remains for some to enter it, and those who formerly had good news preached to them failed to enter because of disobedience, ⁷He again fixes a certain day, "Today," saying through David after so long a time just as has been said before, "Today if you hear His voice, Do not harden your hearts." (Hebrews 4:6-7 NASB95)

At the Sinai church meeting, the gospel went over like a lead balloon. The glitch was that it was not united with faith (trust and obedience). As the Hebrews writer says, the congregation refused to trust God and go into the Land as He said. They "failed to enter because of disobedience" (see also 1 Peter 2:7-8). We can see then that faith has an obedience component as I said a few pages back. To believe in God, or have faith, means to accept the fact of God's existence and also in His right to give instructions. The Law is a wonderful part of the "full gospel" which we live as part of our faith.

In recent times something called "the gospel" has become very self-oriented, or selfish. Instead of presenting a merciful and loving God who does not waver where justice is concerned and commands men everywhere to repent, we hear that if you were the last person on earth Jesus would still die for you. Instead of "for God so loved" we get "Jesus loves you and has a wonderful plan for your life." Some self-interest is expected, but we are not the point. The point is that a holy and righteous God who should rightfully destroy sin wherever it rears its ugly head instead gave the blood of His Son to pay for it. We are obligated to respond positively.

The gospel is something to be obeyed (Romans 10:16; 2 Thessalonians 1:8; 1 Peter 4:17). The good news of the kingdom is that Jesus makes it possible for us and God to live together. After He takes up residence in us, our thoughts and behavior line up with God's will. We must forsake our own ways and live by every word out of His mouth. Call it Law, statutes, commands, charge, bread, living oracles or whatever, but His Word is the gospel. God is with us. Are we with Him?

Inherit Eternal Life

There are three versions of a man asking Jesus "what must I do to inherit eternal life?" (Mark 10; Luke 10 and Luke 18.) Each of the men is wealthy. One is a man (and Mark says that Jesus "loved him"), one a lawyer (who was just testing, apparently), and one a ruler. The man and the ruler might be the same person, because the incidents are similar, but it might be that the question was also common. It certainly is common today.

In each case Jesus leads off His answer by pointing to the Law. Two men were told right off the bat that obedience to the commands was a first step. For them the Law was not the obstacle. It was their wealth. The lawyer was asked which of the commandments were most important, then told he had answered correctly with "love God" and "love your neighbor." Then he was told "do this and you will live." But to "do this" meant something far deeper than the lawyer was willing to go. For him the obstacle again wasn't the Law. It was the effort to self-justify.

These are not tongue in cheek responses from Jesus to see if they know that the Law doesn't save, as some teach. They are not designed to show that the men were going the wrong direction to inherit eternal life as others would have it. Jesus is being serious. He really means that if the men were to follow the Law they would inherit eternal life. Hang with me a minute and I'll tell you why.

The problem is that the men were only following part of the Law. Each thought they were doing what the Law said, but Jesus showed them their following was superficial. To the man (and/or ruler) He gave an instruction to sell what he had and follow Him that would've made sense had the man really been following the whole Law (if he was he would've recognized the Giver). To the lawyer He illustrated love with a parable. All of these are also related to the parables of the Pearl of Great Price (Matthew 13:45-46) or the Field of Treasure (Matthew 13:44). These teach us the same lesson – if you find something valuable you do everything you can to buy it. For the man/ruler with money, he/they loved money more than God or they would've ditched what they had and followed the Lord of Glory. The lawyer doing the testing was himself tested with a definition of love straight from the Law and found to be lacking.

The Law includes love and the Spirit. If these guys really knew and did the Law (or if they were abiding in the Word in the whole Bible sense) then they would know who Jesus was, and who their neighbor was. They would not have needed further instruction. They stopped at following a few laws and did not keep going to love and the Spirit. They were not doing the whole of the Law. Hence they did not recognize Jesus, and the lawyer did not know who his neighbor was.

It's not that Jesus was telling them to follow some rules and you'll be saved. He is saying that the evidence of abiding in God's Word would include the humility to love others such as God and a neighbor. You would sell possessions to follow the God you say you love and who is standing right in front of you. The goal of the Law is Jesus and His love, God in the flesh, who loved us and gave Himself for us. This was evident all through the Law and the Scriptures if one had the heart to see it. So we really can inherit eternal life if indeed the Word of God dwells in us richly, written on a heart of flesh by the Holy Spirit in love.

Free Will

Some argue that people are completely free to choose the gospel (Arminianism from Galatians 5:1 and others), while some argue that God pre-determines who will come to Him (Calvinism from Romans 8:29-30 and others). After years of arguing for Calvinism (the second one), which claims among other things that man's will is totally depraved and therefore we cannot choose God on our own, I've come to the conclusion that either way it's a useless academic argument.[89] God has freed us from being chained to sin. Anyone can come to Him on the basis of His Son's blood given for us on the cross. Righteousness for salvation is a free gift. So we can walk in His ways or Laws without fear. That's why I describe it as salvation by love. It's not that hard. What is hard is giving up our own ways.

It appears to our eyes as if we have the ability to choose left or right, good or bad or right and wrong. So we label that free will. Thinking only of the "free" part however, is like going to bed with a person you meet at a bar. That part seems fun. But the fun is over when we wake up in the morning with the bad results. We forget about two of the main parts of

---

[89] If you really want a cure for insomnia you can try to understand the difference between the five points of Calvinism (using the acronym TULIP) and Arminianism. It's a waste of time for practical purposes because all we have to do is do what God says. This is illustrated for us in such places as the rich men or lawyer discussed earlier.

free will; responsibility and accountability (Romans 14:12). That is, we forget until we're stuck with the hangover, guilt, disease, and/or a baby. Not to mention the bad stuff we do after the bad stuff we did (like abortion). The "free" part of free will is fun, but we're not free of the consequences the morning after.

We don't have a truly "free" will because we are constrained and restrained by all sorts of laws. For instance, there is the law of gravity. We cannot jump off of a tall building without having to obey this law. We might develop a machine for flying, but that only postpones a reckoning with this force of God's creation. Sooner or later, one way or the other, depending on fuel economy (your mileage may vary) we have to come down. In the end, we have a date with dirt, however the choice falls out. I told you the puns were intended. I didn't say they were good.

God purchased a choice for us through His Son, which is why our wills seem to be free. We have the free will to choose how we will respond to His love. If we do not take advantage of the work of Jesus, we will, sooner or later, have another kind of date with dirt. We cannot get away from death if we do not choose the life of God. That's where we have freedom – we can choose to live or continue dying. Not much of a choice, there.

> [16]Do you not know that when you present yourselves to someone as slaves for obedience, you are slaves of the one whom you obey, either of sin resulting in death, or of obedience resulting in righteousness? (Romans 6:16 NASB95)

The Scriptures tell us we are either slaves to sin or slaves to righteousness. There is no middle ground, though it may seem so because believers can do wrong things (and unbelievers can do right things). We sin and payment must be made, just as jumping off a tall building will require a payment. Depending on the height of the building, and how fast we flap our arms, it might take a while to hit the ground. But it doesn't mean a reckoning isn't coming soon.

> [4]In all this, they are surprised that you do not run with them into the same excesses of dissipation, and they malign you; [5]but they will give account to Him who is ready to judge the living and the dead. (1 Peter 4:4-5 NASB95)

We will all have to stand before God and answer for our free will choices, even if in the meantime it looks to us as if we can turn to the left or to the right. We are accountable for all of our "freedom." Free will doesn't mean that we are really, ultimately free to do everything, but it does mean we are free to choose the life that God offers us in His Word.

> And you, O generation, behold the word of the LORD. Have I been a wilderness to Israel, or a land of thick darkness? Why then do my people say, 'We are free, we will come no more to you'? (Jeremiah 2:31, ESV)

Few people realize what the doctrine of free will really means. We tend to think it just means "you can't make me." I suppose this is part of it (at least as far as people dealing with people). But that isn't all of it. Especially when it's between us and God, because yes, He can "make us" if He chooses. He will "make" people reside in a place of their choosing apart from Him eventually (the Lake of Fire). If the will is truly free, and I believe that it is within the boundaries that God gives, then the responsibility for what we choose is also absolute.

If we choose wrong, we cannot say that "the devil made me do it." If we choose right, we will get credit in eternal life, though it is God who makes the right choice possible. We would not be able to choose life no matter how badly we wanted to exercise our free will without the sacrifice of Jesus. It would simply not be available. We give God the glory for making us free. Freedom in Christ means free to choose life in His Word. We are free to live, and free to die.

What About the Temple?

For a while, the temple was where God lived, and was the "heart" of the nation that He wanted to make into a light for all peoples. That didn't work out like He wanted. The temple was torn down, the nation scattered. But wait. Was the temple really gone?

> [24]For Christ did not enter a holy place made with hands, a mere copy of the true one, but into heaven itself, now to appear in the presence of God for us; [25]nor was it that He would offer Himself often, as the high priest enters the holy place year by year with blood that is not his own. (Hebrews 9:24-25 NASB95)

It was a *copy* of the temple that was destroyed. See, the original temple is in heaven.[90] It has always been there. When the tabernacle was built, it was exactly according to the original (Exodus 25:9, 40; Numbers 8:4; Acts 7:44; Hebrews 8:5). When the temples were built,[91] they were also built according to the original specifications (at least Solomon's; see 1 Chronicles 28:11-19). God's temple in heaven is the pattern for the copies. It has never been in danger of being destroyed.

---

[90] Revelation 7:15, 11:19, 14:15-18, 15:5-8 etc.
[91] Solomon's temple, the second temple built during the time of Ezra and Nehemiah, and the later expansion called Herod's Temple.

Many people think that because the temple copy was torn down (about 70 C. E.) the Law was eliminated. For instance, Frank Viola in his book pagan Christianity has this to say.[92]

> "The old Mosaic economy of sacred priests, sacred buildings, sacred rituals, and sacred objects has been forever destroyed by the cross of Jesus Christ. In addition, it has been replaced by a nonhierarchical, nonritualistic, nonliturgical organism called the ekklesia (church)."

Leaders such as Frank speak this way of "shadows" and "copies" being "fulfilled" and thus eliminated. But they speak in part Bible ignorance, because the Temple is still in existence. It's just in heaven, with Jesus as our High Priest. God's holy instructions are still valid, as they have always been. He just moves them into our hearts, along with His Spirit. What is holy is still holy. What is not holy is still not holy.

If the shadows and copies of the Law were supposedly "fulfilled" and thus eliminated as we talked a little about in other places, why was it that the Temple veil was only torn in two? Why wasn't the Temple destroyed in an instant? There is evidence that believers went to the Temple and sacrificed while it was still present (about 40 years after the resurrection of Jesus). This doesn't make sense. And not only did the Temple stay around after the shadows and copies were "fulfilled," another Temple will be built in the future and sacrifices will be made while Jesus is on the throne in an earthly kingdom. The shadows and copies argument doesn't agree with the Bible.

The period we live in now is not the only time the earth has been without a temple. There was also a long period between the destruction of the first temple and the building of the second. From the Garden to the Tabernacle there was no temple either. In fact, the amount of time with a tabernacle or temple (about 1,500 years give or take a century or two) is a much shorter interval than time without it (about 4,500 years).

And guess what? Everyone born during all those different time slots, whether there was a temple or not, Jew or Gentile, still had to live as God wanted them to live. Obedience to God is never based on the presence or absence of a temple.

> You looked for much, and behold, it came to little. And when you brought it home, I blew it away. Why? declares the LORD of hosts. Because of my house that lies in ruins, while each of you busies himself with his own house. Therefore the heavens above

---

[92] From the book 'pagan Christianity?' Frank Viola and George Barna, Tyndale House Publishers, Inc., 2008, p. 27.

you have withheld the dew, and the earth has withheld its produce. (Haggai 1:9–10, ESV)

One of the side effects of claiming that "the old Mosaic economy of sacred priests, sacred buildings, sacred rituals, and sacred objects has been forever destroyed by the cross of Jesus Christ" is that we ignore His house while "each of us busies himself with his own house." Of course "His house" is also the house made up of believers, because we are His temple. He lives in us as He dwelt in a tent and a temple. But in view of this we should be embarrassed that we have no Temple. Our neglect of a temple is related to our neglect of the Body or Temple of believers too. We make money offerings at huge stadiums built for sporting events having some slight benefit for the body but nothing for the soul. Mega-churches haul in millions of dollars and spend them on campuses and monuments to pride like huge meeting halls or TV shows. We build comfortable theater seating for thousands and huge TV's for seeing the star pastor preaching a false gospel of freedom in Christ which then gives license to ignore God's Word.

God's house in the meantime is dust. We hide behind the claim of not knowing where to build, but we put no resources into finding the site. Many churches are "divesting" themselves of investment in Israel when we should be putting everything we've got there. Some cheesy pagan temple for a hateful and unjust moon god stops us in our tracks from tearing the unclean thing down and building God's house. A temple will be built once again (according to Ezekiel) but shame on us that we put more effort into our own comfortable houses and none into His.

Shame on us.

There were times when the Temple fell out of use. Other times it didn't get a lot of respect, and was defiled by idols and idol worship. After a long while of this kind of treatment God's glory finally departed according to Ezekiel. Yet standing or not, filled with idols or neglected, God has never stopped trying to get people into His "house." Or He into ours.

The Temple is a picture of the heart of a nation as well as the heart of an individual. As an illustration of the heart of the nation, it reminds us of lost intimacy with Him and how quickly we forget or take for granted all that He is and has or has done. Though the copy of the heavenly temple was destroyed, the picture still reminds us of heartless lip service and that the mere presence of a temple doesn't grant protection from our lawlessness actions. As an illustration of the heart of the individual, the copy of God's temple shows us the glorious possibilities if He has taken up residence inside.

God's Barbecue

Now let's talk about animal sacrifices, or what I like to call God's barbecue. Animal sacrifices were never, ever, intended to save anyone. There is no mention anywhere in the Word of eternal life given through the blood of an animal.[93] The best that an animal sacrifice could ever do was show obedience.

> [6] By lovingkindness and truth iniquity is atoned for, And by the fear of the LORD one keeps away from evil. (Proverbs 16:6 NASB95)

If a person's sacrifice was accepted, then the person was accepted. Accepted does not mean eternal life. It just means that God hears and approves, and/or forgives sin. This was because the sacrifice was accepted based on a person's heart, as well as his or her actions. A person who loves God and wants to do what He says will try to present a sacrifice the way God wants. Like Able. The sloppy person shows how little they care. Like Cain (Genesis 4:3-5).

Animal sacrifice is a shared experience with God and with others in the community. Most sacrifices are shared by all the people involved (Leviticus 7). Some sacrifices are all God's, and are burned completely. Parts of the other sacrifices are God's (the part that is burned up) part is for the priests (for the work of prep and cooking and they have no land of their own) and part is for the person doing the offering (and family and friends). That's why I call it God's barbecue.

The sacrifices were a reminder of Jesus. They were stand-ins, so to speak, for what would eventually happen with Him. We can think of them as memorials, because that's how God thought of them. The blood and the burning were like a constant prayer, asking God to treat the people with mercy and grace on the basis of the Ultimate Sacrifice (Jesus).

People also needed to be reminded of their sin and the price of disobedience (Hebrews 10:3). That's why the humble submission of the person doing the offering was just as important as the procedure. If sacrifices were offered merely as part of lip service, they didn't work. The death of the animal was not as important as faith (trust and action).

> [10]Hear the word of the Lord, You rulers of Sodom; Give ear to the instruction of our God, You people of Gomorrah. [11]"What are your multiplied sacrifices to Me?" Says the Lord. "I have had enough of burnt offerings of rams And the fat of fed cattle; And I take no pleasure in the blood of bulls, lambs or goats. [12]"When you come to appear before Me, Who requires of you this

---

[93] For it is impossible for the blood of bulls and goats to take away sins. (Hebrews 10:4 NASB95)

> trampling of My courts? ^{13}"Bring your worthless offerings no longer, Incense is an abomination to Me. New moon and sabbath, the calling of assemblies— I cannot endure iniquity and the solemn assembly. ^{14}"I hate your new moon festivals and your appointed feasts, They have become a burden to Me; I am weary of bearing them. ^{15}"So when you spread out your hands in prayer, I will hide My eyes from you; Yes, even though you multiply prayers, I will not listen. Your hands are covered with blood. ^{16}"Wash yourselves, make yourselves clean; Remove the evil of your deeds from My sight. Cease to do evil, ^{17}Learn to do good; Seek justice, Reprove the ruthless, Defend the orphan, Plead for the widow. (Isaiah 1:10-17 NASB95)

God tells Isaiah in this passage that He "had enough of burnt offerings" because they were only lip service. He was not making an arbitrary change. Sacrifices and holy days were (and are) rendered ineffective if they were mixed with iniquity or lawlessness (verse 13).

If our hands are "covered with blood," which isn't from the sacrifices, the sacrifice isn't acceptable. The effectiveness of the sacrifices was based on the future final sacrifice of the only begotten Son of God, or they never would've worked (such as they did) in the first place. The sacrifice of the Christ allowed God to dwell in the midst of Israel in a tent.

> ^{24}"Father, I desire that they also, whom You have given Me, be with Me where I am, so that they may see My glory which You have given Me, for You loved Me before the foundation of the world. (John 17:24 NASB95)

There are lots of reasons for animal sacrifices besides for sin. These include thanksgiving, fellowship, and peace. Isaiah 43 mentions honoring God (verse 23), calling on Him (verse 22), and satisfying Him (verse 24). But salvation was never a reason in and of itself. If salvation were the goal, then when Solomon offers 22,000 oxen and 120,000 sheep (2 Chronicles 7:5) was he "more saved" than the person who could only afford a couple of birds (Leviticus 5:7)? Of course not.

Sacrifices were well known long before Sinai and in many other countries. Most of these were perversions of the original sacrifices God ordained way back with Adam and Eve.[94] None of them "saved" anyone. The 70 bull sacrifices during Tabernacles in Numbers 29:12-35 are

---

[94] Genesis 3:21 they were given "garments of skin" which probably came from a sacrifice and in Genesis 4:4 Able offers "the firstborn of the flock and of their fat portions"

generally understood as being for the nations.[95] Did the sacrifice of bulls "save" the nations? Did the bogus sacrifices performed by many other people save them? The easy answer: no.

The Order of Melchizedek

According to Hebrews, we have a high priest that ministers in the heavenly temple on a continual basis.

> [1]My little children, I am writing these things to you so that you may not sin. And if anyone sins, we have an Advocate with the Father, Jesus Christ the righteous; [2]and He Himself is the propitiation for our sins; and not for ours only, but also for those of the whole world. (1 John 2:1-2 NASB95)

> [23]The former priests, on the one hand, existed in greater numbers because they were prevented by death from continuing, [24]but Jesus, on the other hand, because He continues forever, holds His priesthood permanently. [25]Therefore He is able also to save forever those who draw near to God through Him, since He always lives to make intercession for them. (Hebrews 7:23-25 NASB95)

> [33] Who shall bring any charge against God's elect? It is God who justifies. [34] Who is to condemn? Christ Jesus is the one who died—more than that, who was raised—who is at the right hand of God, who indeed is interceding for us. (Romans 8:33-34 ESV)

So much for a "nonhierarchical, nonritualistic, nonliturgical organism." Just because you can't see it doesn't mean it's not really there. The writer of Hebrews tells us that there was a change in the Law because of a change in the priesthood (Hebrews 7:12) not because God eliminated any part of it. If we had a temple here, we (believers) would still make at the very least freewill offerings of peace, thanksgiving, and fellowship. The apostles used it regularly,[96] including sacrifices (Acts 21:26). There is evidence Gentiles offered sacrifices too (Acts 8:27).

Believers may not (all) be Levitical priests, but we can still perform many similar functions. We can live and teach His Words. We can tell people of God's invitation (nay, command) to become part of His kingdom. We can offer sacrifices of praise (Hebrews 13:15). John the Baptist was a Levitical priest (Luke 1:5-25) who chose a different way to minister than in the corrupt establishment. We can do the same. Believers are part of the kingdom of priests (Exodus 19:6; Revelation 1:6, 5:10).

---

[95] This comes from association with the 70 nations in Genesis 10.
[96] Acts 2:46, 47, 3:1-8, 5:20, 21, 25, 42, 21:26-30, 22:17, 24:6, 12, 24:17,18, 25:8, and 26:21.

> ⁵'Now then, if you will indeed obey My voice and keep My covenant, then you shall be My own possession among all the peoples, for all the earth is Mine; ⁶and you shall be to Me a kingdom of priests and a holy nation.' These are the words that you shall speak to the sons of Israel." (Exodus 19:5-6 NASB95)

All believers are kings and priests as is evident if you read the Word. We are just not priests after the Levitical pattern. Our high priest is after the order of Melchizedek, so we are too. We have direct access to God and can live and teach God's Word to anyone who wants to learn. It's just that as Jesus said, our kingdom is not of this world. Believers are the ones spoken to in the section below. Unbelievers certainly wouldn't be called "priests of the Lord" (verse 6).

> ¹The Spirit of the Lord God is upon me, Because the Lord has anointed me To bring good news to the afflicted; He has sent me to bind up the brokenhearted, To proclaim liberty to captives And freedom to prisoners; ²To proclaim the favorable year of the Lord And the day of vengeance of our God; To comfort all who mourn, ³To grant those who mourn in Zion, Giving them a garland instead of ashes, The oil of gladness instead of mourning, The mantle of praise instead of a spirit of fainting. So they will be called oaks of righteousness, The planting of the Lord, that He may be glorified. ⁴Then they will rebuild the ancient ruins, They will raise up the former devastations; And they will repair the ruined cities, The desolations of many generations. ⁵Strangers will stand and pasture your flocks, And foreigners will be your farmers and your vinedressers. ⁶But you will be called the priests of the Lord; You will be spoken of as ministers of our God. You will eat the wealth of nations, And in their riches you will boast. (Isaiah 61:1-6 NASB95. See also Luke 4:14-21)

Every believer is a priest when we act like priests; serving God and representing Him to others who do not know Him. Paid positions doing "ministry" for us are not ordained by God in any way shape or form in the Scriptures,[97] and those paid people are not given the authority to stop us from following what God says. We don't need their permission to follow the Word. At most, we have elders (old guys) sometimes called

---

[97] 1 Corinthians 12 and Ephesians 4 mention gifts of certain able men and 1 Timothy 5 speaks of 'double honor' given to them, but the system of tithe-receiving pseudo-priesthood that we have now is not mentioned.

shepherds, and we share good things with them. But they do not have the final word on our practice of The Word.

The Temple Rebuilt

Ezekiel describes another temple (chapters 40 through 48; see also Zechariah 6:11-15 for another instance) that hasn't been built yet. It has priests and animal sacrifices. It looks like this temple will be built after the return of the Christ, during His thousand year reign (Ezekiel 44:2).

> ^{14}"Yet I will appoint them to keep charge of the house, of all its service and of all that shall be done in it. ^{15}"But the Levitical priests, the sons of Zadok, who kept charge of My sanctuary when the sons of Israel went astray from Me, shall come near to Me to minister to Me; and they shall stand before Me to offer Me the fat and the blood," declares the Lord God. ^{16}"They shall enter My sanctuary; they shall come near to My table to minister to Me and keep My charge. (Ezekiel 44:14-16 NASB95)

> ^{23}"Moreover, they shall teach My people the difference between the holy and the profane, and cause them to discern between the unclean and the clean. ^{24}"In a dispute they shall take their stand to judge; they shall judge it according to My ordinances. They shall also keep My laws and My statutes in all My appointed feasts and sanctify My sabbaths. (Ezekiel 44:23-24 NASB95)

So how do we square the new temple with the once-for-all sacrifice of Jesus (Romans 6:10, 1 Peter 3:18)? Some try to stick with the idea of two separate programs, one for Israel and one for the church. So the new temple must be for Israel, in their reckoning.

Clearly, however, a temple and animal sacrifices mean something other than salvation. Otherwise why build another temple at all, when Jesus is right there on the throne? It isn't necessary to make up separate programs for separate people groups. All God's people will one day be giving offerings in a brand new temple.

> ^{16}Then it will come about that any who are left of all the nations that went against Jerusalem will go up from year to year to worship the King, the Lord of hosts, and to celebrate the Feast of Booths. ^{17}And it will be that whichever of the families of the earth does not go up to Jerusalem to worship the King, the Lord of hosts, there will be no rain on them. ^{18}If the family of Egypt does not go up or enter, then no rain will fall on them; it will be the plague with which the Lord smites the nations who do not go up to celebrate the Feast of Booths. ^{19}This will be the punishment of Egypt, and the punishment of all the nations who

> do not go up to celebrate the Feast of Booths. (Zechariah 14:16-19 NASB95)

Animal sacrifices in a temple are simply memorials or reminders of the work of Jesus on the cross.[98] When the temple of Ezekiel is built, all of His people will sacrifice there. Salvation will not be the issue, just like it's not the issue now and never was. The issue is abiding.

The presence or absence of a temple copy really doesn't mean all that much in some ways. It is the presence of God in our hearts that makes the difference. Even when the temple copy was around, it was misused.

> [4]"Do not trust in deceptive words, saying, 'This is the temple of the Lord, the temple of the Lord, the temple of the Lord.' [5]"For if you truly amend your ways and your deeds, if you truly practice justice between a man and his neighbor, [6]if you do not oppress the alien, the orphan, or the widow, and do not shed innocent blood in this place, nor walk after other gods to your own ruin, [7]then I will let you dwell in this place, in the land that I gave to your fathers forever and ever. [8]"Behold, you are trusting in deceptive words to no avail. [9]"Will you steal, murder, and commit adultery and swear falsely, and offer sacrifices to Baal and walk after other gods that you have not known, [10]then come and stand before Me in this house, which is called by My name, and say, 'We are delivered!'—that you may do all these abominations? [11]"Has this house, which is called by My name, become a den of robbers in your sight? Behold, I, even I, have seen it," declares the Lord. (Jeremiah 7:4-11 NASB95)

There were times when Israel used the temple (like the Ark of the Covenant) as a talisman. They sinned then went and did the sacrifices (with "bloody hands") to get clean.

Christians are no better. We use the name of Jesus or a crucifix in much the same way. We sin all we want during the week. Then we go to the "temple" on Sunday and weep while we sing songs with raised hands expecting that we will be all clean again. Obviously, temple or no temple, if lip service is all we offer to God, it is never acceptable to Him. We can't depend on a temple, the name Jesus, a communion wafer or a crucifix to protect us from iniquity we harbor.

---

[98] Isaiah 19:19-20 says that there will be an altar to the Lord in the midst of Egypt as a "sign and a witness."

Choose Life

When Josiah found God's book of life, also known as the Law, he was stricken to his core and instantly adjusted his life to it. He jumped whole-heartedly into the living oracles and grabbed all that God commanded. He did not rationalize that the Laws must be "old" so therefore only applied to some earlier group of people. Neither did he reinterpret them as only "spiritual" so he could ignore some.

With his heart of flesh he entered into the covenant (or Promise) that God has had with man since the beginning ("I will be your God and you will be my people"). He could've acted like the wicked kings and ignored what God said, but he chose life. He bought into God's Word to the extent that he led his people in the best observance of a Passover feast ever (2 Chronicles 35). It was so good nobody had seen one like it before. It was better even than the Passovers during the times of the Judges or any other king (2 Kings 23:22 and 2 Chronicles 35:18).

We have the same choice. When we discover all the words of His book of Law we can join in, or we can continue to rebel. The death and resurrection of Jesus makes possible a free-will heart-to-heart relationship with the Father. Our tender heart of flesh responds to all of God's Word by giving our whole life to Him in return. If that means changing what we eat, what we wear or how we act, that's a small enough sacrifice compared to what He gives us.

The gospel includes the law, because the good news is "God with us" and His Word is part of the package. We don't need a temple in order to live it. As priests of the Melchizedek (King of Righteousness) order, we live the Law and teach it to everyone who will listen. "Doing what is right," as Peter says in Acts 10:35, is always in style. The whole-Bible priest knows the Word is one faith given to His one body of believers. It is always fresh and new, and always applicable to all of His people, all of the time. It is never obsolete or outdated.

Temples have no purpose if we only serve God with our lips. If our hearts aren't in it, a temple (or an ark) is just an empty box. Animal sacrifices, whether before or after the cross, are only effective if they are made by a heart obedient to the Spirit of God's Word or Law. We will get to offer these beautiful memorials again at the family barbecues with God and Josiah at the reunion in the kingdom, after a new house is built by Jesus. All people on the earth at the time will come to the house warming, or they'll be sorry they didn't. One way or the other, God will be all in all. From the least to the greatest, everyone will know Him and His Law.

6 A Whole Bible

26"Therefore, I testify to you this day that I am innocent of the blood of all men. 27"For I did not shrink from declaring to you the whole purpose of God. (Acts 20:26-27 NASB95)

Jesus didn't just waltz into the Jewish community and tell them everything they believed in and were doing was wrong. He never said God's Law was wrong, old, eliminated, or outdated. That's the impression we get if we listen to most church teaching. If He had tried something like that, He would've been rejected immediately on good grounds (instead of later with no grounds). Israel had been spanked repeatedly till New Testament times precisely because they *weren't* following God's Word as they should. They had learned the hard way that they should follow only and exactly what God said. Except they didn't learn the lesson quite as completely as God intended. They had finally learned that God was the only god to be worshipped, but in their zeal to obey only Him they had twisted the life out of His living oracles. They developed a "part Bible" way of looking at the Law. Their religious leaders had decided to help God out by interpretations of the Law that added much God didn't command. They had also set aside other parts through tradition, all the while thinking they were still doing what God wanted.

In this section, we're going to do like Jesus did and look at rabbi's teachings, comparing His corrections to current interpretations and tradition. We'll also look at the apostles teachings in the same way. As we'll see, the corrections of Jesus have been "corrected" by the church in much the same way the rabbis corrected God. The corrections by Jesus and the apostles used the "whole Bible" the way God intended. Sadly, the church mostly does not. Like Israel at the time, the church has done a decent job in some ways teaching about Jesus. But also like them we've added a bunch of wrong interpretation and tradition in our zeal to follow Him.

Some teachers read a conflict into the New Testament writings between Law and grace. For instance, the story of the woman caught in the act of adultery (John 8) is frequently presented as Jesus (grace) against the antiquated Law (the accusers). Grace wins because Jesus tears up the arguments from the Law. Now many people think that "you can't judge me because everyone sins." On the contrary, the real conflict was between Jesus using the Law (with grace) correctly against the mob who was not. Grace still wins because grace is a big part of God's Law.

Jesus taught continuity with the Law, and the first century church lived it.[99] There are lots of instances but we'll just look at some of the biggies. Most of these have either been ignored or misinterpreted to remove the absolute, objective aspect of obedience (remember, we can also think of this as abiding). But far from doing away with the Law, or changing it for an imaginary new church, Jesus and the apostles were preaching it and New Testament believers were learning and living it.

There are twenty-seven books in the New Testament, but I challenge you to try and find even one instance in the entire package of a negative word about the Law. There are warnings against misusing it. There are teachings pitting the Law against petrified tradition and attractive but wrong interpretations. It is filled up full with God's love as it should've been all along. But never is there a bad thing said about God's Law. In fact, the Law is established, upheld, referred to and applied to daily living. It could not be otherwise since the books are part of God's Word. So let's take a fresh look at the use of the Law in the New Testament.

The (Second) Sermon on the Mount and the Law

Matthew in chapters five, six and seven of his gospel account records for us the second Sermon on the Mount. Yep, I said second because the first was at Mt. Sinai with Moses, who relayed it to Israel. The second is similar to the first; even identical. Since Jesus actually gave both sermons, we would expect they would sound alike, which they do. In fact, what we really have here is Jesus cutting through man's false teachings about what He set down at Sinai. He repeats His message over and over and over and over in the Bible. Man's *interpretations* or applications of the Law to that point were lacking, so Jesus corrected them.

In 5:17 He says He did not come to abolish the Law and the Prophets, but to fulfill. The word "abolish" is clear – it means eliminate (or destroy, or change). As in "I did not come to eliminate the Law." The word "fulfill" then obviously means something different. It wouldn't make very much sense for Jesus to say, "I did not come to abolish the Law, but to abolish it." It doesn't mean that He came to "fulfill" and then "abolish" it either. The word "fulfill," used as the opposite of "abolish," means to interpret correctly so that words are given their proper meaning. It's clear in this context Jesus is saying He would not destroy the Law through wrong interpretation. So we can read this statement as, "I did not

---

[99] If you want more, try a book like <u>Uses of the Old Testament in the New</u> by Walter C. Kaiser, Jr., Wipf & Stock Publishers, December 1, 2001. It's not specifically about the Law, but it does touch on this and other uses.

come to remove or destroy or change the Law, but to correctly interpret it and put it back on a firm foundation."

The word "fulfill" by itself also means to "fill up full," as in filling up the foundation forms of a house with cement. The religious leaders had the framework (Moses' teachings) but had added empty interpretation and tradition. Jesus cements His intention by telling us that even the tiniest part of God's Law will not change until heaven and earth pass away. Some try to make the phrase "until all is accomplished" to mean Jesus changed the Law through the resurrection. But heaven and earth certainly did not pass away at that time. Therefore the Law still stands, placed on firm foundation by the Giver and Interpreter. It is still absolutely applicable today.

Jesus framed His Matthew teachings in terms of "you have heard (thus and so) but I say to you..." He is NOT saying that "God's Word said this, and I'm changing it to this." Not when He gave the Law in the first place, and when He just said He would not destroy or change it.

Instead, Jesus was saying, "You have heard this other interpretation (limited to action) but I say that this is the correct interpretation" (including motivation or the heart). The teachings Jesus gives in support of this include other parts of the Word and real-world examples. Remember too that behind all of His interpretations is the perfection of God especially as expressed in the Garden before the Fall. In other words, the standard of comparison for sin is not just actions; it is the presence of anything not in line with God's love in the heart.

Religious leaders had limited sin to actions alone. So as long as a person didn't do the action, then in their view they were sinless. Jesus plugs the heart back in, showing that no one is righteous apart from God even in their heart (Psalm 14:1-3 53:1-3; Romans 3:10-18).

What Jesus teaches in the second Sermon on the Mount is also scattered throughout the OT. That is, if one were to look (as one example look at Isaiah 66). The Law, for instance, is summarized as "justice and righteousness," especially for widows and fatherless children, in places such as Deuteronomy 10:18, 24:17, 27:19; Isaiah 1:17, 23, 10:2; and Jeremiah 22:3. His teachings restore the wholeness of His Word, by putting back things taken out by Jewish leaders. These things include motives, love and the Spirit. Otherwise known as "heart."

Examples of Fulfilling the Law

Some of the real-world examples that Jesus properly interpreted or "filled up full" concern murder (5:21-26) adultery and divorce[100] (5:27-

---

[100] Matthew 5:31-32 (and 19:9) could perhaps be translated "Whoever should dismiss (separate from) his wife (a legal wife) let him give to her a certificate of divorce (legally cancelling the

32) vows (5:33-37 – see also Deuteronomy 23:22, 24; Malachi 2:16) and hating enemies (5:43-48). Religious leaders had cut them out of context, robbed them of the Spirit, and sometimes just made things up. Jesus puts the love back into the Law where it belongs, and re-emphasizes God's intentions.

Anger for instance comes from pride. There is no love in pride. That's why it is similar to murder – because anger and hate are so far removed from God's love that murder is not far behind. God hates divorce because love is ignored. We should watch it that we don't pop off and make a vow, because that's pride and God will hold us to it. And "hating your enemy" isn't even in the Law. It's not that hard to see that Jesus isn't rewriting the Law. He's just rewriting other people's opinions about the Law.

Of the available ways of applying God's Word, Jesus tells us that the most accurate is to include the thoughts which give birth to the action. The heart. Anyone that has ever raised children knows that we come out of the womb knowing how to sin. When we get to be adults we are better at hiding it. Sin is a leaning, or intent, and sins are the fruit of the leaning. Sometimes leaning goes all the way to an overt sin, and sometimes it stays hidden. Either way Jesus says we have sin. An example is lust. Lusting is the same as coveting, and Jesus says it is adultery whether acted out or not.

The point is that if all the laws are properly balanced, then the conclusion is a lot different than men's teachings to that point. God's love includes a broad understanding and practice of God's Word in all instances, even down to the roots of actions. The "heart" of the matter, if you will, which takes us right back to the New Covenant.

The so-called "golden rule" is another example of the Law fulfilled. This is plain to see if the real goal is to follow God's Law through its engraving on our hearts of flesh.

> [12]"In everything, therefore, treat people the same way you want them to treat you, for this is the Law and the Prophets. (Matthew 7:12 NASB95)

This is part of both sermons (on the mounts) and fits in nicely with His other expanded meanings. It is another way of saying *"love your neighbor as yourself"* (Leviticus 19:18). In John 15:12 Jesus further fills this up full with an old chestnut *"…love one another as I have loved you."* In this case, He is also dealing with motivations, but in a positive way.

---

marriage). But I say to you, who ever should dismiss (not legally divorce) his wife, except for the matter of prostitution, makes her commit adultery; and who ever marries a dismissed woman (is not legally divorced) commits adultery. Thanks to Shari for this idea.

Instead of saying "don't do this or that," Jesus shifts the focus to the individual. Whatever way a person wants to be treated should be the rule for how they treat others. For more examples of this see verses such as Exodus 12:49, Leviticus 24:22, and Numbers 15:15-16 and 29. This rule makes it easy to follow the Law, and to apply God's Word in any situation.

The Testing of Jesus and the Law

Jesus had a number of tests about the Law given to Him by Jewish leaders. Five major tests were on signs, divorce, paying taxes, the greatest command, and the stoning of the adulterous woman. The tests were designed for Him to fail, though. The leaders thought they had Him trapped, but He surprised them with wise answers using the "fulfilled" Law the way it was intended to be used. He stuck to the letter and the Spirit better than they did. Indeed, Jesus "filled the Law up full" as He said He would. He filled the Law full of love for God; the love it was supposed to have in the first place. He was able to bring both the Spirit and the Letter together in a way that is obvious to anyone not blinded by hypocrisy and pride.

The Test on Signs

The first test was a demand for a sign (Matthew 16:1; Mark 8:11; Luke 11:16). The religious leaders wanted a "sign" because Moses used some. The Prophet that was to come, which Moses spoke about, was supposed to be like him (Deuteronomy 18:15-19). So they reasoned that if Jesus were the Prophet He would use similar signs. They should've reasoned that the Prophet would be humble and hold to God's Law completely. This would in fact be more "like Moses." Remember that Israel wanted signs from Moses too, but were never satisfied with them. They were not really interested in signs, ever. Except maybe as a substitute for TV.

Signs don't do anything to convert anybody. They sure didn't work with Israel, nor do they work now. How can a sign do anything for those who refuse to see? Worse, who see and refuse to obey? It's like a fireworks show where everybody oohs and ahhs. But the end of the show is also the end of the impact.

Jesus again skillfully goes to the heart of the matter. First, He says they couldn't properly interpret or obey a sign from God anyway. This is a biblical equivalent of "blind in one eye and can't see out of the other" as my dad used to say. Second, He said that only the sign of Jonah would be given (Matthew 12:39, 16:4; Luke 11:29). Make a note for yourself here that the people of Nineveh repented at the mere preaching of Jonah. He didn't use any signs.

Of course, signs were on display all around the leaders. Jesus was healing, casting out demons and raising people from the dead left and right. However, they refused to act on the signs. They were like children sitting in the market place, singing to each other in the wisdom of the world. They wanted Him to dance to their music. But Jesus doesn't dance like that for beans.

> [31]"To what then shall I compare the men of this generation, and what are they like? [32]"They are like children who sit in the market place and call to one another, and they say, 'We played the flute for you, and you did not dance; we sang a dirge, and you did not weep.' [33]"For John the Baptist has come eating no bread and drinking no wine, and you say, 'He has a demon!' [34]"The Son of Man has come eating and drinking, and you say, 'Behold, a gluttonous man and a drunkard, a friend of tax collectors and sinners!' [35]"Yet wisdom is vindicated by all her children." (Luke 7:31-35 NASB95)

He wasn't going to give them the dog and pony show they wanted (Matthew 11:16; Luke 7:32). His wisdom, especially in the proper use of the Law, was proven by all of His actions. If the leaders really wanted confirmation that Jesus was the Prophet there was plenty of evidence to go around. The refusal to jump when they said jump went a long way towards His arrest and false conviction. No, signs have about as much chance of making hard-hearted people "see" as the United States Marine Band playing "Stars and Stripes Forever" has of making deaf people hear.

Doing a miracle is related to asking for a sign. People want their senses stimulated with signs and miracles, but this is not the same as a softened heart. Is it better to do miracles, or just do what God says? The false prophet (coming soon to a government near you) will do all sorts of miracles to get people to worship the beast. He will be very successful, for a while, because there are those who want any miracle except the miracle of changing a heart of stone to a heart of flesh.

According to Jesus, many people who merely do miracles (or "signs") *will not* enter His Kingdom. The person acting on His Word *will* enter (this could include miracles, properly done).

> [22]"Many will say to Me on that day, 'Lord, Lord, did we not prophesy in Your name, and in Your name cast out demons, and in Your name perform many miracles?' [23]"And then I will declare to them, 'I never knew you; depart from Me, you who practice lawlessness.' [24]"Therefore everyone who hears these words of Mine and acts on them, may be compared to a wise

man who built his house on the rock. (Matthew 7:22-24 NASB95)

The one who performs a miracle, but is "lawless," will have to depart. The one who did no miracles but does the will of God gets to enter. Later, Jesus will tell Thomas that a person who does not see, yet believes (acts on His Word) is more blessed than the one needing a sign.

> ^{27}Then He said to Thomas, "Reach here with your finger, and see My hands; and reach here your hand and put it into My side; and do not be unbelieving, but believing." ^{28}Thomas answered and said to Him, "My Lord and my God!" ^{29}Jesus said to him, "Because you have seen Me, have you believed? Blessed are they who did not see, and yet believed." (John 20:27-29 NASB95)

A miracle or sign is a piece of cake. What's really hard is taking the small steps of obedience to God on a daily basis, even when no one is looking.

The Test on Divorce

Except for adultery, there is no good reason to divorce[101] (and even adultery is not open and shut). But that didn't stop men in the hardness of their hearts from pursuing wrongness (Matthew 19:3; Mark 10:2). As we already noticed, God never approved divorce and the Law didn't give permission either (allowed because of hard hearts only). Sometimes it might be the only thing to do. Other times it might be beyond one's control. That still doesn't mean it is a good thing. Leaders looked at the Law and decided that divorce for any reason was okay, just because there was no rule saying don't do it. At least for the hard-hearted.

> ^{13}"This is another thing you do: you cover the altar of the Lord with tears, with weeping and with groaning, because He no longer regards the offering or accepts it with favor from your hand. ^{14}"Yet you say, 'For what reason?' Because the Lord has been a witness between you and the wife of your youth, against whom you have dealt treacherously, though she is your companion and your wife by covenant. ^{15}"But not one has done so who has a remnant of the Spirit. And what did that one do while he was seeking a godly offspring? Take heed then to your spirit, and let no one deal treacherously against the wife of your

---

[101] I am not trying to provide an in-depth study on divorce here. The book is almost too long as it is. It seems to me that 1) Divorce is just not good unless absolutely necessary; 2) It is really not all that necessary all that often; and 3) Sometimes a divorce may be the only option, or it might've been forced on someone by no fault of their own.

youth. ¹⁶"For I hate divorce," says the Lord, the God of Israel, "and him who covers his garment with wrong," says the Lord of hosts. "So take heed to your spirit, that you do not deal treacherously." (Malachi 2:13-16 NASB95)

This highlights one of the reasons for the Law in the first place. Instead of following what God says from the heart in the Spirit with love, we look for any excuse to express our sin. Marriage is by vows. Jesus tells us in other places that God will require us to answer for broken ones. What the people testing Jesus were really saying is they had given themselves permission to sin, and wanted Jesus to keep them off the hook. Instead, Jesus trumps their "not-quite-Law card," and hooks them with His own actual Law card – which is the original pattern of one male and one female. This heart response should have told them all they needed to know about divorce. Love does not divorce.

The Test On Paying Taxes

Paying taxes to Caesar (Matthew 22:15-22; Mark 12:15) was a no-brainer. Except the leaders knew that Roman rule was grating on the people, and the tax system was corrupt (gee, our current systems aren't unique!). So popular feeling (they probably thought) would be on their side, and they wanted an excuse to arrest Jesus for dodging taxes. He very practically reminds them that God had decreed the "times of the Gentiles" (Daniel 9-11) because Israel wouldn't obey Him.

God is the one who sets up rulers and pulls them down (Isaiah 40:23; Daniel 4:17, 25; Jeremiah 18:7-10). So if Israel found itself in the hands of another kingdom (where they were dispersed - Ezra 9:7) they had to follow that kingdom's laws (Romans 13:1-2).

Rebellion is not a good idea when it is directed at God's will. Money made by governments represents authority given to them by God. To pay taxes to the government (render what is Caesar's to Caesar) was to acknowledge its authority to govern. A negative answer could've caused more rebellion (or killed the leader). But Jesus used it instead as an object lesson in submitting to God's will.

That coin (Matthew 22:19) in my opinion was a symbol (another "sign" they refused to "see") of Israel's rebellion and God's discipline. Israel resented the rule of Gentiles who didn't use the Law and worshipped man as a god. But the "heart" of their problem was actually with God and His Law. It was God who consigned them to their fate for violating His Laws. The solution was to submit to God in everything. They could've avoided the Romans by submitting to God in the first place. In a way, the coin showed God's will. It served to inflame their hatred because hate filled them. The coin reminded them that God was always going to have His way. One way or the other.

The Test On The Greatest Command

The greatest command mentioned in Matthew 22:34-40 and Luke 10:25-29 had general agreement at the time. So this test question seems to have been more of an effort to make sure Jesus knew the set answer. Surely, the rabbis knew the answer, and the smallest child able to talk would know too.

In modern schools, it is standard to ask questions to make sure the student understands the "right" answers. I found in public schooling (and I've heard the same thing from others) that the teacher didn't want "an answer." He or she wanted me to parrot "their answer." They wanted to teach me what to think (to indoctrinate). I had to learn how to think from other sources (although to be fair some teachers really do try to teach "how to think"). So I learned to give the teachers what they wanted, and passed their tests. This may have been the same with Jesus too.

It just so happens that in this case the answer the leaders wanted was also the correct answer. So Jesus passes, sort of (He still got crucified). Sadly, the religious leaders may have had the "right" answer on their lips (to love God) but they sure didn't have it in their heart.

The Test On Stoning the Adulteress

Stoning of the adulteress (John 8:1-11) was a harder test (to me), because there is more Law that comes to bear on the subject. Some people think this section wasn't in the original manuscripts. Some think it is true even if not in the original. I don't think it matters, because understood in the context of the whole Word it still fits in with all the other teachings of Jesus.

Did Jesus nullify the Law, as the church teaches? Or is there more going on? Did Jesus say, "No one can judge anyone else because everyone has sinned?" If He did, does that mean that each person has the right to do "whatever is right in their own eyes?" I say no, and I think the scriptural position is also no. There is more going on here than is apparent, especially if we don't know the Law.

The only fact of the case given to Jesus was that the woman was caught in the act of adultery. This means having sex with a man who was not her husband. If she was "caught in the very act," isn't there a party to the proceedings that is missing? Like, HELLO, the man? Shouldn't he have been part of the festivities? (Read Deuteronomy 22:22-29 for instruction on 'catching someone in the act.')

In fact, it was par for the course for leaders to blame the woman only. In many cultures even today the woman is blamed for "provoking" men to lust. This is false. Men lust all by themselves. Sure, a woman should be modest, and if "caught in the act" should be punished right along with her partner. But in this case, that wasn't happening as it should.

Two or more witnesses are required for any offense, especially any capital offense, and they are not supposed to bear false witness (Exodus 20:16, 23:1, 7; Deuteronomy 5:20, 19:15-21). If they did, they got the same punishment as the accused would've gotten (Exodus 21:14, Leviticus 24:19; and Deuteronomy 19:18-19). The witnesses are also supposed to be the first to cast stones after a conviction is legally (according to Torah) obtained. So if they were legally correct, Jesus says go for it.

This is the main reason why Jesus says, "He who is without sin cast the first stone." Since the man was missing, and since "caught in the act" is a little suspicious unless the two had sold tickets, then the testimony was very likely false. If there were witnesses to "the very act," then their first act was to stop it. Instead, they grab the woman only and take her to a kangaroo court.

> [1]"You shall not bear a false report; do not join your hand with a wicked man to be a malicious witness. (Exodus 23:1 NASB95, see also Exodus 20:16 and Deuteronomy 5:20.)
>
> [6]"On the evidence of two witnesses or three witnesses, he who is to die shall be put to death; he shall not be put to death on the evidence of one witness. [7]"The hand of the witnesses shall be first against him to put him to death, and afterward the hand of all the people. So you shall purge the evil from your midst. (Deuteronomy 17:6-7 NASB95. See also Numbers 35:30)

The issue was equal justice according to Torah. It wasn't to shove the Law out of the way. Speaking of kangaroos, it doesn't appear that the court here had been convened according to Torah, and they are being way too quick in jumping to a conclusion. There are elders that are supposed to judge these matters. The mob might have been a group of elders, but doesn't seem like it from the text.

Even if it was, they would have to be the elders designated for hearing cases, not just any person walking by on the street (Leviticus 19:15-18). We are also not privy to other factors. Were the alleged adulterers caught in the city, or in the country? Was she a virgin? Did she fight or cry out? But Jesus, in a masterful stroke, gathers all of these questions together with one statement, "He who is without sin." In other words, if you've followed Torah, start chucking.

Obviously, there were lots of Torah sections ignored by the accusers, many of which were even more important than the issue of adultery. No one in the mob was following the Law; they were acting on their own. This is also against the Law (Leviticus 19:15-19).

It wasn't that Jesus was being all that sympathetic to the woman. He wasn't thinking of some lame idea that "we all sin" so she couldn't be punished. Of course she could've been punished, if in fact justice (following Torah) were the issue. She was evidently guilty. But there was enough doubt that capital punishment couldn't be administered legally.

Justice obviously wasn't a concern of the mob. Due to the number of laws broken, the statement of Jesus brought everyone up short. If they had kept going, they would have been subject to the death penalty also. That is why the mob backs off.

In all this testing, did you note that Jesus never said, "Don't worry about this, the Law is going away?" Not once. In fact, He kept using the Law in order to correct the false teachings. Wouldn't it have been easier to just wave His magic wand and make it all go away? Easier, perhaps. Instead, He kept going back to what God had been saying all along.

Many other examples of Jesus fulfilling the Law revolve around traditions, not the Law itself. Plucking heads of grain (Matthew 12; Mark 2; Luke 6) was allowed (Deuteronomy 23:24, 25) because making a meal was allowed on Sabbath (Exodus 16:25). The leaders had wrongly classified plucking grain as work, which was banned on Sabbath.

Healing on the Sabbath (Matthew 12; Mark 3; Luke 6, 13, 14; John 5) and eating with unwashed hands (Matthew 15; Mark 7) were never banned by God.[102] But the rabbi's, for the sake of their authority, set aside God's Word on a regular basis with rulings like these. As time went by the rulings became a heavy yoke. In contrast, the yoke of Jesus (Matthew 11:29, 30) which is His Law, is light and easy.

The Acts 15 Council and the Law

People wrongly use Acts chapter 15 to teach "we don't have to do the Law." But then they have to backpedal quite a bit and come up with something like, "Well, we don't have to do the 'civil' or 'ceremonial' laws. We still have to do the 'moral' ones." There are two problems with this kind of teaching. Well, there are lots of problems, but we'll look at two now. One is that the teaching of "we don't have to" doesn't come either from a heart of flesh or Scripture. It's not a matter of "have to," it's a matter of love. The second is that the reasoning of "we don't have to" is used by other people to reject any other Law they don't want to follow. Make a crack in a dam and pretty soon the whole thing tumbles down.

---

[102] See also the section of this book on the subject of clean and unclean in Chapter 10.

The truth of "we don't have to" follow the Law depends on your viewpoint. It's true that God is not standing around with a stick to whack us upside the head if we don't. He doesn't kill us immediately when we show signs of imperfection. He's far too gracious and loving. It's also true that we "don't have to" enter in to life. "We don't have to" eat good things as opposed to eating pig slop. "We don't have to" love Him back for the tremendous love He's given us. "We don't have to" accept the death and resurrection of God in the flesh as payment for our sin. "We don't have to" have blessings if we don't want. There's a lot of things we "don't have to" do. We can choose self-will, sin and death instead. Looked at that way, it doesn't make any sense at all to say "we don't have to."

By the time this gets to our street level theology, the second problem with the "we don't have to" doctrine is that it is used by others to dismiss *any* part of the Law they don't like. Many don't even pay attention to categories such as "moral" and "ceremonial." Lots of churches have taken the "we don't have to" view of staying married to one spouse, or one spouse of the opposite gender, for instance. By the time the "don't have to" theology works its way down to street level from the seminaries, many churchgoers think "we don't have to" do very much of God's Word at all.

There's no Scriptural support at all for the "we don't have to" teaching. Certainly not from this chapter of Acts. The council had no authority to erase any Law. Any attempt to do so would mark them as false teachers. The subject is stated in 15:1 & 5.

> [1]Some men came down from Judea and began teaching the brethren, "Unless you are circumcised according to the custom of Moses, you cannot be saved." (Acts 15:1 NASB95)
>
> [5]But some of the sect of the Pharisees who had believed stood up, saying, "It is necessary to circumcise them and to direct them to observe the Law of Moses." (Acts 15:5 NASB95)

The first part of the subject concerns conversion by circumcision; the second part was whether the new converts (Gentiles) should observe the Law, which would include the rabbi's rulings known as Talmud or oral law. After a great deal of discussion by a number of learned people and witnesses from field work, the disciples conclude that the Gentiles are saved by grace through faith *just as they were*. Obviously, Gentiles were receiving the Holy Spirit in spite of the fact they weren't circumcised. This follows the pattern of Abraham who obeyed God and was chosen by Him. His circumcision (Genesis 17) came 14 or more years after several promises from God and after "cutting a covenant" with him in Genesis

15. Abraham was saved by grace through faith same as the Jews. There is no such thing as salvation by circumcision in the Word.

The second part of the subject, Gentiles observing the Law, was answered in verse 20 and 21. By giving the Gentiles a few starting rules, fellowship with their Jewish brethren could be sustained. Both would continue to learn in the synagogue as they heard Moses preached. Just like it took a while for Abram to change to Abraham (Genesis 17).

> [21] "For Moses from ancient generations has in every city those who preach him, since he is read in the synagogues every Sabbath." (Acts 15:21 NASB95)

Salvation by circumcision was a tradition created by priests and rabbis. This tradition and others were in the oral law but not in Scripture. The traditions (oral law) had become a "yoke which neither our fathers nor we have been able to bear" (verse 10). The application of the Word to Gentiles is not being discussed here. It is the traditions of men.

If we interpret this chapter, as many do, that the council said Gentiles don't have to follow the Law, it doesn't make sense they would immediately list four commands to follow. Either the Law is gone or it isn't. It is also curious that three of those commands are dietary in view of the assertion that dietary Law is part of the so-called ceremonial law (and so eliminated). A true believer's council would not say the Law was gone (especially the "ceremonial" and "civil" laws) then on top of that tell everyone what to avoid eating.

It also doesn't make sense that, if the Law was gone except for the "moral" laws, the council would pick laws to follow that were not "moral." If the laws mentioned in Acts 15 are the only ones believers are supposed to follow, as is alleged by those who teach exactly that, aren't there some major laws missing? Like for instance, oh, I don't know, "thou shall not murder," and "thou shall not commit adultery?"

The four laws actually contradict the idea that the council changed anything. God's living oracles were given their proper place by clear teaching. The council went right to the Law when trying to figure out the answer to these dilemmas. They said we are to abstain from things polluted by idols, sexual immorality, from what has been strangled, and from blood. Three of these are dietary, and the fourth could be considered related to diet.[103] If the Laws are gone, then they wouldn't pick four that were "shadows" for believers to follow. James could've

---

[103] Sexual immorality was a big part of pagan worship. Temples were set up with prostitutes and all sorts of other similar disgusting practices. Sacrifices were worked into cultic practices. Later the meat was sold at market (probably what is meant by "things sacrificed to idols" in verse 29). Blood and strangling are self-explanatory.

just said, "Hey, Pete and Cornelius worked it all out with God. The Law doesn't apply anymore."

The actions of the council make more sense and match the rest of the Word when we realize that the four laws mentioned were "starter laws" so that Jews and Gentiles could socialize together. The idea was to make a little common ground to enable both groups to have dinner together. Gradually over time Gentiles and Jews would learn more about how to behave through the teaching of Moses on Sabbath.

All the council did was put down some groundwork to avoid misusing the Law for salvation. If anything, the Law is reinforced quite strongly. It was used by the council to answer the challenges. It was taught in every synagogue. It was taught on the Sabbath (Saturday). And it was preached in "every city." The concept that this council changed God's Laws, or any part of God's Word, is foreign to the Word.

Paul Teaches the Law

Usually we hear that Paul converted to Christianity, except there was no Christianity such as we know it today in his time. He was a model of a Law-following Jew (see chapter 7 Paul Tells Us It's Okay), and never stopped abiding in His Messiah's Word. He taught the Law, filled with the Spirit and love, as it was intended – a lifestyle and discipleship method. Many of his teachings have been sliced and diced and taught differently. But when we just read the Word, we can see he held to the ancient, unified message of the Father and Jesus.

Keep three things firmly in mind as you are reading Paul's writings. One is that he doesn't downgrade or speak negatively about God's Law. Ever. But like his Messiah he's not so fond of man's laws (at least the ones that interfere with God's Law). Two is that the Law was never meant to save anyone. Law was added as a guidepost because of transgressions increasing. Israel was "saved" first then given instruction on living a saved life. Three is that the word "law" can mean any law including natural law, Roman law, God's Law, man's traditions especially Jewish ones, and physical laws. Law is improperly thought of as a legal relationship to earn merit which can be traded for salvation.

If you don't like the Law and have been trained to reject it, then Paul's writings will look anti-Law. However, if you have a heart of flesh with His Law written on it, then Paul's writings are easy to understand and completely fit in with the rest of Scripture.

Paul Governs Stepmother Relations by the Law

If the Law had been "fulfilled," (improperly interpreted to mean "eliminated") then the following is a very curious thing for Paul to say.

> ¹It is actually reported that there is immorality among you, and immorality of such a kind as does not exist even among the Gentiles, that someone has his father's wife. ²You have become arrogant and have not mourned instead, so that the one who had done this deed would be removed from your midst. (1 Corinthians 5:1-2 NASB95)

He would not care about a man who marries ("has his father's wife" refers to sex in marriage) his stepmother[104] if he was practicing his "freedom in Christ." Instead, he frowns on this marriage because it is against the Law. According to the modern church, everything and everyone is clean, but according to Paul that is wrong. He appeals to the Law (Leviticus 18:8; Deuteronomy 22:30 and 27:30) in order to correct iniquity. He also appeals to the fact that this is something even Gentiles didn't do (natural law).

There might be a thin argument here for the fictitious "moral law." Except did you know there is almost nothing in the Law about marriage? There are rules against marrying any of the seven tribes already in the Land (Deuteronomy 7:3). There's a rule about a slave (Exodus 21:10). There are Laws about improper sex (to which Paul was appealing here) and Laws about divorce paperwork (due to hard hearts Mark 10:2-12). But there are no regulations about marriage. That's because everyone knew what it was supposed to be. The pattern was set in the Garden. So is marriage civil, ceremonial, or moral? (Hint: it's all three.) Again I point out that everything God says is by definition "moral," and Paul reinforces that idea here. It appears to me that the Corinthians, like the modern church, had changed the law to say that everything was clean. They were probably practicing their "freedom in Christ."

Paul doesn't make up any new commandment here. He certainly doesn't cherry-pick nor does he apply only the law he chooses. Not only does he say that the Corinthians should be following this Law, he implies it is a natural fact everyone (even the non-believing Gentiles) knows. In other words, God's people should at least have the sense God gave a pagan. He also gives the punishment for the sin outlined in Torah – "purge the evil from among you." (Deuteronomy 13:5, 17:7, 12, 21:21, 22:21). Later, it looks like they were "obedient in all things" (2 Corinthians 2:1-11) although they didn't stone the guy with the stepmom wife because we don't have the power of capital punishment. Our alternative is from Matthew 18 – confront for repentance and cast out if we have to.

---

[104] "His father's wife" must be his step-mom or she would be called his mother. Either way, it's still wrong.

This is the essence of whole-heartedly abiding in all of God's Word. The congregation was doing something wrong according to the Law and was corrected by Paul. Then they stopped doing the wrong thing and started doing the right thing. This is how a heart of flesh chooses the tree of life over the tree of knowledge.

Paul Corrects Passover Observance

In 1 Corinthians 11:23-34 it is obvious that the meal is the Passover (verse 23 "the night (our Lord) was betrayed"). The misnamed "Lord's Supper" is in reality the Passover before His crucifixion (Matthew 17:7; Mark 14:12; Luke 22:8, 15). It is not communion. This is a problem for those who insist on separating the Law into civil, ceremonial, and moral sections. The Passover is clearly ceremonial in their view. But the Corinthians (and probably the rest of the "church") are celebrating the feast. The reason we don't spot this is because it is taught wrongly that they are celebrating some sort of "communion" ceremony. Here the New Covenant and Passover are linked (verse 25 "this cup is the new covenant").

The plain meaning is that the churches were still following the "ceremonial" laws, but in this case the Corinthian believers were doing it improperly. Apparently, the congregations didn't think that "ceremonial" laws were no longer to be practiced. They were also aware of the meaning of Passover. Or at least Paul was teaching them the meaning.

Paul Teaches the Validity of Circumcision

This is mentioned by Paul in about 36 verses in his writings.[105] For a doctrine that was supposed to be abolished according to modern church teaching, it sure does show up a lot. Paul is circumcised (Philippians 3:5) and circumcises Timothy (Acts 16:3). Timothy, evidently, was not circumcised at the time of the Acts 15 council where circumcision for salvation is the main issue (Acts 15:1, 5).

Mentioned first in Genesis 17 for Abraham's household, he did it even though his faith was credited to him as righteousness in Genesis 15. So he was "saved" then followed the Law anyway. Circumcision also has a few mentions in the Gospels and Acts, mostly for Jews, and "the circumcision" is a way of referring to members of Judaism. Remember too that real circumcision includes circumcision of the heart according to Deuteronomy 10:16, 30:6; Jeremiah 4:4; Joel 2:13 and Romans 2:29.

Romans 2 is probably the best look at what Paul tries to convey about circumcision.

---

[105] The main sections are Romans 2 and 4, Galatians 2, 5 and 6, Philippians 3, and Colossians 2, 3, and 4.

> [23] You who boast in the Law, through your breaking the Law, do you dishonor God? [24] For "the name of God is blasphemed among the Gentiles because of you," just as it is written. [25] For indeed circumcision is of value if you practice the Law; but if you are a transgressor of the Law, your circumcision has become uncircumcision. [26] So if the uncircumcised man keeps the requirements of the Law, will not his uncircumcision be regarded as circumcision? [27] And he who is physically uncircumcised, if he keeps the Law, will he not judge you who though having the letter of the Law and circumcision are a transgressor of the Law? [28] For he is not a Jew who is one outwardly, nor is circumcision that which is outward in the flesh. [29] But he is a Jew who is one inwardly; and circumcision is that which is of the heart, by the Spirit, not by the letter; and his praise is not from men, but from God. (Romans 2:23-29 NASB95)

Verse 27 is telling. Paul says that a physically uncircumcised person, who keeps the Law, is in a better position than a person who is circumcised yet breaks it. He says, "Circumcision is of value if you practice (follow, obey, abide in, remain in) the Law." So rightly understood circumcision isn't bad. But circumcision shouldn't be by itself. It's part of the whole Word or Law, and goes together with a circumcised heart. This heart is none other than the heart of flesh given by God written with His Law as part of the new covenant.

The issue here is the same as other places, which is that circumcision doesn't save anyone. Never has, never will. Becoming a Jew or following some Laws does not save a person and never has. A person follows the Laws because they are saved. In other words, a person following God by faith is justified. Circumcision is a sign after the fact (as in Genesis 17). Now the hard question – would a circumcised person who stopped following God's Law be "saved?" Answer: if a person stops following God their circumcision becomes like uncircumcision. In my opinion they were never "saved" in the first place.

Paul Judges Romans 14 Opinions by the Law

Paul gives his opinion of other people's opinions in Romans 14. The very first verse tells us about the chapter. It's about opinions, not God's Word.

> [1] Now accept the one who is weak in faith, but not for the purpose of passing judgment on his *opinions*. (Romans 14:1 NASB95 italics added)

At least 5 or 6 times in the chapter Paul tells us directly not to be judging each other. His admonishments are specifically for things not found in the Word. The message is to avoid getting on each other's case about stuff that doesn't matter. But this does not mean anything goes. Nor does it mean that all things are opinion only. The Word of God is not an opinion in the way a man has one. Therefore, Paul is excluding the Word from this chapter, and looking at man's opinions. Including man's opinions about the application of God's Word.

He speaks of one person eating vegetables only. Another person will eat meat. To eat or not to eat are both opinions. They might come from an attempt to practice what God preaches, but the opinions are not actual laws.[106] The meat here probably refers to meat that was sold at market. One did not know for sure whether it was from idol sacrifices or had touched the sacrifices.

One guy tries to avoid all meat, just in case, so he eats vegetables only. Another guy knows the meat is clean. If the weak faith guy still has a problem, then don't rub his face in it. Since this is all opinion anyway, we are to accept one another's opinions and give each other time to figure out what's what. This is not a reason to ignore God's Words. Not even close.

Some people say that Paul here is teaching that all things are a matter of opinion, using verse 23 as back up ("whatever is not from faith is sin"). In other words, something is only wrong if a person "thinks" it is wrong. This is a big error on the meaning of faith. They try to make a point that if a person wants to eat ham, it is just a matter of opinion. If another person wants to avoid ham it is also a matter of opinion (though forbidden to believers in the Word).

It's true that in a very loose way everything is an opinion. My opinion is that the Bible is one absolute truth that applies to every person. Another person's opinion might be that they can pick and choose. But the Bible is God's opinion, and that's the only opinion that counts with believers. God's Word (the Law) is not a matter of our opinions. He sets down what is right and wrong in very concrete terms. A person may have an opinion that they don't want to follow God's Law, but that does not mean God's Law is open to question. To follow, or not to follow, is between each person and God. I am not assigned to tell anyone what to believe. I just tell them what the Book says. Men's opinions on eating are a far different thing than what God says we can eat and what we can't.

If it were true that all things are simply a matter of opinion (or "of faith), then if, in someone's opinion adultery or homosexual behavior was acceptable, there isn't anything wrong with it. And in fact many so-

---

[106] See Exodus 34:15; Leviticus 7:21; Deuteronomy 14:3; and 1 Corinthians 8 and 10.

called Christians are reasoning exactly this way. If we know something to be wrong and do it anyway then it really is sin. But even if a person doesn't think something is wrong, it's still wrong according to Scripture. Remember the guy marrying the step-mom. Read the book of Judges, where "doing what is right in their own eyes" is a condemnation. We see the fruit of opinions that are not God's all through the Word and in the current destruction of our society.

There are a great many bad things that go along with sin, regardless of whether the sinner believes it's sin or not. Cain was banished for manslaughter (killing Abel). David lost a son for adultery with Bathsheba. I'm sure the residents of Sodom and Gomorrah were claiming innocence all the way to the grave – but they still went because they were wrong. Making sin a matter of opinion, then calling it a "disputatious matter," is not what Paul is talking about.

> [12]For all who have sinned without the Law will also perish without the Law, and all who have sinned under the Law will be judged by the Law; [13]for it is not the hearers of the Law who are just before God, but the doers of the Law will be justified. [14]For when Gentiles who do not have the Law do instinctively the things of the Law, these, not having the Law, are a law to themselves, [15]in that they show the work of the Law written in their hearts, their conscience bearing witness and their thoughts alternately accusing or else defending them, [16]on the day when, according to my gospel, God will judge the secrets of men through Christ Jesus. (Romans 2:12-16 NASB95)

Notice that whether a person has the Law or not, everyone is judged. Having the Law is an advantage that carries a greater responsibility (and greater intimacy with God). But it is "doers of the Law," Paul says, who are justified. Of course, he means the whole thing including love from a heart of flesh filled with the Spirit.

Some argue that what we put in our mouths is not as important as adultery or murder, so therefore we can safely ignore God's Word on the subject. But this is wrong because 1) the one saying so is sitting in judgment on God's Word (James 4:11) and 2) God says that eating unclean things is an abomination in the same way homosexuality (Leviticus 18:22) and adultery are. Besides, the very first sin (in the Garden) was ignoring a diet command.

We don't have leeway to be so arbitrary with His Word. If you don't want to follow His living oracle, if life more abundant doesn't appeal to you, then don't follow it. However, one should always remember the millstone effect (causing other people to sin), and at least try to avoid making God out to be a liar.

Paul Nails the Law in Colossians 2

Paul's next teaching here, when read carefully, will show that he is again speaking of the teachings of men. He would never attribute these to God.

> [4]I say this so that no one will delude you with persuasive argument. (Colossians 2:4 NASB95)
>
> [8]See to it that no one takes you captive through philosophy and empty deception, according to the tradition of men, according to the elementary principles of the world, rather than according to Christ. (Colossians 2:8 NASB95)
>
> [20]If you have died with Christ to the elementary principles of the world, why, as if you were living in the world, do you submit yourself to decrees, such as, [21]"Do not handle, do not taste, do not touch!" [22](which all refer to things destined to perish with use)—in accordance with the commandments and teachings of men? [23]These are matters which have, to be sure, the appearance of wisdom in self-made religion and self-abasement and severe treatment of the body, but are of no value against fleshly indulgence. (Colossians 2:20-23 NASB95)

What Paul is talking about is plain – "commandments and teachings of men," and "self-made religion." In context, by the time the reader gets to verse 21 where it says, "Do not handle, do not taste, do not touch!" Paul is obviously NOT talking about God's Word. These types of rulings are interpretations and applications ("decrees") made by teachers (such as the traditions and oral law) that were (and are) added to the Word on a regular basis.

My paraphrase of what Paul is saying here I think fits the whole context of Scripture much better. He says to walk in Jesus rooted and built up in Him and established in the faith (v. 6, 7), and not to be taken captive by philosophy and empty deceit according to human tradition that agrees with the elemental spirits of the world (v. 8). Since Christ, who has the fullness of God in Him (v. 9-15) has nailed our sins (the record of debt v. 14) to the cross, paying the debt, then we should not let the traditions of men disqualify us (v. 18) from partaking of God's Word. We have died to the elemental spirits of the world and are dead to the world, so why should we buy into them again? Those who get lost in visions and details about angels, adding human precepts and teachings along the lines of "do not handle, do not taste, do not touch" to God's

Word, have sensuous minds and are not holding fast to the Head (that is Christ Colossians 2:19). Their extra regulations have the appearance of wisdom but have no value in stopping the indulgence of the flesh (v. 20-23).

Colossians 2:16 is not an admonition to avoid God's Word; it is an admonition to avoid the elemental spirits of the world.

> [16]Therefore no one is to act as your judge in regard to food or drink or in respect to a festival or a new moon or a Sabbath day— [17]things which are a mere shadow of what is to come; but the substance belongs to Christ. (Colossians 2:16-17 NASB95)

Remember, this was written after the crucifixion and resurrection. Does it mean "don't observe festivals or new moons (months) or Sabbaths?" Or does it mean "don't let anyone judge how you observe them within the context of God's Word?" Obviously, to me, a heart of flesh would choose the latter meaning. The next verses in Colossians 2 confirm it.

> Let no one disqualify you, insisting on asceticism and worship of angels, going on in detail about visions, puffed up without reason by his sensuous mind, and not holding fast to the Head, from whom the whole body, nourished and knit together through its joints and ligaments, grows with a growth that is from God.(Colossians 2:18–19, ESV)

"Let no one disqualify you" seems pretty clear. I'm sure there was people at the time (as there are now) who try to say that you can't observe God's holidays if you don't do it the way they specify. Paul means that we shouldn't allow others to keep us from following God's Word.

A heart of stone looks for excuses to reject His Law. A heart of flesh searches them out and puts them everywhere. In context, with the references to the "elementary principles of the world" and "teachings of men," the statements in Colossians 2:16 & 17 do not mean "avoid God's Laws."

What Paul is plainly saying is that people's opinions shouldn't have any bearing on one's practice of God's Word. In other words, as I practice the Sabbath, new moon (month) or festival, I do it according to what is in the Word, not someone's opinion. I don't let anyone "disqualify" me based on their opinions. Besides, Jews were not the only ones to observe certain days or seasons or years (Galatians 4:10). You ever try to tell someone that Christmas and Easter is not God pleasing and should not be part of a believer's practice?

The opinions of men have no bearing on what I do or don't do. There is no central authority (outside of the Word), though lots of people still set them up. If someone thinks I'm "not resting" enough on the Sabbath (or, say, healing as Jesus did) it's between me and God. I don't have to use an egg and lamb shank bone on a Seder plate to enjoy the Passover the way God intended. I don't have to skip Passover entirely and celebrate a non-biblical pagan feast called Easter with a ham entrée instead either. No one has been appointed judge and jury for other people's practice of the Word. If things aren't written, it's men's opinions.

Romans chapter 14 is connected here too. Believers are to receive one another, no matter our opinions outside the Word. If someone wants to eat vegetables so they don't eat the wrong meat, it is up to them. If someone thinks the meat (probably offered to idols) is okay and wants to eat it, just don't stomp on the guy who doesn't. Paul's teaching in Colossians 2 is a far cry from what many think they find here. He very obviously teaches that man-made tradition should not get in the way of doing what God says.

Paul Justifies the Law to the Galatians

As Peter says, some of the teachings of Paul are hard to understand.

> [14]Therefore, beloved, since you look for these things, be diligent to be found by Him in peace, spotless and blameless, [15]and regard the patience of our Lord as salvation; just as also our beloved brother Paul, according to the wisdom given him, wrote to you, [16]as also in all his letters, speaking in them of these things, in which are some things hard to understand, which the untaught and unstable distort, as they do also the rest of the Scriptures, to their own destruction. [17]You therefore, beloved, knowing this beforehand, be on your guard so that you are not carried away by the error of unprincipled men and fall from your own steadfastness, [18]but grow in the grace and knowledge of our Lord and Savior Jesus Christ. To Him be the glory, both now and to the day of eternity. Amen. (2 Peter 3:14-18 NASB95)

The letter to the assemblies of Galatia is right up there with difficult things that the untaught and unstable distort. Most of the time, the book of Galatians is presented as a teaching against God's Laws. But when we get into the book, and read carefully, we find that Paul is not telling us to ignore God's Word, especially the Law. What he is doing is contrasting merit with grace through faith. The key verse (in my opinion) says it all.

> ⁴You have been severed from Christ, you who are seeking to be justified by law; you have fallen from grace. (Galatians 5:4 NASB95)

To be justified by law (another of those places where "the Law" should just be translated "law") as we've already talked about means to be righteous enough in observing some rules that a person could demand eternal life from God. People who try this want to focus on selected actions but ignore the condition of the heart. Some of the Galatians (probably either visitors of the "circumcision party" or Jewish leaders) were seeking to be justified by their own actions described as "righteousness through the law" (2:16) and "desires of the flesh" (5:16).

These leaders wanted other Galatians to undergo an extra-biblical circumcision ritual to get points with God (6:13; see also 2 Corinthians 11:18; 2 Peter 2:18; 1 John 2:16). Attempting a trade using one's own works such as a circumcision ceremony (nowhere found in the Word) renders the sacrifice of the Christ useless (2:21). Paul points out that the Galatians received the Spirit by hearing with faith (3:2, 5, 14) and are justified by that faith (3:7, 11), not by works.

Merit is the idea that we have earned something, like wages for work. Some try to trade their (perceived) merit for eternal life. This is a mistake because it's just not worth it to God. "For all who rely on works of the law are under a curse..." (Galatians 3:10). If we can be justified on our own merit by cutting off a little piece of skin, then we should just go the whole way and cut it all off (5:12). Then we will be really, really justified!

Just like in Colossians, Paul here speaks of "elementary principles of the world" (4:3, 4:9) and how the Galatians were formerly "enslaved to those that by nature are not gods" (4:8). This is not how Paul describes either God or God's Law. It is how he describes religious leaders and the laws of men. The laws of men might include some of God's Laws but are interpreted in man's way. As he says in 6:13, *"even those who are circumcised do not themselves keep the Law, but they desire to have* (the Galatians) *circumcised that they may boast in the flesh"* (works of law). The issue was not God's Law at all. It was misusing God's Law by faulty interpretation to gain supposed merit.

Observing "days and months and seasons and years" (4:10) is like the phrase in Colossians for "do not handle, do not taste, do not touch" (Colossians 2:21). Neither concerns God's Law. Both are "weak and worthless elementary principles of the world." They are a "yoke of slavery" (5:1) coming from people who are not gods.

In other words, Paul is saying that following man-made laws (especially circumcision (4:3) which for some at the time meant to become a Jew) is not the way to gain a place in God's kingdom. It is only by grace through faith (3:11) that anybody – Jew or Gentile, circumcised or not – has a place at all. The Law is for living life after salvation, not the means to get salvation.

Paul Knocks Down the Wall with the Law

There was a low wall in the outer court of the second temple (part of Herod's improvements) that marked a boundary past which Gentiles could not go. They were not allowed past the wall deeper into the Temple on pain of death. This was an extra wall not specified by God. It was built at the direction of Jewish leadership to keep Gentiles out. This is probably the dividing wall that Paul is referring to metaphorically in Ephesians 2:14-16.

You'll have to look in a concordance to find out what is really meant by some of the words in this passage because they are not translated very well. This is another of those places I told you about, where the word *nomos* (Greek for law – little "l") is translated with a capital L when it should just be "law" ("law of commandments").[107] Paul is writing to congregations consisting of both Jews and Gentiles. The Law was not meant to divide, it was meant to unify. It applied to everyone equally in Israel. Laws made by men are the main agents in a "dividing wall."

> [14]For He Himself is our peace, who made both groups into one and broke down the barrier of the dividing wall, [15]by abolishing in His flesh the enmity, which is the Law of commandments contained in ordinances, so that in Himself He might make the two into one new man, thus establishing peace, [16]and might reconcile them both in one body to God through the cross, by it having put to death the enmity. (Ephesians 2:14-16 NASB95)

The word for "ordinances" (verse 15) is the Greek "dogma."[108] This doesn't apply to God's living oracles (though some say it does). He's talking about the Jew's oral law, not God's Law. The phrase in verse 15 should read closer to "law commands in dogma or opinions." A "law command in dogma" means tradition or oral law. This is a much different idea than The Law. But even if we use the translation as it is given, what is put to death is the *enmity* between the Jews and Gentiles, not the Law.

---

[107] The ESV does a little better, translating nomos to 'law' as it should be, but still trying to imply Law is bad.
[108] In Strong's Concordance δόγμα (dogma 1378) is also 'opinions' or 'decree' and now is used for statements not having proof (and in our case biblical proof).

The dividing wall (either real or metaphor) is created by rules and regulations outside of the Bible. It was built on men's opinions calcified in false interpretation and tradition.[109] Men's laws are where Peter, for instance, got his idea that Gentiles were unclean (Acts 10). Gentiles were (and are) reconciled to God through the sacrifice of His Son directly. Jesus was crucified outside the city because He went to His own and His own received Him not. The Temple veil was torn in two, showing we have direct access now. These things smashed down the dividing wall of enmity created by unbiblical laws or other opinions of men. God tears down the wall but men can't wait to put it back up.

Spirit and Law

The Spirit and The Law are not in conflict. They couldn't be. The Spirit repeats what He hears, and what He hears is the Law. We might use the Law without the Spirit for something like self-justification, and many people try just that. But then the Law kills because we cannot use it to gain salvation righteousness. God has to change a willing heart to flesh first, and give the gift of the Spirit. Some people persist in the belief that the Spirit is somehow split apart from God's Word (including the Law) but He isn't.

> [26]"Moreover, I will give you a new heart and put a new spirit within you; and I will remove the heart of stone from your flesh and give you a heart of flesh. [27]"I will put My Spirit within you and cause you to walk in My statutes, and you will be careful to observe My ordinances. (Ezekiel 36:26-27 NASB95)

We can't have the Spirit without His statutes and His ordinances. If we have the Spirit, we have the Law. It is the Spirit, working through God's Word, which produces the fruit of the Spirit. Fruit of the Spirit naturally occurs when we abide in God's statutes and ordinances.

> [34]"For He whom God has sent speaks the words of God; for He gives the Spirit without measure. (John 3:34 NASB95)

> [13]"But when He, the Spirit of truth, comes, He will guide you into all the truth; for He will not speak on His own initiative, but whatever He hears, He will speak; and He will disclose to you what is to come. [14]"He will glorify Me, for He will take of Mine and will disclose it to you. [15]"All things that the Father has are

---

[109] There was never a 'court of women' and a 'court of Gentiles' at the tabernacle or Solomon's temple. In Solomon's temple there was an inner court and an outer court, but Jew and non-Jew were treated equally.

> Mine; therefore I said that He takes of Mine and will disclose it to you. (John 16:13-15 NASB95)

There are more of these Laws we could look at, but I trust you've seen enough to help sort through the others. What some people think of as the new covenant, meaning the New Testament, is simply loaded with Law. From Matthew to Revelation, from the (first) Sermon on the Mount to the New Jerusalem, the Law, far from being eliminated, is interpreted and applied properly by a host of Spirit-filled people.

The incarnate ministry of Jesus is filled with examples of His defense of the written Word and the proper "whole" interpretation. He was tested in many ways that were not a part of the Word or Torah. But even in those, He perfectly obeyed Torah in every way. Not only was He a walking example of obedience to every part of Torah in every test He faced, but He also without exception directed every person who wants to follow Him to repent of their own ways and return to God's. In fact, I think it was very logical and appropriate for Jesus to stick with God's Law while all around Him people were breaking it. He was steadfast in His obedience, no matter what was thrown at Him.

Paul continued in the same vein. The Jew of Jews who was "blameless according to the Law" never once departed from the correct application of the Law. He lived it completely, and taught everyone else who would listen to do the same. Much of his teaching was the contrast between merit and grace, which has been wrongly understood to mean we should avoid the Law. But anyone who claims to be from God will have a message or teaching consistent with Torah in every way, as did Paul. All the apostles and all the writers of Scripture learned it, lived it, and taught it. How can we who profess to love Him and follow Him do any less?

7 Whole Bible Objections

> [16] Your words were found, and I ate them, and your words became to me a joy and the delight of my heart, for I am called by your name, O LORD, God of hosts. (Jeremiah 15:16 ESV)

The Law is one of the most explosive issues in Christianity. But why should it be? It doesn't make any sense that it would cause such hard reactions from people who claim to know Him. There is so much intense opposition to the Law that if it is even *lightly* mentioned in many circles, it gets a heavy negative response. If a Christian dares to practice the actual new covenant (remember, the law written on a heart of flesh), there is grave risk of censure and expulsion from the circles. There's another pun in there somewhere.

If the Bible is just read naturally, and by that I mean without explanation from others, it seems plain we are to follow the Law. We keep seeing hints of this as we read, like flickers of motion at the edge of our vision. When we ask about it, we get a lot of excuses for why we shouldn't follow the Law. I know this because I've heard them all, and before I discovered the truth of whole Bible Christianity used some of them myself to explain why I didn't follow. I also used them to "help" other people understand.

Here are 20 of the major objections or "helpful explanations." Some of them we've gone over a little already because most of the time you can't even get a conversation started without dealing with them up front. We might want to ask ourselves why there are so many. How come people who wear His name have so many objections to His Word? I had to think long and hard to pick just a few examples for this chapter. I'm hoping you'll see the patterns in them, and see how they are really all the same argument. You can learn how to respond biblically to these and others you may hear. After a while they all sound the same, and at the heart they are simply excuses to go our own way. All objections are made up, in my opinion, by hearts of stone. As we shall see, they don't come from the Word.

"All I Commanded You" (Not)

Jesus tells us in the "great commission" to go to the nations and make disciples.

> "Go therefore and make disciples of all the nations, baptizing them in the name of the Father and the Son and the Holy Spirit,

teaching them to observe all that I commanded you; and lo, I am with you always, even to the end of the age." (Matthew 28:19-20 NASB95)

But some object to Jesus' statement. They want to redefine what "all I commanded" means. Apparently, the words of Jesus for these people don't include the "old" words. So what do we do with the people in these verses?

> ^{24}'Do not defile yourselves by any of these things; for by all these the nations which I am casting out before you have become defiled. ^{25}'For the land has become defiled, therefore I have brought its punishment upon it, so the land has spewed out its inhabitants. ^{26}'But as for you, you are to keep My statutes and My judgments and shall not do any of these abominations, neither the native, nor the alien who sojourns among you ^{27}(for the men of the land who have been before you have done all these abominations, and the land has become defiled); ^{28}so that the land will not spew you out, should you defile it, as it has spewed out the nation which has been before you. (Leviticus 18:24-28 NASB95)

> ^{22}'You are therefore to keep all My statutes and all My ordinances and do them, so that the land to which I am bringing you to live will not spew you out. ^{23}'Moreover, you shall not follow the customs of the nation which I will drive out before you, for they did all these things, and therefore I have abhorred them. (Leviticus 20:22-23 NASB95)

The people in these references (and others) were all Gentiles, and they didn't have the stone tablets. They are getting "spewed out" even though they didn't have the Law. The reason? They did the abominations that God forbade.[110] Perhaps it's just poetic imagery, but the abominations were so bad that even the dirt was disgusted. Unfair blanket statements? No. They knew right and wrong. They just refused to do right.

God created the earth and upholds it by the word of His power. Our fight is against spiritual wickedness, and nature is connected with God's Spirit. His Word is universal and constant, and has been around forever. The abominations are a perversion of the nature that God created. So it's not a big stretch to think the Land literally vomited the offending nations out.

---

[110] See also Deuteronomy 9:4-6 where God says it is not Israel's righteousness that is causing the spewing.

The Gentile nations in the Land paid a penalty for doing the same abominations that were prohibited to Israel in the Law. But why would those nations have to be spewed out if the Law doesn't apply? The answer is it really *does* apply.

One thing is very clear: God's Law applies to everyone, everywhere, at every time. No one is off the hook because they "don't know" God's Law. "All I commanded" includes the Law. Solomon tells us this point blank.

> [13]The conclusion, when all has been heard, is: fear God and keep His commandments, because this applies to every person. [14]For God will bring every act to judgment, everything which is hidden, whether it is good or evil. (Ecclesiastes 12:13-14 NASB95)

Only the Moral

We've covered the next objection a little already but there are a couple more things to say about the Law being split into three parts: ceremonial, civil, and moral. Ceremonial commands are supposed to be about sacrifices and holidays, laws of clean and unclean, and similar stuff. Civil commands, it is claimed, are the ones for government and punishment for violations. Moral commands are said to be universal in nature. These commands are allegedly fewer in number and include laws such as the prohibition of murder or stealing. We talked some about this in the first chapter (page 20), but here I want to expand a little on the reasons I disagree with these categories.

After dividing the Word into these non-biblical sections, some teachers pass judgment (James 4:11) on which parts apply to modern believers. In their opinion, the civil or ceremonial laws don't apply. But I say to you the Bible doesn't divide itself this way. No believer described in the Bible ever sets aside any part of it. There is nothing that gives us the right to toss anything out, no matter what extra-biblical divisions we make.

The rich truth is that the designations of civil, ceremonial, and moral are not found in the Word. We simply cannot split them apart into categories then ignore some. We are warned on many occasions in the Word not to add to or take away from it.[111] There is no hint that God thinks of any part of His Word as simply "ceremonial" and therefore not worth doing, or limited only to Jewish people.

Everything God says is moral, whether we call it moral or invent some other category. All of His Words are eternal, and we are not to

---

[111] Deuteronomy 4:2, 12:32; Ecclesiastes 3:14; Revelation 22:18, 19 for starters.

change any. That, of course, doesn't keep us from trying, which we've been doing ever since the Garden. Here's a riddle for you: Is the following command to bury our toilet leavings civil, ceremonial, or moral?

> [12] "You shall also have a place outside the camp and go out there, [13] and you shall have a spade among your tools, and it shall be when you sit down outside, you shall dig with it and shall turn to cover up your excrement. [14] "Since the LORD your God walks in the midst of your camp to deliver you and to defeat your enemies before you, therefore your camp must be holy; and He must not see anything indecent among you or He will turn away from you. (Deuteronomy 23:12-14 NASB95)

The answer is (envelope please) all of the above. Civil is in the "defeat your enemies" (and perhaps general sanitation) clause. There is some ceremonial in the holy/clean/unclean aspect, and there is moral in the "indecent" aspect. So much for the three-fold division.

There are many commands that are similar and just cannot be split. One of these days someone will have to explain to me in which category the broken law leading to the "original sin" falls into. You know, the law about eating some fruit from the wrong tree. Was it civil, merely ceremonial, or moral? Wasn't it dietary? Doesn't that mean it was ceremonial? Does it matter? Of course not. Another explanation I need is how we preserve the tithe, which is ceremonial, but chuck all of the other ceremonial laws. Why is it that the one about money is preserved? And how did it come to cover paychecks in the first place? Wasn't it primarily agricultural? In other words, how did it morph from giving the priests part of our crops to giving pastors some cash? Obviously if we are going to throw out ceremonial commands, this is at the top of the list. Gee, I wonder why it is still around.

A simple reading of the Word, by a humble and tender heart willing to respond, is sufficient to overturn the complicated, extra-biblical arguments for disobedience. Anything He asks us to do is part of His morality, whether we think it's important or not.

Paul Tells Us It Is Okay

A standard Christian teaching in favor of ditching the Law is that Paul tells us we can. Many teachers think that Paul converted to Christianity, and with his newfound faith came the realization that the

Law was mostly gone.[112] The Scriptures teach something different, however. Among other things, Paul still followed the Law.

> [5]circumcised the eighth day, of the nation of Israel, of the tribe of Benjamin, a Hebrew of Hebrews; as to the Law, a Pharisee; [6]as to zeal, a persecutor of the church; as to the righteousness which is in the Law, found blameless. (Philippians 3:5-6 NASB95)

A quick look at the book of Acts shows Paul observing feasts (20:6,16, 24:17, 18) fasts (27:9) vows (18:18; 21:23-26) Sabbath (13:14, 42, 44, 16:13, 17:2, 18:4) circumcision (16:3) temple worship (22:17, 24:11, 17, 18) teaching from the Law and the Prophets (28:23) and keeping the Law (21:24, 22:3, 23:6, 24:14). Paul was obviously a model of a law-following Jew before and after conversion.

Paul did not teach that the law was over with. He had no authority to do so, and would never claim that he did. It was not granted to him to change the unchanging Word of God.

> [20]'But the prophet who speaks a word presumptuously in My name which I have not commanded him to speak, or which he speaks in the name of other gods, that prophet shall die.' (Deuteronomy 18:20 NASB95)

He never converted to Christianity because there was no Christianity such as we know it today at the time. He was a "partisan of the Christ" but that is not the same as converting to Christianity. He did, however, meet his long-awaited Messiah in the person of Jesus. These are two very different things.

Can't Do the Law

Another mask for rich biblical truth is the teaching that we "can't do the law" as in "we are unable." You've heard it said that if you follow the Law you have to follow it perfectly (citing Galatians 5:3 or James 2:10). Since that is impossible, goes the theory, then the Law must be replaced by the righteousness of Jesus. Again, the Scriptures tell a different story. God tells His people at Sinai that the Law He is proclaiming is not out of reach.

> [11]"For this commandment which I command you today is not too difficult for you, nor is it out of reach. [12]"It is not in heaven, that you should say, 'Who will go up to heaven for us to get it for us and make us hear it, that we may observe it?' [13]"Nor is it beyond

---

[112] In that seminar video from Mark Driscoll I quoted earlier in the book he said, "Saul becomes a Christian." As I said before, I can't find it now but before his fall from grace it was at http://theresurgence.com/mark_driscoll_2008-02-25_video_putting_preachers_in_their_place.

> the sea, that you should say, 'Who will cross the sea for us to get it for us and make us hear it, that we may observe it?' [14]"But the word is very near you, in your mouth and in your heart, that you may observe it. (Deuteronomy 30:11-14 NASB95)

Paul echoes this principle in Romans 10:1-11. In another place Paul agrees with Moses yet again, and tells us that with Christ all things are possible. *"I can do all things through Him who strengthens me"* (Philippians 4:13 NASB95). Jesus wouldn't have told us we could be perfect (before the resurrection even) unless it was within our grasp.

> "Therefore you are to be perfect, as your heavenly Father is perfect. (Matthew 5:48, NASB95)

Our faith (trust and obedience) is counted as righteousness (Romans 4) but we must continue in faith, abiding in every Word from His mouth. It's not the Law that can't be done. God's Word can easily be "done," or He would not have given it to us. The Law is an easy yoke and a light burden (Matthew 11:25-30). What *cannot be done* is to *earn God's salvation* through following some rules (or Laws). We can't trade our own righteousness (it is "filthy rags" according to Isaiah 64:6) for salvation. No one can earn enough merit before God to claim any sort of righteous standing sufficient for salvation. Let me say it again: you can't earn salvation by following the Law. Faith saves; Law pursued as works doesn't. We are justified by faith (Romans 1:17, 3:20, etc.).

Obviously, though, there are Laws we cannot observe. Some of them involve a Temple or a priesthood, which we do not have on earth at the moment. Others involve the administering of penalties. This is mostly impossible now because His body is not a sovereign state recognized by all the other states.[113] At the present time, our kingdom is like leaven working its way through a lump of dough (the earth, Matthew 13:33). We don't yet have a separate state, with borders and a capital city.

One of the side effects of teaching "we can't do the law" is that it makes God out to be a sadist. That's the conclusion if God actually does give us a code we can't follow. Or we make God out to be a liar, because we create two different teachings that contradict but are supposed to come from God. What we've really done with this teaching is to mix truth and error.

Just because there are some things in the Law we can't do today, that doesn't mean what we *can* do should be left by the wayside. We can take His holidays as our own and forsake the pagan ones. We can go on His diet, which doesn't include pork, shellfish, or animals that eat carrion.

---

[113] By the way, governments *could* follow the Law if they wanted to, up to and including the penalties. They just don't because they don't want God either.

We can share His Word and exercise mercy, justice and compassion as much as we are able. In short, there are more things we *can* do than can't.

It's a Curse

There is a non-scriptural concept pedaled by some teachers that the Law is a curse. They get this from an incorrect view of Galatians 3:13-14.

> [13]Christ redeemed us from the curse of the Law, having become a curse for us—for it is written, "Cursed is everyone who hangs on a tree"— [14]in order that in Christ Jesus the blessing of Abraham might come to the Gentiles, so that we would receive the promise of the Spirit through faith. (Galatians 3:13-14 NASB95)

It is not that *the law is a curse.* It is that the curse connected with disobeying the Law is *death.* Obviously the curse of the law is for those who do not follow the Law, or try to use the Law in a lawless manner. The Law includes love, a heart of flesh, and the Spirit. If any of these are missing, the Law is being used lawlessly. As Paul says, it is impossible to earn salvation.

> For all who rely on works of the law are under a curse; for it is written, "Cursed be everyone who does not abide by all things written in the Book of the Law, and do them." (Galatians 3:10, ESV)

The Word says that the Law is part of God's Words to man, and they are life and blessing. Remember while you're reading the following verses that a blessing is the presence of God, and a curse is, at its root, the absence of God.

> [15]"See, I have set before you today life and prosperity, and death and adversity; [16]in that I command you today to love the Lord your God, to walk in His ways and to keep His commandments and His statutes and His judgments, that you may live and multiply, and that the Lord your God may bless you in the land where you are entering to possess it. (Deuteronomy 30:15-16 NASB95)

> [19]"I call heaven and earth to witness against you today, that I have set before you life and death, the blessing and the curse. So choose life in order that you may live, you and your descendants, [20]by loving the Lord your God, by obeying His voice, and by holding fast to Him; for this is your life and the length of your

days, that you may live in the land which the Lord swore to your fathers, to Abraham, Isaac, and Jacob, to give them." (Deuteronomy 30:19-20 NASB95)

Choosing God's Word or Law is choosing "life, blessing, and prosperity." It is not "death, adversity or a curse." The curse comes when we don't "choose life" and instead choose from the tree of our own Knowledge. Knowledge alone is death and/or lack of life if you want to look at it that way. When Jesus redeemed us from the "curse of the Law" by becoming "a curse for us," He died in our place to pay for violations of the Law. Death is the penalty for not following God's Word (Deuteronomy 27:26). The curse of the Law is death or separation from God (1 Corinthians 15:55, 56). It is not the Law itself that is the curse. Jesus didn't redeem us from the Law. Jesus redeemed us from the *curse* of the Law. Why in the world would He have had to redeem us from His own Word of Life? Only someone who wants an excuse to jettison God's Words will confuse the curse of the Law with the Law itself.

So why does the letter kill as Paul says in 2 Corinthians 3:6? Because God's holy Word kills anything unholy. Perfection destroys imperfection, like disinfectant destroys germs. We are less than perfect in ourselves, so if we mishandle the Law, or use it to try and justify ourselves without Jesus, it will kill us. The Law kills what needs to die, that is, the flesh or pride. If pride is all we've got, the Law will make us dead meat. If we have Jesus (faith), the Law is more like the ointment we use for athlete's foot, which kills the fungus but not the healthy tissue. If we are spiritual, the Law, which is also spiritual (Romans 7:14) will not harm us. We can follow it without fear of death because the blood of Jesus has cleansed us and made us holy, and His Spirit gives us the power.

Nailed To The Cross

Sometimes you'll hear that the Law was nailed to the cross, therefore we don't have to do it anymore. But you couldn't construct a doctrine with less truth in it from a plain reading of His Word if you did it on purpose. Some teachers base this false statement on one passage of Scripture. Here it is in two versions.

> [13] When you were dead in your transgressions and the uncircumcision of your flesh, He made you alive together with Him, having forgiven us all our transgressions, [14] having canceled out the certificate of debt consisting of decrees against us, which was hostile to us; and He has taken it out of the way, having nailed it to the cross. [15] When He had disarmed the rulers and authorities, He made a public display of them, having

> triumphed over them through Him. (Colossians 2:13-15 NASB95)

> ¹³ And you, who were dead in your trespasses and the uncircumcision of your flesh, God made alive together with him, having forgiven us all our trespasses, ¹⁴ by canceling the record of debt that stood against us with its legal demands. This he set aside, nailing it to the cross. ¹⁵ He disarmed the rulers and authorities and put them to open shame, by triumphing over them in him. (Colossians 2:13-15 ESV)

The "certificate of debt" is assumed by some teachers to be the Law, but this makes no sense from a Bible perspective. A certificate or record of debt is a list of wrong or lawless actions, not the law itself. In our court system, when someone is charged with law breaking, a list of the lawless behavior is read aloud. These are "decrees against us." It is this certificate of decrees that was nailed to the cross, not the Word of God. Jesus "became sin" for us, He didn't "become the Law." The nailing of the certificate of debt to the cross in no way implies termination of the Word or Law. God's Word continues. In verse 15 He "disarmed the rulers and authorities" meaning He paid the "certificate of debt against us" so certain spiritual powers lost their claim on us. The "accuser of the brethren" (Revelation 12:10) has lost his court case.

God says His Word will never pass away, nor will it change (Isaiah 40:8; Matthew 5:18; 1 Peter 1:25). His Word is love, life, grace, and mercy. It is not hostile to law-abiding citizens in the least (1 Timothy 1:8). Breaking the law gets us into trouble, not the Law itself. Jesus came to pay the penalty for our sin, not to eliminate any part of God's Word.

> ²¹He made Him who knew no sin to be sin on our behalf, so that we might become the righteousness of God in Him. (2 Corinthians 5:21 NASB95)

It is ridiculous to think the Law is eliminated by nailing it to a cross. It is eternal, and still in effect for everyone. Including the law-breaker should he or she choose to break it again. The certificate of debt is hostile, not God's Word. Put another way, the Word is only hostile to us when we break it.

> ⁴Everyone who practices sin also practices lawlessness; and sin is lawlessness. ⁵You know that He appeared in order to take away sins; and in Him there is no sin. (1 John 3:4-5 NASB95)

The verse above means that sin is "without Torah" or the Law. That's what "lawlessness" means – behavior outside the Law. The word "lawless" is also translated "iniquity" or sin. The King James Version of Matthew 7:23 is a good example of how the two words relate.

It's Legalism

Legalism is an English term (not in the Word) that means to misuse a law, usually to gain merit before God – in other words, to "earn" salvation. It does not mean that following laws is wrong. We follow many hundreds of laws nowadays just driving back and forth to church! We are not "saved" because we didn't go over the speed limit.

Besides, it's not that we have no laws in our congregations. God's laws in many instances have just been replaced by traditions. There are many "laws" which are made apart from the Scriptures and used like a legal hammer by the church or synagogue. Image 2 shows examples of some of those laws.

No musical instruments	Women must wear skirts
Can't watch 'R' rated movies	'Secular' music is sinful
Baptism is required for salvation	Smoking is sinful
Christians observe Christmas	Men and women can't swim together
Alcohol is sinful	Milk and dairy must be separate
Can't turn on a light on Sabbath	Men must wear a small hat
Dancing is sinful	Jews have to go to shul on Saturday
Men should not wear a hat	The pastor has to wear a suit and tie
Christians go to church on Sunday	Makeup is forbidden
Don't eat lamb on Passover	Christians observe Easter

Image 2

Many Christians or Jews live by these laws and others like them. They are simply not in God's Word. But if you are quiet long enough in many congregations, sooner or later you will hear these "laws" formalized and taught as if they were Scripture. If you break these "laws," you risk your membership in the Kingdom and even your salvation is suspect. You could be expelled from some congregations for violating some of them. So the misuse of law is alive and well, even if God's Laws are rejected.

I remember when I was about 18 my two older friends, call them Gary and Dan, decided that they needed to get rid of all their secular music albums in an effort to "remove what was ungodly" and get closer to God. Like a lamb, I just followed their lead and gave mine away too.

Perhaps this really helped them, but ever since, I've regretted it. Music is not sinful just because it's secular. There is good music and bad music. The labels of "Christian" and "secular" don't give us enough information. Dan and Gary got rid of the albums but continued with many unbiblical practices such as Christmas and Easter. Go figure. Whatever you think about the music, my point is legalism is always alive and well whether or not the Law is included. Legalism is falsely defined as following the Mosaic Law, but the Scriptures teach differently.

> ¹²So then, the Law is holy, and the commandment is holy and righteous and good. (Romans 7:12 NASB95)

> ¹⁴For we know that the Law is spiritual, but I am of flesh, sold into bondage to sin. (Romans 7:14 NASB95)

God's laws are life, but misusing or ignoring them can cause death (as it did for the First Parents). Many think of themselves as "saved" simply because they attend a church service once a week. There are also many who follow some of God's laws to the letter but only as traditions learned by rote (Isaiah 29:13). A whole-Bible Christian realizes that the law may be misused as an attempt to gain merit before God, or as an empty formula, but misuse does not mean God's Word is wrong. People can be wrong. Never God's Word.

Works of The Law Are Bad

Still another excuse some use to ignore the Law is the claim that "works of the Law" are bad. A section of this group even goes so far as to say actions done without "feeling like we are led by the Spirit" are "works of the Law." They discourage any activity if it isn't "felt" – the church version of "if it feels good, do it." If they do something, such as work in a soup kitchen, without "feeling" it, then it must be a "work of the flesh" or by association one of those terrible "works of the Law." So they avoid doing what God plainly commands because they don't "feel led." Feelings are king, and simple obedience to the whole of the Word is reduced to a sin.

Let's expand a little bit on what we talked about in the first chapter. On the surface it *does* look like parts of the Bible teach that works of the Law are not "from the Spirit," that they don't belong in a believer's walk, and should be avoided. The NASB (and others) translates words from Paul in Romans 3, Galatians 2 and Galatians 3 as "works of the Law" (capital L and with the added definite article "the").[114] Paul is made to look very negative about "works of the Law" at first glance.

Yet the translation is not correct according to the Greek. It also doesn't stand up to a balanced scrutiny from the whole of the Word. The word "Law" in those references should be lowercase and without the article. As in, "works of law" instead of "works of the Law." You might think it doesn't make a difference, but it does. "Works of the Law" is an

---

[114] The ESV doesn't usually capitalize it, but they still have the definite article and it isn't in the Greek.

attempt to limit works to the Mosaic Law, and castes obedience as wrong. The more accurate statement, "works of law," includes any legal relationship, any "work of the flesh," or any try at trading merit for grace. Works of law includes a misuse of The Law but isn't limited to The (Mosaic) Law. Roman law can be included, as well as natural law, oral law, and even tradition.

"Works of law" describes a legal relationship. A legal relationship is where I do things that I get paid for, and I only do them if I get paid. It is the use of any law to try and gain justification from God. This was the basis of the Satan's accusation against Job. He said that Job only worshipped God because he got paid (Job 1:9-11). He thought that if God took away the pay or the "hedge" (God's protection) that Job would falter.

"Works of the Law" makes it sound as if following God's Law is bad. But works of the Law by themselves are not bad. It's when we try to trade our works for God's salvation that they are bad. We cannot be justified by following a few rules. It's like not having enough money at the grocery store checkout. Even if our wallets are full of money, but we come up a few dollars short, we can't buy what we want. With God, even if our pockets are stuffed with works of law, this "money" just isn't enough to buy eternal life.

If an accused criminal tries to argue in court that he shouldn't be guilty of murder because he obeyed the speed limit, the judge would rightfully disregard it. This is sort of how we bargain with God (and frequently with each other). We want our good behavior to wipe out the consequences of our sin. It doesn't matter how many laws a criminal has NOT broken. The only thing that matters to the court is the one he broke. In God's court, if we try to argue our own righteousness, we will lose. We just won't have enough works of law to get paid.

Hananiah (Shadrach), Mishael (Meshach), and Azariah (Abednego) weren't interested in pay for following God's Word (Daniel 3). They were threatened with death by furnace for not worshiping an idol, but even if God wouldn't "pay off" with a rescue they were still going to stick with Him.

> [17] "If it be so, our God whom we serve is able to deliver us from the furnace of blazing fire; and He will deliver us out of your hand, O king. [18] "But even if He does not, let it be known to you, O king, that we are not going to serve your gods or worship the golden image that you have set up."(Daniel 3:17-18 NASB95)

Paul uses "works of law" to mean that some do an action connected with the Law, and then try to get paid for it (justification, Romans 4:4). It's like telling God that we deserve His blessing, including the blessing of eternal life, because we worked for it. Under this relationship, we try to trade our merit for His blessings. But we simply cannot do enough "right stuff" to make it worth a trade for eternal life. Our works (any works) are worthless for buying God's salvation. That does not mean works are worthless. They are just not legal tender for buying salvation.

> [19]Now we know that whatever the Law says, it speaks to those who are under the Law, so that every mouth may be closed and all the world may become accountable to God; [20]because by the works of the Law no flesh will be justified in His sight; for through the Law comes the knowledge of sin. (Romans 3:19-20 NASB95)
>
> [28]For we maintain that a man is justified by faith apart from works of the Law. (Romans 3:28 NASB95)

Not Under the Law

A similar term is "under law" (also mostly translated wrong as "under the Law"). This also means a legal, merit based trade. Paul says we are not "under the Law" (should be "under law") in Romans 6:14. We do not have a legal relationship with God (thank you Jesus). We have a grace relationship. Law has always been "under grace." Law is supposed to be in our hearts of flesh and we are all under grace. Grace is much better than a legal relationship, because God gives blessings to us in love. We give our obedience to Him because we love Him. Under grace, merit isn't even an issue.

One of the dumbest things I've ever heard smart men say is in the notes of the English Standard Version Study Bible on Galatians 5:16-26. This section of Galatians is where Paul describes the "works of the flesh." The note says, "Life under the law expresses itself in the works of the flesh, but those who live by the Spirit bear fruit pleasing to God." Sounds good, on the surface. Except that "works of the flesh" is most assuredly the *opposite* of God's Law. Paul in Romans says that the Law is "spiritual" (7:14) and "holy and righteous and good" (7:12). Remember that in the new covenant God says He will put His Spirit within us and "cause you to walk in my statutes and be careful to obey my rules" (Ezekiel 36:27). The ESV note is contrasting Spirit and Law as if the two are separate and opposite. Biblically, they go together.

I've got some news for you (and the ESV note writer). We never were "under the law" (in the sense of using it for salvation). Humans have always been "under grace." Certain people try to get "under the law" like Adam and Eve got under fig leaves. They misuse the Law to try and justify themselves. But that doesn't mean law has gone away.

The law has always been with us, just as grace always has. Grace, law and Spirit go together. They are all from the same living and loving God. Law is supposed to be in our hearts by the Spirit, not over our heads in the flesh. (See more on this subject in the chapter 8 "Produces the Fruit of the Spirit" section.)

When Adam was created, that was grace. He was placed in a beautiful paradise God had created, lacking nothing. More grace. Then God gave Adam a chance to look over all the animals. After Adam found the animals lacking in companionship, God made Eve. Grace again. Adam did not have to work for anything, and he didn't have to work for Eve. God just graciously provided.

We lived in Grace to start with, and God would've continued with us like that forever if not for sin. But since the first couple rebelled, they were expelled from the easy living situation and barred forever from returning (on their own, anyway). Ever since then man has been trying to figure out a way to buy a ticket back in with "works of law" (or even works of The Law). We try to sneak past the angel with the flaming sword (Genesis 3:24) with our own merit. It just cannot be done.

We want to arrange it that our "good things" can be traded for entry back into Paradise. We try to convince God that we deserve re-entry on our own merit. Imagine taking a stab at trying to barter with the flaming sword angel to look the other way so we can stroll on in to God's presence. But that angel is a little too cantankerous. He tends to chop first and ask questions later. Happily for us, the re-entry fee to paradise has been graciously provided by Jesus. The "cost" to us is our repentance and loving obedience. This brings us full circle, because obedience (or abiding) was all that was required of Adam and Eve in the first place.

It is a common human trait to desire payment for any and every effort, and not entirely bad. But when we try to get more from God than our effort is worth it doesn't fly. Scripture cautions against a legal relationship with God, because we just don't have a case.

Grace is the only way to go, and when we get grace and law in proper order, obedience takes on a completely different character. We start with grace, and then become slaves to His righteousness. Paul tells us to "work out your salvation," so working is not all wrong.

> [12] So then, my beloved, just as you have always obeyed, not as in my presence only, but now much more in my absence, work out your salvation with fear and trembling; [13] for it is God who is at work in you, both to will and to work for His good pleasure. (Philippians 2:12-13 NASB95)

We *do* get some "pay," in abundant blessings, for following each tiny little instruction that our Father gives us. We just aren't overpaid, in the sense of gaining eternal life for doing a few commands. Being overpaid wouldn't be reasonable for an earthly job. It's not reasonable to expect it from God for the "job" of doing some of His commands, either.

Humans in general get quite a few blessings from God even though many do not follow His commands. Bunches of them don't even acknowledge the giver of the blessings. God's children gain more, because the relationship is based on gracious love. It is through love that God's abundant blessings flow.

No Punishment

Then there is the idea that we don't have to do the Law because we don't get punished right away. This is a typical attitude from Christians, which many don't say aloud. Usually this objection comes up when speaking of the (perceived) small commands such as avoiding pork and shellfish. Because God does not seem to stand around and whack us upside the head with a stick when we don't obey, some think that implies permission to sin.

> [11] Because the sentence against an evil deed is not executed quickly, therefore the hearts of the sons of men among them are given fully to do evil. (Ecclesiastes 8:11 NASB95)

But we really should make sure of our idea of punishment. Connection to actions is not always seen. We may not be immediately punished with a lightning bolt or by the ground opening up and swallowing us (Numbers 16:30). But that doesn't mean we won't suffer when we ignore His command. Many times suffering is slow in coming because God wants us to repent.

We have no idea of the effects of eating flesh that is not food. For instance, we don't know for sure whether some of our diseases come from ingesting pork or shellfish on a regular basis. Science doesn't know enough to figure it all out because it's too complex.

Many effects of sin take a while to manifest, such as a pregnancy or disease from illicit sex. Jehoiakim, the son of Josiah we talked about in chapter 5, gets a scroll from God addressed directly to him. He cuts pieces of it off as they are read and burns them (Jeremiah 36) because he doesn't like the message. He is not immediately punished, but punishment surely falls. Not only did God do what He said He was going to do to Israel with the king of Babylon, but Jehoiakim is not allowed to have his son sit on the throne.

God is gracious in protecting us from some consequences of sin on some occasions. But should we continue to presume on, or cheapen, His grace this way?

> ¹What shall we say then? Are we to continue in sin so that grace may increase? ²May it never be! How shall we who died to sin still live in it? (Romans 6:1-2 NASB95)

This is part of the discussion we had under the Idolatry section of chapter 2. Remember that idolatry is cheating on God. We walk in the stubbornness of our hearts ignoring His Law thinking we'll get away with it because we (seemingly) don't get punished. It is obvious the church is reaping the poisonous fruit from this root of bitterness. The idea of avoiding immediate punishment does not fit in with love. Is it part of love to say I can do what I want because I'm not being hit with a stick? Not really. Love means God gives us commands that are good for us. A loving response is to do whatever He asks, simply because He asks. He is the source of light and life and love, so when we do what He says we share in His goodness. A stick isn't even part of the equation.

No Pay

On the flip side of the punish coin is reward. Or lack of it. Some just don't see the profit in following God's laws. In fact, it looks like many who follow His ways seem to have more problems than those who don't. There doesn't appear to be any big payoff for obedience.

> ¹³ "Your words have been hard against me, says the LORD. But you say, 'How have we spoken against you?' ¹⁴ You have said, 'It is vain to serve God. What is the profit of our keeping his charge or of walking as in mourning before the LORD of hosts? ¹⁵ And now we call the arrogant blessed. Evildoers not only prosper but they put God to the test and they escape.' " (Malachi 3:13-15 ESV)

Malachi was written a long time ago, but this problem is still around. Many think that "keeping his charge" (following his commands) is vain or not profitable. It's supposed to be all smooth sailing after we get our new heart of flesh, or that there should be some huge visible benefit like wealth or not getting sick or something. But pay is not the issue. Love is. Eternal life is. Of course we will have problems in this world. It isn't our world. It's filled with perverse people who hate God and do everything in their power to subvert and besmirch every aspect of His kingdom. They murdered the Son of God. How much more will they revile, slander, attack and murder us? The problems we have will all produce a positive blessing because "all things work together for good to them that love God and are called according to His purpose" (Romans 8:28). The sting of death is eliminated, and the comfort of His presence tames the problems by giving us wisdom and power to deal with them well.

There are blessings that accrue to believers, some of which we get now, like peace. Some we will get later, like a new body. The pay is good, and there is lots of it, but it's not measured in gold. It's not even measured in time. It's measured in love, which has no limit when you are joined together with the source of love.

It's Judaizing

The word "Judaizing" has been wrongly used to describe a person who wants to follow all of God's Word, including the Law. It implies that following the Law is a Jewish thing, and that Jewish things are bad (which isn't necessarily true). Judaizing[115] just means "to live like a Jew."

> ¹⁴But when I saw that they were not straightforward about the truth of the gospel, I said to Cephas in the presence of all, "If you, being a Jew, live like the Gentiles and not like the Jews, how is it that you compel the Gentiles to <u>live like Jews</u>? (Galatians 2:14 NASB95, underline added)

To live like a Jew is to adopt Jewish customs. These are mostly added on to the Law, and are spelled out in the oral law (Talmud). Like the modern church, Judaism doesn't have much in common with the Bible. It elevates tradition and rabbi's rulings over the Law. Jesus (John 7:19) Stephen (Acts 7:53) and Paul (Galatians 6:13) say that Jews do not follow the Law. There are also places like 2 Kings 17 that describe "living like a Jew" as a lot different than following God's Word. Through Judaism prophets of God are killed, and the kingdom of heaven suffers violence (Matthew 11:12). Of course, Christianity has the same problems. The "violent take it by force" means that unbelievers abuse His Word and assault His servants, as they did John the Baptist and ultimately God's Son. Trying to get in to the kingdom on their own merit, they get violent when told that just won't work.

Israel (as a group) has only truly followed Torah (the Law) a few brief times in their history. All sorts of tradition and interpretation were added at various times that took them far away from His Word. That's why God got on their case so much. He managed to beat disobedience back on occasion with a prophet like Samuel or a king like Josiah. Jesus made some progress getting His disciples and a few others to properly follow all of the Law. But generally Israel does not follow the Law. The

---

[115] It comes from the Greek word *Ioudaizo* (ee-yo-deh-ee-zo) mentioned once by Paul in Galatians 2:14 and once in Esther 8:17 in the Septuagint. Enhanced Strong's Lexicon G2450: "to adopt Jewish customs and rites; imitate Jews; one who observes the ritual law of the Jews." This is in contrast to living the Laws of God.

Law is mixed in with Judaism, but Judaism is not solely a practice of the Law.

> "You stiff-necked people, uncircumcised in heart and ears, you always resist the Holy Spirit. As your fathers did, so do you. Which of the prophets did your fathers not persecute? And they killed those who announced beforehand the coming of the Righteous One, whom you have now betrayed and murdered, you who received the law as delivered by angels and did not keep it." (Acts 7:51–53, ESV)

A whole Bible Christian strives for a balance between blindly embracing all of Jewish tradition bound up in Judaism, and rejecting anything and everything Jewish. Living the Law is different and better than living like a Jew.

The Crucifixion

Some argue that the crucifixion changed everything, including eliminating the Law. In some ways, yes the crucifixion did change everything. When Jesus was crucified and resurrected there were many areas affected. Lewis Sperry Chafer, for instance, lists 14 major areas affected by the crucifixion such as "the purification of things in heaven" (Hebrews 9:27).[116]

However, in many ways things were as they always had been, just reestablished. For instance, salvation was and is always, always, always by grace through faith. Or like I said earlier, by love through love. Salvation never came through observing some rules, no matter how righteous the rules.

The Bible does tell us of a change in law. However, this change was for the qualifications of priest. Before Jesus, according to the Law only people from the tribe of Levi could be priests. Jesus is from the tribe of Judah and is a priest after the order of Melchizedek, and the Law doesn't mention priests in connection with either Judah or Melchizedek. So when Jesus assumed the office of High Priest it was because of a change somewhere. He is a different kind of priest in a different place (the heavenly temple). The change was only concerning a transfer[117] of, or addition to, the priesthood (Hebrews 7:12-28). The writer of Hebrews was not suggesting a wholesale change of any kind in the Law.

Think for a minute. Actually, we should think for more than a minute, but devote at least a minute or two to this concept. If Jesus is

---

[116] Lewis Sperry Chafer Systematic Theology; unabridged; Dallas Seminary Press; 15th printing August 1983; volume III chapter IV page 55. He's the founder of DTS; I don't agree with every item, but it's an interesting read.

[117] Hebrews 7:12, the first word 'change' is Enhanced Strong's Lexicon 3346a, which means change or transfer.

God, and God is unbounded by time (He is eternal), then His crucifixion would have eternal effects, both forward and backward. The crucifixion was truly a monumental event. So monumental in fact that its effects echo throughout infinity. Time only looks to us like there is a backward and forward. It doesn't look like that to God.

> [8]Therefore do not be ashamed of the testimony of our Lord or of me His prisoner, but join with me in suffering for the gospel according to the power of God, [9]who has saved us and called us with a holy calling, not according to our works, but according to His own purpose and grace which was granted us in Christ Jesus *from all eternity*, (2 Timothy 1:8-9 NASB95, italics added.)

In fact, probably the only reason God didn't wipe out the creation, instead of just purifying it with a flood, was the anticipated (in time and space) sacrifice of the Son of God. In other words, the death and resurrection of Christ happened at a particular time and place from our viewpoint. But not God's. To God, who is eternal, the death and resurrection of His Son is, for lack of a better term, always "fresh in His mind."

We are not the only ones who can take advantage of the sacrifice of Jesus even though we exist 2,000 years after it happened. The people who lived thousands of years before it happened could do the same thing. How else would God be able to deal with sin-filled humans?

Do you really think the Law, with a few animal sacrifices and a tent, was enough to make the people sinless? Enough that God could dwell amongst them? Of course not. The tabernacle was a concrete reminder of the death and resurrection of Jesus, and the animal sacrifices were memorials and a testing of faith. The issue then was not salvation, it was trust and obedience. Just like it is now.

It's a Shadow

We covered this some before, but here I wanted to expand a little more on the concept of shadows in the context of application. Because a shadow is insubstantial, and Paul mentions that parts of the Law are a shadow, some conclude we don't have to follow the Law.

> [16]Therefore no one is to act as your judge in regard to food or drink or in respect to a festival or a new moon or a Sabbath day— [17]things which are a mere shadow of what is to come; but the substance belongs to Christ. (Colossians 2:16-17 NASB95)

Trouble is, the idea that shadows are meaningless is false. There are many uses of the word "shadow" in the Word, but the shadows are real.

For instance, in Matthew 4:16 people are said to be under the shadow of death, and death is very real. Isaiah speaks of a type of shadow.

> ¹⁶"I have put My words in your mouth and have covered you with the shadow of My hand, to establish the heavens, to found the earth, and to say to Zion, 'You are My people.' " (Isaiah 51:16 NASB95)

The "shadow of (God's) hand" is obviously real too, and has a very real effect on us. Just because Paul used the concept of a shadow does not mean that the Law isn't real and isn't to be followed. A shadow can only be cast by the real thing. If you have the shadow, you have the reality too. We'll cover more of Colossians 2 a little later in the book.

The life that we live here and now is a shadow of the next one, but that doesn't mean it is any less substantial or real. What we do in this "shadow" life will determine substance in the next life. What we do with the "shadows" God gives us in His Law will be part. If we are faithful with very little "shadows" it means we are faithful also in much bigger things, shadows or not.

> ¹⁰"He who is faithful in a very little thing is faithful also in much; and he who is unrighteous in a very little thing is unrighteous also in much. (Luke 16:10 NASB95)

If it is true that God gave a "mere shadow" of things in the Law, then why give them in the first place? Why not just say (at Mount Sinai) "Oh, just do what you want because My Anointed will make everything cool in a thousand years or so?" It doesn't make any sense. Yes, some of the things God gave at Sinai could be termed shadows of things to come. But that does not mean they are not worth doing.

"No one is to act as your judge" means no one should tell me how I observe the days outside of what the Bible says. For instance, there are people who celebrate Passover with an egg on the Seder plate. If I don't have an egg (or a beef bone) because it's not in the Word, then I shouldn't be judged for not having it. In fact, if I don't observe the traditional Seder and prefer the simple biblical order of Exodus 12, I shouldn't be judged for that either.

It's All Good (Genesis 9, Acts 10)

The whole issue of food somehow sticks in the craw of many. For some reason we want to justify eating whatever we want. We use Scripture like this to do it.

> ¹But the Spirit explicitly says that in later times some will fall away from the faith, paying attention to deceitful spirits and doctrines of demons, ²by means of the hypocrisy of liars seared

in their own conscience as with a branding iron, [3]men who forbid marriage and advocate abstaining from foods which God has created to be gratefully shared in by those who believe and know the truth. [4]For everything created by God is good, and nothing is to be rejected if it is received with gratitude; [5]for it is sanctified by means of the word of God and prayer. (1 Timothy 4:1-5 NASB95)

This is one of the Scriptures (see also Mark 7:18-19) used to excuse what a person wants to eat before they even read the Bible. In other words, they want to eat pork or shellfish and they look around in the Word to see if they can find permission. Here they think they find a magic formula where they can pray over anything, consume it, and be okay. But believers know that doesn't really work. If something is "sanctified by the Word of God," that means the Word tells us how to "set it apart" (the definition of sanctified). That's what Leviticus 11 does, for instance. God "sanctifies" or sets apart things in that chapter that are food and things that are not. "Those who believe and know the truth" are those who know the Word and follow what He says. The "truth" is God's Word, and God says there are certain things that we shouldn't be eating. That is much different than a doctrine or teaching of demons.

The two situations mentioned here don't have anything to do with God's Law. Obviously forbidding marriage would not come under the heading of God's command. Equally obviously, not everything is good to eat even if it is "sanctified by the word of God and prayer." We can't just pray over some poison hemlock, say, and turn it into sugar. Even if it's clean (Hemlock is a plant) it's still poison. There are lots of things we can't or shouldn't eat, no matter how much we pray.

"*Foods which God has created to be gratefully shared*" does not include pork or shellfish or any of the other things He told us were not food. Even Noah knew the difference between clean and unclean animals (Genesis 7:2). God did not ever say that pork, shellfish, dog, cat, horse, or rabbit were food. Somewhere along the line, somebody decided that if it tasted good it was okay to eat. But God designed certain animals for purposes which did not include barbecues.

He told us there are things that are food, and things that are not food. If Jesus declared "all foods clean" (Mark 7:19) then He wasn't talking about stuff that isn't food. Leviticus 11 tells us that there are things we can eat, and things we can't. God doesn't say "food we can eat," and "food we can't eat." Things we can't eat are, by definition, not food. Clean things are food, unclean things are not food. And even if a food item is clean that still doesn't mean it is okay to eat (like spoiled potatoes). Besides, in Matthew 15:20 Jesus said that the lack of hand washing does not make food unclean. He didn't say that suddenly everything is okay to eat.

Genesis 9:3 is another argument people use to justify eating anything they want.

> Every moving thing that lives shall be food for you. And as I gave you the green plants, I give you everything. (Genesis 9:3, ESV)

A small problem, however. "Every moving thing that lives" doesn't mean everything can be eaten. For instance, though people are included in "every moving thing that lives" obviously they are not to be eaten. All green plants cannot be eaten either. Some are poisonous. Others are distasteful, like moldy bread or rotten fruit. There are meats that are deadly poison too, or are deadly if they are not handled just so (like lobster). We even treat plain water with caution, boiling and filtering it to "clean" it. Meat was made available, but there is nothing in the text to suggest all meat is okay to eat. God nailed the issue down further at Sinai. Probably because there were a lot of people who ate anything without exercising the sense God gave a turnip.

Peter's vision (Acts 10) is another Scripture improperly applied. First, he didn't "rise, kill and eat." Second, the account does not say that everything in the sheet was declared clean by God. The sheet wasn't the point. The point was to make sure clean and unclean were rightly labeled. Clean and unclean animals mix together all the time. The unclean animals do not make the clean ones unclean.

Only in relation to eating is there a difference. Under the Scriptural Law Peter would've been fine if he had taken a clean animal and had a barbecue. But according to rabbi's reasoning, unclean animals made the clean ones unclean (which doesn't make sense). Peter was refusing to eat because of the rabbinical ruling, not the Law. God reminded Pete, through a refresher course from His Word, that He (not rabbis) makes the call on what is clean and what is unclean. Jews wrongly thought (and many still think) that only Jews (clean) are saved and Gentiles (unclean) are not. Therefore many rabbis teach that the clean (Jews) can't mix with the unclean (Gentiles) or they will themselves become unclean. Peter didn't want to eat because the unclean and clean animals were mixed together (as in nature, if you think about it). God was pointing Peter back to His Word and away from rabbinical tradition.

Third, Peter tells us the meaning of the vision.

> [28]And he said to them, "You yourselves know how unlawful it is for a man who is a Jew to associate with a foreigner or to visit

him; and yet God has shown me that I should not call any man unholy or unclean. (Acts 10:28 NASB95)

³⁴Opening his mouth, Peter said: "I most certainly understand now that God is not one to show partiality, ³⁵but in every nation the man who fears Him and does what is right is welcome to Him. (Acts 10:34-35 NASB95)

The vision had nothing to do with changing the Laws of clean and unclean animals, but had everything to do with removing the "unclean" label from Gentiles. This label was falsely applied by Jewish leaders against what God intended. In the vision, God was getting the situation back to right. Obviously not all Gentiles are clean unless they "[fear] Him and [do] what is right." Cornelius was such a "right doing" person, but there was still a roadblock to being included in the local church. Not because of the Law, but because of "elementary principles of the world" in Judaism.

Freedom In Christ

As taught by most of the visible church, this short statement carries with it a huge amount of power, even to the erasing of that which Jesus said could not be erased (Luke 16:17, John 10:35). Many cling to this statement in its dogmatic form as meaning, "I don't gotta do what God says." In other words, by the dogma of pastors or other supposedly learned men, this "freedom in Christ" frees us from God's Words. However, that is not what Paul meant.

> ¹It was for freedom that Christ set us free; therefore keep standing firm and do not be subject again to a yoke of slavery. ²Behold I, Paul, say to you that if you receive circumcision, Christ will be of no benefit to you. ³And I testify again to every man who receives circumcision, that he is under obligation to keep the whole Law. ⁴You have been severed from Christ, you who are seeking to be justified by law; you have fallen from grace. (Galatians 5:1-4 NASB95)

Pay careful attention to verse four, especially the phrase "you who are seeking to be justified by law." With a few moments reflection it is obvious that circumcision was equated to being justified by the Law in some minds. Therefore, those minds were pursuing circumcision and rejecting God's grace. They were trying to earn salvation through a legal relationship. Paul rightly condemns such attitudes in very strong terms. Grace has always been God's way.

> And you, O generation, behold the word of the LORD. Have I been a wilderness to Israel, or a land of thick darkness? Why then do my people say, 'We are free, we will come no more to you'? (Jeremiah 2:31, ESV)

The mistake with people has always been to seek acceptance through merit. As if somehow we could live righteously enough in ourselves that we don't need God. Following God's Word is not wrong; it is misusing God's Word as a means of self-justification that is wrong. Peter says, *"Don't use your freedom as a covering for evil"* (1 Peter 2:16).

"Freedom in Christ" means freedom from the impossible tyranny of trying to buy our way into heaven. It also includes freedom from another person's idea of righteousness. When we are free in Christ, we choose servitude to God through love. There is great freedom in His Word; His Law. We are marked with the Holy Spirit in a similar way as the servant with a pierced ear (Exodus 21:5-6) who voluntarily continued to serve his master. Freedom in Christ also means we are free from sin, not free from the Law or Word of God.

> ^{5}For if we have become united with Him in the likeness of His death, certainly we shall also be in the likeness of His resurrection, ^{6}knowing this, that our old self was crucified with Him, in order that our body of sin might be done away with, so that we would no longer be slaves to sin; ^{7}for he who has died is freed from sin. (Romans 6:5-7 NASB95)

Freedom in Christ has changed us from slaves of sin to willing servants of righteousness. This is because we have become "obedient from the heart."

> ^{15}What then? Shall we sin because we are not under law but under grace? May it never be! ^{16}Do you not know that when you present yourselves to someone as slaves for obedience, you are slaves of the one whom you obey, either of sin resulting in death, or of obedience resulting in righteousness? ^{17}But thanks be to God that though you were slaves of sin, you became <u>obedient from the heart</u> to that form of teaching to which you were committed, ^{18}and having been freed from sin, you became slaves of righteousness. (Romans 6:15-18 NASB95 underline added.)

Salvation Is Enough

So many people halt in the "salvation moment," as if that was all there was to a relationship with God. It is like saying "I got what I want and that's that." But He has so much more for us, and requires that we continue our transformation by taking every thought and action captive for the Christ (2 Corinthians 10:5).

A person who was dying of cancer and had four broken limbs wouldn't want to be cured of the cancer only. I'm sure he'd be grateful to be alive, but the broken limbs would make living a little difficult. This is sort of like people who stop at the salvation moment.

To say "I got what I want," and not give God what He wants (our life), is not genuine love. The Law, as part of the whole of the Word, is love, and love does not hold still. It moves us through the salvation moment and into abundant life.

I Don't Hear Jesus

One of the big objections I get when I talk about abiding in His Word, or obedience, or anything to do with the Law, is that "I don't hear Jesus" (in my teaching). What they mean is that I don't say "Jesus" every other word. Or that I don't constantly refer everything back to the crucifixion. I usually pose this question in reply – Is it that you don't *hear Jesus*, or that you don't *hear*? Am I not *saying*, or are you not *hearing*?

> [47] Whoever is of God hears the words of God. The reason why you do not hear them is that you are not of God." (John 8:47 ESV)

Jesus is all about obedience (or abiding). It's His Word in the first place that we obey and abide in. He showed up all through the Old Testament preaching and reinforcing the Law He delivered and had Moses write down at Sinai. After He was born as a human, He consistently taught repentance and a return to God's Law. He instructed the disciples to take this gospel (good news which is God with us so live like it) to the whole world, making other disciples (a word related to "discipline"). We have His Spirit who only repeats what He hears from Jesus (John 16:14) and leads us into all truth, which is the Word. Jesus is God's Word, with the Law, in form and action. You can't read more than a few verses in the Scriptures without tripping over the issue of staying true to His Word, or returning to His Word, or teaching His Word. There is nothing about obedience that is not intimately connected to Jesus.

If someone doesn't "hear Jesus" in the Law, or in teachings on obedience to His Law, they are probably 100% correct. They don't hear (Matthew 13:13, Luke 16:31, John 8:43).

Lifting Jesus Up

Along the same lines as the objection about "hearing Jesus" is the one about lifting Jesus up. The argument is that we need to focus on

Jesus only, and "lift Him up."

> ^{32} And I, when I am lifted up from the earth, will draw all people to myself." (John 12:32 ESV) (Compare also verses such as John 3:14 and 8:28.)

However, most who object to teaching the Law or obedience, and use this argument, do not understand these verses. To lift Jesus up is to crucify Him. He *was* lifted up, and He *does* draw all men to Himself. But when these people use the word "lifting" they mean "glorify" or "remind" or even "speak of constantly or only." They are confusing two meanings with one word. This verse conveys what they mean a little better.

> ^{2} For I decided to know nothing among you except Jesus Christ and him crucified. (1 Corinthians 2:2 ESV)

"Lifting Him up" does not mean that the only thing we ever talk about is the crucifixion. There are other things He wants us to do. We don't leave Him on the fence as they do in the play Godspell (one of the big objections to that play is there is no resurrection).

Don't get me wrong, the crucifixion is one of the most, if not *the* most, important event ever. We can't talk enough about it. But part of the crucifixion is that through it we have life. Now we walk in that life, eating and drinking His body and blood, from the body which was broken for us. We crucify our own flesh by turning from our ways to His. We lift Jesus up (glorify) when we eat His body and drink His blood, meaning we abide in and glorify Him when we obey His commands (John 6:56, 8:31, 1 John 2:6, 17, 24; 3:6, 9).

> ^{8} By this my Father is glorified, that you bear much fruit and so prove to be my disciples. ^{9} As the Father has loved me, so have I loved you. Abide in my love. ^{10} If you keep my commandments, you will abide in my love, just as I have kept my Father's commandments and abide in his love. ^{11} These things I have spoken to you, that my joy may be in you, and that your joy may be full. (John 15:8-11 ESV)

So there are two ways to look at "lifting up." One way is to crucify, the other is to obey. The more we obey or abide, the more we "lift Him up" in the sense of giving Him glory. This means much more than just using His name all the time. It means to abide or remain with Him and His Words. If we do not obey His commands we "lift Him up" or crucify Him again (Hebrews 6:4-6).

It's Not Restated

There are a few people who teach that the Law is not restated in the New Testament in the same way as the Old, so we don't have to follow. I have to say, "Oh c'mon now, how many times does God have to tell us something? Why would the Law need to be restated (a fourth or fifth time, not counting the summaries)? Would it really change anything if He did?" Considering all the lame excuses to avoid it we've seen, I think not.

> [12] Were I to write for him my laws by the ten thousands, they would be regarded as a strange thing. (Hosea 8:12 ESV)

It's not restated because it was already written twice (two sets of tablets) and was assumed to be in effect. Jesus directed His message first to the Jews, so of course they already knew the Law. The apostles went first to the Jews, so it *still* didn't need to be restated. If you read the New Testament carefully, though, you'll find that it *is* restated many times. Just not on stone tablets. It's universal, and has always been around. Nowhere in Scripture do we find that the Law is now gone. It would be simple enough to write this, wouldn't it? And wouldn't that be momentous news? You betcha it would. It would also disqualify the person who said it from being a godly teacher.

We're like teenagers with a curfew, or an adulterous President. As soon as we get the curfew, we start looking for ways around it. If we get caught having sex outside of marriage, we redefine sex. Take time to read through the laws on immoral relations in Leviticus 18. After a moment or two you should almost hear the sound of people in the background saying over and over, "But what if..." like a teenager trying to weasel out of a curfew. Sometimes it seems like we're almost frantic in looking for any loophole to do what is in our hearts. Or to jump the fence surrounding His pasture.

After we jump the fence He set up for us with His Law, we are chased around by lions, bears, and wolves. We get frazzled, and wonder why we suffer so much, and wonder why God doesn't rescue us. There's a reason He doesn't always rescue us. He already rescued us, and we left His safe area on our own. He tells us, "Come back into the sheepfold ringed about with the protection of my Laws!"

> [17]These are springs without water and mists driven by a storm, for whom the black darkness has been reserved. [18]For speaking out arrogant words of vanity they entice by fleshly desires, by sensuality, those who barely escape from the ones who live in error, [19]promising them freedom while they themselves are

> slaves of corruption; for by what a man is overcome, by this he is enslaved. ²⁰For if, after they have escaped the defilements of the world by the knowledge of the Lord and Savior Jesus Christ, they are again entangled in them and are overcome, the last state has become worse for them than the first. ²¹For it would be better for them not to have known the way of righteousness, than having known it, to turn away from the holy commandment handed on to them. ²²It has happened to them according to the true proverb, "A DOG RETURNS TO ITS OWN VOMIT," and, "A sow, after washing, returns to wallowing in the mire." (2 Peter 2:17-22 NASB95)

I could go on and on with people's objections to God's Word, but enough has been presented that we can see the many ways people question what God says, and how to get the simple answers. The Great Commission of Matthew 28:19-20 was to make disciples and teach them all of His commands. We aren't to pick and choose which commands to teach by dividing them into false categories and sitting in judgment picking which ones are "moral." After Paul was introduced to His Messiah he helped show us the way while remaining a Jew and practicing the Law he was teaching. Of course we can do the Law, or a gracious and loving God would not have given it.

The curse in the Law is death for ignoring it. It is not the Law itself. What was nailed to the cross were our violations of the Law; He died in our place bearing the sins of the world (John 1:29; 1 John 2:2). Trying to find merit in legalism then is a poor substitute for His Word, because works of law were not intended for salvation. We don't wait for God to punish, because we are too busy loving Him through obedience. In this we do not ask for pay. As humble servants we ask only that we can continue to serve Him.

Following the Law is not living like a Jew, or Judaizing, because living like a Jew includes traditions outside of God's Law and they rarely follow as they should. There's nothing Jewish about the Law; it is for all His people. Traditions of all sorts, not just Jewish, have blocked access to the easy yoke of His living oracles. We groan under the weight of man-made legal rulings that do more to rob us of life than aide us in finding it. The crucifixion made big changes, helping creation in many ways, but one thing it did not change was the unchangeable Law. Even shadows from the law have more substance than all the concrete opinions of man. The shadows help us discern what is good and not good, clean and unclean, holy and not holy.

We walk in the freedom of Christ way past the salvation moment, lifting Him up and glorifying Him by abiding in steady obedience. We preach the "good news" of "God with us" with repentance and returning to His Word as His Kingdom gospel. He doesn't need to restate His Law for true believers to recognize that He wants us to live by it. The changeless God did not change His Word either arbitrarily or due to the crucifixion; He changes our hearts.

8 Whole Bible Blessings

¹³"Thus says the LORD of hosts, the God of Israel, 'Go and say to the men of Judah and the inhabitants of Jerusalem, "Will you not receive instruction by listening to My words?" declares the LORD. ¹⁴"The words of Jonadab the son of Rechab, which he commanded his sons not to drink wine, are observed. So they do not drink wine to this day, for they have obeyed their father's command. But I have spoken to you again and again; yet you have not listened to Me. (Jeremiah 35:13-14 NASB95)

The descendants of Rechab spoken of in these verses followed the commands of their father Jonadab. They were not to drink wine, and they were supposed to live in tents and take care of livestock. These things they did faithfully. So God used them as a good example of obedience, and blessed them for it. However, Israel did not compare favorably. The Rechabites did as their father said, but Israel wouldn't obey *their* Father. God asks His people for simple obedience, and blesses us when we honor Him. Just as the Rechabites honored their father. The modern church is not obeying their Father in exactly the same way.

God's gracious Law is a perfect gift with a number of benefits attached that we also call blessings. There are 24 listed here. They are not the only blessings, but they are a good cross-section. We get benefits when we get the Law. God's purpose is to bless, and His Law has tremendous blessings. Some people only get a few benefits because they only accept a little of what God has to offer. But if we plunge in with whole hearts, we will gain the approval of our Father and we reap a full harvest of blessings, pressed down and overflowing. Just like the Rechabites.

Connects

One of the first blessings believers get when we embrace the whole of God's Word is it helps connect the spiritual and the physical worlds. The inside and the outside. God's Word is not only spiritual (unseen, if you prefer) or only physical (the seen or sensed). It is both spiritual *and* physical. His intentions are for the Spirit and the Word to work as one on both the material (body) and immaterial (soul/spirit) parts of believers.

> ¹ Therefore I urge you, brethren, by the mercies of God, to present your bodies a living and holy sacrifice, acceptable to God, *which is* your spiritual service of worship. ² And do not be

conformed to this world, but be transformed by the renewing of your mind, so that you may prove what the will of God is, that which is good and acceptable and perfect. (Romans 12:1-2 NASB95)

Paul tells us in the verses above to present our bodies a living sacrifice, and to be transformed by the renewing of our minds. We train our bodies with God's action regimen (the physical part of the Word). We transform our minds by rightly dividing the Word to help our practice. Both are critical ingredients of working out our salvation with fear and trembling.

And beside this, giving all diligence, add to your faith virtue; and to virtue knowledge; And to knowledge temperance; and to temperance patience; and to patience godliness; And to godliness brotherly kindness; and to brotherly kindness charity. (2 Peter 1:5–7, AV)

Some in the church are afraid of the Law because they are convinced that you shouldn't do something unless you feel like it first. For them, doing something (like avoiding pork) without feeling like it is "works." "Works" to them is the same as "works of the flesh" or even "works of the Law." Working is somehow wrong in their opinion. Feelings, for these people, are the same as the Spirit and therefore good. Obedience without feeling like it, on the other hand, to this group is merely physical and therefore bad. If you've ever heard someone use the term "I don't feel led," even when faced with a clear biblical command, then you've heard it too.

Western Christians get this "physical is bad" thinking handed down to us from the Greeks. Among other things, Greek thinking is very linear and assumes that material and spiritual things are separate, and only spiritual things are good. They think it is wrong to do something without feeling like it. According to them, a person can't just obey God; we have to feel like it too.

Mixed in with the Greek thinking people are the hippies who entered the church in the '60's from the "Jesus people" movement. But the Jesus they followed was the false Christ of <u>Godspell</u> and <u>Jesus Christ Superstar</u>. And they didn't leave their eastern, sentimental, sort-of-spiritualism at the door. They simply Christianized some of their practices such as transcendental meditation.[118] Instead of changing to

---

[118] TM, or transcendental meditation, was really big in the '60's. You may remember the chant of "ohm, ohm" or "oh-ma-na-pahd-me-ohm." The chant is supposed to focus attention outside of the physical world on the so-called 'god-mind,' and is an attempt to connect with it. It is from eastern

God's standard, they remade Jesus in their own image. Now they just sing songs over and over (and over and over) instead of chanting ohm. The hippies went establishment, and they changed their outside somewhat. Inside, however, they were, and are, still the same.

To maximize the fruit of the Spirit, we have to pursue changes with a whole effort. Inside and out. If we love God and want to do His will, then His Laws will help us change and grow. As we move forward in obedience, we continue to remove bad practices from our lives and replace them with good ones.

> "For no good tree bears bad fruit, nor again does a bad tree bear good fruit, for each tree is known by its own fruit. For figs are not gathered from thornbushes, nor are grapes picked from a bramble bush. The good person out of the good treasure of his heart produces good, and the evil person out of his evil treasure produces evil, for out of the abundance of the heart his mouth speaks. (Luke 6:43–45, ESV)

We do not have to wait for our minds to renew first and then do what God says. Nor do we have to disconnect our actions from our minds. Out of the abundance of our heart our mouth speaks. We present our bodies (the outside) as a sacrifice by doing what God commands. We transform our mind (the inside) by continued reading. Then the Word and the Spirit train us in righteousness and the blessings flow freely. In the following verses, Isaiah connects the fruit of the Spirit with things like fruitful fields, justice, and righteousness, which in turn leads to peace, quietness and trust forever.

> [14] For the palace is forsaken, the populous city deserted; the hill and the watchtower will become dens forever, a joy of wild donkeys, a pasture of flocks; [15] until the Spirit is poured upon us from on high, and the wilderness becomes a fruitful field, and the fruitful field is deemed a forest. [16] Then justice will dwell in the wilderness, and righteousness abide in the fruitful field. [17] And the effect of righteousness will be peace, and the result of righteousness, quietness and trust forever. (Isaiah 32:14-17 ESV)

Justice

Another blessing from the Law that could use a whole book is justice. Everything God gives us is connected together and balanced, and justice is right there in the mix, with love and mercy. Micah tells us this

---

mysticism and thoroughly pagan, but has found its way into the church in the form of endless song and prayer repetitions. Matthew 6:7.

in a summary of the Law, which is similar to the "two commands" and many other summaries.

> [8] He has told you, O man, what is good; and what does the LORD require of you but to do justice, and to love kindness, and to walk humbly with your God? (Micah 6:8 ESV)

His Law teaches us real justice, which is mixed with mercy, love and humility. Everyone has some sense of justice. Anyone who has raised children, or been a child, knows how they have a laser-like focus on justice. Especially when mom is handing out deserts and a sibling has a larger helping. Generally, though, our innate sense of justice is very self-centered and lopsided. God's justice, outlined in the Law, is much more balanced.

Many, many blessings flow from learning and applying His brand of justice in the Law. Sadly, in modern culture, justice is falling by the wayside. Lawyers tell me that juries convict on appearance and feelings rather than testimony and facts. Jail has replaced paying restitution. The death penalty is taking a holiday, but the blood of innocents aborted cries out for justice, and surely deafens heavenly watchers. Murderers, kidnappers and rapists go free (or become president), but trumped up tax problems get you jailed for a long time.

The church is right in there with modern culture in what it approves.[119] We do not make thorough investigations (Deuteronomy 13:14, 17:14, and 19:18). We judge by appearances (John 7:24). More weight is given to a wealthy person's opinions over a poor person's (Exodus 23:6). In general we do not speak out against abortion, homosexuality, adultery, witchcraft, drugs, and other behavior as we should. Nor do we restrict it in our assemblies. Matthew 18 is rarely applied correctly to my knowledge. Well, maybe to weed out the disagreeable people. We throw a coat of "social justice" over the deep gaping mud holes made by ignoring His real justice and call it good. Until we step in the hole and find ourselves up to our armpits in alligators.

Remember, the root of blessing is the presence of God. A curse, at its root, is the absence of God. Creation is under a curse, meaning that God has withdrawn to some extent. That's why we have thorns and poisonous critters to fight all the time. If we reject the Law, we compound the curse with a lack of justice, and God will not allow injustice to continue forever.

---

[119] Remember we're talking about the whole of the Book, not just lip-service to some alleged 'moral' laws.

Protects

Believers need protection from the opinions of men, and God's Law provides it. His protection keeps us from having to jump through the hoops formed by teachings based on extreme feelings or tradition. He has told us which actions are approved and which actions are not. If we are doing His approved actions we don't have to worry about the opinions of men. For instance, if I don't want to eat ham and someone doesn't like my choice, I am still at peace because I am abiding in His Word. When I rest on Sabbath, my love for God and His Word protects me from the judgment of others who don't want to rest. I have confidence in His Law, and as I seek His approval I do not worry about the approval of men (Colossians 2:16-23).

Moves

Yes, our reliance on Jesus' sacrifice is the one and only action needed to gain right standing with God. But instead of just standing there, God requires that the life be changed to match up with His Word ("put on the new man" Ephesians 4:20-24, "be filled with the Spirit" Ephesians 5:18-21, etc.). The message of the Law is don't just stand there, do something! We are supposed to keep moving toward the Christ and His example.

> [4]For Christ is the end of the law for righteousness to everyone who believes. (Romans 10:4 NASB95)

Jesus is the "end" (the Greek word *telos* Strong's 5056 in this context means "goal" "aim" or "purpose") of the Law, so doing the Law takes us to Jesus. It's like taking a train (the "gospel train?" the "peace train?"). It takes believers where we want to go. But your goal has to be Jesus; because that is the only place the Law train goes. If you want to go someplace besides the Jesus stop, you'll either ride in circles or have to take a different train.

Frequently someone who is newly "saved" will ask, "What do I do now?" The standard answer is, "Nothing. Jesus did it all." We are so thoroughly conditioned against "works," we take great pains to educate the newbies away from "doing." This "do nothing" attitude discourages maturity. The new believer is robbed of independence (from groups) and goals, not to mention abundant life blessings. He or she is not taught to rely on the Word as a guide for righteousness.

Eating and drinking His body and blood fosters dependence on God instead of a pastor or church. This may explain at least part of the reason why His Law isn't taught or followed very well. In following the Law, a new believer is encouraged to develop his or her own relationship directly with the Father through the Son (by His Word). His goals are given to Him by God. He's got the guidebook (the Bible) right there in front of him, an absolute, objective standard needing no improvement. A pastor or church doesn't want this because it might wreck the machine.

The Law has been routinely and falsely portrayed as impossible to follow. But it is much easier to follow a few simple written rules than it is to do some of the other things He asks us to do. Sometimes we are tasked with things that are really difficult, such as dying for our faith or having to flee a home or country because of persecution.

Straightens

One of the reasons Law was given is because man is perverse. This is defined as doing differently than God has directed.[120] I do a lot of woodworking, and I use an L shaped piece of metal called a carpenter's square to check if the wood is square or straight. God's Law is like a carpenter's square. It is a straight path for our feet and a light to our way. We compare our will and actions with it, and we find out if we are straight and square. When we aren't, He makes adjustments to bring us in line. Sometimes with sandpaper. Ouch.

Perversion is as obvious as homosexuality or as simple as ignoring His holidays. Or even eating fruit from the wrong tree. Humans in general are quite creative when it comes to acting perverse. We seem to take delight in exploring just how many ways we can pervert anything God says (Deuteronomy 32:5, 20; Acts 2:40, 20:29-30). We'll even go so far as to take the carpenter's square of His Word and tweak it so it fits us, instead of using it to keep us straight.

No matter what God tells us to do, in our perversity we've gotta do it at least slightly different. If He says stay away from the tree of knowledge, we make it into a buffet, complete with fancy lighting and a sneeze shield. He created man and woman to be together in marriage; we come up with sterile and destructive "alternate lifestyles." He says don't eat certain things; we go out of our way to farm and mass market pork and shellfish.

The church would like to think that somehow we are different, and more apt to follow what God says. But we have the same tendency toward perversity as the non-churched. We're just a little more creative in how we go about it. We come up with all kinds of nifty theories to help give ourselves permission to sin.

We've got "different ages" with separate commands for "other people." There are spiritualized covenants that distance us from actually doing His Word. There's the "anti-theology" crowd and the touchy-feely

---

[120] Some dictionaries say "willfully determined, or disposed, to go counter to what is right, good or proper."

"social justice" crowd. It seems there's no end to our dodging. But no matter how artfully we decorate the fig leaves, or how well we hide in the bushes (Genesis 3:7-8); no matter how we tweak the carpenter's square, the Word is always there to straighten out our lack of obedience. Or measure us for judgment.

Perfect Practice

Another purpose of the Law is practice. My high school band teacher was the first one to tell me that "perfect practice makes perfect." Practice alone doesn't make perfect. If you practice sloppy, you will play sloppy. We had to get it right in practice because in performances you will play as you practiced. It's true. If I didn't get it right in practice, I would blow it in the performance. I would play just like I practiced. God wants us to practice each part of Torah (the Law) to perfection, so we will act the same no matter who is watching.

When we start to learn almost any skill or task, we get simple things first. More complicated things are added as we get familiar with the basics. God's law functions this way for the believer too. We can start with simple things like diet changes and a day of rest. Then we progress to more complicated principles such as patience and self-control. We work back and forth between easy and hard stuff, like a kid learning to play a musical instrument. We learn notes and simple songs first. Later we get a symphony solo.

Learning the simple, concrete things helps to pave the way for learning the more difficult actions. It's the difference between a ladder with the first few rungs missing and one with all the rungs. We find out that God is concerned about every area of His children's life, from what we eat and wear to the fruit of the Spirit. The more we practice right things the more sanctified (set apart) we become.

> ^{22} But the fruit of the Spirit is love, joy, peace, patience, kindness, goodness, faithfulness, ^{23}gentleness, self-control; against such things there is no law. (Galatians 5:22-23 ESV)

Of course there's no law against such things as patience, kindness and self-control. That's because if we have those things we have the Law. All those things are what God wants for us in the first place, and why He gives us His living oracles.

Universal

God's law or Word applies to everyone, not just to believers. There are a number of places in Scripture, for instance, that speak of God's judgment on nations other than Israel. God has the right to judge them. And what does He judge them by?

> ⁵The earth is also polluted by its inhabitants, for they transgressed laws, violated statutes, broke the everlasting covenant. ⁶Therefore, a curse devours the earth, and those who live in it are held guilty. Therefore, the inhabitants of the earth are burned, and few men are left. (Isaiah 24:5-6 NASB95)

> ⁵"Thus says the Lord GOD, 'This is Jerusalem; I have set her at the center of the nations, with lands around her. ⁶'But she has rebelled against My ordinances more wickedly than the nations and against My statutes more than the lands which surround her; for they have rejected My ordinances and have not walked in My statutes.' (Ezekiel 5:5-6 NASB95)

That's right; God judges by the Law (also called the "everlasting covenant"). How can God judge people who aren't part of the covenant? Because everyone knows what is right and wrong, even if they don't have the Bible.

> ¹⁸For the wrath of God is revealed from heaven against all ungodliness and unrighteousness of men who suppress the truth in unrighteousness, ¹⁹because that which is known about God is evident within them; for God made it evident to them. ²⁰For since the creation of the world His invisible attributes, His eternal power and divine nature, have been clearly seen, being understood through what has been made, so that they are without excuse. ²¹For even though they knew God, they did not honor Him as God or give thanks, but they became futile in their speculations, and their foolish heart was darkened. (Romans 1:18-21 NASB95)

It's not that people don't know what God wants. Verse 19 says *"that which is known about God is evident within them, for God made it evident to them."* They *know* what God requires, they just don't want to *give* it (verse 21). We all have sinned, whether we possess the written commands or not. Ignorance is not bliss. Everyone will have to answer for their actions. God's Law is an opportunity to understand what God requires and adjust ourselves to it. It is universal, so everyone knows what He wants. Everyone knows, so we don't have to guess.

Life Abundant

The Law is life and health to our being, because it's a part of the whole Word of God. It is the Bread of Life. It is blessing and vitality for the soul. With it we live; without it we merely exist. A fly exists but spends its life in filth. A mouse exists but is constantly fearful. Believers live because they are connected with the Source of life through hearing and doing His Word.

A malnourished child lives, yes, but just barely. Every day is a struggle to find enough food to make it through the next day. He or she is weak, listless, and incapable of much more than trying to find more food. The well-nourished child on the other hand is healthy, happy, and well able to pursue any activity. God's complete Word is the nutrition His children need to be healthy, content, mature, and have life abundant. Blessings pressed down and overflowing.

There are two attitudes we are talking about here. The first attitude says that the Law has been nullified by some "new thing" that Jesus did. The second attitude sees the Word eternally existing and unchangeable. The Law is part of God's gracious promise and God is The Rock.

The first attitude leads to viewing God as capricious and constantly shifting the relationships between Himself and others. He plays games like giving Israel a covenant they supposedly couldn't follow. The second attitude sees God as always loving, always merciful and ever constant (Exodus 34:5-7). He uses a progressive revelation that builds on previous revelations to unfold His unfailing promise.

The first attitude causes anxiety because one never knows what the capricious God will do next. The second produces the fruit of the Spirit because God can be counted on always to do what He says He will do. The first rips away the anchor of God's Word because the plain meaning is destroyed. The second attitude generates confidence because the Word is understandable as it is read by the average person.

It Marks His Children

The Law (God's Word) is a sign or mark of those who follow God. It is not necessarily a physical mark such as a stamp on the hand, although there are some physical marks too such as circumcision (including circumcision of the heart Deuteronomy 10:16, 30:6; Jeremiah 4:4; Joel 2:13 and Romans 2:29).

> [11] "And you shall be circumcised in the flesh of your foreskin, and it shall be the sign of the covenant between Me and you. (Genesis 17:11 NASB95)

A physical mark can accompany those who are unhappy with the ways of the world and long for a society that follows God's ways.

> [4] The LORD said to him, "Go through the midst of the city, even through the midst of Jerusalem, and put a mark on the foreheads of the men who sigh and groan over all the abominations which are being committed in its midst." (Ezekiel 9:4 NASB95)

The Sabbath is a sign of those who know that He is the Lord our God. All who "sanctify" it or set it apart like it's supposed to be are God's children. Sanctifying Sabbaths is the same as walking in His statutes and keeping (observing) His ordinances (Laws).

> [19] 'I am the LORD your God; walk in My statutes and keep My ordinances and observe them. [20] 'Sanctify My sabbaths; and they shall be a sign between Me and you, that you may know that I am the LORD your God.' (Ezekiel 20:19-20 NASB95)

The "mark of the beast" (Revelation 13:16-17) may be a physical mark, but the mark is just an outward sign of what the people have already chosen. They've already sold out to the beast and his image (Revelation 14:9, 11). People in the Bible are marked because of obedience. Believers are marked as belonging to God by observing God's ordinances and statutes, just as worship of (or obedience to) the beast "marks" those who belong to the deceiver. External marks certify (or signify) like a nametag or a badge. But our behavior identifies us more surely than paint or ink to God. External marks are for those who can't see as He does, such as angels and people.

Best Discipleship Method Ever

The Law is not for salvation. It never has been, although following God's Word by repentance and obedience certainly gives life, and salvation *is* a command. Instead, the Law is a tried and true method to condition us and train us for righteousness. It is the best discipleship system ever devised. God's Law, or Word, trains us to be like the Kingdom version of the U.S. Navy Seals. We handle any of life's problems under any conditions and still reach the target. That target is Jesus, our hearts desire. That's what Romans 10:4 really means – that Jesus is the goal of the Law. Jews, who had the Law, did not accept God's righteousness (Jesus) but sought to establish their own. They did not follow the Law to its goal.

There have been many attempts by man to develop discipleship or training systems, and some of them are even based on the Word. But they are not the Word, and therefore even the best of them are just not as effective as His. Even the methods of Bill Gothard and Ray Comfort, who are closer than many others, still do not reach the effectiveness of God's whole Law.

The Spirit uses God's Word to work on the flesh and transform the mind. That is exactly what it is designed to do by the Creator of our bodies and souls. It is an objective standard that takes the guesswork out of what is right behavior and what isn't. It is backed by the authority of

God. So if He says a practice will work a certain way, then if followed in faith (remember, trusting obedience) it will do exactly what He promises.

> [19]I am speaking in human terms because of the weakness of your flesh. For just as you presented your members as slaves to impurity and to lawlessness, resulting in further lawlessness, so now present your members as slaves to righteousness, resulting in sanctification. (Romans 6:19 NASB95)

Paul gives us another metaphor to help our understanding about training.

> [24]Do you not know that those who run in a race all run, but only one receives the prize? Run in such a way that you may win. [25]Everyone who competes in the games exercises self-control in all things. They then do it to receive a perishable wreath, but we an imperishable. [26]Therefore I run in such a way, as not without aim; I box in such a way, as not beating the air; [27]but I discipline my body and make it my slave, so that, after I have preached to others, I myself will not be disqualified. (1 Corinthians 9:24-27 NASB95)

Paul says he disciplines his body, or trains, in such a way as to win the race. The Law, as part of the whole Word of God, helps us with this training. Salvation is not the only issue—there is also walking in a manner worthy of the God who calls us.

> [10]You are witnesses, and so is God, how devoutly and uprightly and blamelessly we behaved toward you believers; [11]just as you know how we were exhorting and encouraging and imploring each one of you as a father would his own children, [12]so that you would walk in a manner worthy of the God who calls you into His own kingdom and glory. (1 Thessalonians 2:10-12 NASB95)

> [7]But have nothing to do with worldly fables fit only for old women. On the other hand, discipline yourself for the purpose of godliness; [8]for bodily discipline is only of little profit, but godliness is profitable for all things, since it holds promise for the present life and also for the life to come. (1 Timothy 4:7-8 NASB95)

The single biggest factor in our growth as believers is probably the switch from thinking of God's Word in negative terms to positive ones. Part of this depends on how we see God. If we see Him as a big, capricious meany thumping on people all the time, we think of His Laws as tools for mistreatment. But if we see Him as the source of good, then His Law is life for us.

Teaches Children

I was talking to a guy from Voice of the Martyrs magazine at my church a few years ago. He was there with a special speaker warning of the danger of Islam. We got into a discussion because of the tassels on my pants (see chapter 10). He was familiar with some of the concepts in this book on the positive portrayal of the Law, and he made an interesting comment.

He said we (the church) are losing kids in the inner cities to Islam because of the attraction of discipline.[121] Islam offers a discipleship method that is more structured than Christianity, and uses parts of God's Law. Many of our youth have become tired of floating in an endless sea of subjective sentiment. Our culture has cut itself loose from too many anchors. So young people are looking for something solid, something they can build with.

Islam is attractive to the kids because it provides structure in an unstructured world. You might think this is merely anecdotal and not proof that something is wrong in the church. But it illustrates that youngsters are looking for more than what the watered-down church is offering.

Following God's ways doesn't guarantee a lack of problems, but it certainly works better than man-made rules or drifting aimlessly in a shifting sea of ever-changing feelings. In my opinion, God's instructions are way more effective than the ones we make up. God desires of us godly offspring, and the most effective way to raise them is to teach His Laws in word and deed.

> [15] Did he not make them one, with a portion of the Spirit in their union? And what was the one God seeking? Godly offspring. So guard yourselves in your spirit, and let none of you be faithless to the wife of your youth. (Malachi 2:15 ESV)

A few years ago a good friend in a Sunday school asked how he could help keep his kids in the faith. It seems his teenagers were starting to drift away, and he was concerned. I listened in some amazement as another friend took ten minutes to advise the first friend to keep his kids from watching R rated movies and make sure they went to church every week. My advice was a little different. I told both friends to teach the Word through God's traditions, especially the feasts (Leviticus 23). I told them how we observed Sabbath with a family meal as a kick off on Friday night, and how my daughter who went to college in Hawaii for a

---

[121] A more recent article mentions the loss of Hispanics from Catholicism to Islam also. http://beforeitsnews.com/opinion-conservative/2013/08/report-u-s-hispanics-leaving-catholicism-for-islam-2702638.html

while still participated even though she was far away. She would call on Friday nights and we would put her on speaker phone. Then we would say blessings and eat together.

Later her fiancé, a Marine training in North Carolina, would call too and we had to find a second speaker phone for him (we already had two phone lines). It was a lot of fun, and helped keep our separated kids involved in and connected with the family and with the Word. The key to this of course was to practice God's Word all the time, not just after they left home. I lost touch with that friend, so I don't know if he ever took me up on my advice. I hope so.

Practicing the whole Bible has made a huge, wonderful difference in our lives. We still have a family meal once a week, even though my daughter and her husband have been married for 14 years. I am so pleased that my children (and now grand children) have been taught the Law and they are still following its precepts. They tell me that the Word is much more meaningful to them than ever before. God's Word is guaranteed to work because it is backed by His authority and power. *We don't always cooperate, but the Word works.* If we follow His directions, we will end up right where He wants us.

Esteems God

Our culture in the last few decades has placed a great emphasis on self-esteem. We think we need to work hard on building ourselves up and feeding our egos. The Bible, however, accurately informs us that we don't need more self-esteem. We already have an over-inflated sense of self-worth. The problem is not what we think of ourselves, but how we treat God and others.

We love ourselves just fine without having to bolster it or have it bolstered by others. *"For no one ever hated his own flesh, but nourishes it and cherishes it"* (Ephesians 5:28-30). This is why verses like Leviticus 19:18 assume a love of self as a starting point for loving others. Notice too that "lovers of self" turns up in a very negative list in 2 Timothy.

> [1] But realize this, that in the last days difficult times will come. [2] For men will be *lovers of self*, lovers of money, boastful, arrogant, revilers, disobedient to parents, ungrateful, unholy, [3] unloving, irreconcilable, malicious gossips, without self-control, brutal, haters of good, [4] treacherous, reckless, conceited, lovers of pleasure rather than lovers of God, [5] holding to a form of godliness, although they have denied its power; Avoid such men as these. (2 Timothy 3:1-5 NASB95 italics added)

In general, people want what God *has* but they do not want what God *is*. We want His power, His life, His blessings and all the other nice things that He has. But we do not want Him in charge of any of it. We love Psalm 23, but Psalm 119 doesn't exactly fan our flames.

Magic and other practices He prohibits are self-esteem related attempts to get what God has without God. We overrate our importance, then try to use that inflated sense of self-worth to manipulate and get what we want – minus the whole sovereign God thing. Self-esteem doctrines tell us that what is important is what each person thinks or feels. They don't include what God thinks or feels.

> ⁹"For the eyes of the LORD move to and fro throughout the earth that He may strongly support those whose heart is completely His. You have acted foolishly in this. Indeed, from now on you will surely have wars." (2 Chronicles 16:9 NASB95)

We've got plenty of self-esteem built in. What we really need is "God esteem." Obedience to the smallest instruction from God shows our esteem. When every jot and tittle of His Word, even the least command, is accepted and followed with love in the Spirit, we speak volumes about how we esteem our God. Self-esteem follows in its proper place.

Draw near, Touch God

One of my favorite terms, and one that comes the closest to the reason for following the Law, is "draw near" (or "come near" see Exodus 12:48). In my view this is what Torah is all about. The gospel tells us that God is with us, and His Law tells us we can draw near to Him by obedience or abiding in His Word. The term can be used for simply getting together (if we are talking about a pair or group of people), but when one of the parties is God it takes on a whole different character. We can "come near" God for judgment as in Malachi 3:5, or we can come near in love and intimacy. A similar term is "draw near."

> Draw near to God, and he will draw near to you. Cleanse your hands, you sinners, and purify your hearts, you double-minded. (James 4:8, ESV)

We "draw near" to God as we do what He says. The more we do, the closer we get. In humility we use His living oracles to wash the parts of us that get dirty. Though He has cleansed us wholly, we still need to wash occasionally.

> Jesus said to him, "The one who has bathed does not need to wash, except for his feet, but is completely clean. And you are clean, but not every one of you." (John 13:10, ESV)

We are clean, but we still need to wash some in order to continue "drawing near." Notice that Jesus did the foot washing during the Passover meal. Jesus continues to wash our feet by the washing of the Word as we "draw near" to Him through His commands. There is a continual cleansing by His Law because we are in a dirty world and sometimes we step in something odoriferous that needs to be removed. If we judge (cleanse) ourselves and wash our hands (or feet) then Jesus doesn't have to judge us.

Every time we implement another instruction from our Father we draw near, and it is as if we touch Him and He touches us. When we trust Him and do what He says, like a little child, love flows between Him and us and our siblings in the Body. People long for a touch from God. They don't find it as often as they'd like because usually they want His touch on their own terms. Submitting to His Law allows more of His light inside. As we abide in His Word it is like we open windows one at a time in a dark, musty house.

One of the many things Jews have right is to refer to a command from God as a *mitzvah*, and liken each one to a thread between the believer and God. The more commands we do, the more threads are established and the more we are "tied" to Him. The more threads we have the harder it is to wander away.

Still a Tutor

The Law is called a tutor by Paul. In his time, usually in Greek households, a tutor would be sort of a guardian of a person's child. This was until the child reached the age when he or she could make their own decisions and be responsible for their own behavior. The tutor was responsible for teaching the child to function as an adult, and led them to maturity.

> [24]Therefore the Law has become our tutor to lead us to Christ, so that we may be justified by faith. [25]But now that faith has come, we are no longer under a tutor. [26]For you are all sons of God through faith in Christ Jesus. (Galatians 3:24-26 NASB95)

Once a person reaches maturity, it does not mean that all of the principles taught by the tutor disappear. We simply incorporate them into daily living without having to be told what to do every second. Even if we are not "under the law," that doesn't mean we don't follow it, because "not under the Law" does not mean "don't obey the Law." It means that something else is "over" us (and the Law), which in this case is God's grace. We are under grace with the Law written on our hearts.

If Paul had meant for us to avoid obedience to God's Word, he would have said exactly that. And he didn't. Maturity means we take the Law (all of God's Word) filled with the Spirit, and do it with a new, whole, soft heart of flesh. When we do this, we don't need to be told every little move to make. We already know what our Father wants, by heart.

Some people think and teach that if we have the Christ, then we "don't need the Law" (there's that lucky rabbit's foot again). "Having Christ" to these teachers' means to like Him a lot. Or "believe" without action. Or to think that He's a great teacher or prophet and nothing more. There's a technical term for the "we don't need the Law" teaching, which is "horse hockey." If we have the Christ, we have God, and we get God's Words, including the Law. If we reject the Law, we are rejecting God's Word to His people, which would show that we do not "have Christ." It's a package deal.

If we say we "have Christ" yet do not do what the Christ says, then we are nothing more than clashing gongs and clanging cymbals (1 Corinthians 13:1). And that not even in time with God's music. When we pick and choose through the Word for what we will do and what we won't, it does not jive with the example that Jesus set. He did it all, and perfectly. He expects us to do the same. And perfectly means confessing and repenting when we make mistakes instead of looking for excuses or rationalizing. It means a circumcised heart (Deuteronomy 10:16, 30:6; Jeremiah 4:4; Joel 2:13; Romans 2:29).

We need to understand that the Law still functions as a tutor to lead a person to the Christ. It tutors anyone on their way to maturity with God. This means that God still uses it to draw people to His Son, and by living it, we can draw people to Him, too.

Further, the Laws do not go away just because we are now old enough or "have Christ." When I was a child I learned not to stick the wrong object into an electrical socket, but when I "grew up" that law did not cease to be. I just graduated to the proper use of the socket without having to be told. I still don't stick the wrong object in the socket. I learned it is injury or death to ignore or mishandle the law. In the same way, when we graduate to Christ, the Law still functions. It's just that I don't need to be told. It is written on my heart. Having reached maturity, the Law does not cease to function. Instead, it is written on my heart so that I do what it says automatically. The Law becomes second nature.

Besides that, what kind of arrogance do you have to have to claim that you are so "grown up" that you don't need the helping hand of

God's Law? I suppose it might be a reasonable claim, if in fact we could see a bunch of grownups behaving in a mature, Spirit filled fashion. But we don't. What we see are mostly squalling, fighting, unloving, cut-you-off-at-the-drop-of-a-hat teenagers. Hypocritical at best and wearing sheep's clothing at worst. If there was ever a desperate need for the tutoring of God's Law, it is now.

The Fruit of The Spirit

In Galatians Paul speaks of the fruit of the Spirit in contrast to the deeds of the flesh. It is obvious that he is contrasting two different types of actions, not feelings or intentions. Fruit is real, concrete action coming from inside.

> [18] But if you are led by the Spirit, you are not under the Law. [19] Now the deeds of the flesh are evident, which are: immorality, impurity, sensuality, [20] idolatry, sorcery, enmities, strife, jealousy, outbursts of anger, disputes, dissensions, factions, [21] envying, drunkenness, carousing, and things like these, of which I forewarn you, just as I have forewarned you, that those who practice such things will not inherit the kingdom of God. [22] But the fruit of the Spirit is love, joy, peace, patience, kindness, goodness, faithfulness, [23] gentleness, self-control; against such things there is no law. [24] Now those who belong to Christ Jesus have crucified the flesh with its passions and desires. [25] If we live by the Spirit, let us also walk by the Spirit. (Galatians 5:18-25 NASB95)

Remember that verse 18 should read "you are not under law" rather than "you are not under the Law." To tweak it a little so the meaning is plainer, we might say, "You are not operating by a legal relationship." The "deeds of the flesh" are actions, and so is the "fruit of the Spirit." If we are "under the Spirit" (a grace relationship) then we act like it and continue to act like it. To get the Spirit we need to get the Law. Law includes following every one of His Words.

The church trains people to see the fruit of the Spirit and obedience to the Law as two different things, when in reality they go hand in hand. You cannot have the Spirit without the Law, and you cannot properly do what God instructs without the Spirit (Ezekiel 11:19-20). This is the "heart" of the new covenant.

> [26] "Moreover, I will give you a new heart and put a new spirit within you; and I will remove the heart of stone from your flesh and give you a heart of flesh. [27] "I will put My Spirit within you and cause you to walk in My statutes, and you will be careful to observe My ordinances. (Ezekiel 36:26-27 NASB95)

There are people who try to follow laws without the Spirit. This is the essence of legalism – perform an action and demand to be accepted by God because of it. There are other people who regard themselves as spiritual but ignore God's Law. This leads one to inquire just exactly what sort of spirit energizes them.

We should not seek a legal relationship with Him anyway because like I already said, we don't have a case. He sent His Son to die for us because He loved us, not because He had to, and not because our "righteous" actions required it. John 3:16 is about God's love translated into action in the giving of His Son. It is not about sentiment.

When God took up residence in the Tabernacle, it wasn't because Israel had done everything right (Deuteronomy 9:4-6). It was because He loved Israel and wanted to make them into a great nation who knew their God in a personal, loving way. Love causes loving actions, and loving actions are a result of love, whether one "feels" love or not. Love is action. Action is fruit. You don't have to feel it; you just have to do it. Feelings will come later.

Faith is trust and obedience, with love mixed in, around and through. Love is greater than faith and hope (1 Corinthians 13:13) but it does not stand on its own. Neither does faith, nor hope. We do not fracture faith, hope and love into sections and get them piecemeal. They are part of God's whole package to us. All of them work together to bring forth the fruit of the Spirit, and the Law provides the framework.

He's in There

Some of you may remember a TV commercial in the 70's with the famous Italian opera singer and actress Anna Maria Alberghetti. She advertised some brand of spaghetti sauce (I forget which one), telling us that all kinds of good stuff was "in there." Somebody would ask her if a certain spice was in it, and she'd say, "It's in there." Paul sort of says the same thing. He tells us another blessing of the Law is that the Messiah's glory is "in there." This is why Moses had to put a veil over his face.

> [7]But if the ministry of death, in letters engraved on stones, came with glory, so that the sons of Israel could not look intently at the face of Moses because of the glory of his face, fading as it was, [8]how will the ministry of the Spirit fail to be even more with glory? [9]For if the ministry of condemnation has glory, much more does the ministry of righteousness abound in glory. [10]For indeed what had glory, in this case has no glory because of the glory that surpasses it. [11]For if that which fades away was with glory, much more that which remains is in glory. [12]Therefore having such a hope, we use great boldness in our speech, [13]and

are not like Moses, who used to put a veil over his face so that the sons of Israel would not look intently at the end of what was fading away. ¹⁴But their minds were hardened; for until this very day at the reading of the old covenant the same veil remains unlifted, because it is removed in Christ. ¹⁵But to this day whenever Moses is read, a veil lies over their heart; ¹⁶but whenever a person turns to the Lord, the veil is taken away. (2 Corinthians 3:7-16 NASB95)

The reason for the veil was the glory Moses had seen, and the glory was Jesus. In Moses' time the law wasn't fading, it had just been given. What was fading was the glory of the Messiah that he had seen in the Law. The glory of Jesus had to be veiled because the minds of the people were hardened (verse 14). They did not want to obey, and they did not love God. The veil is removed when someone turns to the Christ, so the glory in the Law (Jesus) can be seen.

People teach perverse things about the Law because their hearts are hardened, and when they read the Law, the veil remains. It is only when we humble ourselves (or accept humbling by God) and abide or obey that God transforms the tablet of our heart from stone to flesh. Then the Spirit can write the new covenant on it (2 Corinthians 3:3). What is written is the Law of God (Jeremiah 31:31-34) and because the Spirit writes it and the heart responds in love, the letter does not kill (2 Corinthians 3:6). Everything God has is "in there" waiting for us to taste and see.

An Effective Mirror

Paul calls the Law a mirror, and says if we look into this mirror, we are transformed by the glory of Jesus in the Law.

> ¹⁸But we all, with unveiled face, beholding as in a mirror the glory of the Lord, are being transformed into the same image from glory to glory, just as from the Lord, the Spirit. (2 Corinthians 3:18 NASB95)

According to Paul, the glory of Jesus transforms us as we gaze with unveiled face (without a hard heart) into the mirror of the Law. We turn to the Christ and the veil is removed. James also says the Law is like a better mirror.

> ²³For if anyone is a hearer of the word and not a doer, he is like a man who looks at his natural face in a mirror; ²⁴for once he has looked at himself and gone away, he has immediately forgotten what kind of person he was. ²⁵But one who looks intently at the perfect law, the law of liberty, and abides by it, not having

> become a forgetful hearer but an effectual doer, this man will be blessed in what he does. (James 1:23-25 NASB95)

James' mirror and Paul's mirror are the same. It is the "perfect law," and the "law of liberty" – the whole absolutely true Word of God. James is just a little more specific. He mentions being an effectual doer of the law. Not just a lookie lou. It doesn't do enough good just to look. We have to copy what we see to make the changes complete. Both Paul and James convey the very real idea that the law helps us see ourselves as we are (another reason we're not real comfortable with it). The glory of Jesus in the law accurately reflects His image and shows us what we are. He gives us the reflection we need to guide and change our ways.

The Key to Understanding

Submitting to God's will, including the part of His will revealed in the Law, amazingly adds to and enhances the understanding of God's whole plan and purpose. When the Spirit begins his (or her) work in the believer with the Law, the whole Word of God becomes easier to understand and follow. Something about humble submission to the Word imparts an ability to understand it better.

> [10]The fear of the Lord is the beginning of wisdom; A good understanding have all those who do His commandments; His praise endures forever. (Psalm 111:10 NASB95)

> [3]Seek the Lord, All you humble of the earth Who have carried out His ordinances; Seek righteousness, seek humility. Perhaps you will be hidden In the day of the Lord's anger. (Zephaniah 2:3 NASB95)

> [6]"So keep and do them, for that is your wisdom and your understanding in the sight of the peoples who will hear all these statutes and say, 'Surely this great nation is a wise and understanding people.' [7]"For what great nation is there that has a god so near to it as is the Lord our God whenever we call on Him? [8]"Or what great nation is there that has statutes and judgments as righteous as this whole law which I am setting before you today? [9]"Only give heed to yourself and keep your soul diligently, so that you do not forget the things which your eyes have seen and they do not depart from your heart all the days of your life; but make them known to your sons and your grandsons. (Deuteronomy 4:6-9 NASB95)

> [18] Where there is no prophetic vision the people cast off restraint, but blessed is he who keeps the law. (Proverbs 29:18 ESV)

Without the Law, we build on a shaky foundation (like building a house on sand). We also find whole chunks of the New Testament more obscure and harder to understand. However, head knowledge alone of the Law is not enough. We need to read it and do it, like we are eating His body and drinking His blood. Accepting His will as expressed in the Law requires humility, and humility brings understanding.

It's Love

Speaking of immersion and submission, Jesus says that His disciples abide in His love by doing what God says.

> [23] Jesus answered and said to him, "If anyone loves Me, he will keep My word; and My Father will love him, and We will come to him and make Our abode with him. [24] "He who does not love Me does not keep My words; and the word which you hear is not Mine, but the Father's who sent Me. (John 14:23-24 NASB95)

> [9] "Just as the Father has loved Me, I have also loved you; abide in My love. [10] "If you keep My commandments, you will abide in My love; just as I have kept My Father's commandments and abide in His love. (John 15:9-10 NASB95)

According to Jesus, God's word (or Law) is the same as Jesus' words. There are not two different words for two different peoples. The words we hear from Jesus are the Father's words, and Jesus speaks what God tells Him to speak. So we abide in the love of the Father and the Son when we take in what they say and do it. Love is the aim of everything a believer does. As we do what He says, He makes His abode (or abides) with us, and we abide in love with each other.

> [4] I was very glad to find some of your children walking in truth, just as we have received commandment to do from the Father. [5] Now I ask you, lady, not as though I were writing to you a new commandment, but the one which we have had from the beginning, that we love one another. [6] And this is love, that we walk according to His commandments. This is the commandment, just as you have heard from the beginning, that you should walk in it. (2 John 4-6 NASB95)

The beginning that John speaks of is not the alleged beginning of the church but the beginning in the Garden. "His commandments" are not some abbreviated or changed version of the Law, but the eternal Law itself. God's Law to love one another has always been around; it just hasn't always been followed. The message has always been "walk in it."

Remember that when Jesus says to eat His body and drink His blood (John 6:50-58) He is saying that hearing and doing is like partaking of

Him. Each time we obey a command, we make another connection to God and to each other. The more we obey the more we abide. It is like the food we eat distributed to every cell in our body, keeping our life going. The more we bring in what He says to daily living, the more it helps us "take every thought captive."

> [3] For though we walk in the flesh, we do not war according to the flesh, [4] for the weapons of our warfare are not of the flesh, but divinely powerful for the destruction of fortresses. [5] We are destroying speculations and every lofty thing raised up against the knowledge of God, and we are taking every thought captive to the obedience of Christ, (2 Corinthians 10:3-5 NASB95)

It doesn't matter if the Testament is old or new, there is an implied obligation—not from fear but from love. It is not lip-service, nor is there a take-it-or-leave-it option. God's child is "obliged" to follow God's Words in their completeness because God gives us so much love. It is reasonable to love God back by giving Him obedience with all of our heart, mind or soul, and strength. In view of His love and sacrifice for us, it doesn't make any sense to ask, "Do I *have* to follow the Law?"

> [18] Little children, let us not love with word or with tongue, but in deed and truth. [19] We will know by this that we are of the truth, and will assure our heart before Him [20] in whatever our heart condemns us; for God is greater than our heart and knows all things. [21] Beloved, if our heart does not condemn us, we have confidence before God; [22] and whatever we ask we receive from Him, because we keep His commandments and do the things that are pleasing in His sight. [23] This is His commandment, that we believe in the name of His Son Jesus Christ, and love one another, just as He commanded us. [24] The one who keeps His commandments abides in Him, and He in him. We know by this that He abides in us, by the Spirit whom He has given us. (1 John 3:18-24 NASB95)

It's Worship

This is a good place to talk about the blessing of worship. If you look in the Word (gee, what a concept!) worship is generally spoken of in connection with doing what God says. Worship, obedience, and blessing go hand in hand with humility and truth.

> [23] "But an hour is coming, and now is, when the true worshipers will worship the Father in spirit and truth; for such people the Father seeks to be His worshipers. [24] "God is spirit, and those

> who worship Him must worship in spirit and truth." (John 4:23-24 NASB95)
>
> ⁸Jesus answered him, "It is written, 'You shall worship the Lord your God and serve Him only.' " (Luke 4:8 NASB95)

We worship or serve God when we do what He says. Obedience is the most basic form of worship, and the one form that He desires above all others. There is no grey area. We are either for Him or against Him. *"For he who is not against us is for us."* (Mark 9:40 NASB95)

We cannot roll around on the ground, sing songs over and over with many tears, give money, or speak in mysterious languages, yet ignore His Word, and then expect these histrionics will be acceptable worship. We may "acquire the fire" but it won't keep going without loving obedience to fuel it. Acquiring the fire is easy. Tending it throughout the years is a lot harder.

If you had a child that spoke of how devoted to you they were, then went out and behaved in ways that caused harm to you or others, would you think the way they spoke about you was genuine? If you had a spouse that spoke of devotion to your face, but behind your back was getting in bed with other people, would the devotion be real? God doesn't think so either.

Many times Israel is chastised by God because their worship of Him consisted of mere lip service. They would "go through the motions" of sacrificing, then do things that were directly against what God had commanded. The church has not escaped the same fault, nor will we escape the same judgment if we continue in it. Worship of God was and is always to be done with a whole heart in every action. Loving the Lord includes all our heart soul and strength.

> ¹⁷But thanks be to God that though you were slaves of sin, you became obedient from the heart to that form of teaching to which you were committed, ¹⁸and having been freed from sin, you became slaves of righteousness. (Romans 6:17-18 NASB95)

Worship can include singing or what have you, but for these outward expressions to be genuine they will be coupled with an inside condition of obedience. They spring from a right relationship with God. When we obey God in the smallest area, it is worship. In this way, we can worship Him minute by minute by following as many of the commands as we can. We don't need a special building with a special music team and special leaders. We don't have to have "worship music" on the radio or something either. We don't need signs and wonders. Obedience is the key to worship; it's abiding as a living sacrifice (that Romans 12:1-2 section again).

Are we also glad of heart in the doing? Sure. Obeying God imparts life and brings forth joy on a regular basis, and we express this joy in song. Are we thankful? Oh yeah, especially when we think about all He has done for us. But worship is as regular as breathing, and is not limited to a few songs on Sunday or grace before a meal.

> ⁹For to this end also I wrote, so that I might put you to the test, whether you are obedient in all things. (2 Corinthians 2:9 NASB95)

It cracks me up (and not in a humorous way) when we sing songs in the church, with subjects that sound godly, but then we refuse to actually do what we sing. "Anywhere you go I'll follow;" at least till we get out the door. He makes a right turn and we make a left.

I like music – I play drums and guitar. I enjoy "rocking out" on occasion (most drummers are a little nuts). My CD collection would get me thrown out of a lot of churches. The sad thing is, I've been part of music teams that said music was an offering to God, yet refused to offer their best effort in practicing or showing up on time. I've been barred from other music teams because I wasn't "holy" enough. Others told me I couldn't produce a "spirit" of worship in a fashion acceptable to them (I'm not big on endless repetitions, Matthew 6:7). I've been hammered for playing "secular" music, whatever that means, and rejected for playing, and not playing, hymns.

As a matter of fact, my perspective is that there is a lot of ungodliness in the music programs of most of the visible church. It's amazing that any part of it comes together in such a way as to please God at all. Much less make it acceptable to Him as "worship." It might please the people who are doing it, but I wouldn't expect it to please God. Not any more than sacrifices mixed with iniquity (Isaiah 1:10-17). Worshipping God is constant, and sometimes we sing too.

Trains Our Hearing

The more we follow the written form of God's ways, the better we can hear when He speaks to us outside of the Word. In other words, if we don't pay attention to what He already said, how would we hear it if He told us something additional? For instance, if we ignore His Word on what we eat, how would we hear His response when we prayed for healing? He is our physician and healer, and He gives us preventative medicine in His Law.

He doesn't always answer our prayers with miraculous cures. Sometimes He just has to tell us to stop being stupid about what we stick in our mouths. If we don't listen to His prescription, we'll just keep getting sick. Some preach the opposite – eat whatever we feel like, then pray for a miracle when we get sick. If it doesn't work, then it must be your fault. You don't have enough of some mystical ingredient they call faith. Well, duh. But the reason the faith isn't working is that we are ignoring the obedience part in the first place!

Our hearing gets sharper when we practice listening to His written Word. We have to develop the spiritual "hearing muscles" of humility and obedience. We get used to the sound of His voice from the Word, so we can automatically distinguish His voice from all the other chatter around us. Just like a young child can tell the difference between mom's voice and others in a crowded room. When God speaks directly to us, the character of what He says will match the character of His written Word, and we pick it up by association. The Law trains us in righteousness so that rightness always stands out for us no matter where we see it or hear it.

Helps Prayer

The training in righteousness from following His Word assists in discerning what to pray for and when. I'm convinced it improves communication with God.

> [16]Therefore, confess your sins to one another, and pray for one another so that you may be healed. The effective prayer of a righteous man can accomplish much. (James 5:16 NASB95)

> [29]The LORD is far from the wicked, But He hears the prayer of the righteous. (Proverbs 15:29 NASB95)

Some think that Jesus provides righteousness to such an extent that we do not need to practice right behavior ourselves. This is a misunderstanding of the Word. It is clear that God does not hear the prayers of sinful people. The exception is if it is His will for His purpose. Or if it is a prayer of humble repentance and request for forgiveness.[122]

> [12]"There they cry out, but He does not answer Because of the pride of evil men. [13]"Surely God will not listen to an empty cry, Nor will the Almighty regard it. (Job 35:12-13 NASB95)

> [31] We know that God does not listen to sinners, but if anyone is a worshiper of God and does his will, God listens to him. (John 9:31 ESV)

Sin is like a cloud that hangs between us and God's love, or like one of those loud, thumping stereos that drowns out conversation. We need to remove it with confession and repentance (or a really big hammer in

---

[122] See Jeremiah 7:16 and the context, where God refuses to hear prayer due to idolatry.

the case of the stereo) before He will do much else for us. The Law outlines righteous behavior. Sin, as we have already seen, is transgression of the Law. Ignoring His Law causes Him to ignore us.

Did you know that during the middle ages, the bubonic plague did not affect the Jews nearly as much as the Gentiles (even church goers)? Could it be that the Jewish practice of God's laws protected them? Did their refusal to eat unclean animals help them avoid the disease? Was washing and separation from things that God said were to be avoided creating in them a better resistance to getting sick? I think so. Perhaps the church's practice of "freedom in Christ" is the reason for so many sick and dying in the church, then and now.[123] Remember; before sin entered the world there was no sickness or disease. A person may get sick through no direct fault of their own (John 9:1-7). Perhaps it is a test from God. But sickness in general is due to the presence of sin. God is our healer, and righteousness His prescription.

Putting On Christ

The church frequently comes up short when teaching how to do the things God wants us to do. The popular question asking "What would Jesus do?" is as much an admission of ignorance as it is a motivating interrogative. I've heard all sorts of strange, subjective advice such as, "allow Jesus to be the person in you that He wants you to be." Another was "quit, confess, face," which was trying to match the death, burial and resurrection of Jesus. Still another was, "actively yield." Huh? What in the world do these things mean, anyway? They are confused and incomplete mush because they come from pagan mystical principles. It's like listening for the sound of one hand clapping. The average person cannot walk with Him using this drivel.

In contrast, Paul in Romans 13:8-14 speaks about how to "put on Christ." He uses examples from the Law, and reminds us that love is part of the equation. We "fulfill" (fill up full) the Law as we "lay aside the deeds of darkness" and follow His instructions in love. Step by step we "put on Christ" when we do the things He did, in the same way He did them.

Doing His Law fills a person with the Word, and the Word has the authority to make the changes needed. When I started abiding in or obeying all of His instructions in my life, I got a better handle on my temper. Now things don't bug me like they used to because I abide in His Word. I have more peace than I ever had under lame, anti-law church teachings. The best that can be hoped for with most current church

---

[123] See Exodus 23:25-27; Deuteronomy 7:15, 28:58-61; 2 Chronicles 6:28-33; 1 Corinthians 11:27-32; Revelation 2:22-23.

dogma is to cover up something like an anger problem. But a cork is just not a good substitute for change.

You might not realize it because you haven't tried it, but avoiding pork and shellfish, for instance, has a positive effect on gaining control of the emotions such as anger. As I practice this command, I am more aware of what I eat. The more aware I become, the more I put His instructions into effect everywhere. This keeps me mindful of His Word. Since His Word is ever in my mind as I choose my food, His Word is present when I begin to feel anger also. The same determination to avoid eating things that are not food helps to infuse my spirit with peace and produces more patience. Anger disappears or is channeled more properly. Plus I become more aware of hypocrisy in that it doesn't make sense to control what I eat and not control what's more important. I know it sounds funny, but try it and you'll see what I mean after a while.

Restores integrity

Integrity means "wholeness." The integrity of the Word has been broken to such an extent that it is often ineffective. Just like breaking a sentence into individual letters eliminates meaning. We have a tendency to look at God as if He were fractured and pieced out too, so we don't get a good idea of who He is and what He can do.

Many people, especially the young, criticize the church for hypocritical, judgmental, and insincere attitudes. In short, lack of integrity. A large contribution to these perceptions is the refusal to follow all that the Bible says without compromise. If the Word is put back together and placed in a central role in the believer's life, we can put these perceptions in the ground where they belong. God hasn't changed, and we shouldn't be changeable either. Since we know His Word hasn't changed, we know He will do all He said He would do. We can rest in Him because we know He isn't fractured, pieced out, or schizophrenic. Whole Bible belief and practice puts it all back together, so we get a better and more complete picture of everything God is and will do. Communicating that to others by the way we live says more to the doubters than all the sacraments, liturgy, and tradition ever did.

What's The Big Deal?

Besides, what is the big deal with doing what our Father says, even in minor details? A few holidays, what we eat, and some clothing choices don't seem like all that huge of an issue do they? No, they aren't. What does make a big difference, however, is our attitude about God's Word. Either it is all important or none of it is.

We can't get all mystical about "Christ lives in us" then ignore the things He commanded us. At least not and have an effective walk with Him. If we keep making excuse after excuse to dodge His Word, we will miss out on life and that more abundantly. We will also continue to present a hypocritical and cracked-up picture of our Father to others. We end up driving the rest of the world away from what they desperately need also.

Doesn't Dad (the Father) have a right, nay, a fatherly responsibility to tell us what is right and wrong, what is good and bad, what is clean and unclean? How else should our Father deal with His children? Birth them into new creations and then leave them by the side of the road? Give 'em a few vague instructions like "love your God and neighbor" and then let 'em go off by themselves? That doesn't make any sense at all.

God loves us and provides guidance for growing and strengthening the Life that He gives us. We can love Him back by adoring every Word He speaks and striving to put it everywhere in our lives that it belongs. Isn't it wonderful that we have something like His Law to tell us where the boundaries are, where we should go and where we shouldn't go?

God never intends for His people to stand in one place once we gain right standing with Him. He wants us to move. The beginning of our movement should be in taking on all of His ways as spelled out in His Law. It is the best discipleship system ever designed, and is guaranteed to produce fruit that is pleasing to God.

The Holy Spirit uses it to tutor us in the way we should go, and when we get "all grown up," it still functions to guard and protect. His Word is the foundation on which we can build a house that honors Him in every area. His Law is love in action, and through it we learn how to love Him and how to love others as well.

As we obey each command we touch our Lord and Master and Friend and He touches us. From this flows worship, thanksgiving, praise and testimony to His provision and blessed love. It is no big deal to incorporate all of God's requirements for holy living, because He doesn't ask very much of us. As our Father, of course, He's not going to leave us hanging after making us new creations. He shepherds us with tender loving care, making boundaries and warning us away from dangerous situations. His Word works.

9 Whole Bible Instruction

> [7] "Listen to Me, you who know righteousness, A people in whose heart is My law; Do not fear the reproach of man, Nor be dismayed at their revilings. [8] "For the moth will eat them like a garment, And the grub will eat them like wool. But My righteousness will be forever, And My salvation to all generations." (Isaiah 51:7-8 NASB95)

Now we move on to some helps that God has given us in His Word for how to get the most out of His Word. He doesn't leave it to guesswork. God gives us great tips for interpreting and applying what He says. A first century congregation might've had an apostle around to help teach them. But mostly they had to make do with what they had, which was perhaps just a copy of the Old Testament and maybe second or even third hand testimony. Nowadays it's not much different. Happily for us God put lots of helps in both Testaments. Copies are widespread, and we have the benefit of scholar's hard work in multiple translations. God doesn't keep people in the dark about life applications.

There are books that cover details of interpretation, such as the Walter Kaiser book on hermeneutics or interpretation I mentioned in chapter 4, and this is another area where I could write a book too. But these are principles direct from the Person who wrote the Book. I've chosen some of His guidelines that mostly focus on how to apply the Word to daily living. Other author's works on the subject are very complete and worth studying, so I just want to cover what I think are the keys to practical application given to us from the Word. I think of these as God's helpful explanations of His Word that I use to counter the enemy's "helpful" explanations.

These 12 rules or principles all have to do with action, which is natural considering that when God speaks life springs forth (if His Word falls on good ground). They are not really separate rules. They're actually very similar; we could even say they are all aspects of the same rule: abide in His Word. Here they are in no particular order.

1. **Read** the Word.
2. **Do** the Word.
3. **Hold s**till the Word.
4. **Live** on the Word.
5. **Test** God by the Word.
6. **Worship** with the Word.
7. **Follow** the Leaders of the Word.
8. **Value** the Word.
9. **Weigh** the Word.
10. **Investigate** with the Word.
11. **Judge** with the Word.
12. **Balance** the Word.

1. Read the Word

"Where do I start a whole Bible walk?" you might be asking. The easy answer is: just start reading. "Oh no," you say, "It couldn't be so simple." But I kid you not, it actually is that simple. The complications pop up when trying to read every day. Stuff just keeps getting in the way. But I can't emphasize enough how critical reading is. Take time to sit down, even for a few minutes and a chapter or three, and read every day. Give His Word better attention than you do your favorite TV show or soap opera.

It is the Book of Life. When you think you don't have time, read anyway. If you get distracted, make space to read. It doesn't matter if you are a fast or slow reader; stop whining and just read. If you don't completely understand every word just keep reading, because it will gradually become clearer.

> [130]The unfolding of Your words gives light; It gives understanding to the simple. (Psalm 119:130 NASB95)

We need a frame of reference when God wants to speak through us. Jesus tells us that when we are brought before governors and kings for His sake we will be given what to say by the Holy Spirit.

> [19]"But when they hand you over, do not worry about how or what you are to say; for it will be given you in that hour what you are to say. [20]"For it is not you who speak, but it is the Spirit of your Father who speaks in you. (Matthew 10:19-20 NASB95. See also Mark 13:11 and Luke 12:11)

How will we know what to say unless we have His Words filling our hearts? I suppose He could do it like a supernatural ventriloquist, but that's not the way He usually does things. Except maybe as a last resort with donkeys (Numbers 22) or something.

> [26]"But the Helper, the Holy Spirit, whom the Father will send in My name, He will teach you all things, and bring to your remembrance all that I said to you. (John 14:26 NASB95)

The Spirit needs something with which to work. We aren't dummies (I'll refrain from the puns. Okay, I can't stop the puns) so it's much more likely that He will bring to our remembrance what has been laid up inside of us for just that occasion. If we read His Words and do them on a regular basis, the Spirit has a full storehouse of living oracles from which to draw.

Every time someone tells me things aren't going so great in their life, I'll ask if they are reading the Word. Sure enough, when they think back on it, problems increased after they stopped. Or, they've been having a lot of frustration, and they haven't been reading in the first place. Funny, but it seems that problems increase when reading the Word decreases. Not to say it is some magic elixir, but there is a definite connection between reading, doing, and peace.

There are several different ways to read the Word. 1) Casually, every once in a while, and because it's mildly interesting. 2) The same 16 verses over and over again. 3) Maybe as an academic exercise, breaking it into pieces and analyzing grammar and syntax. 4) Like an atheist. They read it, grabbing proof texts here and there to support non-belief (or another peculiar belief) but the effect is limited because of a stone heart. 5) Or, like starving people at a buffet, we can read the whole thing seriously and regularly because it is our life. As I said before, take ownership of the Bible, and the teachings in it. Read it and do it as if it was directly addressed to you, because it is. It is addressed to all of His children for our benefit.

I was standing at my window one winter morning looking out at the early morning sunshine on the snow. A flurry of bird activity around a corner of the shop roof caught my eye. Six or eight mountain bluebirds had all their attention focused on doing something. What was really odd was that one of the birds was hanging upside down by one claw from the thin fascia board at the edge of the roof. Every few seconds, that bird would fly up to the top of the roof corner, and one of the waiting birds would fly down and take his turn hanging upside down.

This was a little unusual in my experience. After a minute of trying to solve the puzzle of their odd behavior, I figured out that the upside down bird was getting a drink of water from snowmelt running down the fascia board. Then it dawned on me (I told you the puns are intended) that all their water was frozen, except for the little bit dripping from the corner of my shop roof facing the rising sun. Not only is this a picture of God's providence for even little birdies, but it is also a picture of the lengths one will go to when one really, really needs a drink.

How we regard God's Word has a lot to do with its effectiveness, because the manner of our regard translates into understanding and actions (or lack of them). If we do not regard His Word very highly, we might think it sounds great, but probably won't want to follow it. If we regard it highly, then we must act on it. We would even hang upside down by one hand from the corner of a roof to get every drop if we had to.

If you are not sure about something, just keep reading. Or do a word study,[124] or ask another who is also following the whole of the Word. Keep going. If you have trouble figuring out what to read, start at the front of the book and work your way back. Or there are several schedules around; try 'em all. Mix 'n match. Just keep reading.

I developed a schedule I call <u>Manna for Whole Bible Christians</u> that is like one used in many synagogues for the annual reading cycle.[125] I like this one because it has readings for God's festivals (Passover, Tabernacles, etc.) and it's nice to be unified with other people. You can always add more readings if you want. Another schedule is to read three chapters a day and five on Saturday (or whatever day you want – 20 chapters a week) and you will read through the whole Bible in a year. We have that one also in the Manna schedule. Shari developed a schedule so that you read through the whole Book in about 30 weeks.

There should also be lots of reading of Scripture in public. In any meeting I lead we read out loud using the Manna schedule. We go through as many as eight to ten chapters with different readers. We just ask people on the spot to read as much as they want (usually a chapter), and rotate readers frequently. God speaks first, then if there's time left over, we speak.

> [13]Until I come, give attention to the public reading of Scripture, to exhortation and teaching. (1 Timothy 4:13 NASB95)

It takes about 40 minutes to read through about 10 or 12 chapters out loud with different people. This is just about the amount of time taken by pastors preaching on just a few verses. Then we have a discussion time for anyone to ask questions if they want. Participation is encouraged both by reading and by inviting responses. Everyone can contribute whatever God has given them for the edification of our local part of the Body.

> [26]What is the outcome then, brethren? When you assemble, each one has a psalm, has a teaching, has a revelation, has a tongue, has an interpretation. Let all things be done for edification. (1 Corinthians 14:26 NASB95)

Some people say lots of reading is too hard. They can't grasp it all. There is a preference for only doing a few verses at a time and "covering them in depth." But what does examining a few verses in-depth really mean? Are we really sure it's not just an excuse to avoid doing what God

---

[124] Be careful with word studies. Include similar words, and also the concepts and context. Remember, just because words look the same doesn't mean they have the same meaning. Looking at the context and comparing large chunks of the Word together will give better understanding. Don't get lazy and stop with a dictionary definition.

[125] We've got it on the website www.wholebible.com/manna_for_whole_bible_christians.htm for personal use.

says by implying it is complicated and "deep?" How many times have you read a section over and over, only to find out after years of "in-depth" study there was something you missed? How many centuries have been devoted to "in-depth" analysis and commentary, and we ignore Him still?

If we really want to understand the Word, we have to read a lot of it. Sitting and listening to a pastor or rabbi drone on and on with opinions or philosophy about the Bible is not going to produce what God wants. It certainly doesn't make fruit. All we've got to do is look at the church honestly and we can see that. Eating His body and drinking His blood is the ticket to life.

The first time reading through the whole book, there will be sections you do not understand. They won't seem to have a place in your daily living. Trust me (better yet, trust God) they will eventually make sense. What is happening is that as you read and do, your frame of reference, your worldview and the cubbyholes in your brain that you've been using to store information are getting enlarged and rearranged. The first time through (remember, with the determination to do what you read) is the toughest. You will stop and start and retrace your steps a lot. You will ask a lot of questions. Just be patient and give yourself time to absorb it.

The second time through the Bible you will have a changed perspective. Many of the sections you struggled with before will start to become clearer. This is because the larger cubbyholes can handle more of what He's trying to get across to you. The cubbyholes will also be arranged better, in more God-centered ways. You will remember a little better, and you will see connections between sections of the Word that you didn't see before. This second time through the Bible might scare you a little, because you are getting better at taking God at His Word. The fear of God at some point will become sharper and more defined. You might wince when some unbeliever uses His name in vain or an alleged believer speaks things that aren't in the Word. Stay calm, focus on the Word, and brace yourself for the third time through.

The third time eating and drinking the whole of His body and blood from cover to cover will be even better. You will add depth to your realization that God is always in control, and you are His child not because of what you believe but because you love Him and can't imagine leaving. You will know He loves you too, and will continue to guide you and bring forth fruit from within you, sometimes even when you don't realize it. Connections between all of the previously misunderstood sections will become clearer. As His Word works its way through your heart, mind and literally your muscles and body parts, filling and changing you, you will wonder how you were making it in life before when you were so deaf, dumb, and blind.

Reading, and re-reading, over and over again, is all part of the salvation process. The more you read, the more you will understand. This is called being filled with the Word or "knowledge of His will" (Colossians 1:9-12). As your understanding grows, then teach it to others. Sooner or later (hopefully sooner) the Law (a.k.a. all of the Word) will be written on your heart, and you will know it and do it without having to be told. But keep reading and doing and teaching. This is love in action – love for God, and love for each other.

> [4]"Hear, O Israel! The Lord is our God, the Lord is one! [5]"You shall love the Lord your God with all your heart and with all your soul and with all your might. [6]"These words, which I am commanding you today, shall be on your heart. [7]"You shall teach them diligently to your sons and shall talk of them when you sit in your house and when you walk by the way and when you lie down and when you rise up. [8]"You shall bind them as a sign on your hand and they shall be as frontals on your forehead. [9]"You shall write them on the doorposts of your house and on your gates. (Deuteronomy 6:4-9 NASB95. See also Deuteronomy 11:19)

2. Do the Word

Of course, not only do we have to read we also have to do His Word. Complications will pop up when you are reading, and more of them pop up when you try to do what you read. One of the hardest things a believer has to do is faithfully take in His words and just as faithfully do them. Even the small commands. It's a daily process of abiding in His love and law; consuming His body and blood. Perhaps the most important aspect of reading and understanding is the determination to actually do everything God tells His people to do, no matter how minor or major. For believers there is no subdividing His Words into old or new, civil or ceremonial, Jewish or Gentile. All of them are life, and that more abundant. We return His love for us by treating every word as the absolute truth, fully applicable and relevant to daily living.

So when you get to something in the Word you think you should do, do it. If it's something you should stop, then stop. It's not that hard to figure out. Reading and doing, doing and reading work hand in hand to bring forth the blessings of chapter eight, and more. Blessings pressed down and overflowing. Reading is good, but we also have to respond. The more you act, the more your behavior changes. The more your behavior changes, the more of your reading you will understand.

3. Hold Still the Word

The third guideline to help us apply the Word is to hold it. Hold it still. Leave it like God gave it.

The Bible warns us in a number of places not to add to His words, and not to take away from them.

> [2]"You shall not add to the word which I am commanding you, nor take away from it, that you may keep the commandments of the Lord your God which I command you. (Deuteronomy 4:2 NASB95)
>
> [32]"Whatever I command you, you shall be careful to do; you shall not add to nor take away from it. (Deuteronomy 12:32 NASB95)
>
> [14]I know that everything God does will remain forever; there is nothing to add to it and there is nothing to take from it, for God has so worked that men should fear Him. (Ecclesiastes 3:14 NASB95)
>
> [5]Every word of God is tested; He is a shield to those who take refuge in Him. [6]Do not add to His words Or He will reprove you, and you will be proved a liar. (Proverbs 30:5-6 NASB95)
>
> [18]I testify to everyone who hears the words of the prophecy of this book: if anyone adds to them, God will add to him the plagues which are written in this book; [19]and if anyone takes away from the words of the book of this prophecy, God will take away his part from the tree of life and from the holy city, which are written in this book. (Revelation 22:18-19 NASB95)

This is not as easy as it sounds. How many times have you heard of a law that you can't find in the Word? And how many times are you tempted to subtract something?

I remember one time a self-appointed pastor was frustrated with me because I told him that his teaching about generational curses was not in the Word. He believed that people suffering from alcoholism or other "besetting sins" inherited a curse from someone in their family tree (though he had no Scripture for this). His answer was for the "cursed person" to confess and get immersed (baptized) or "clean;" repeatedly if necessary (wash, rinse, repeat?). So I pointed out Ezekiel 18 (see also Scripture such as Romans 6:6 and following). There we are told by God that each person will pay the penalty for their own sin, not the sins of their fathers. It didn't help to point back to the Bible.

Obviously, the clear teaching of the Word wasn't appealing to this man. He had added to the Word, made up his mind, and didn't want to be confused with facts. It's true there are some tendencies we inherit from the people who raised us. But as new creations, we are no longer slaves to them. Of course, this guy thought of his teachings as biblical, even if he couldn't find any verses in the Word to back up his teaching. Perhaps he wanted the credit for healing people. It might be that this wolf wanted people to come to his church and tithe so they could get access to the healing ritual. Charge for admission, as it were.

> But we have renounced disgraceful, underhanded ways. We refuse to practice cunning or to tamper with God's word, but by the open statement of the truth we would commend ourselves to everyone's conscience in the sight of God. (2 Corinthians 4:2, ESV)

I suggest there are at least two things we can establish from verses like those concerning adding and subtracting. One is, if we are uncertain of an application of a law, then it is better to leave things unclear than to add to the Word. Just hold it. Since the Word leaves some meanings open, then we should also. We can't get into trouble if we just leave things as the Bible seems to leave them. I can't see any biblical reason why we have to clear it up if God left it murky. Usually only minor things are a little murky anyway, because the major things are clear. Why not let people make their own determination about what to do in the minor things?

The other thing I see in this idea of not adding to, or taking away, from the Word is that the Word is the Authority for every decision a whole-Bible Christian makes. I've been called a "Bible-ist" a few times, which I think was an attempt at an insult. Except it didn't work, because I wasn't insulted, I was pleased. A Bible-ist is, in fact, just what I am; at least as far as authoritative influence goes.

There are lots of good rules for living that don't show up in the Bible. The difference is these rules are not God's Law. The key is not in the extra laws we make up. It is in the way we handle His Word. Something might not be a good thing to do (whatever it is). But there's a big difference between what we think is good and putting words in God's mouth. Adding or subtracting is a big temptation that we give in to all the time. But it's a temptation that whole Bible Christians work at resisting. We work at doing only what is written.

> [6]Now these things, brethren, I have figuratively applied to myself and Apollos for your sakes, so that in us you may learn not to exceed what is written, so that no one of you will become arrogant in behalf of one against the other. (1 Corinthians 4:6 NASB95)

Paul says in another place not to pay attention to "strange doctrines," "mere speculation" or "fruitless discussion."

> ³As I urged you upon my departure for Macedonia, remain on at Ephesus so that you may instruct certain men not to teach strange doctrines, ⁴nor to pay attention to myths and endless genealogies, which give rise to mere speculation rather than furthering the administration of God which is by faith. ⁵But the goal of our instruction is love from a pure heart and a good conscience and a sincere faith. ⁶For some men, straying from these things, have turned aside to fruitless discussion, ⁷wanting to be teachers of the Law, even though they do not understand either what they are saying or the matters about which they make confident assertions. ⁸But we know that the Law is good, if one uses it lawfully, ⁹realizing the fact that law is not made for a righteous person, but for those who are lawless and rebellious, for the ungodly and sinners, for the unholy and profane, for those who kill their fathers or mothers, for murderers ¹⁰and immoral men and homosexuals and kidnappers and liars and perjurers, and whatever else is contrary to sound teaching, ¹¹according to the glorious gospel of the blessed God, with which I have been entrusted. (1 Timothy 1:3-11 NASB95)

The myths at that time were probably added things like the Sadducee teaching against the resurrection. The "endless genealogies" had to do with tracing Jewish lineage to prove how Jewish (meaning righteous in their own eyes) they were (or are). Understand that these teachings are not in The Word. They are teachings from outside the Word. All these (and others) are "strange doctrines" not of faith. The "Law is good if one uses it lawfully," that is, consistent with the whole of the Law (all of God's Word).

Some try to say that a person can prove anything by the Bible. This is not the case in the least. A person might be able to pick a single verse or two and build a doctrine. In the same way I can use the letters of the alphabet to make up any teaching I want. But if we really use the whole of the Word as He intended, we find it's a lot more difficult to prove just any teaching.

Love fills up everything that God commands us to do; the letter needs the Spirit. Too often, we try to cut the process of blending and balancing short and just throw a verse at somebody. Often with condemnation mixed in. A lot of people use the law "unlawfully," without the Spirit and without love. They use only part of it to justify actions, or prove a teaching. But if we are going to use His Word for anything, stay in the lines. Hold still. Take it in without adding to it or taking away from it.

4. Live on the Word

When confronted by evil, Jesus shows us a practical defense. In Matthew chapter four, He made three statements to counter the Satan's temptations, and all three statements came from "what is written" meaning Torah or the Law.

> [4]But He answered and said, "It is written, 'Man shall not live on bread alone, but on every word that proceeds out of the mouth of God.' " (Matthew 4:4 NASB95)
>
> [7]Jesus said to him, "On the other hand, it is written, 'You shall not put the Lord your God to the test.' " (Matthew 4:7 NASB95)
>
> [10]Then Jesus said to him, "Go, Satan! For it is written, 'You shall worship the Lord your God, and serve Him only.' " (Matthew 4:10 NASB95)

Guidelines four, five, and six come from these three temptation responses. Each one is saying essentially the same thing in three different ways. On the surface what looks like three different temptations have the same goal. The Satan tries to get Jesus to abandon God's will and do His own thing (in reality the Satan's own thing). They may have been in a desert but the scene recalls the Garden of Eden, when Satan also used part of God's Word to tempt Eve (and Adam) to go against God's will. Jesus responds as Eve (and Adam) should have – "It is also written." We still get hammered with the same sort of temptations on a regular basis, and the defense used by the Master works just as well now as it did then.

So guideline four we get from the first temptation – making stones into bread. Jesus says instead we are to live on God's Word in addition to our physical meals. Choosing to make bread out of the stones would ignore God's way of doing things. Jesus has the power to change the stones, but he chooses God's will.

> [1]"The whole commandment that I command you today you shall be careful to do, that you may live and multiply, and go in and possess the land that the Lord swore to give to your fathers. [2]And you shall remember the whole way that the Lord your God has led you these forty years in the wilderness, that he might humble you, testing you to know what was in your heart, whether you would keep his commandments or not. [3]And he humbled you and let you hunger and fed you with manna, which you did not know, nor did your fathers know, that he might make you know that

man does not live by bread alone, but man lives by every word that comes from the mouth of the Lord. (Deuteronomy 8:1-3 ESV)

The Law, even at the time of Sinai, was to be followed "from the heart" (verse 2). All of God's Words, whether viewed as "commands" or not, are similar to bread feeding us, providing nourishment, and keeping us strong. We are to live by all that God says, including any statute, ruling, decision, decree, rule, instruction, suggestion, charge, idea, or whim. It doesn't matter whether we hear it in a shout that shakes the earth, a whisper like the still small voice heard by Elijah, or from the letters on a page.

Jesus tells Satan that all Words from God are life, and the first priority of every living thing is to do exactly as God directs. No more and no less. The Spirit led Jesus out into the wilderness, so God wanted Him to fast. Making bread out of rocks would sidestep what God wanted Jesus to do. So Jesus says He's not going to do it. All we have to do is check with God first before we do anything on our own, and modify our thoughts and actions accordingly.

The will of the Father is like bread to Jesus. The Father was certainly capable of turning stones into bread, or providing something else to eat. He did it for Israel in the wilderness when He provided the daily manna, and He could do it again if He so desired. But Jesus was going to wait on the Father. He clung to God's Word, and when it was time God sent angels (Matthew 4:11) to help Him recover from His ordeal.

We are to do the same thing. God knows we need bread, a place to sleep and other things. But our first task and priority is to do what He says. He will provide all the other stuff (assuming of course that those who can will work too). I know trusting God is hard to do on many occasions. Life is tough and there are hard choices. But we need to cling to what He says in spite of what we see and hear to the contrary. Constantly hunger and thirst after every tiny syllable He may utter. This is the path to life more abundant.

5. Test God by the Word

Guideline five is to test God by the Word. It's from the second temptation (Matthew 4:7 don't put God to the test) but might be a little more obvious if we realize that the word "put" is the same word as "test." Literally, "do not test God with a test." The opposite would be to test God by doing what He says. There are two kinds of biblical testing of God. One is through obedience, and one is through disobedience. Malachi tells us about the correct way to test. This testing is approved by God.

> ¹⁰"Bring the whole tithe into the storehouse, so that there may be food in My house, and test Me now in this," says the Lord of hosts, "if I will not open for you the windows of heaven and pour out for you a blessing until it overflows. (Malachi 3:10 NASB95)

The testing mentioned here is within the bounds of obedience, as in "obey the Lord, and in so doing test Him and see that His Word is true. He will deliver as He promised." We don't test God by disobedience; we test Him by trusting His Word and obeying it.

Testing by disobedience is not the way to go. We do not make God prove Himself with tests of our own making. This is what the deceiver was trying to get Jesus to do by throwing Himself off of the Temple. Testing like this includes a lack of belief and even outright disobedience. The Satan quoted parts of Scripture (he's skilled at part-Bible doctrine) in his theological arguments to boost his point, but Jesus responds with the missing sections.

> ¹⁶"You shall not put the Lord your God to the test, as you tested Him at Massah. ¹⁷"You should diligently keep the commandments of the Lord your God, and His testimonies and His statutes which He has commanded you. (Deuteronomy 6:16-17 NASB95)

We don't move away from abiding in the Word because things look bad. Jesus "tested" God the right way by doing as He said. Israel "tested" God the wrong way at Massah (a word that means "test") by moaning and complaining about the lack of water, and faulting God for failing to provide. They were questioning whether God was present, and disobedience followed. In a way they were accusing God of wrong doing. Instead, they should've had patience and trusted that God would not have led them to that place without providing water.

> ⁷He named the place Massah and Meribah because of the quarrel of the sons of Israel, and because they tested the Lord, saying, "Is the Lord among us, or not?" (Exodus 17:7 NASB95)

In effect, they were saying that God couldn't or wouldn't follow through. That implied either He was too dumb to know they needed water or was deliberately messing with them. They were also in effect saying that God did something wrong on purpose. They made up a fault in God and were using that to remove Him from the throne and put themselves in His place. Testing God in this way is nothing more than high-handed disobedience, and shows we do not trust God's Word. When we test Him by disobedience, it is because we are afraid He won't live up to His Word. Or that we want to use a perceived failure of the test for an excuse to go our own way.

When we decide on our own to switch the Sabbath to another day, this is also testing God with a test (the wrong way). He doesn't immediately (or apparently) zap us, so we think we're okay. Then we go on to break other laws. If we eat bacon and don't drop dead we keep eating. We presume on His grace, making it cheaper. Then we compound our sin by sharing the results of the test with others like Eve shared the fruit with Adam. We encourage them to test Him in a sinful way also. It just keeps getting worse and worse. Either we stick with the whole of His Word as Jesus did, filling in the missing parts when the enemy's minions try to detour us with part Bible arguments, or we test Him to justify our own knowledge and pride. I think I'll pick the testing of obedience, myself.

6. Worship with the Word

The sixth guideline comes from the response of Jesus to the third desert temptation (Matthew 4:10 "worship me"). Satan abandons misquoting of Scripture and tries a direct approach, offering cash and power if Jesus will turn from the Father. And again, Jesus quotes from what is written.

> [13]"You shall fear only the Lord your God; and you shall worship Him and swear by His name. [14]"You shall not follow other gods, any of the gods of the peoples who surround you, (Deuteronomy 6:13-14 NASB95)

To "fall down and worship me" (Matthew 4:9) would be to do what Satan commanded. This is equated to "follow other gods" in verse 14 above, and to "fear" or "swear by" in verse 13 above. Each of these terms means the same thing. We "worship" (fear, swear by, follow) God when we do what He says.

How many of us buy into the kingdoms of the world every day! We may not buy them all at once, but we often make payments on the mortgage. To worship God, first and foremost, requires a heart of loving obedience. Anything else is mere lip-service, as stated in Isaiah (Isaiah 29:13-14). To worship God and Him only is, in essence, to obey or abide. It happens that God is the only God, and He is the source of all light, life and love. So it doesn't make any sense to move away from Him in the first place.

Worshipping God is a whole person effort. If we say we love Him, praise Him and adore Him, but we don't do what He says, we only have our lips involved. That is not enough for God. He wants everything we've got. After all, He gave it to us in the first place.

Jesus gives us the pattern for responding to any challenge. Even when part of the Word was used to tempt Him, He responded with another part of the Bible in a balanced way (or even a "whole Bible" way). He always had perfect loyalty to God uppermost.

Jesus knew God and God's Words intimately, and His worship of God included the whole of His heart, soul, and strength. He always referred back to God's Word as the basis for meeting the challenges thrown at Him by the father of lies. Each time He was tempted He clung to the Word for defense. In doing so, He showed that His intent and actions were submitted to God in complete obedience.

For me to have the same steadiness and fearless response to temptation means I have to eat His body and drink His blood all the time. I need to read and do the whole of His Word, all of the parts together. I worship God alone by submitting myself to His Word alone through continual and loyal obedience to Him.

> [12]For though by this time you ought to be teachers, you have need again for someone to teach you the elementary principles of the oracles of God, and you have come to need milk and not solid food. [13]For everyone who partakes only of milk is not accustomed to the word of righteousness, for he is an infant. [14]But solid food is for the mature, who because of practice have their senses trained to discern good and evil. (Hebrews 5:12-14 NASB95)

"Solid food is for the mature." We become mature by practice. If He says "Do this" then that's what we do. If He says "Don't do that" then we should avoid it. And if He's not specific, maybe we shouldn't try to help Him out by adding to or subtracting from what He says. If He left it open, we should also. The Bible shouldn't have to be extremely detailed about every tiny little thing. There is enough in there that a heart of flesh coupled with our God-given conscience can figure out what is right and what is wrong in every situation and worship accordingly. It takes time to understand the Word and fit every new thing into daily living. We can encourage growth in others by sharing our insights and methods too.

7. Follow the Leaders of the Word

Our seventh guideline is to follow leaders only as they lead from the Word. The Leader is Jesus, and His leaders follow Him. We follow our leaders only as they follow Jesus. When inquiring about the validity of the Law in a believer's life, sooner or later this Scripture will pop up.

> [1]Then Jesus spoke to the crowds and to His disciples, [2]saying: "The scribes and the Pharisees have seated themselves in the

chair of Moses; ³therefore all that they tell you, do and observe, but do not do according to their deeds; for they say things and do not do them. (Matthew 23:1-3 NASB95)

On the surface, it looks like we should do everything the scribes and Pharisees say. But let's look closer. Notice that the leaders "seated themselves." This I think is a clear indication of usurping God's authority. There's no provision for Pharisees or Sadducees in the Law. Even if we could classify them under the term "elders," Jesus says they're hypocrites. They tell people to observe the Law, but they do not follow it themselves.

Jesus is teaching us to follow the leaders only as long as they follow Moses (the written Law). Deuteronomy 18:9 (NASB95) says not to imitate the "detestable things" of the nations. Paul says "imitate me as I imitate Christ" in 1 Corinthians 11:1 and "imitate God" in Ephesians 5:1. John says something similar.

Beloved, do not imitate evil but imitate good. Whoever does good is from God; whoever does evil has not seen God. (3 John 11, ESV)

Why just the written Law, and not the oral law (Talmud)? Because the written is the only standard that we can verify came from God through Moses. The Talmud also only has validity if it matches the whole of God's Word. Some claim the oral law also came from Moses, but there are many ways that the oral law doesn't match the written Law, or only matches part of it. The complete written Word is the guide. Plus, we can tell what comes from the Father because it glorifies the Father. If it doesn't glorify God (and much of the oral law and church tradition does not) then it's from men and not from God. The claim that rabbi's, priests, or pastor's teachings are on the same level as God's Word (even if they depart from the Word) is one of those power grabs that some leaders attempt and which we should ignore.

Many times in Israel's past, the leaders led into idolatry and many horrible practices. Is Jesus saying we are required to follow leaders when they lead off the path? Emphatically not. When they take a left turn, we should keep on going straight. The church routinely leads believers away from the Word; all we have to do is look at the results. We shouldn't be blindly following those leaders any more than Jesus followed the rabbis.

As long as the teaching fits in the framework and on the foundation that Moses laid down (Genesis through Deuteronomy) then we should follow. All other books that were added to the Bible had to pass this muster, and so should every other teaching that claims to be God's.

When a teacher departs from the Word, true believers should depart from the teacher and keep going towards God.

8. Value the Word

Jesus encourages us with an eighth guideline when He speaks of jots and tittles in Matthew 5:18. Every tiny part of His Law is still in effect. He said clearly that none of it was going away. We need to value everything, even the tiniest letter. A jot or a tittle is a small part of Hebrew letters, like the dot on an i or the cross of a t. The ESV calls them an "iota" and "dot." When Jesus speaks of small things like this in Matthew 5:18, He is comparing them to the tiniest parts of God's Word.

> [18] For verily I say unto you, Till heaven and earth pass, one jot or one tittle shall in no wise pass from the law, till all be fulfilled. [19] Whosoever therefore shall break one of these least commandments, and shall teach men so, he shall be called the least in the kingdom of heaven: but whosoever shall do and teach them, the same shall be called great in the kingdom of heaven. (Matthew 5:18-19 KJV)

Every part of every letter of God's Word is important, and will not pass away at the whim of any man. In case there is any misunderstanding, Jesus goes on to say that any who break the smallest command and teach others to break it shall be called least in the kingdom.

"Least" may mean the lowest rewards but still in the kingdom, or it might mean being assigned to the lowest part of the kingdom (like hell). Whatever it means, it is certain that Jesus takes God's commands seriously and wants all of His followers to do the same. Who in their right (godly) minds would shoot for "the least" in anything?

Paul brings focus to this by reminding us that word wrangling is not the same thing as minding our p's and q's (jots and tittles). Every jot, tittle, dot and iota in the Law (the Word) is important, but we've also got to watch that we don't make big doctrines out of little words (or one or two verses) as it says in 2 Timothy 2:14 (NASB95).

> [14] Remind them of these things, and solemnly charge them in the presence of God not to wrangle about words, which is useless and leads to the ruin of the hearers.

Augustine (354-430 A. D.) stated something like this in his work on hermeneutics titled *De Doctrina Christiana*. It's called the "analogy of the faith," and "he meant that no teaching contrary to the general tenor of the Scriptures should be developed from any particular passage."[126] It's all consistent, and one verse or word does not override the rest of the Word.

Some people like to use a concordance (sort of a dictionary for Hebrew and Greek if you don't know) and thumb through it until they find a word definition that suits them. Others take an English word, translate it back into the Greek, and then look for the Hebrew equivalent. They translate that word back into English, and build a huge doctrine that just doesn't have any support (or very little support) from the Word. All that really gets them is a lot of exercise in making stuff up. If something was that important, I'm sure God would've spelled it out plainly in His own Words.

Wrangling over words is the last refuge of someone who is intent on shoving a pet doctrine down everyone's throat. These people also tend to discount the ability of God to convey His Word in a way that is easily understood by the average man. To shove their viewpoint effectively they need to scrounge authority from the Word by word wrangling (1 Timothy 6:3-5).

Really, do you think God would hide His will in some obscure word ending or dictionary definition? No. His will is plain and easy to understand and plastered repeatedly all over the Bible. It doesn't take a genius word wrangler to find out His meaning.

It seems clear from a plain reading of the Word that God said what He meant and meant what He said. We don't have to go through a lengthy bunch of grammatical gymnastics to get His point. Oh, sometimes it helps to clarify a word or two here and there. But if we are responsible in comparing Scripture with Scripture and maybe comparing translations, along with judicious use of the concordance, we'll generally be fine. Mostly we need to read it and heed it. But we do need to remember that every part of every one of our Father's words is important. Our best bet is to shoot for "greatest" in the kingdom and devote ourselves to a serious understanding and application of every tiny piece.

9. Weigh the Word

Speaking of small pieces, in the section of the Word below Jesus tells us in our ninth guideline to avoid neglecting any law, big or little.

> [23]"Woe to you, scribes and Pharisees, hypocrites! For you tithe mint and dill and cummin, and have neglected the weightier provisions of the law: justice and mercy and faithfulness; but

---

[126] Earle E. Cairns, 'Christianity through the Centuries,' Zondervan, 1981 page 147.

these are the things you should have done without neglecting the others. (Matthew 23:23 NASB95)

While it is a good thing to measure out the spices, we should pay equal or even greater attention to weightier issues. The tithing of small things is good. We should do that. But we are not to neglect justice, mercy, and faithfulness while we are measuring our spices. These should weigh more in our measuring than something like tithing spices. This is like a child with a laser sense of judgment when eyeing a sibling's dessert, but steals money out of mom's purse when she's not looking. If I am nit-picky about tithing some spices, yet ignore more important issues that have a far greater effect on people, something is out of whack.

Feast days, diet, and laws of clean and unclean are important. But we must not forget that love, grace, patience, self-control and longsuffering are weightier. The fruit of the Spirit is just as much a law as avoiding pork and shellfish (except weightier). Jesus tells us not to neglect the weightier commands while obeying the lighter commands. The lighter helps us learn the weightier, and the weightier reinforces that even the lighter words from God are important.

This is one of those teachings from Jesus that is skipped over by people who divide the Law into civil, ceremonial and moral sections. They tell us to ignore what they deem "small things" in His precious Word. How they make the determination of a small thing and a weightier thing is unclear. But Jesus clearly says all the commands are important. Some are weightier than others, but none of them are neglected by the believer. As I said before, Jesus also tells us that if we are faithful in small things we will be faithful in larger things (Luke 16:10).

10. Investigate the Word

Our tenth guideline is where quite a few people falter in spectacular fashion. We jump to a conclusion based on what little we see instead of thoroughly investigating. Or we react by our own set of laws instead of God's. Jumping to conclusions is such a common occurrence now, especially in the church, that it is easy to lose sight of the fact that a thorough investigation is a standard part of God's Word. After all, everyone should have a fair trial before the hanging!

> ^{14}then you shall investigate and search out and inquire thoroughly. If it is true and the matter established that this abomination has been done among you, (Deuteronomy 13:14 NASB95)
>
> ^{18}"The judges shall investigate thoroughly, and if the witness is a false witness and he has accused his brother falsely, ^{19}then you

shall do to him just as he had intended to do to his brother. Thus you shall purge the evil from among you. (Deuteronomy 19:18-19 NASB95)

I'm sure we've all experienced a rushed judgment directed at ourselves. We desperately wish that people would give us a chance to explain the circumstances. But they've already passed sentence and consigned you or me to the outer darkness. Sometimes there's another agenda, such as someone just wanting to get rid of you or smear your reputation. This is another reason people don't want to have an objective standard like the Law around. The standard makes it harder to railroad people.

If I am on the receiving end of this, there's not much I can do except heave a large sigh of regret and move on. Actually, I'm quite practiced at this by now, because it seems very few people care enough to investigate thoroughly. But it can be frustrating when people are judging you on their own personal criteria not connected with the Word. This is especially true when they are judging whether your teaching is biblical, or if you can remain in their assembly, or similar issues.

A thorough investigation is when facts are gathered, witnesses come forward and we evaluate their testimony. We compare the facts to the whole of the Word in order to render an impartial and just verdict. The accused is allowed a defense. At least, this is what's supposed to happen. Sadly we know how very rare this is in most modern congregations. Our God is a just God, and He expects His people to pursue justice too. But influence pedaling in congregations is a major past time. Pastors or rabbis are frequently untouchable. Money is king with a lot of people. Real justice is scarce. Many want to commit the Law to the rubbish heap so they can pursue their agendas unburdened by accountability or humility.

This is where some might interject that justice and love are separate. Somehow if we judge things are unjust or wrong we are being unloving. But if we use the Word properly, we are doing both. Justice is love; love without justice isn't love. The reason Jesus had to die is because justice and love both had to be satisfied. One could not be exercised by God without the other. It was a very difficult thing for God to justify sinners without merely "overlooking" sin. The resolution was the death and resurrection of God in human form. There is such a thing as being too harsh. But that is generally connected with condemnation, not justice. We condemn when we try to practice justice outside of God's Word, and fail to investigate according to the Word.

People ask me questions quite a bit about the Law. Most of the questions don't really qualify as questions but are more like accusations.

These usually center on the penalty aspect of the Law, such as whether or not we should stone homosexuals or adulterers. The answer is most emphatically not. The original idea for "due process" comes from God. He tells us not to take the Law into our own hands, especially to "act against the life of your neighbor."

> ^{15}'You shall do no injustice in judgment; you shall not be partial to the poor nor defer to the great, but you are to judge your neighbor fairly. ^{16}'You shall not go about as a slanderer among your people, and you are not to act against the life of your neighbor; I am the Lord. ^{17}'You shall not hate your fellow countryman in your heart; you may surely reprove your neighbor, but shall not incur sin because of him. ^{18}'You shall not take vengeance, nor bear any grudge against the sons of your people, but you shall love your neighbor as yourself; I am the Lord. (Leviticus 19:15-18 NASB95)

Believers do not have a sovereign state with the power for capital punishment. That was removed when Israel was booted out of the Land. Since they've returned they have yet to decide to follow God's Laws. We now live amongst Canaanites, and the only power we have is over ourselves. Even if we had the state and the power, we would still have to carry out other provisions, such as a thorough investigation. We are not allowed to go around throwing rocks at someone on a whim just because we think they broke the Law. There's too much of that going on as it is. We are not to act as judge and jury by ourselves, nor are we to sit in judgment on His Word.

If there was a question about the Law in a dispute, it went to the elders. If the elders could not settle it, the case went to the priests.[127] But since we don't have Levitical priests anymore, we go right to the Word of God for the final authority. Both elders and priests would have used the Word, so we can also. This is where we might use a couple of other principles clarified for us in the New Testament.

> ^{7}Actually, then, it is already a defeat for you, that you have lawsuits with one another. Why not rather be wronged? Why not rather be defrauded? ^{8}On the contrary, you yourselves wrong and defraud. You do this even to your brethren. (1 Corinthians 6:7-8 NASB95)

If you can't reach agreement with someone, perhaps there is too much reliance on the letter and not enough on the Spirit. I think there is a

---

[127] Exodus 18:25-27; Numbers 11:17; Deuteronomy 17:8-12.

good possibility that in such a case the grievance is probably a small one. Existing "case law" covers the major sins. So if the legal wrangling drags on, there's a good chance it is more a matter of pride than of justice. Either that or the Law is ignored in the first place. In that case, maybe it's just better to let it go.

11. Judge with the Word

Speaking of judging, did you know it's okay to judge? That's what Jesus tells us. So our eleventh guideline is about judging. We'll talk about it more in a minute, but I want to lead into that subject by first looking at some verses for judging using weights and measures. The verses we're going to look at are about scales or measuring sticks. But the principles apply to all of our dealings with each other, especially in the field of justice and discernment.

We are to be honest and fair in all of our dealings, not just the merchant transactions. Everyone who doesn't is an "abomination to the Lord." Not being honest and fair is an abomination to God, right up there with homosexuality and eating pork.[128]

> [13]"You shall not have in your bag differing weights, a large and a small. [14]"You shall not have in your house differing measures, a large and a small. [15]"You shall have a full and just weight; you shall have a full and just measure, that your days may be prolonged in the land which the Lord your God gives you. [16]"For everyone who does these things, everyone who acts unjustly is an abomination to the Lord your God. (Deuteronomy 25:13-16 NASB95)

God is always concerned about honesty and fairness. Accurate weights and measures are just one aspect of His desire for what is right and true. His Word is the standard, and we are supposed to use it without cheating. We are to avoid taking a tiny verse out of context and making a big doctrine out of it while ignoring other, larger parts of the Word. God wants honesty and right judging even in small things like weights and measures in merchant transactions. As I mentioned at the beginning of this section, weights and measures are not a separate issue. Other living oracles from God bear on this subject too, such as that if we are "faithful in little" we will be faithful in much.

This is why weights and measures take us very smoothly into the broader subject of judging. The next verse on judging is frequently used

---

[128] Deuteronomy 22:5, wearing the opposite gender's clothing; see also 'detestable' in places like Leviticus 7, 11 and 20, or 'abhorrent' in Leviticus 11:12 and Leviticus 20:21. These are interchangeable words.

by people to avoid responsibility or say they shouldn't answer for their behavior.

> [37]"Do not judge, and you will not be judged; and do not condemn, and you will not be condemned; pardon, and you will be pardoned. (Luke 6:37 NASB95)

Jesus seems to be saying we should avoid judging. But let's add another verse on the same subject to our measuring stick to get a whole picture.

> [24]"Do not judge according to appearance, but judge with righteous judgment." (John 7:24 NASB95)

It might appear on the surface that Jesus is contradicting Himself. But of course, that's not the case. It might help to realize that judging has several different meanings. Sometimes we can think of judging as condemning[129] and sometimes as discernment.

I think when Jesus says "don't judge" He means not to pass sentence by ourselves. When He says "judge with righteous judgment," He means to use discernment (according to the Word). This includes removing the log from our own eye so we can have clear vision to judge (Matthew 7:3-5). We condemn when we step outside of the spirit-filled Word and consign someone to punishment without proper discernment (like that in a thorough investigation). Judging apart from the Word is the proper definition of "judgmental."

Judging by appearance is also wrong because there is not enough information to render a fair and balanced verdict according to the legal principles He gave us. We use discernment when we balance the whole of the Word together in justice, compassion, and mercy. Each of these is part and parcel of the Law of love. This is why God doesn't like bribes – they pervert justice. We are not to be so stiff-necked. Instead, we must operate with a circumcised heart of flesh, tender toward God's Word and ways.

> [16]"So circumcise your heart, and stiffen your neck no longer. [17]"For the Lord your God is the God of gods and the Lord of lords, the great, the mighty, and the awesome God who does not show partiality nor take a bribe. [18]"He executes justice for the orphan and the widow, and shows His love for the alien by giving him food and clothing. (Deuteronomy 10:16-18 NASB95)

---

[129] The word in Luke 6:37 translated 'condemned' (G2613a *katadikazo*) means much the same as the word translated 'judge' (G2919 *krino*) but the gist of the meaning I believe is to practice discernment according to the Word.

> [8]"You shall not take a bribe, for a bribe blinds the clear-sighted and subverts the cause of the just. [9]"You shall not oppress a stranger, since you yourselves know the feelings of a stranger, for you also were strangers in the land of Egypt. (Exodus 23:8-9 NASB95. See also Deuteronomy 16:19-20.)

Bribes take a multitude of forms from tangible to intangible, and direct to indirect. They could be something as simple as acceptance by the crowd. Or they can be as complex and harder to buy as political office.

The sad fact is that in many cases people who wear His name don't even have to be paid to turn a blind eye to the plight of others. Frequently we do it for free or just on the promise of payment. We cater to the whims of wealthy people, for instance, simply because they might favor us with a reward eventually. We don't seem to realize that many wealthy people have their money because they don't give it away!

> [1]My brethren, do not hold your faith in our glorious Lord Jesus Christ with an attitude of personal favoritism. (James 2:1 NASB95)

12. Balance the Word

The twelfth guideline is to balance the Word. In 2 Samuel 6:6-8 (also 1 Chronicles 13) a priest named Uzza (or Uzzah) touches the Ark, as it is being brought to Jerusalem by David on a cart, and dies. In 1 Chronicles 15:13 David speaks of the reason for Uzza's death – the priests were not carrying the Ark as specified.

> [13]"Because you did not carry it at the first, the LORD our God made an outburst on us, for we did not seek Him according to the ordinance." (1 Chronicles 15:13 NASB95)

Later, we read of Hezekiah and his Passover, where he prays for the people because they were not observing it exactly.

> [18]For a multitude of the people, even many from Ephraim and Manasseh, Issachar and Zebulun, had not purified themselves, yet they ate the Passover otherwise than prescribed. For Hezekiah prayed for them, saying, "May the good LORD pardon [19]everyone who prepares his heart to seek God, the LORD God of his fathers, though not according to the purification rules of the sanctuary." [20]So the LORD heard Hezekiah and healed the people. (2 Chronicles 30:18-20 NASB95)

There are two attitudes represented by these references. Do we fear to make a wrong move unless we do it according to "the rule," or do we think Jesus is our passport to do whatever we want? The answer lies in balance. We balance the Word together with love and the Spirit and prayerfully consider how to follow Him. Consult God first; try to obey exactly as He says; but make allowance for good faith effort. Lack of understanding is one thing; deliberately avoiding what is clearly taught is another.

An unbalanced extreme is the standard Christian idea that Jesus came to eliminate the Law. Now we think we can do anything we want because He paid the price of our disobedience. "Let us sin that grace may abound." Other unbalanced extremes are in legalism or Jewish orthodoxy, where particular attention is paid to outward appearance and only parts of the Word. Legalism is misuse of the Law for earning salvation. Orthodoxy is restrictive traditions that override the Word, squeezing Jesus out. The extra restrictions make us feel like we are paying our own price. This means ignoring grace in favor of personal holiness or merit.

A cup of flour is not a cookie, and a tomato is not lasagna. Balancing the Word means all of it comes into play in any area of life, and all the ingredients have to be there in proportion to get something sweet or tasty. Satan tries to derail our practice of God's Word in any way he can by trying to shove us to one extreme or the other. Applying the whole of the Word to our lives is abhorrent, detestable and an abomination to him and his minions. He just can't stand the smell of well-balanced practice of God's Word. The guidelines in this chapter are designed by God to avoid extremes.

The guy executed for gathering sticks (Numbers 15:32-36) on the Sabbath was ignoring what God said in a "high-handed" or deliberate way. If he ignored God in the little things, he would ignore God in the big things. It's like the broken window theory of crime prevention.[130] In addition to his own disobedient action, if left unpunished the stick guy's attitude would give others permission to sin.

It's obvious that attitudes in Israel weren't all that great in the first place. Note for instance that this episode came right between two of the worst examples of disobedience ever committed. Right before this they refused to go into the Land (Numbers 14). Right after this was Korah's rebellion (Numbers 16). Wild swings in obedience are not what God desires from His people.

When a marriage ends up on the rocks, the cause can generally be traced to a series of small slights that paved the way for bigger sins. In

---

[130] If a window (a small crime) is broken and nobody does anything about it, then more windows get broken (bigger crimes). Rudy Giuliani, the mayor of New York, caused drastic reduction in crime a few years ago by directing the police to enforce the 'little laws' as well as the big ones.

my opinion, people don't usually jump to big sins right away. We get used to sinning in small steps. The problem with a "little white lie" is that it generally leads to a whole bunch of big black ones. Little white lies are like a gateway drug to a life of sin addiction.

On the flip side, we also learn righteousness by a series of small steps. That's why we call it a "walk with God." Whether raised in faith as a child or converting as an adult, we should keep trying to choose what God wants instead of what our flesh wants one step at a time, minute by minute, one day at a time. Our walk should be balanced with a determination to follow what we think of as the small stuff as well as the big stuff. Like the first broken command in Genesis we realize there is no such thing as small stuff with God. It's all in the heart. We love God and strive to please Him by balance in everything.

Do What Jesus Did

I've always been fascinated by the statement from Jesus that Satan has "nothing" in Him.

> "I will not speak much more with you, for the ruler of the world is coming, and he has nothing in Me; (John 14:30, NASB95)

The ESV says "no claim" and the Amplified New Testament says "nothing in common," "nothing in Me that belongs to him" and "he has no power over Me." To me Jesus is saying that He's pure. Satan does not have anything to hold over the head of Jesus, or any foothold or lever to make Jesus do what he wants. Jesus simply has no reaction to the temptations that Satan throws at Him from every direction. He is inert to sin. A rock. He doesn't move away from God, He doesn't flinch. He's not drawn to sin, or to a particular sin. There is no "shadow of turning" in Him. He's perfectly balanced in God's will and Word, having the Spirit and rightly applying every whisper from God inside and out. This is purity.

Purity means we are not moved by anything outside of God's will. Believers are moved by His will and His will alone. Learning to balance the Law is part of purity. A big part of purity is confession and repentance when we find ourselves doing something wrong. Doing His Word requires quite a bit of self-examination and adjusting behavior to match. We learn the will of God minute by minute with every command we weigh, value, and follow. We also will become inert to sin. Sort of like a rock. His Spirit-filled Law, written on our heart of flesh beating in time with His love, makes us immune to the offerings of the world and everything it thinks is important.

The Word itself tells us how to handle the Word if we just read it and do it as if we are taking in His body and blood. It doesn't get any simpler. Man lives and worships by every word from God. Testing Him is by obedience, not by disobedience. Adding, editing, opinions or teachings of men are not needed. A soft heart intent on doing the will of God will easily find out what pleases God.

> So Jesus answered them, "My teaching is not mine, but his who sent me. If anyone's will is to do God's will, he will know whether the teaching is from God or whether I am speaking on my own authority. 18 The one who speaks on his own authority seeks his own glory; but the one who seeks the glory of him who sent him is true, and in him there is no falsehood. (John 7:16-18 ESV)

Teaching from God glorifies God (John 7:18; 3 John 11). Teaching from man glorifies man (or the teacher). Jesus gave concrete examples of how to follow God when challenged by Satan. Each time He went back to the whole plain meaning of what is written by God, properly balanced, valued and followed. Each time He gave the same response to every part-Bible temptation – "It is written." Paul echoes the Messiah with caution not to go beyond what is written. Of course both are referring to the Word of God, not the opinions of men.

Believers follow the leader that follows the Word. I've got file cabinets full of commentary that helpfully explains why we don't have to follow the Law, and in the end it's mostly fire starter. Every jot and tittle of God's Word, on the other hand, stays fresh and relevant and as full of life as ever. Careful judging is to do the weightier commands while not neglecting the lighter commands. True discipleship strives for accurate discernment and justice without the corruption of bribes or appearance. We use the Law as a scale for thorough investigations, balancing all of His living oracles together for defense against the Satan's attacks.

Jesus leads the way (as always) by correcting the partial use of Scriptures and giving us guidelines on how to do the same ourselves. He puts it all together with, I might say, a "whole Bible" view. These twelve guidelines help keep us on track and reap the many blessings of the application of the whole of His Word to every area of our lives.

10 Whole Bible Applications

> [20]Thus Hezekiah did throughout all Judah; and he did what was good, right and true before the LORD his God. [21]Every work which he began in the service of the house of God in law and in commandment, seeking his God, he did with all his heart and prospered. (2 Chronicles 31:20-21 NASB95)

Well. You've made it this far, which is good. The path believers walk is not easy and this book isn't either. I'm sure many of the subjects we've talked about have shocked you and rearranged a lot of your thinking. It did me. It takes a long time to reverse the effects of standard and current church teaching using the whole Bible. But I keep digging, trying to connect with my God and the fruit of His Spirit in an ever more real and practical way. I encourage you to keep digging too. Though I may have only a mustard seed faith it is secure and growing because His Words and ways are living and true. His yoke is easy, but the way is hard because of the pressure we get from unbelievers around us.

> "Enter by the narrow gate. For the gate is wide and the way is easy that leads to destruction, and those who enter by it are many. For the gate is narrow and the way is hard that leads to life, and those who find it are few. (Matthew. 7:13–14, ESV)

A New Definition of Cult

There is a strong chance, maybe even a guarantee, that some will accuse me of being in a cult because of this book. That word gets thrown around a lot, sometimes rightly. But lots of times it's a nice little hay maker intending to dismiss and bury whatever teaching is uncomfortable. Never mind that many of the church (and a lot of the synagogue) teachings cannot be sustained from the Word as a whole. Never mind that new churches were thought to be cults by the established church of the time when they first got started. The only reason they don't think they are cults now is that they've been around a while. Hardly a ringing endorsement.

Oh sure, parts of the Bible are used all the time to support weird cult teachings. In fact, considering how few people actually follow the Word, it is amazing how many parts of it get plastered on buildings, bumpers, and signs at football games. But when the whole of the Word is brought to bear on the weird teachings they just sort of dwindle away. I think this book gives a viewpoint that is unique and very un-cult like. The difference is in balancing all of His Word together to arrive at the conclusions.

Cults are traditionally defined by somebody's opinion of orthodoxy. The dictionary definition of orthodox is "conforming to the approved form of any doctrine." In other words, orthodox means accepted opinion. Orthodoxy can include the Bible, but usually includes a lot of men's opinions too. If a person or group is lacking in any of the "orthodox" or accepted doctrine or dogma, then in the opinion of the "orthodox" they must be a cult or part of one. Dr. Walter Martin says it this way.

> "By cultism we mean the adherence to doctrines which are pointedly contradictory to orthodox Christianity and which yet claim the distinction of either tracing their origin to orthodox sources or of being in essential harmony with those sources. Cultism, in short, is any major deviation from orthodox Christianity relative to the cardinal doctrines of the Christian faith."[131]

I propose a better definition of orthodox, and of a cult or cultist. My definition of a cult or a cult member is a group or a person who at most gives only lip service to God. Orthodox then would be those who actually do what God says.

Lip service can be seen in those claiming to follow Jesus, for instance, yet refusing to do what He says in the Law. It's in a person who says he "runs to Jesus" telling us to "ask Jesus for guidance" (which sounds good) but also encouraging us to ignore the plain meaning of the Bible (for instance saying that the Bible is not the Word of God).

These two definitions of orthodox and cult take into account all those who smugly wrap themselves in church or synagogue doctrine, yet have no intention of anything more than lip synching the Word of God. They include anyone who is in a "religion" and denies the whole truth of the Word. They also cover those on the flip side who talk bad about "religion" but who also include following the Bible in their definition of religion. The definitions of orthodox and cult also gathers up all those part-Bible people who sit in judgment on the Word, picking and choosing what part of it they want to follow. We can throw in all those people with outside-the-Bible doctrines that are used to separate us from abiding in His living oracles too.

Lots of cult people want to be in the kingdom without having to do what God really commands. You know, "Everyone wants to go to heaven, but nobody wants to die." Real orthodoxy is the whole of the

---

[131] Walter R. Martin, 'The Rise of the Cults,' Grand Rapids: Zondervan, pp. 11-12.

Word, including the Law. And orthodox people are those who do the whole of His Word as if it was life itself, eating the body and drinking the blood of our Messiah Jesus. This orthodoxy was the key for the first century church to turn their world upside down.

Some ideas I have presented here have been advanced by cults (by the Martin definition) but that's not very surprising, is it? Satan is the original part-Bible person, and loves to mix truth with his lies. Otherwise, they just wouldn't be that easy to take. If he didn't mix, we would laugh him right out of the room. But just because he misuses the Word does not mean the parts he uses are invalid. It's just the way he uses them that is invalid. And like Jesus, we can fight part-truth simply by applying the whole of the Word. I'm not trying to imply that repeating a few words from the page is some magic elixir for curing all that ails us. That would be occultism. But much good comes from humbly submitting to His will. Humility, especially the humility that must be present when following the Law, is a big factor in all that we do with the Father.

He doesn't take us out of the world when we become new creations (John 17:15). We don't change into some sort of angel-type being unaffected by what goes on around us. We have bodies that hurt and spirits that lose courage and minds that still make dumb decisions. But when we lay down our lives for Him, and observe all His instructions on a minute-by-minute basis, the Spirit flows freely and the fruit of the Spirit pops out all over.

We do have to watch for the typical cult-trap of misusing the Word though, especially The Law. Some cults create tons of extra laws outside the Bible. They are trying to be seen as "more holy" than their brothers and sisters because they follow more rules. I call these "more observant" people Torah tyrants. A cult can beat people up with man-made laws (or even a few of God's) and still not follow God's Law. As with medications, more is not better. Laws can be plastered all over the surface of a person like a bunch of ads on a downtown wall in a gritty TV drama. Or whitewash on a tomb. But while it might make the outside look better, the Bible message is lost in the clutter.

Other cults swing the opposite way and ignore the bulk of the Law. Or they consign it to "the Jews" or "another age," thinking that the magic eraser of Jesus is enough to wipe out any sort of lawless thought or action even as we refuse to repent. Both extremes have been raised to an art form. The whole Bible lived and loved and balanced and filled up full with the Spirit and love is what He wants from us.

We really shouldn't need a bunch of laws from God. His ways should be as normal and natural as breathing or heartbeats. But they're not, because we've wandered off into the wasteland of our own limited knowledge. Generally, we are discontent yet lethargic in our stupidity, floating toward the Niagara Falls of life.

We keep thinking if we're in the barrel of "church" (synagogue, mosque, and cult, whatever) we must be okay. But we're just sleeping with our eyes open. So He slaps us with the Word on occasion, attempting to rouse us from our stupor. His law is a gracious effort extended from His bottomless love, attempting to pluck us from disaster and place us firmly on His Rock.

I'm not advocating the breakup of existing groups. I'm just saying that wherever people claim to follow Him they should go all the way. The ideal is one body living by one biblical faith humbly obedient to one Lord in the one household of our one God and Father. Anything that gets in the way should go bye-bye, including Nicolaitan tradition and sectarian[132] infighting.

We need His Word, His Law, more than ever before. We find ourselves now like Israel spoken of in Isaiah.

> [9] "To whom will he teach knowledge, and to whom will he explain the message? Those who are weaned from the milk, those taken from the breast? [10] For it is precept upon precept, precept upon precept, line upon line, line upon line, here a little, there a little." [11] For by people of strange lips and with a foreign tongue the LORD will speak to this people, [12] to whom he has said, "This is rest; give rest to the weary; and this is repose"; yet they would not hear. [13] And the word of the LORD will be to them precept upon precept, precept upon precept, line upon line, line upon line, here a little, there a little, that they may go, and fall backward, and be broken, and snared, and taken. (Isaiah 28:9-13 ESV)

Because of our refusal to do it, the Word sounds like the stuttering, broken language of a foreigner. Instead of maturity, we are stuck in baby land, needing constant repetition and only grasping the most basic instruction. If we understand it at all. Our ears are so stopped up with pride that only bits and pieces of His Word come through. If we continue in our stubbornness we will, as Isaiah says, be broken, snared and taken.

Some use this reference as if it was a proper teaching method. However, it is really a lament and an insult. It also means that Israel will hear the Word from Gentiles, who have embraced it better than their

---

[132] Sectarian means narrowly confined or devoted to a sect. Literally, a section of people who believe a certain way.

elder brothers. But we haven't been living it (again, in general) so they haven't been listening either.

In this chapter, I'm going to give you some suggestions for bringing all of God's Word into your daily living. I'm not going to give you a step-by-step manual for all of it, because most of it can be easily figured out. You don't need me making decisions for you.

I'll just give you some starting points and a basic outline with some Scripture references you'll need to get you started. Part of the fun of doing everything God has for a believer is in sifting and deciding how to work it all in. I prefer to figure out how many different ways I can obey His commands instead of making them harder to bear.

The Feasts of Jesus

A real good place to start living His Ways is the feasts of the Lord (Sabbath, Passover,[133] Pentecost, Trumpets, Atonement and Tabernacles, see Leviticus 23). They are not "Jewish," they are God's (these are "the appointed feasts of the Lord" as it says in Leviticus 23:2) and like Him they belong to all believers.

Sabbath

The Sabbath was given to man by God right after creation, and He set the example by resting on the first one. He didn't wait until Sinai (Exodus 20:8-10, see also Exodus 16) and create some new holiday. Sabbath is on Saturday, and the Bible says we are to rest from work (you and all your household Leviticus 23:3) set it apart, and make it holy. You haven't experienced rest until you experience a Sabbath set apart for you by God. The Law protects you on the Sabbath because you are required by God to avoid work. No one can legally make you work. When we "rest" from working to make a living it's a picture of the eternal rest we will have one day.

The work of making a meal is okay, but other work is not (Exodus 16:23-26). There are also a couple of rules for not kindling a fire (Exodus 35:3) and staying in your place (Exodus 16:29). Nehemiah locked merchants out of Jerusalem on Sabbath (Nehemiah 13:15-22 see also 10:31). This is where some get the belief that we shouldn't buy or sell on Sabbath (in addition to the "everyone should rest" instruction). But it wasn't the buying and selling. It was the work.

Orthodox Jews get radical about what they consider making a fire by not turning on even a light switch on Sabbath. Or they get uptight about the distance of a home from the synagogue (it needs to be in walking distance of, I think, a mile). However, these things are tough to support from the Word. In an ideal world the meeting place would be a short

---

[133] Passover includes Unleavened Bread and First Fruits.

walk from home, but finding a godly assembly close to home is pretty tough.

I live in Colorado, and we use a wood stove for heat in the winter. I hardly think God meant my family should freeze or run up an electric bill (making others working on Sabbath) in order to avoid a fire. There's not much labor in striking a match. We make sure we have wood inside so we don't have to carry a burden. Taken as a whole I don't see where God would have a problem with our fire.

As Jesus said, man was not made for the Sabbath but the Sabbath was made for man (Mark 2:27). Religious leaders got uptight with Him, not because He was changing God's Words, but because He sent them back to the Word. Examine carefully Matthew 12:1; Mark 6:1-11, Luke 13:10-17, 14:1-6; John 7:22 and 9:13-16. You'll see that what He did was different than their traditions but not different than the Law. See also Matthew 15:3, 6 and Mark 7:8, 9, and 13. If we get radical about how many details we can load up on His day, we end up working to hold a weight that God did not intend for us to bear.

The Sabbath is a delight and a beautiful way to rest from our cares for a while. Taking the day off refreshes me and strengthens me for the coming week. Giving God one day out of seven is not a sacrifice at all. You'll hear some excuses for avoiding the Sabbath, such as we don't know which day it is or "all days are a Sabbath." These are false. All anyone has to do to track the day of the Sabbath is count to seven. And if we don't know which day is the last day of the week, how do we know Sunday is the first day of the week?[134] Oh please. Just look at any calendar and you'll see Saturday is the seventh day and Sunday is the first.

As far as every day being the Sabbath, you can choose to rest on any one of them if you want. But there is only one day that is God's day of rest.[135] Hebrews 4:10 is used a lot to justify ignoring the real Sabbath, but the whole context is obedience, and "there remains a Sabbath rest" (Hebrews 4:9). People don't enter it by "believing in Jesus," they enter it by obeying God (which includes the belief in Jesus). The lack of obedience was the reason the Sinai church did *not* enter His rest.

> [1]Thus says the LORD, "Preserve justice and do righteousness, For My salvation is about to come And My righteousness to be revealed. [2]"How blessed is the man who does this, And the son of man who takes hold of it; Who keeps from profaning the sabbath, And keeps his hand from doing any evil." [3]Let not the

---

[134] Matthew 28:1; Mark 16:2, 9; Luke 24:1; John 20:1, 19; Acts 20:7; 1 Corinthians 16:2.
[135] Although God did say to work the other six. Being blasé about something so important isn't love.

foreigner who has joined himself to the LORD say, "The LORD will surely separate me from His people." Nor let the eunuch say, "Behold, I am a dry tree." ⁴For thus says the LORD, "To the eunuchs who keep My sabbaths, And choose what pleases Me, And hold fast My covenant, ⁵To them I will give in My house and within My walls a memorial, And a name better than that of sons and daughters; I will give them an everlasting name which will not be cut off. ⁶"Also the foreigners who join themselves to the LORD, To minister to Him, and to love the name of the LORD, To be His servants, every one who keeps from profaning the sabbath And holds fast My covenant; ⁷Even those I will bring to My holy mountain And make them joyful in My house of prayer. Their burnt offerings and their sacrifices will be acceptable on My altar; For My house will be called a house of prayer for all the peoples." ⁸The Lord GOD, who gathers the dispersed of Israel, declares, "Yet others I will gather to them, to those already gathered." (Isaiah 56:1-8 NASB95)

Passover

Passover can include Unleavened Bread and First Fruits, and in modern times does. The Passover meal is on the first evening of the seven-day Unleavened Bread feast. First Fruits is the day after the first Sabbath[136] after Passover. So they all get sort of lumped together. Specifics for Passover and Unleavened Bread are mostly in Exodus 12 and Leviticus 23. Some helpful hints are also given by Paul in 1 Corinthians 11:23-34. An exception is that we don't put the blood on the doorway. The first and seventh days of the feast are Sabbaths in addition to regular Sabbaths.

Unleavened Bread, Pentecost, and Tabernacles are referred to as the Pilgrimage feasts because all males were to travel to (eventually) Jerusalem to present offerings and sacrifices. This is why so many different people were present in Acts 2 to hear the disciples speaking in their own languages. There is an exception to travel, however, in Deuteronomy 12:21 and 14:24 if the place where God puts His Name is too far away.

Some object to eating lamb because of the lack of a temple, but the first Passover didn't have a temple either. My family has a lamb barbecue. We just make sure to burn up the leftovers (Exodus 12:10). One of these days, we might even go from scratch with a lamb if we can find other families to share it with.

---

[136] Somewhat confusing, because it's a little unclear whether it's the day after the regular weekly Sabbath or not.

We eat with a staff close by and our shoes on, and we use some of the good traditions we have learned. At this meal and all week long we eat unleavened bread too. Jesus is our Passover lamb, and He is the unleavened bread that feeds us all year round, so these things we speak of and teach our children. The first century church obviously observed this feast too according to Paul. For First Fruits there isn't much to do, other than start counting weeks until Pentecost.

Pentecost

The second of the pilgrimage feasts, Pentecost is a Sabbath 50 days after First Fruits (Leviticus 23:15-22) as near as we can tell from the text. There is not much to do here except perhaps socialize together. Reading the Law is a good tradition to follow if you'd like. We can also remember the ascension of Jesus and bake two loaves of leavened bread to share at a party. It is interesting to note that the Law was given to Israel at this time, and the Holy Spirit visited the apostles. Coincidence?

The Feast of Trumpets

Trumpets is the first of the fall feasts. Like the name implies, it is for blowing horns. We purchased some large shofars (curly horns) but you can use a trombone (or other horn) if you'd like. It is a Sabbath and called the Day of the Awakening Blast. We borrow the Jewish tradition of eating sweet stuff (like apples with honey). My family buys (or makes) fancy caramel apples just for this day. There are not many specifics in the Word for this holiday. So we go up on a high point overlooking our valley and blow our shofars while praying for spiritual walls to come down (like the walls at Jericho in Joshua 6).[137] Traditionally this is also a wakeup call for the Day of Atonement.

Atonement

Also known as Yom Kippur, this holy day is ten days after the feast of Trumpets. It's a special Sabbath, so even the work of preparing a meal is absent and we fast all day. My family will walk around a little (one year we walked around Main Street of our town) and blow shofars. At the end of the day, we'll go out to a nice restaurant to eat. Small children, of course, and nursing mothers are exempt from fasting, as are any people with medical problems. This is a day to "afflict ourselves" but not a day to grind people into the ground. Sometimes we'll go down to the river to read our Bibles and pray for those who need to repent before the actual Day of Judgment.

---

[137] There was a group called 'Shofars Around the World' (www.shofarsaroundtheworld.net) that informally tried to coordinate the blowing of shofars worldwide on Trumpets. Can't find them now, but we still try.

Lately, we've been staying home and having quiet prayer all day. This is really the best thing, I think. We focus on God all day long. Around about the middle of the afternoon, it seems as if we can actually touch God and hear His voice, responding to our prayers. This isn't the only day we can reach Him, but it just seems to bring it all together so that the signal is clearer.

Tabernacles

The third pilgrimage feast, called the feast of Booths or Tabernacles, is a holiday (actually a holy week) we have taken to calling "God's camping trip." The basics are to wave pleasant smelling branches and spend time in booths or tents. One day soon all people will be traveling to Jerusalem every year, and we'll probably camp out there too. Our family sleeps in tents in the back yard for the week. Some Jews make special booths. The feast is eight days long with the first and eighth as Sabbaths. Nice meals with sweet things are routine, and we'll try to come up with special things to do in keeping with the holidays.

Every day the shofars are blown, and during the week, we read all five books of the Law. When the temple was up then sacrifices were made for the nations (70 bulls). This is one of the feasts that are specifically mentioned to continue into the reign of Jesus on earth the second time according to Zechariah 14:16-19.

The Calendar

You're going to need a calendar to track God's holidays. A standard Jewish one is good or you can go online at www.wholebible.com where the booklet <u>Manna for Whole Bible Christian</u> can be printed for personal use. It has the dates, and you get the reading schedule too. A day, by tradition, starts the evening before (Genesis 1:5).

God sets up the holidays on a lunar schedule and our calendar (the Gregorian) is a solar calendar. That's why the dates move around. There are groups that think the lunar schedule is the only way to go, and there are some who take the extreme (and unwarranted) position that if we don't observe the feasts at a specific time we will miss God or "lose our salvation."

If it is important to you, do some investigating and make your choice for a calendar. I can find no law equating the specific day of a feast with salvation. Nor do I find instruction that if we don't have the days right we will be penalized. I think it is more important to do it together, but that's just my opinion.

Food

Much of the arguments for and against the pagan menu items of pork and shellfish we covered in chapter 7 under the heading It's All Good.

Here were going to look at applications for food from Leviticus 11 and Deuteronomy 14. According to God there is food and there is not-food. Animals with cloven hoof that chew the cud are food. Animals with solid hooves or no cud chewing are not food. Pigs have split hooves but do not chew cud, so they are not food. Neither are horses, or rabbits, or carrion eaters.

For water critters, if they have scales and fins they are food. If not, they are not food. Simple. Read the labels of the food you eat, because you'll be surprised at how much pork is in a lot of processed items. We were eating a certain brand of turkey bacon for a while until we read the fine print on the package and discovered it had pork in it. We switched brands, and now we read very closely.

We get the frozen cheese pizzas from the grocery store and add our own turkey pepperoni. Are we extreme? Not at all. Unless trying to put His Word into every tiny area of our lives is extreme. We don't get neurotic about it, but we try to be thorough because we love Him.

Some think that Israel at Sinai did not know how to cook pork (or shellfish) and didn't have refrigeration.[138] Since we "know better" now, it's okay to eat what we want. Well, Israel may not have known, but God sure did.[139] He didn't say, "You gotta cook it real well and stick it in an ice cave." He said it wasn't food. He didn't want us playing Russian roulette with meals. The people who think up these brilliant arguments obviously aren't thinking with a heart of flesh.

Tassels

Numbers 15:37-38 tells us about wearing tassels with one blue thread on the four corners of our garments. Some people want to make an issue about the definition of a corner (has to be a right angle in their opinion) and what shade of blue should be on the thread. This is too nitpicky if you ask me, and can't be sustained from the Word.

The earth is round, and yet it has four corners. Any circle has at least four corners. All you have to do is draw a plus sign, like the crosshairs on a rifle scope, on the circle to see where they are. I'm round, so I must have four corners too! That's why I wear tassels on my pants in four spots. I tie them myself in the Jewish prayer shawl style in order to identify with Israel, but you can have any kind you want. I've seen

---

[138] By the way, did you know there is a virus in pork that cannot be cooked out? It's not supposed to affect humans, but how do we know it really doesn't? Pigs are also plagued with arthritis, and it's a problem in humans. Connection? Could it be that we are what we eat?

[139] This is from people who have bought in to evolutionary theory, thinking that a long time ago people were dumber than they are now. I think it's the opposite – people 3,500 years ago were more likely much smarter.

rainbow colored (just make sure to include a blue one) short ones and long ones. The more different kinds we have the better it is I think.

We wear the tassels as reminders to follow God's ways instead of our own. You might think that wearing tassels is no big deal, but it helps more than you know if you haven't tried it. They don't guarantee you won't sin. They only work as well as you allow them to work.

Sometimes, after I've messed up (again) and said or done something I shouldn't, I look at them and think, "Well, at least I've done one thing right." And from that, I can rebuild, remembering all the things God has done for me. I refresh myself by touching Him through this command. Wearing tassels as He instructs helps me feel I am surrounded by His love. I renew my love for Him by a determination not to fail again.

Tithe and Money

Ever wonder why the tithe, which is ceremonial, is kept by the church, after they throw most of the other ceremonial laws out? Originally it was used to support the priests who couldn't own land, and some of it was to be used for the poor (Deuteronomy 26:12). The tithe was mainly agricultural in nature; people would give a tenth of their gardens and orchards to help feed the priests. Money really wasn't a part of it.[140]

Now of course the tithe has been used to hit the paycheck and is only monetary. Funny how that happened. It doesn't make much sense that the church keeps the tithe in view of their "ceremonial rejection." Unless, of course, you need a method to obtain money for keeping the Nicolaitans in power.

God expects us to be generous with the things He has given us (Deuteronomy 15:7-11) because it's all His in the first place (Exodus 9:29). Exodus 22:24-25 has rules on collateral. Leviticus 19:9-10 and Deuteronomy 24:19-20 concern sloppy harvesting so the poor can maintain some self-respect and work the harvest some too.

The teachings by Jesus in Matthew 6:19-24 on a "good eye" and a "bad eye" are related to the concept of generosity (good eye, light) and stinginess (bad eye, dark). Clearly, God doesn't want to have to flog us to get us to part with our money or produce or whatever. That doesn't mean we should just go around handing it out to anyone, because we are supposed to be good stewards (Luke 12:41) of what He gives. But being loose is better than being tight.

I think the national average for paycheck giving at churches is 3% or something. I don't know how they arrive at that figure, but the thing is we don't have to give to a church. That whole system is out of whack

---

[140] Deuteronomy 14:22-26 says that we eat of the tithe, or sell it for money if we have to go a long way.

with what God intended. We use it wrongly to make our leaders "do ministry" for us, or to construct buildings that aren't big enough for our egos.

A small argument can be made not to muzzle the oxen[141] (pastors, rabbis) that are treading out the grain. But it's stretching the Word past the breaking point to find support for huge buildings or big mission networks. Tithe was intended for support of the poor and people who were not allowed to have land or other jobs (priests). It wasn't intended for starting priesthoods outside of the Scripture, or for building monuments to vanity.

Circumcision

The first reference to circumcision in the Word is God's command to Abraham to circumcise all the males of his household as a sign of the covenant (promise) between them (Genesis 17). Another reference is the debacle at Shechem (Genesis 34). Moses errs in not circumcising his son and his wife has to do it (Exodus 4). Exodus 12 (the Passover) has another mention of circumcision, where no one can partake unless he is circumcised. Notice that this is only for males, and notice further that all of these were before Mt. Sinai.

Other body parts can be circumcised, and with greater effect. Twice in Deuteronomy circumcision of the heart is mentioned, one of these connecting circumcision with loving God.

> [16]"So circumcise your heart, and stiffen your neck no longer. (Deuteronomy 10:16 NASB95)

> [6]"Moreover the Lord your God will circumcise your heart and the heart of your descendants, to love the Lord your God with all your heart and with all your soul, so that you may live. (Deuteronomy 30:6 NASB95)

Jeremiah also speaks of circumcising the heart (4:4, 9:25, 26) and that ears can be uncircumcised (6:10). It seems clear that circumcision has more to do with a response to God than a cutting of the flesh. To have ears that refuse to listen and a heart of stone that won't abide is the same as being uncircumcised. Even if a piece of flesh has been removed here and there.

The other main references to circumcision simply tell of a command for Israel to circumcise a male child on the eighth day after birth. The child was already part of Israel, but had to be circumcised as part of the covenant (involuntarily, I might add). As already mentioned, everyone

---

[141] See 1 Corinthians 9:9-18; 1 Timothy 5:17-18; and Deuteronomy 25:4.

who eats the Passover meal has to be circumcised, which of course meant only the males. This is a sign of response to God, but it goes along with loving Him and doing whatever He says whenever we can. As a side note, there is nothing in the Word for female circumcision.

Circumcision was practiced by a number of ancient cultures besides Israel's. Generally, however, much of the practices seem to have been for older children and adults. Israel seems to be one of the few, if not the only culture, that did it to 8 day-old male babies.

By the time of Jesus, circumcision had become a required religious ceremony for becoming a part of Israel, or in other words becoming "Jewish." It was thought that in order to be "saved" one had to become Jewish by converting to Judaism. But nowhere in the Word do we find instructions linking circumcision to salvation, or even linking Jewishness to salvation. Paul speaks rather negatively about the misuse of circumcision in several places, most notably the book of Galatians, and yet also practiced it. He circumcised Timothy (Acts 16:3) seemingly to avoid arguments with Jews so Timothy could travel with him. The big difference seems to be the false use of circumcision as a salvation requirement.

Acts 15 was all about this controversy. It wasn't that circumcision wasn't valid; it was the misuse of circumcision for salvation that was the real problem. The council in Acts 15 decided circumcision wasn't necessary for salvation, yet pointed out that "Moses is taught in the synagogues every Sabbath" (Acts 15:21). Paul strenuously teaches that if a person tries to gain some sort of merit sufficient for salvation through following the Law, especially through getting circumcised, the Messiah loses value. The Christ is the only basis for approaching God, not merit. Again I note that *this has always been true*, since the beginning.

There are debates raging worldwide at the moment over circumcision. Some try to argue that it is medically beneficial, while others decry it as a "mark of uniformity and servitude." I'm sure there are many logical sounding arguments either way. But God never said to do it for health or any other reason. He simply instructed Abraham, and Israel, to circumcise all male children as part of the covenant to follow Him. It wasn't necessarily for health, but it certainly could be seen as a mark of uniformity and servitude. And what's wrong with that? In fact, it seems that the anti-circumcision crowd is really attacking the practice for religious reasons. In other words, the anti-circumcision arguments are, at heart, anti-God arguments. This is odd; until you consider that it really is more of a spiritual battle than a purely medical or physical one.

There might be a question in some people's minds about whether to seek circumcision as an adult, because of the desire to follow all of God's Words. Jesus was circumcised (Luke 2:21), and there is an argument there along the lines of "what would Jesus do." I know I'm glad I was circumcised when I was a baby, because I wouldn't look forward to it now. But, for myself, I would probably seek it if I wasn't already. Not because of any identity with Israel, or any thought that I needed it for conversion or salvation, but just because God wants His people to do it. I would do it because I think it's what God would want me to do.

However, for other people, I cannot say. You will have to make up your own mind, just like you will have to make up your mind about the Law and whole Bible Christianity. I know that a person who wants to submit in every way possible to every Word God says experiences many, many blessings. But if a person does not think he should, then don't. I'm not going to say that blessings will not be forthcoming for that person. But I will say that partaking of the Word even to the point of circumcision, out of a desire to please God and as part of living life more abundantly, will not go awry.

Clean and Unclean

One of the things that infuriated God about Israel was the failure of her priests to teach His Word properly, especially the differences between clean and unclean.

> [26]"Her priests have done violence to My law and have profaned My holy things; they have made no distinction between the holy and the profane, and they have not taught the difference between the unclean and the clean; and they hide their eyes from My sabbaths, and I am profaned among them. (Ezekiel 22:26 NASB95)

Clean and unclean are not identical to sinless and sinful, although disobeying the law is sinful. The general procedure for getting clean was by bathing, washing clothes, and waiting till evening (the three "eengs"). Uncleanness from touching a dead human body was a different process, which we'll talk about in a minute.

Becoming unclean was easy too. A certain kind of disease or sore could do it, as well as certain body discharges (Leviticus 15) and childbirth or a woman's menses (Leviticus 12 and 15). It's good to be aware of what is clean and what is unclean, and remember to follow through on the steps to get clean. It's not a salvation issue, it's a love issue.

Most everyone bathes and launders clothes now, and evening still rolls around like clockwork every night. Some will argue that a certain kind of bathing is required (for instance a bath in a pool with running water rather than a shower) but the text isn't so specific. Israel was in the desert when the rules were given and water was in short supply, so perhaps a quick shower or even a sponge bath might've been the norm. Later on Naaman the Syrian (2 Kings 5) would get clean in the Jordan, and even later John the Baptist was helping people get clean in the Jordan River. The idea behind the baptism of repentance for sins (Mark 1:4; Luke 3:3; Acts 19:4, 5) comes from the rules for cleansing. One of the reasons for changing Israel's diet was to teach the difference between clean and unclean (Leviticus 10:10, 11:47).

Some people will isolate a woman for two weeks during her monthly cycle (the law says only during the flow, about 1 week). They will refuse to sit on a chair that she sat in and other similar actions. Yet they ignore the fact that a man makes a woman unclean through a discharge of semen. This kind of skewed practice is an addition to the Law that gives it a bad name. Nowhere does God require isolation except for certain instances. This is a shameful way to treat a woman. There's way more uncleanness in the way some misuse the Law than is specified by the Law.

The issue of clean and unclean is both very simple (dirt) and complex (holiness). Jesus is said to have cleansed everything, and in a way that is true, but I still wash my hands before I prepare food. There is still a difference between clean and unclean. Ideally, we should continue to observe and teach the differences instead of teaching there are none (Ezekiel 44:23) as the priests did.

One form of uncleanness cannot be taken care of by the three "eengs" (bathing, laundering and evening) and that is contact with a dead human. The only way to cleanse this was by the red heifer solution, which we haven't had for thousands of years.[142] Anyone touching a body is unclean, and anyone they touch is unclean. After all this time, you'd think everyone would be permanently unclean by now, with no hope of cleansing. Happily, we have the "solution" in Jesus. His blood really does cleanse, even from the effects of death.

However, it is one thing to have His blood and quite another to wallow in filth again, physically or spiritually. If we presume on God's grace by ignoring His instructions, we can't just keep going back and taking a bath in the Blood. This is worse than lip service (Hebrews 10:26-30). We can be clean and yet still have to be cleansed every now and again, much like the washing of the feet Jesus did for the disciples (John 13:5-15).[143]

---

[142] See Numbers 19 for an outline of what this is and its applications.
[143] A side note: if everything has been declared 'clean,' then why in Revelation 18:2 is fallen Babylon said to be the dwelling place of "demons and a prison of every unclean spirit" and "every unclean and hateful bird?"

¹⁵ To the pure, all things are pure, but to the defiled and unbelieving, nothing is pure; but both their minds and their consciences are defiled. ¹⁶ They profess to know God, but they deny him by their works. They are detestable, disobedient, unfit for any good work. (Titus 1:15-16 ESV)

Sex

This always gets people's attention, doesn't it? God's Word tells us that sex is for a man and a woman in a marriage. There is no other place for it, even though perverse people keep pushing the envelope.

In the beginning, it seems that genetics weren't such an issue. By the time of Sinai, it was important enough to make a rule against sex with close relatives.[144] So God tells us that near relations are off-limits for sex (Leviticus 18:7-18, 1 Corinthians 5:1-2).

But wait, not all the forbidden relationships are strictly genetic. In-laws and relation by marriage (like step-moms or step-sisters) are included. So there is something more going on here. While we might not understand all the whys and wherefores (there's that stupidity thing again) we just avoid what God says to avoid.

The only law about the sex act is to avoid it during the woman's menses (Leviticus 18:19, 20:18). This is usually about six or seven days and is not that big of a hardship. Other than that, we shouldn't deny each other except by agreement for a short time (1 Corinthians 7:1-5). A woman's body is not her own, and a husband's body is not his own (in spite of current cultural teachings). When we start a marriage, we give up our "rights" of independence in exchange for the benefits of an interdependent relationship.

Some of the sex laws overlap with clean and unclean. Most of these are in Leviticus 15 and can be followed with great profit. There have been studies done, for instance, on people who avoid sex during a woman's cycle having lower rates of some types of cancer. As I've said, we don't always know the connection between laws and consequences, but that doesn't mean they don't exist. It also doesn't mean that consequences are the only reason for the law.

Rules concerning sex are some of the clearest examples of our stupidity. How far has the person drifted from God who needs a law about sex with animals? (Leviticus 18:23.) What soul is so cut off from the light of God that it gives itself over to sex with the same gender? (Leviticus 18:22, Romans 1.)

---

[144] Obviously, in the beginning people married sisters and brothers. After the flood, genetics was more of a concern, perhaps because the canopy of water protecting us from the sun's radiation was destroyed at the flood.

Perverse acts arise from lightless depths of hatred for God and all He is or has created. It is very clear that people who practice perversion are driven by hatred to the extent they want to destroy God, starting with His Word. In the process, they destroy other people in addition to themselves. If we are in the light as He is in the light, hate cannot continue.

Vows

God is a person of His Word, and expects the same from the people He created. A vow is a statement of action. There's usually a penalty if we fail to carry out what we vow (Numbers 30). We should avoid vowing when we cannot or will not follow through. A vow is a permanent, concrete promise that God will hold us to (believers or non-believers). If we make a vow, God demands that we follow through on the terms. He always follows through with His.

In the present day, vows are common, and just as commonly ignored. A driver's license is a vow or promise to drive according to the laws of the licensing government. Yet we frequently drive as if we are rewriting the laws to suit ourselves. A marriage vow is heavy with commitment, and just because civil courts allow divorce doesn't make the bad consequences go away.

> [21]"When you make a vow to the LORD your God, you shall not delay to pay it, for it would be sin in you, and the LORD your God will surely require it of you. [22]"However, if you refrain from vowing, it would not be sin in you. [23]"You shall be careful to perform what goes out from your lips, just as you have voluntarily vowed to the LORD your God, what you have promised. (Deuteronomy 23:21-23 NASB95)

In general, we should be very careful about making vows. The responsibility for a vow has not gone away, so we should simply give a "yes" or a "no" more often than invoking one (Matthew 5:37; James 5:12). Our word should be our bond. There are some foolish enough to tell you that vows aren't very important anymore and can be ignored. That's not biblical.

Stuff That Is Not Commanded

It's tragic that God's laws are rejected by so many who turn right around and make their own. Or extra laws are added to God's laws (calling them "fences") in an attempt to help people avoid breaking the Law. Asceticism, which is self-denial as in living like a monk, plays a part sometimes. Other times it might be a desire for power or a transfer of authority from the Bible to a man. Whatever the reason, we've got lots of laws that don't belong on the same level as God's laws. Strange that rejecting God's Laws seems to make other laws multiply like rabbits. Here's a brief list of some examples of self-created laws that in my opinion are not at the level of God's Law at all.

Head Coverings

The kippah for men and scarves for women are not commanded. There are a couple items on hats for priests, and a small section in 1 Corinthians 11:1-16 that some take as a head covering for women. Some trace the kippah back to the Babylonian captivity, but at any rate there is no law for it.

Lots and lots (and lots and lots) has been written about head coverings for women. One of the top pages viewed on our website www.wholebible.com (and the related video on our Youtube channel Whole Bible Christian) is an article on head coverings. The reason it is pushed, I think, is mostly because of that desire for asceticism and authority transfer rather than a desire for the Word. Paul is speaking of hair (verse 15 in the NASB95 even says outright that "For her hair was given to her for a covering") and it takes a severe stretch to read a cloth into that section. Six times words for hair are mentioned here. Bottom line is, at worst it isn't very clear there is a cloth involved, so let's avoid adding one, shall we? I like to wear Levi's button-fly shrink to fit 501 jeans. I like them so much I wear them to church (my good ones) when I'm allowed to go. I haven't worn another type of pant in a long time. But I can't find any biblical admonition that I should wear them, and I certainly do not tell other people that the only "right" pants are Levi's 501's. Even if they are 100% cotton and the Bible tells us not to mix threads.

Day of Meeting

There is also no regulation for which day to meet together. It is no big deal to have a church meeting on Sunday (or any other day) if you want. Meeting on Sabbath is great because you have the day off anyway, but then the people putting the service together have to work. The specific Day of Rest is not in dispute (even the people who switched it admit this) but the day of meeting is frequently an argument. It doesn't matter. If you want to get together on Sunday, fine. If Saturday is better for you, fine and dandy. This issue should be disconnected from the Sabbath because it is not related.

Christmas and Easter

This might sound harsh, but these two holidays are examples of the church's perversity. Look. As with a day of meeting or head covering, if you want to celebrate Christmas and Easter, feel "free in Christ." However, they are not biblical holidays and never have been. I object to two things about these holidays in particular: one is rejecting others for wanting to be biblical and two is mixing God's things with pagan things. Both of these so-called holy days include idols such as bunnies and evergreen trees, and neither is commanded by God's instructions. In fact, God specifically commands us not to make images, and not to learn the ways of the pagans (Deuteronomy 12:29-32; 2 Kings 17:15; Jeremiah 10).

If you don't think bunnies and evergreens are worshipped as idols, try telling someone about the likely pagan associations. You will find an almost vicious defense of them in almost every "worshipper." The roots of the pagan symbols go far back into the past, and these "holy days" contain teachings that are humanistic at best, and obscure God's promise at worst. None of the practices are in the Word. We can slap Christian labels on them, and throw some Bible stories in there to make them more appealing, but that's like throwing flowers in a cesspool before taking a dip.

You know what's really funny? These are the types of things mentioned in places like Galatians and Colossians 2:22. The pagans are the ones who observe worthless and elemental days, months, seasons and years!

> [9]But now that you have come to know God, or rather to be known by God, how is it that you turn back again to the weak and worthless elemental things, to which you desire to be enslaved all over again? [10]You observe days and months and seasons and years. (Galatians 4:9-10 NASB95)

How strange is it that many in the church get very mad about a believer observing God-ordained holidays and avoiding the pagan holidays? Why is it more acceptable to observe the pagan ones and avoid God's? Has wrong become right and right become wrong (Isaiah 5:20)?

What is bad about these so-called holidays is that many people think you are not a Christian if you don't swim in the cesspool with them. My son got dumped by several ladies he dated who didn't like his stand on keeping paganism out of his future home. My mom thinks that I've somehow traded in my salvation because I've stopped observing Christmas and Easter. Members of our former church were uncomfortable when we wouldn't volunteer to help with special events around those times. All of this and more over minor practices that specifically go against what God instructs.

If you get to the point where you want to ditch the paganism in these days, you may have to deal with family and friends who can't see the smelly chunks in the cesspool for the flowers. It is better in those instances to refrain from condemning and give them time to see the truth.

If you have to go to family functions, try to keep the peace as best you can by not preaching behavior that they can't understand anyway. You risk getting only a legalistic response from them.

Calmly explain your reasoning if you get a chance. You may not have a tree in your home. But someone else might want one, and it's no big deal to be at their house if they do. I still don't eat the ham (amazing isn't it that this is the "Christian" choice for a meal?). I tell my kids who Santa really is. But I don't have to jam my beliefs down the relative's throats, either.

Two Sacraments

Baptism and Communion are said by many in the church to be the only two sacraments given to the church, but this is not biblical. Aren't these two, um, ceremonial? And didn't the church throw out the ceremonial commands?

Baptism comes from the bathing concepts in the clean and unclean laws (the "ceremonial" for those so inclined) such as that for the leper in Leviticus 14. The physical cleansing helps us understand spiritual cleansing and a new beginning, and it seems it was used by the apostles as a public testimony of the new life in Jesus.

It is important, and I think everyone who is able should be baptized by immersion, but it is not required. The thief on the cross next to Jesus wasn't baptized, but was going to be with Him in paradise (Luke 23:43). There are many who die suddenly who might be chosen by God, but did not have the opportunity for a bath (such as aborted babies).

Communion might come from Passover and Unleavened bread, but it isn't the same thing. The Lord's Supper of 1 Corinthians 11 is Passover. It is not a separate ceremony newly instituted and given to some separate entity called the church. There may have been other meals where unleavened bread and wine were used for a memorial. I don't see a problem with this "shadow," but we should not forget the substance. Paul uses the example of Jesus in 1 Corinthians 11 to remind the Corinthians that there is a proper way to do the Feast, and it should not be done haphazardly. This is not the same thing as creating a new sacrament.

Meat and Dairy

Some Jewish people refuse to put meat and dairy together, such as with a cheeseburger. You wouldn't know it to look at the verse, but this practice comes from a law given to His people concerning what is thought by many to be an obscure pagan practice.

> [19]"You shall bring the choice first fruits of your soil into the house of the Lord your God. "You are not to boil a young goat in

the milk of its mother. (Exodus 23:19 NASB95, see also Exodus 34:26 and Deuteronomy 14:21)

It is not clear where this practice came from, but from the context of this reference it seems to be related to the pagan ritual from Egypt where this was done at the end of the harvest. The resulting liquid was sprinkled on the ground before planting again as a sort of invocation for the pagan deities to make it fertile. Somehow, over the centuries, rabbis made one of those "fences" to protect people from possibly disobeying the command not to do the kid and milk thing. I guess they didn't know if the milk product came from the mother of the meat product.

On the one hand we can respect the seriousness of the way the rabbis looked at the Word, but on the other this is just nuts. There is no way that putting cheese on a burger would ever be mistaken by God for the pagan ritual. This is one of those examples of good intentions run amok, of adding to the Word one more burden, and making the whole thing harder to bear.

Drinking Alcohol

Lots of people want to make spiritual legislation[145] from the Word prohibiting the drinking of alcohol, but there are no commands that God made anywhere that do so. Of over 300 references to wine or strong drink in the Scriptures, the vast majority of these speak of wine as having alcohol, and there are no prohibitions anywhere against drinking it.[146] The references to "strong drink" suggest an alcohol content that is greater than wine, but still there are no drinking prohibitions even for this product.

However, this doesn't mean that drinking is recommended either. The Word has a bit to say about the negative effects, and the consequences of drunkenness (abuse of alcohol). Very frequently drinking a little can lead to drinking a lot and even to alcoholism, so caution is indicated whenever dealing with it.

Jesus undeniably made wine, and very good wine, at the wedding in Cana (John 2). At least 25 times in the Old Testament "new wine" (Hebrew *tirosh*) is connected with fruitfulness and blessings from God. In one reference wine, strong drink, and grape juice are included together, showing that they were separate products and that when wine is mentioned it is not just grape juice but alcohol.

---

[145] For one effort among many, see www.biblicalperspectives.com for the book by Seventh Day Adventist Samuele Bacchiocchi titled 'Wine in the Bible,' Signal Press and Biblical Perspectives, June 30, 1989.

[146] For more information, or a good cure for insomnia, see 'In Vino, Veritas' by Bruce S. Bertram, March 2003. It can be found under Commentary on www.wholebible.com, or you can email info@wholebible.com for a copy.

²"Speak to the sons of Israel and say to them, 'When a man or woman makes a special vow, the vow of a Nazirite, to dedicate himself to the Lord, ³he shall abstain from wine and strong drink; he shall drink no vinegar, whether made from wine or strong drink, nor shall he drink any grape juice nor eat fresh or dried grapes. (Numbers 6:2-3 NASB95)

If we take a complete look at all Scripture concerning alcohol and balance the various meanings together, we can see that alcohol by itself is not a bad thing in moderation. It is not the consumption but the overuse or abuse that produces "bad fruit." There are a lot of people who cannot handle it at all, however, and for those it would seem that total abstinence is the only sure-fire method of avoiding the consequences. But we should all seek to be filled with the Spirit through His Word, which would go a long way toward avoiding argument.

There are many "laws," some of which are good applications of biblical principles, but they are not really law. If you don't think you should watch certain movies then don't. But try to avoid making a law about it for others. I watch a lot of movies because I don't like commercials. When I watch TV I drive my family crackers because I keep switching channels when the commercials come on. I get tired of the inane babble that passes for news and entertainment. Four hundred channels and nothing on. I think I've just outgrown it.

However, that doesn't mean that another person can't watch TV if they want. In my opinion, we should be careful of the time spent on it (and on video games, etc.) and we should devote more time to reading the Word. It's much more productive to spend time with the Lord and with each other, but it doesn't quite come up to the status of a law. Philippians 4:8 has a good thought on this, but if it has to be a law then something is wrong somewhere.

Bad Things And Good People

The whole Bible lifestyle has many benefits and blessings, but there is also a downside. I sometimes get discouraged because some people ignore God's Word in the Law yet have wealth and fame and other (seemingly) good things given to them. Bad things seem to happen to good people who hunger and thirst after righteousness. It's tough to follow God, because He said there would be thorns and thistles, sweat and pain for a while.

But through living a whole Bible life I realize that not everything is as good as I think, and not everything is as bad. I have had to realign my thoughts of good and bad by the Word.

> [^12] Although a sinner does evil a hundred times and may lengthen his life, still I know that it will be well for those who fear God, who fear Him openly. [^13] But it will not be well for the evil man and he will not lengthen his days like a shadow, because he does not fear God. (Ecclesiastes 8:12-13 NASB95)

For instance, winning the lottery might look good (and sometimes I wish I could win it) but it is not necessarily good. It destroys lives and introduces all sorts of evil that wasn't present before. In order for you to win, everyone else has to lose. So if you are a whole Bible believer, you can actually thank God that He doesn't "bless" you with winning the lottery!

Some of what we consider bad is not really that way either. A financial setback might just cause you to look for a more beneficial path. For instance, you could go into business for yourself after losing a job. I remember one time I lost a job while building our house, but we managed to convert the construction loan to a mortgage and I ended up starting my own business. God allows some hard events for His children's benefit. It might be the only way to get something through our hard heads.

I've gone on many trips to the proverbial woodshed with my Father. While the momentary experience was certainly unpleasant, He made some good changes in me. And I've gotta admit that generally the trips were my own fault too. The "rod" and "staff" of Psalm 23:4 are His Word, and will indeed discipline and comfort us.

> [^11]My son, do not reject the discipline of the LORD Or loathe His reproof, [^12]For whom the LORD loves He reproves, Even as a father corrects the son in whom he delights. (Proverbs 3:11-12 NASB95)

> [^7]It is for discipline that you endure; God deals with you as with sons; for what son is there whom his father does not discipline? [^8]But if you are without discipline, of which all have become partakers, then you are illegitimate children and not sons. (Hebrews 12:7-8 NASB95)

We have to be careful also of characterizing people as good or bad. Living is a process of decision making, and as long as we are alive, there is opportunity for change. There are believers and non-believers, and people who look like one or the other, but actions tell the true story.

Some people switch back and forth a few times, and some well-meaning people are just momentarily led astray. The only thing we can judge by is consistent action. We cannot tell (and we are not tasked with deciding) whether or not someone is "saved" or "unsaved." That is for

God to decide at the end. All we can do is encourage people to do what He says and govern affairs in our own sphere of influence according to His Word.

I find that because I want to embrace all of God's Word, I'm frequently cast in the "bad" mold. Most often, this comes from people who consider themselves "good" because of "mainstream Protestant doctrine" (or even Jewish doctrine). Outwardly they appear righteous by their own standards, but inside they are full of lawlessness and hypocrisy (as in Matthew 23:28). Don't be surprised by their vicious attacks; our fight isn't against flesh and blood. I know you will have heartache as you attempt to bring the whole Word into your life, but there isn't much we can do about other people's actions. We can take comfort in eating and drinking His body and blood, and in the community of our family and those others who have seen and live in the light of the whole Bible.

> [1]Righteous are You, O LORD, that I would plead my case with You; Indeed I would discuss matters of justice with You: Why has the way of the wicked prospered? Why are all those who deal in treachery at ease? [2]You have planted them, they have also taken root; They grow, they have even produced fruit. You are near to their lips But far from their mind. (Jeremiah 12:1-2 NASB95)

One odd thing (among several) about our concept of bad and good is that we insist on free will, and then blame God for all the things we think are going wrong. But we can't have it both ways. If we insist on free will choosing, we'd better choose correctly or face the consequences. It is true we have a certain amount of volition purchased for us by God. But that volition is subject to His sovereignty.

God has ultimate control, but He gives us the power to do as He commands. Sometimes He allows things to happen that challenge us to continue choosing Him, and other times we are protected and sheltered. Partly He has His own plans; partly He's exercising grace in waiting for repentance. Sometimes we are a demonstration like Job (Job 1:8-11) and sometimes He's training and disciplining (1 Peter 5:10). Jesus was "perfected through suffering" (Hebrews 2:10) and we are not greater than our Master. We are tested, tried, disciplined, chastised and purified through all life situations, good or bad. The answer to the challenge is "God in all things" (Romans 8:28).

You will have difficulties. Some will come from people who follow the Law but add all sorts of extra tradition, such as Jewish orthodoxy. Sadly, a large amount will come from those who call themselves Christian (church orthodoxy). They will hammer you with all the excuses to disobey that we've covered, and then some. Members of my family have been literally cornered by three or four alleged Christians at a time shooting away like a firing squad with their standard objections. We've been called "dangerous" because we make too much sense when defending the Word.

Why do we get such a response? In my opinion it is because by nature people do not want to obey, abide, or remain in His Word. We started clumsily dodging Him in the Garden, but since then have raised it to an art form with six thousand years of practice. We've developed all sorts of complicated interpretation methods to give ourselves permission to avoid obedience. So we don't like to be reminded that all of it is smoke and mirrors.

We don't want to carve a day a week out of our busy lives doing our own thing to rest and honor God, especially when it has become a favorite day to catch up on chores. We don't want to be told what to eat or what to wear. Much less do we want to be told what is true or honorable or right or pure or lovely or of good repute (Philippians 4:8). We want to pick and choose our own holidays and our own traditions. We want to decide things for ourselves, and we resent being reminded that God and His absolute standard is the foundation for all good things. The sentiment and tradition we've loaded onto the pagan holidays we've stolen is more fun than an objective standard that takes away wiggle room.

There are those who refuse to accept objective, absolute standards. Instead they want to judge everything by feelings. Trying to be "right in their own eyes," they will do all in their power to discourage and dissuade you from following the Law. There will be resentment as the Word pierces the dark places, shining light on what some would rather stayed hidden. They don't want to be reminded that they are dodging God's Word. The fear is that carefully built, hypocritical facades won't stand biblical examination.

Your armor and weapons for these occasions will be the Word of God as it says in Ephesians 6 among other places. You will probably be faced with censure and expulsion from your current church or synagogue if you have one. It's going to be a fight, but I encourage you to persevere. We can reclaim ourselves as well as modern culture with His absolute truth. We've done it before. The Remnant has always been in tough situations like this. And we will always win. But we have to live it, not just preach parts of it. You can feel "free in Christ" to live as you choose, just don't tell me that His living oracles aren't for me. You can call His Word "old;" kick it into a distant age and spiritualize it out of existence for yourself, but count me out of that lawlessness.

Our True Identity

Balancing the Word causes identity problems. Most Christians reject whole Bible beliefs because of the Law, and many Jewish people won't accept us because of Jesus. So are we Christians or Jews? I don't think we have to decide. "Whole Bible" can apply anywhere, anytime. You can be a whole Bible Lutheran, a whole Bible Baptist, and even a whole Bible Jew (if those groups will let you). Just remember His Word comes first. Nothing should get between you and Him.

Of course, in trying to live out the whole of the Word we are not going to be able to maintain any sort of sectarianism (dividing into sects) for long. The name Christian simply means "partisan of the Christ," which is what we are. Lots of people wear the name but there are many degrees of partisanship. It depends on actual obedience. Some partisans don't know any better because of false teaching. Some know better and don't care. But just because many Christians (or Jews) have dragged His name through the mud doesn't make the name invalid.

Okay, I'm a partisan of the Christ, but what kind? There are many types that are heavy on words and light on biblical living. So many people want to use His name and claim His blessings without actually living His Word. Accepting the whole of the Word as a valid lifestyle and discipleship method makes me distinct from most of them. So almost by default, I'm a "whole Bible Christian."

We don't really need a name, but a short hand way to refer to ourselves is simpler for those with short attention spans. Many labels have been co-opted by people for whom hypocrisy is an art form, and I'm sure this will get the same treatment. Lots of partisans of the Christ want to think of themselves as whole Bible because they "believe" it.

One lady told me she was whole Bible but "not like you." What she meant was that she "believed" the whole Bible, but she didn't follow the feasts or many other parts of the Law. Ye-e-ah. That's like a Pharisee who "believed" the Old Testament (the Tanakh) and crucified Jesus. This is a clear example of one thing this whole book is about – Christians who "believe" but don't follow. Believing without acting doesn't make sense. Faith without works is dead (James 2:14-26). Seems to me we are either whole Bible or not. That word "whole" nails it down pretty well. There is no end to some people's hypocrisy, but whole Bible Christians are intent on returning God's love by living out the whole of His Word everywhere.

In Matthew 15:21-28 Jesus resists a little giving help to a Gentile woman (Mark calls her a Syrophoenician[147] in Mark 7:26, a part of the Canaanites) who was asking healing for her daughter. This is where Jesus says that it is not right to give the children's bread to dogs. Jews at the time generally referred to Gentiles as dogs. She has an amazing response, saying that "even dogs eat the crumbs that fall from the master's table." She doesn't argue the point, but humbly accepts the fact that she wasn't first in line for help. Jesus is so impressed with her faith He tells her the demon has left her daughter. Her faith was shown by her humble submission and obedience.

At first it might seem off-putting that Jesus would regard her (or me) as a dog. But I think this was more of a statement of where He was focusing His work at that time ("to the Jew first and also to the Gentile") rather than a judgment against either the lady or me. Although come to think of it, Canaanites were historically pretty "doggy." (Ephesians 2:12, Hebrews 11:6).[148] Those who by nature do what God requires, even if non-Jewish, belong to Him because of their faith, and aren't dogs at all. But even if it's true that my identity (in the eyes of some) is that of a dog in the kingdom, I'm okay with it. He made me and can assign me any place He chooses. I'd much rather be a dog in heaven than a lion in hell!

The material in this book is not for the purpose of creating yet another separate group or doing away with existing groups. It may (and probably will) happen that we cannot fellowship with existing groups. Those of us who believe and practice the whole of God's Word might have to find solace in meeting separately like the first century believers, but that is not our desire. Our desire is to be one Body. If you have to split because of the Word, remember you are not alone. God scatters His people like salt among the unbelievers, whether they have nothing to do with a church or attend religiously.

He wants us to be like priests, after the order of Melchizedek, representing His interests wherever we are. We are one Body with one faith and one God, and we don't need to create a unity or identity for ourselves. Our identity is in the Messiah Jesus, our root and head and life force. All we need to do is maintain or preserve that unity in a bond of peace.

> ¹Therefore I, the prisoner of the Lord, implore you to walk in a manner worthy of the calling with which you have been called,

---

[147] Literally a Phoenician from Syria, north of Israel. The Phoenicians were probably the ancestors of the Philistines.

[148] Canaanites were very bad in general. They made up the population of Sodom and Gomorrah (Genesis 10:19), they practiced all sorts of sexual immorality, they sacrificed children, and they were some of the people to be eliminated from the Promised Land (Exodus 23:23). They were descended from Canaan, the son of Ham, who saw his father's nakedness (Genesis 9:22-25). The Philistines were also part of the Canaanite family (through Ham).

> ²with all humility and gentleness, with patience, showing tolerance for one another in love, ³being diligent to preserve the unity of the Spirit in the bond of peace. (Ephesians 4:1-3 NASB95)

Represent

Those of you who embrace all of what God has for believers remember that not everyone shares your understanding and may need extra time and gentleness. The whole-Bible way is not for sissies or fair weather fans. But we don't have to smack people upside the head either.

You may be quite aggravated about the lies you have been taught. You may be unhappy with the stone-hearted refusal of people who've been part of your circle of friends and leaders to listen to the truth. I was very angry for a short while against everything church or Christian. Take my advice, and don't waste your time. For one thing, not everything church or Christian is bad. For another, anger and hatred only affect you. It's like drinking poison expecting the other guy to drop dead. If God cannot reach them, you certainly won't.

What is better is to plunge yourself into learning God's ways and teaching them to your family. Let's face it – if everyone did that, there'd be no need for evangelism or teachers in the first place. Be filled with the Word and be ready to give a defense for what you believe.

> ¹I solemnly charge you in the presence of God and of Christ Jesus, who is to judge the living and the dead, and by His appearing and His kingdom: ²preach the word; be ready in season and out of season; reprove, rebuke, exhort, with great patience and instruction. (2 Timothy 4:1-2 NASB95)

Some self-appointed part-Bible pastor one time told me how frustrated he was with people who were learning from the Word as I have suggested in this book. They would constantly respond to his non-biblical teachings with, "That's not in the Word." I failed to see the problem, and he refused to pay attention to the stupidity in his own protests. Either his teaching was in the Word or it wasn't. If it's just opinion, he shouldn't have said it was from the Word.

Of course we should know the Word inside and out so that we can respond as Jesus did in His desert experience – "It is written." When part-Bible people try to justify their actions and teachings with fragmented verses torn out of context, all we have to do is say, "It is also written." The whole-Bible response does not have to be in anger (although there is a godly anger available when we need it). The more you know and do the Word, the more it fills you and governs you, and the more peace will reign in you.

Don't be afraid to engage in discussions or even heated debates, because there's nothing wrong with Spirit-controlled passion. As long as you think it is productive, and as long as people will stay in it with you, continue presenting the Word (2 Timothy 2:22-26). But try to avoid arguments with people who will not investigate the truth for themselves, because those will go nowhere. Some are searching; others are looking for confirmation of what they want to believe. The second group becomes obvious when they keep going in circles looking for reasons not to do what God says. Save your precious time for those few who really are searching for their God.

You can find out where someone is in a few minutes of conversation simply by asking basic questions. One type of question is to ask for Scriptural support for dogmatic statements ("Where is that in the Word?"). When they show you a verse, look at the context (read a few verses or chapters before and after to find out how the verses are really being used – like we did with Colossians 2). Show them what they missed in the context (such as Peter's vision explained by Peter in Acts 10:28, 34-35). Show them the context of the whole of the living oracles.

The standard tactic for a typical non-searching Christian is to try one or two times to explain their view with a couple of verses (from their favorite 16). Then they get mad when you show them the truth from the Word. The antinomian (against the Law) teachings of the church in general have attracted many others who resist the Law. Birds of a feather and all that. They will either shut you down ("I don't want to argue") or they will run for their leader to get fresh ammunition. Of course they don't want to argue. They have no biblical argument to make. This might continue for a few exchanges, but eventually their leaders will encourage them to have nothing to do with you (saying something about "divisive people"). Their part-Bible approach ignores what Jesus and Paul said. Jesus did not come to bring peace but a sword with division. Paul said there must be divisions to show who is approved.

> [19]For there must also be factions among you, so that those who are approved may become evident among you. (1 Corinthians 11:19 NASB95)

You might get fortunate and find a person who really wants to learn and will continue to study with you. As long as you can do it, help them learn and practice the Word, being careful to distinguish between your opinions and the Author's meaning. Don't count on finding a lot of these people though. Remember only a few really believe God's Word. You will usually find it easier to talk with non-believers (or the unchurched) than with people for whom lip service is the limit.

Show anyone who will listen where your position comes from in the Word and be ready to learn yourself. Use this book as a guide. Avoid turning your opinions into Scripture, and just live and teach the Word. If someone seems to be lagging where you think they should be, you are not assigned to keep them in line. If we are in a leadership position, that requires a different approach, but even then, we work to include rather than exclude. There's a big difference between helping and shoving.

Torah Tyrants
Not all who follow the Law are whole-Bible either. There are those who make a career out of coming up with all sorts of legal rulings on just about every letter and syllable of the Word. They pride themselves on how much more observant they are than others. Others insist on "Hebrew only" language, and some are heavy into Jewish tradition. Some of these people are just bullies, and we relegate them to the status of "Torah tyrants" while trying to repair the damage they cause. Funny, it seems the more observant they get, the further away from God and His Son they go. They also have form down pat, but deny the power.[149]

Rest On The Rock
I hope you see now how to restore the wholeness of your God, the Body, and the Bible in your thinking and acting in order to reap the harvest of the fruit of the Spirit. It's amazing how eating His body and drinking His blood clears the eyesight. It stops the bleeding, binds up the wounds, and restores the hearts of all believers. It truly is the healing medicine we need. My thoughts on this are not original, but they are quite radical in view of the many attempts to dodge God. Some of us at least can now stop diving into the bushes and grabbing for fig leaves.

He hasn't hidden Himself, and the path to finding Him is right in front of our eyes. We discover the Way when we just take Him at His Word and move forward in trusting obedience. Abide in His Word like a branch to a vine. Follow the footsteps of Jesus and you'll find Him every time.

Taking on the whole of the Word is tough. It's like putting your feet down while floating in a river. As long as you float, there is no resistance. As soon as you take a stand, you will feel a lot of pressure. Jesus will give you the heart, and the Spirit will give you the power, but it can still be a mighty struggle.

---

[149] See for instance 1 Corinthians 5:11 ("immoral so-called brothers") 2 John 7; Jude 19; 1 John 3:10.

> [4] For whatever was written in earlier times was written for our instruction, so that through perseverance and the encouragement of the Scriptures we might have hope. (Romans 15:4 NASB95)

I can't even promise that you'll get a "payoff" when you commit to the whole of the Word. You might suffer real economic harm if you own a store and you decide to close on Saturdays (the Sabbath). You will be ridiculed for not eating pork and shellfish, though other diets sell a lot of books. People will think you are not Christian if you switch from the pagan holidays to His. You will be outcast from many so-called Christian groups, Jewish groups will not accept you, and even the pagans will think you are just weird. Although the pagans tend to leave you alone, where many Christians and Jews will actively hate you. And yes, it's hard to tell who's a pagan nowadays anyway.

But like Peter said, "Lord, to whom shall we go? You have the Words of life." Even if we don't get a payoff in this life; if we are despised and spat upon; if our material wealth suffers, or if we get thrown into a furnace and He doesn't rescue us, He is still God and He still has the Words of life. To whom else would we go? Who else would we stand with?

When all is crumbling around you, and the hypocritical façade of the church dissolves in your hand as you reach for it; when mountains shake, and it seems there is no firm footing anywhere and no one to turn to for help, rest your hope on the Rock. Shalom.

> [11] For the grace of God has appeared, bringing salvation to all men, [12] instructing us to deny ungodliness and worldly desires and to live sensibly, righteously and godly in the present age, [13] looking for the blessed hope and the appearing of the glory of our great God and Savior, Christ Jesus, [14] who gave Himself for us to redeem us from every lawless deed, and to purify for Himself a people for His own possession, zealous for good deeds. [15] These things speak and exhort and reprove with all authority. Let no one disregard you. (Titus 2:11-15 NASB95)

> [4] "Remember the law of my servant Moses, the statutes and rules that I commanded him at Horeb for all Israel. [5] "Behold, I will send you Elijah the prophet before the great and awesome day of the LORD comes. [6] And he will turn the hearts of fathers to their children and the hearts of children to their fathers, lest I come and strike the land with a decree of utter destruction." (Malachi 4:4-6 ESV)

Acknowledgements

I thank God for His grace and patience with me, forgiving over and over and staying with me even when I thought He wasn't there. All my thoughts written here were given to me by Him, but if anything turns out not to be in line with His Word it is not His fault but mine.

There are many people in my life who have been positive influences and helped me get to where I am now. My adoptive parents stabilized my life at a critical time, and they put in the effort and gave me a loving home.

My wife Susan deserves a medal or three for putting up with me, loving her God and sticking around for 37 years (so far), sometimes just because she loves her God so much. She helped edit this book, and also helps me edit what I say so I don't put my foot in my mouth. On occasion she has to help extract my foot anyway.

Several pastors have chipped in with words of wisdom over the years. John Lockhart of Mapleview Baptist church in Lakeside tried to teach unruly high-schoolers hermeneutics (I still have his book) and got fired. He bucked the Nicolaitans and wanted the congregation to get more involved in the community. Wesleyan Pastor Dave Holmquist helped keep our young marriage together. From Tim Hegg I learned excellent lessons on Bible interpretation and the difference between meaning and application. Dr. Walter C. Kaiser Jr. deserves much praise for his books and for taking a chance on writing a recommendation for this book. Tony Ford, Shari Freeland and Mike Florian were friends when I needed them and/or helped with critical thinking also.

There are people also in my life who were and are bad examples, but I learn(ed) from them anyway. Some of their wrong teachings ended up in this book. One of them said he would destroy me but I'm still around. I think I will keep from mentioning their names because they might repent, and mom always said if you can't say anything nice don't say anything at all. Not that I listened to her as much as I should've.

Scripture Index

1 Chronicles 12:18 ref 99
1 Chronicles 13 ref 280
1 Chronicles 15:13 quote 280
1 Chronicles 15:13 ref 280
1 Chronicles 16:14-18 quote 129
1 Chronicles 16:15 ref 129
1 Chronicles 16:22 ref 114
1 Chronicles 21 ref 51
1 Chronicles 28:11-19 ref 165
1 Corinthians 1:10 ref 109
1 Corinthians 1:18 ref 134
1 Corinthians 10 ref 192
1 Corinthians 10:16 ref 18
1 Corinthians 10:4 ref 53
1 Corinthians 11 ref 12, 303
1 Corinthians 11:1 ref 272
1 Corinthians 11:1-16 ref 301
1 Corinthians 11:19 quote 312
1 Corinthians 11:19 ref 109
1 Corinthians 11:23-34 ref 190, 290
1 Corinthians 11:25 ref 150, 151
1 Corinthians 11:27-32 ref 255
1 Corinthians 11:31–32 quote 43
1 Corinthians 12 ref 171
1 Corinthians 12:12-14 quote 87
1 Corinthians 13:1 ref 245
1 Corinthians 13:12-13 quote 74
1 Corinthians 13:13 ref 247
1 Corinthians 13:4–7 quote 14
1 Corinthians 14:20 ref 71
1 Corinthians 14:26 quote 261
1 Corinthians 14:26 ref 134
1 Corinthians 15 ref 125
1 Corinthians 15:2 ref 134
1 Corinthians 15:24 ref 58
1 Corinthians 15:55, 56 ref 208
1 Corinthians 16:2 ref 289
1 Corinthians 2:11–16 quote 135
1 Corinthians 2:2 quote 226
1 Corinthians 3:16 ref 90
1 Corinthians 4:6 quote 265
1 Corinthians 4:6 ref 9
1 Corinthians 5:11 ref 313
1 Corinthians 5:1-2 quote 189
1 Corinthians 5:12 ref 43

1 Corinthians 5:1-2 ref 299
1 Corinthians 6:2-3 ref 43
1 Corinthians 6:7-8 quote 277
1 Corinthians 7:1-5 ref 299
1 Corinthians 7:19 quote 102
1 Corinthians 7:19 ref 10, 104
1 Corinthians 8 ref 192
1 Corinthians 9:24-27 quote 240
1 Corinthians 9:9 ref 142
1 Corinthians 9:9-18 ref 295
1 John 1:8–10 quote 43
1 John 2:1-2 quote 170
1 John 2:16 ref 197
1 John 2:2 ref 228
1 John 2:25 quote 131
1 John 2:27 quote 116
1 John 2:3-6 quote 81
1 John 2:6, 17, 24 ref 226
1 John 3:10 ref 313
1 John 3:16 ref 72
1 John 3:18-24 quote 251
1 John 3:4-5 quote 209
1 John 3:6, 9 ref 226
1 John 4:12 ref 50, 51
1 John 4:1-3 ref 20
1 John 4:9-14 ref 53
1 John 5:10, 11 ref 20
1 John 5:1-12 ref 17
1 Kings 19:1-2 ref 108
1 Kings 19:18 quote 96
1 Kings 2:3-4 (AV) ref 134
1 Kings 8:47 ref 78
1 Kings 8:56 ref 128
1 Peter 1:10-13 ref 90
1 Peter 1:11 ref 100
1 Peter 1:20-21 quote 151
1 Peter 1:25 ref 209
1 Peter 2:16 quote 224
1 Peter 2:4-5 quote 116
1 Peter 2:5, 9 ref 91
1 Peter 2:7-8 ref 161
1 Peter 3:15 ref 116
1 Peter 3:18 ref 172
1 Peter 4:16 ref 89
1 Peter 4:17 ref 162

1 Peter 4:4, 5 ref 43
1 Peter 4:4-5 quote 164
1 Peter 5:10 ref 307
1 Samuel 10:6, 10 ref 99
1 Samuel 11:6 ref 99
1 Samuel 13:14 ref 115
1 Samuel 16:13 ref 99
1 Samuel 19:20 ref 99
1 Samuel 2:25 ref 50
1 Thessalonians 2:10-12 quote 240
1 Thessalonians 4:1 ref 134
1 Thessalonians 5:12 ref 134
1 Thessalonians 5:8 ref 42
1 Timothy 1:3-11 quote 266
1 Timothy 1:5 ref 134
1 Timothy 1:8 ref 24, 209
1 Timothy 3:14-15 quote 140
1 Timothy 3:16 ref 20
1 Timothy 4:10 quote 69
1 Timothy 4:13 quote 261
1 Timothy 4:1-5 quote 221
1 Timothy 4:3 ref 107
1 Timothy 4:7-8 quote 240
1 Timothy 5 ref 171
1 Timothy 5:17-18 ref 295
1 Timothy 6:3-5 ref 274
2 Chronicles 15:1 ref........................ 99
2 Chronicles 15:1-7 ref................... 134
2 Chronicles 16:9 quote 243
2 Chronicles 2:13-14 ref.................. 92
2 Chronicles 20:14 ref..................... 99
2 Chronicles 30:18-20 quote........... 280
2 Chronicles 31:20-21 quote........... 284
2 Chronicles 35:18 ref.................... 174
2 Chronicles 5:14 ref 50
2 Chronicles 6:28-33 ref................. 255
2 Chronicles 6:37 ref 78
2 Chronicles 7:5 ref 169
2 Corinthians 1:22 ref 78
2 Corinthians 10:3-5 quote 251
2 Corinthians 10:5 ref 225
2 Corinthians 11:12-15 quote 115
2 Corinthians 11:18 ref 197
2 Corinthians 2:1-11 ref 189
2 Corinthians 2:15-16 ref 60
2 Corinthians 2:9 quote 253
2 Corinthians 3:18 quote 248
2 Corinthians 3:3 ref 248

2 Corinthians 3:5-6 ref 21
2 Corinthians 3:6 ref 21, 150, 151, 208,
   248
2 Corinthians 3:7-16 quote 248
2 Corinthians 4:2 quote 265
2 Corinthians 4:4 ref 50
2 Corinthians 5:21 quote 209
2 Corinthians 5:21 ref 72
2 Corinthians 7:10 quote 79
2 Corinthians 7:9-10 ref 78
2 John 4-6 quote 250
2 John 7 ref 313
2 Kings 17:15 ref 302
2 Kings 22 and 23 ref 149
2 Kings 22:13 quote 149
2 Kings 22:2 ref 149
2 Kings 23:22 ref 174
2 Kings 23:3 ref 150
2 Kings 5 ref 298
2 Peter 1:16 ref 133
2 Peter 1:20-21 quote..................... 133
2 Peter 1:5–7 quote 231
2 Peter 2:17-22 quote 228
2 Peter 2:18 ref 197
2 Peter 3:14-18 quote..................... 196
2 Peter 3:16 ref 154
2 Peter 3:5-6 ref 126
2 Peter 3:9 quote 131
2 Samuel 22:26-28 ref..................... 134
2 Samuel 6:6-8 ref........................... 280
2 Samuel 7 ref 38
2 Samuel 7:11-16 ref....................... 129
2 Thessalonians 1:6-10 quote 66
2 Thessalonians 1:8 ref 162
2 Timothy 1:8-9 quote 219
2 Timothy 2:14 quote 273
2 Timothy 2:15 quote 20
2 Timothy 2:22-26 ref 312
2 Timothy 3:14–15 quote 52
2 Timothy 3:1-5 quote 242
2 Timothy 3:16-17 quote 135
2 Timothy 3:16-17 ref 132
2 Timothy 4:1-2 quote 311
2 Timothy 4:2 ref 134
2 Timothy 4:3 ref 29
3 John 11 quote 272
3 John 11 ref 283
Acts 10 ref............................... 199, 222

Acts 10:28 quote 223
Acts 10:28, 34-35 ref 312
Acts 10:34-35 quote 159, 223
Acts 10:34-35 ref 85
Acts 11:26 ref 89
Acts 12:4 ref 146
Acts 13:14, 42, 44 ref 12, 205
Acts 13:42-43 ref 87
Acts 13:44, 48, 49 ref 134
Acts 14:16, 17 ref 75
Acts 15 ref 185, 187
Acts 15:1 ref 186
Acts 15:1, 5 ref 190
Acts 15:16-17 ref 96
Acts 15:17 ref 90
Acts 15:20 ref 123
Acts 15:20, 21 ref 187
Acts 15:21 quote 187
Acts 15:21 ref 296
Acts 15:29 ref 187
Acts 15:30 ref 88
Acts 15:5 ref 186
Acts 16:13 ref 12, 205
Acts 16:3 ref 190, 205, 296
Acts 17:10, 11 ref 116
Acts 17:10-12 ref 20
Acts 17:2 ref 12, 205
Acts 17:24-28 ref 50
Acts 17:30-31 quote 155
Acts 18:11 ref 134
Acts 18:18 ref 205
Acts 18:4 ref 205
Acts 18:6 ref 104
Acts 19:13–16 34
Acts 19:13–16 quote 34
Acts 19:15 ref 20
Acts 19:4, 5 ref 298
Acts 2 ref 27, 33, 87, 117, 290
Acts 2:33 ref 50
Acts 2:38 ref 32
Acts 2:40 ref 235
Acts 2:42 ref 134
Acts 2:44 ref 27
Acts 2:46, 47 ref 170
Acts 2:5 ref 32
Acts 20:26-27 quote 175
Acts 20:29-30 ref 235
Acts 20:6,16 ref 205
Acts 20:7 ref 289

Acts 21:23-26 ref 205
Acts 21:24 ref 205
Acts 21:26 ref 12, 170
Acts 21:26-30 ref 170
Acts 22:1-22 ref 105
Acts 22:17 ref 170, 205
Acts 22:3 ref 205
Acts 23:6 ref 205
Acts 24:11, 17, 18 ref 205
Acts 24:14 ref 205
Acts 24:17, 18 ref 205
Acts 24:17,18 ref 170
Acts 24:6, 12 ref 170
Acts 25:8 ref 170
Acts 26:21 ref 170
Acts 26:28 ref 89
Acts 27:9 ref 205
Acts 28:23 134
Acts 28:23 ref 9, 205
Acts 3:1-8 ref 170
Acts 4:2 ref 134
Acts 5 ref 25
Acts 5:20, 21, 25, 42 ref 170
Acts 5:31 ref 50
Acts 6:2-4,7 ref 134
Acts 7 ref 87
Acts 7:38 quote 87
Acts 7:38 ref 8, 88, 161
Acts 7:44 ref 165
Acts 7:51–53 quote 108, 218
Acts 7:51-53 ref 102, 140
Acts 7:53 ref 111, 217
Acts 7:55-56 ref 50
Acts 8:27 ref 12, 170
Amos 3:7 quote 139
Amos 4:13 quote 139
Amos 5:7 ref 58
Amos 6:12 ref 58
Amos 7:7, 8 ref 52
Amos 9 ref 52
Colossians 1:18 ref 50
Colossians 1:9-12 ref 263
Colossians 2 ref 190, 194, 220, 312
Colossians 2:13-15 quote 209
Colossians 2:16 ref 195
Colossians 2:16-17 quote 195, 219
Colossians 2:16-23 ref 234
Colossians 2:17 ref 36
Colossians 2:18–19 quote 195

Colossians 2:19 ref	195
Colossians 2:20-23 quote	194
Colossians 2:21 ref	197
Colossians 2:22 ref	302
Colossians 2:4 quote	194
Colossians 2:8 quote	194
Colossians 2:8 ref	145
Colossians 3 ref	190
Colossians 3:1 ref	50
Colossians 3:16 ref	34
Colossians 4 ref	190
Daniel 10:12-13 ref	133
Daniel 12:10 quote	6
Daniel 12:1-3 quote	69
Daniel 2:20-22 ref	53
Daniel 3 ref	212
Daniel 3:17-18 quote	212
Daniel 4:17, 25 ref	182
Daniel 6:26 ref	129
Daniel 7 ref	51
Daniel 7:13-14 ref	52
Daniel 9-11 ref	182
Deuteronomy 10:12 ref	157
Deuteronomy 10:12-13 ref	81
Deuteronomy 10:14 ref	53, 67
Deuteronomy 10:15, 18 ref	157
Deuteronomy 10:16 quote	295
Deuteronomy 10:16 ref	190, 238, 245
Deuteronomy 10:16-18 quote	279
Deuteronomy 10:18 ref	177
Deuteronomy 10:19 ref	157
Deuteronomy 11:1, 13, 22 ref	157
Deuteronomy 11:19 ref	263
Deuteronomy 12:21 ref	290
Deuteronomy 12:29-32 ref	302
Deuteronomy 12:32 quote	264
Deuteronomy 12:32 ref	203
Deuteronomy 12:6 ref	123
Deuteronomy 13:14 quote	275
Deuteronomy 13:14 ref	233
Deuteronomy 13:3 ref	157
Deuteronomy 13:5 ref	189
Deuteronomy 14 ref	293
Deuteronomy 14:21 ref	304
Deuteronomy 14:23 ref	60
Deuteronomy 14:24 ref	290
Deuteronomy 14:3 ref	192
Deuteronomy 15:19 ref	123
Deuteronomy 15:7-11 ref	294
Deuteronomy 16:19-20 ref	280
Deuteronomy 17:11 ref	134
Deuteronomy 17:14 ref	233
Deuteronomy 17:19 ref	60
Deuteronomy 17:6-7 quote	184
Deuteronomy 17:7, 12 ref	189
Deuteronomy 17:8-12 ref	277
Deuteronomy 18:15-19 ref	179
Deuteronomy 18:20 quote	205
Deuteronomy 18:9 ref	272
Deuteronomy 19:18 ref	233
Deuteronomy 19:18-19 quote	276
Deuteronomy 19:18-19 ref	184
Deuteronomy 19:20 quote	61
Deuteronomy 19:9 ref	157
Deuteronomy 21:15-17 ref	124
Deuteronomy 21:21 ref	189
Deuteronomy 22:21 ref	189
Deuteronomy 22:22-29 ref	183
Deuteronomy 22:30 ref	189
Deuteronomy 22:5 ref	278
Deuteronomy 23:12-14 quote	204
Deuteronomy 23:21-23 quote	300
Deuteronomy 23:22, 24 ref	178
Deuteronomy 23:24, 25 ref	185
Deuteronomy 23:5	157
Deuteronomy 24:17 ref	177
Deuteronomy 24:19-20 ref	294
Deuteronomy 25:13-16 ref	278
Deuteronomy 25:4 ref	142, 295
Deuteronomy 25:5 ref	124
Deuteronomy 26:12 ref	294
Deuteronomy 27:1-3, 26 ref	134
Deuteronomy 27:19 ref	177
Deuteronomy 27:26 ref	208
Deuteronomy 27:30 ref	189
Deuteronomy 28:58-61 ref	255
Deuteronomy 29:18–19 quote	58
Deuteronomy 29:29 quote	139
Deuteronomy 30:10,14 ref	134
Deuteronomy 30:11 quote	36
Deuteronomy 30:11-14 quote	206
Deuteronomy 30:11–14 quote	13
Deuteronomy 30:11-20 ref	36
Deuteronomy 30:15-16 quote	207
Deuteronomy 30:19 ref	123
Deuteronomy 30:19-20 quote	208

Deuteronomy 30:6 quote 295
Deuteronomy 30:6 ref ... 157, 190, 238, 245
Deuteronomy 30:6, 16, 20.............. 157
Deuteronomy 31:13 ref 60
Deuteronomy 31:27........................ 102
Deuteronomy 32:46,47 ref 134
Deuteronomy 32:46-47 ref 134
Deuteronomy 32:5, 20 ref 235
Deuteronomy 33:3........................ 157
Deuteronomy 34:10 ref 51
Deuteronomy 34:9 ref 99
Deuteronomy 4:1 ref 134
Deuteronomy 4:10 ref 60
Deuteronomy 4:2 quote 264
Deuteronomy 4:2 ref 203
Deuteronomy 4:37 ref 157
Deuteronomy 4:6 ref 18, 140
Deuteronomy 4:6-9 quote 249
Deuteronomy 5:10 ref 7, 157
Deuteronomy 5:20 ref 184
Deuteronomy 5:24 ref 50
Deuteronomy 5:27 ref 18
Deuteronomy 5:5 ref 134
Deuteronomy 5:6-21 ref 156
Deuteronomy 6:13-14 quote 270
Deuteronomy 6:16-17 quote 269
Deuteronomy 6:4-5 quote 45
Deuteronomy 6:4-9 quote 263
Deuteronomy 6:5 quote 15
Deuteronomy 6:5 ref 15, 157
Deuteronomy 7:15 ref 255
Deuteronomy 7:3 ref 124, 189
Deuteronomy 7:7-8, 13 ref 157
Deuteronomy 7:9 quote 15
Deuteronomy 7:9 ref 157
Deuteronomy 8:1-3 quote 268
Deuteronomy 8:3 ref 21
Deuteronomy 9:4-6 ref 202, 247
Deuteronomy 9:6 ref 102
Ecclesiastes 12:13-14 quote 203
Ecclesiastes 12:13–14 quote............. 22
Ecclesiastes 3:14 quote............. 62, 264
Ecclesiastes 3:14 ref....................... 203
Ecclesiastes 8:11 quote................... 215
Ecclesiastes 8:12-13 quote 306
Ephesians 1:13 ref 78
Ephesians 1:21 ref 58
Ephesians 2:10 ref 41

Ephesians 2:12 quote..................... 131
Ephesians 2:12 ref..................... 93, 310
Ephesians 2:14-16 quote 198
Ephesians 2:14-16 ref 198
Ephesians 2:19-22 ref 95
Ephesians 2:8 ref............................. 41
Ephesians 3:4-7 ref 93
Ephesians 4 ref.............................. 171
Ephesians 4:1-3 quote 311
Ephesians 4:17-19 ref 140
Ephesians 4:20-24 ref 234
Ephesians 4:3 ref............................ 118
Ephesians 4:30 ref............................ 78
Ephesians 4:4-6 ref 2
Ephesians 5:1 ref............................ 272
Ephesians 5:15-21 ref 71
Ephesians 5:18-21 ref 234
Ephesians 5:28-30 ref 242
Ephesians 5:5 ref...................... 42, 57
Ephesians 6 ref.............................. 308
Ephesians 6:4 ref............................ 134
Esther 8:17 ref 217
Exodus 1:5 ref 31, 84
Exodus 11 ref 124
Exodus 12 ref 124, 220, 290, 295
Exodus 12:10 ref 290
Exodus 12:25 quote 129
Exodus 12:38 quote 91
Exodus 12:48 ref 243
Exodus 12:49 quote 159
Exodus 12:49 ref 179
Exodus 13:16 ref 124
Exodus 13:2 ref 124
Exodus 16 ref 288
Exodus 16:23-26 ref 288
Exodus 16:25 ref 185
Exodus 16:26-28 ref 124
Exodus 16:29 ref 288
Exodus 16:4 ref 124, 134
Exodus 17:7 quote 269
Exodus 18:16 ref 124
Exodus 18:25-27 ref 277
Exodus 19:10, 14............................ 124
Exodus 19:34 ref 93
Exodus 19:5 ref 22
Exodus 19:5, 6 ref 91
Exodus 19:5-6 quote 171
Exodus 19:6 ref 118, 170
Exodus 2:24 quote 128

Exodus 20:1-17 quote 156	Exodus 40:20 ref 160
Exodus 20:1-17 ref 157	Exodus 6:8 ref 129
Exodus 20:16 ref 184	Exodus 9:16-17 ref 96
Exodus 20:20 quote 60	Exodus 9:20-21 quote 91
Exodus 20:5-6 ref 157	Exodus 9:29 ref 294
Exodus 20:6 ref 7, 74, 129	Ezekiel 11:19 ref 16
Exodus 20:8-10 ref 288	Ezekiel 11:19-20 quote 151
Exodus 21:14 ref 184	Ezekiel 11:19-20 ref 150, 246
Exodus 21:5-6 ref 224	Ezekiel 11:19-21 ref 7
Exodus 22:2, 7 ref 79	Ezekiel 11:5 ref 99
Exodus 22:21 ref 92	Ezekiel 12:2 ref 18, 22
Exodus 22:24-25 ref 294	Ezekiel 14:6 ref 78
Exodus 22:29 ref 124	Ezekiel 16 ref 94
Exodus 23:1 quote 184	Ezekiel 18:4-9 ref 157
Exodus 23:1, 7 ref 184	Ezekiel 20:19-20 quote 239
Exodus 23:14 ref 11	Ezekiel 22:23-31 ref 42
Exodus 23:19 quote 304	Ezekiel 22:26 quote 297
Exodus 23:23 ref 310	Ezekiel 22:26 ref 42
Exodus 23:25-27 ref 255	Ezekiel 3 ref 18
Exodus 23:6 ref 233	Ezekiel 3:12, 14, 24 ref 99
Exodus 23:8-9 quote 280	Ezekiel 3:7 ref 102
Exodus 23:9 ref 93	Ezekiel 33:31, 32 ref 18
Exodus 24:12 ref 134	Ezekiel 33:32 quote 80
Exodus 24:16 ref 52	Ezekiel 34:17 ref 68
Exodus 24:7 ref 18	Ezekiel 36:22-37 ref 150
Exodus 25:9 ref 165	Ezekiel 36:26-27 quote ... 151, 199, 246
Exodus 27:26 ref 124	Ezekiel 36:26–27 quote 8
Exodus 3:2, 3 ref 51	Ezekiel 36:27 ref 213
Exodus 31:3 ref 99	Ezekiel 37:15-28 ref 91
Exodus 32:10 ref 160	Ezekiel 37:24 quote 83
Exodus 32:3-4 quote 59	Ezekiel 40 through 48 ref 172
Exodus 32:9 ref 102	Ezekiel 40-47 ref 9
Exodus 33:11 ref 51	Ezekiel 44:14-16 quote 172
Exodus 33:13 quote 79	Ezekiel 44:2 ref 172
Exodus 33:18 ref 79	Ezekiel 44:23 ref 298
Exodus 33:19-23 ref 79	Ezekiel 44:23-24 quote 172
Exodus 33:20-23 ref 52	Ezekiel 5:5-6 quote 237
Exodus 33:3-5 ref 102	Ezekiel 7:25–26 quote 106
Exodus 34:1 ref 79	Ezekiel 8:17 quote 93
Exodus 34:15 ref 192	Ezekiel 9:3 ref 50
Exodus 34:26 ref 304	Ezekiel 9:4 quote 238
Exodus 34:5-7 ref 52, 238	Ezekiel. 2:2 ref 99
Exodus 34:6 ref 15	Ezra 6:21 ref 92
Exodus 34:6–7 quote 55	Ezra 9 and 10 ref 92
Exodus 34:7 ref 74, 129	Ezra 9:13-14 ref 92
Exodus 35:31 ref 99	Ezra 9:7 ref 182
Exodus 4 ref 295	Galatians 2 ref 190, 211
Exodus 4:26 ref 124	Galatians 2:14 quote 217

Galatians 2:14 ref 217
Galatians 2:16 ref 197
Galatians 2:21 ref 197
Galatians 3 ref 211
Galatians 3:10 quote 207
Galatians 3:10 ref 197
Galatians 3:11 ref 198
Galatians 3:13-14 quote 207
Galatians 3:13-14 ref 207
Galatians 3:19 ref 54, 56
Galatians 3:24-26 quote 244
Galatians 3:28 quote 94
Galatians 3:29 quote 131
Galatians 3:29 ref 136
Galatians 3:7, 11 ref 197
Galatians 4 ref 128
Galatians 4:10 ref 195, 197
Galatians 4:24 ref 144
Galatians 4:3 ref 197, 198
Galatians 4:4-6 ref 53
Galatians 4:8 ref 197
Galatians 4:9 ref 197
Galatians 4:9-10 quote 302
Galatians 5 ref 190
Galatians 5:1 ref 163, 197
Galatians 5:12 ref 197
Galatians 5:1-4 quote 223
Galatians 5:14 ref 134
Galatians 5:16 ref 197
Galatians 5:16-26 ref 213
Galatians 5:18 ref 23
Galatians 5:18-25 quote 246
Galatians 5:21 ref 42
Galatians 5:22-23 quote 236
Galatians 5:3 ref 205
Galatians 5:3-4 ref 23
Galatians 5:4 quote 197
Galatians 5:6 quote 102
Galatians 6 ref 190
Galatians 6:13 quote 197
Galatians 6:13 ref 197, 217
Galatians 6:2 ref 106
Galtaians 3:2, 5, 14 ref 197
Genesis 1 ref 12
Genesis 1:2 ref 49
Genesis 1:26 ref 47, 48
Genesis 1:5 ref 292
Genesis 10 ref 170
Genesis 10:19 ref 310

Genesis 12:1-3 ref 128
Genesis 12:3 ref 100
Genesis 13 ref 128
Genesis 13:13 ref 125
Genesis 14:14 ref 84
Genesis 14:20 ref 124
Genesis 14:8 ref 118
Genesis 15 ref 51, 128, 187, 190
Genesis 15:13 ref 93
Genesis 15:6 ref 84
Genesis 16:7-11 ref 51
Genesis 17 ref .128, 186, 187, 190, 191, 295
Genesis 17:11 quote 238
Genesis 17:13-14 ref 124
Genesis 17:23 ref 84
Genesis 18:19 ref 75
Genesis 18:20 ref 125
Genesis 19:4-7 ref 124
Genesis 2:17 ref 123
Genesis 2:2-3 ref 123
Genesis 2:23-25 ref 123
Genesis 2:7 ref 14, 49
Genesis 20:3 ref 124
Genesis 21 ref 53, 84
Genesis 22 ref 53, 84, 124, 128
Genesis 22:11 ref 51
Genesis 22:13 ref 124
Genesis 22:18 ref 22
Genesis 24 ref 128
Genesis 24:27 ref 15
Genesis 24:3 ref 124
Genesis 25 ref 25
Genesis 26 ref 128
Genesis 26:4, 5 ref 124
Genesis 26:5 ref 22, 25, 84, 136
Genesis 27 ref 124
Genesis 28 ref 128
Genesis 28:1 ref 124
Genesis 28:22 ref 124
Genesis 29:26 ref 124
Genesis 3 ref 123
Genesis 3:1-3 quote 146
Genesis 3:15 quote 127
Genesis 3:15 ref 38, 104, 128, 148
Genesis 3:21 ref 169
Genesis 3:24 ref 214
Genesis 3:7-8 ref 236
Genesis 30 ref 124

Genesis 31:35 ref	124
Genesis 31:54 ref	124
Genesis 32:30 ref	52
Genesis 34 ref	295
Genesis 35:14 ref	124
Genesis 35:2 ref	124
Genesis 35:22 ref	124
Genesis 38:6-26 ref	124
Genesis 4:10 ref	123
Genesis 4:3-5 ref	168
Genesis 4:3-7 ref	123
Genesis 4:4 ref	123, 169
Genesis 46:1 ref	124
Genesis 46:27 ref	31
Genesis 48:16 ref	49
Genesis 48:18 ref	124
Genesis 49:3, 4 ref	124
Genesis 5:24 ref	125
Genesis 6:18 ref	128
Genesis 6:5 ref	125
Genesis 6:5, 11-13, 17 ref	123
Genesis 6:8 ref	75
Genesis 7:2 ref	221
Genesis 7:2, 8 ref	123
Genesis 8 ref	123
Genesis 9:20-27 ref	123
Genesis 9:22-25 ref	310
Genesis 9:25-27 ref	128
Genesis 9:3 quote	222
Genesis 9:3 ref	222
Genesis 9:4 ref	123
Genesis 9:6 ref	123
Genesis 9:9 ref	128
Habakkuk 1:11 quote	57
Haggai 1:9–10 quote	167
Haggai 2:5 ref	99
Hebrews 1:1-2 quote	123
Hebrews 1:3 ref	50, 132
Hebrews 10:1 ref	37
Hebrews 10:22 ref	124
Hebrews 10:3 ref	168
Hebrews 10:4 quote	168
Hebrews 11:13-16 ref	90
Hebrews 11:39, 40 ref	90
Hebrews 11:6 ref	310
Hebrews 12:24 ref	150
Hebrews 12:5, 8, 10, 11 ref	43
Hebrews 12:7-8 quote	306
Hebrews 13:15 ref	170
Hebrews 13:8 ref	53
Hebrews 2:10 ref	307
Hebrews 2:12 ref	87
Hebrews 3:14-19 ref	70
Hebrews 4:10 ref	289
Hebrews 4:12 ref	117
Hebrews 4:2 quote	160
Hebrews 4:2 ref	9, 38, 40
Hebrews 4:6-7 quote	161
Hebrews 4:9 ref	289
Hebrews 5:12-14 quote	271
Hebrews 5:13 ref	30
Hebrews 5:14 ref	71
Hebrews 6:1 ref	71
Hebrews 6:4-8 ref	70
Hebrews 7 ref	118
Hebrews 7:12 ref	170, 218
Hebrews 7:12-28 ref	218
Hebrews 7:1-3 ref	50
Hebrews 7:23-25 quote	170
Hebrews 8:5 ref	37, 165
Hebrews 8:8 ref	150
Hebrews 9:15 ref	150
Hebrews 9:24-25 quote	165
Hebrews 9:27 ref	125, 218
Hosea 10:12 quote	15
Hosea 11:1 ref	142
Hosea 6:6 ref	140
Hosea 6:6-7 quote	125
Hosea 6:7 ref	150
Hosea 8:12 quote	158, 227
Isaiah 1:10 ref	134
Isaiah 1:10-17 quote	169
Isaiah 1:10-17 ref	253
Isaiah 1:16-17 ref	157
Isaiah 1:17, 23 ref	177
Isaiah 10:2 ref	177
Isaiah 11:10 ref	104
Isaiah 11:16-12:6 ref	90
Isaiah 11:2 ref	99
Isaiah 19:19-20 ref	173
Isaiah 2:1-4 quote	127
Isaiah 2:3 ref	134
Isaiah 24:5-6 quote	237
Isaiah 28:5, 6 ref	90
Isaiah 28:9-13 quote	287
Isaiah 29:13 ref	211

Isaiah 29:13-14 ref	270
Isaiah 32:14-17 quote	232
Isaiah 35:1-10 ref	49
Isaiah 35:2 ref	50
Isaiah 40:23 ref	182
Isaiah 40:8 quote	132
Isaiah 40:8 ref	209
Isaiah 41:10 ref	50
Isaiah 41:14 ref	49
Isaiah 41:8 ref	84
Isaiah 42:1 ref	99
Isaiah 42:8 quote	59
Isaiah 45:23 ref	20
Isaiah 45:7 quote	62
Isaiah 47:4 ref	50
Isaiah 48:16-18 quote	139
Isaiah 5:20 ref	302
Isaiah 51:16 quote	220
Isaiah 51:7-8 quote	258
Isaiah 53:2 ref	104
Isaiah 54:5 ref	50
Isaiah 55:10-11 ref	33
Isaiah 56:1-8 quote	290
Isaiah 56:3-8 quote	94
Isaiah 56:7 ref	93
Isaiah 56:8 quote	153
Isaiah 59:1–2 quote	55
Isaiah 59:20-21 ref	50
Isaiah 6 ref	52
Isaiah 6:1-5 quote	64
Isaiah 61 ref	91
Isaiah 61:1 ref	99
Isaiah 61:10 ref	90
Isaiah 61:1-6 quote	171
Isaiah 63:10-14 ref	100
Isaiah 63:11 ref	99
Isaiah 64:6 ref	206
Isaiah 65:9 ref	90
Isaiah 66 ref	177
Isaiah 66:2 ref	141
Isaiah 66:23-24 quote	66
Isaiah 7:14 ref	160
Isaiah 8:12-13 quote	62
Isaiah 8:20 quote	147
Isaiah 8:20 ref	134
James 1:17 ref	53
James 1:18 ref	134
James 1:21-25 quote	145
James 1:22-27 ref	20
James 1:23-25 quote	249
James 1:26, 27 ref	20
James 2:1 quote	280
James 2:10 ref	205
James 2:14-26 ref	309
James 2:18 quote	23
James 2:2 ref	89
James 2:21 ref	72
James 2:5 ref	71
James 4:11 ref	193, 203
James 4:8 quote	243
James 5:12 ref	300
James 5:16 quote	254
Jeremiah 10 ref	302
Jeremiah 10:12 ref	53
Jeremiah 11:6 ref	18
Jeremiah 12:1-2 quote	307
Jeremiah 12:16-17 quote	17
Jeremiah 15:16 quote	201
Jeremiah 15:16 ref	18
Jeremiah 18:7-10 ref	182
Jeremiah 2:31 quote	165, 224
Jeremiah 22:3 ref	157, 177
Jeremiah 23:23-24 ref	53
Jeremiah 27:5 ref	53
Jeremiah 3:1-10 quote	57
Jeremiah 30:2 ref	133
Jeremiah 31 ref	150
Jeremiah 31:31–34 quote	7
Jeremiah 31:31-34 ref	248
Jeremiah 32:33 ref	134
Jeremiah 35:13 ref	134
Jeremiah 35:13-14 quote	230
Jeremiah 36 ref	215
Jeremiah 36:2 ref	133
Jeremiah 4:4 ref	190, 238, 245, 295
Jeremiah 42:4 quote	119
Jeremiah 5:21 ref	18, 22
Jeremiah 5:3 quote	70
Jeremiah 6:10 quote	6
Jeremiah 6:10 ref	22, 295
Jeremiah 6:18-19 ref	134
Jeremiah 7, 8 ref	80
Jeremiah 7:16 ref	254
Jeremiah 7:28 ref	140
Jeremiah 7:4-11 quote	173
Jeremiah 7:4-11 ref	20
Jeremiah 7:5-11 ref	157
Jeremiah 8:4-13 ref	78

Jeremiah 9:25, 26 ref 295
Job 1:8-11 ref 307
Job 1:9-11 ref 212
Job 16:9 ref 70
Job 22:22 ref 134
Job 35:12-13 quote 254
Job 36:10 ref 134
Job 42:12 ref 71
Job 42:6 ref 78
Joel 2:13 ref 78, 190, 238, 245
John 1:16-17 quote 160
John 1:18 quote 51
John 1:18 ref 50
John 1:2 ref 50
John 1:29 ref 228
John 1:3 ref 50, 132
John 10:10 ref 71
John 10:11 ref 72
John 10:16 quote 83, 153
John 10:16, 27 ref 22
John 10:18 ref 41
John 10:27 ref 102, 110
John 10:30 ref 47, 53
John 10:35 ref 223
John 11:48 quote 85
John 11:48 ref 84
John 12 ref 134
John 12:25 ref 42
John 12:32 quote 226
John 12:50 quote 19
John 13 ref 134
John 13:10 quote 244
John 13:12 ref 124
John 13:33 ref 71
John 13:5-15 ref 298
John 14 ref 134
John 14:15 ref 14
John 14:15, 21 ref 8
John 14:23-24 quote 250
John 14:26 quote 259
John 14:30 quote 282
John 14:6 quote 21
John 14:6 ref 72
John 14:7 quote 51
John 14:7 ref 47
John 14:9 ref 47, 51
John 14:9-10 quote 19
John 14-16 ref 71

John 15:10 ref 8, 134
John 15:1-16 ref 22
John 15:12 quote 15, 158, 178
John 15:12 ref 72, 156
John 15:13 ref 72
John 15:24 ref 51
John 15:25 ref 134
John 15:5 ref 50
John 15:8-11 quote 226
John 15:9-10 quote 250
John 16:13-15 quote 200
John 16:14 ref 225
John 17:11 ref 47
John 17:15 ref 286
John 17:17 ref 134
John 17:2 ref 53
John 17:24 quote 169
John 18:28 ref 64
John 18:37 ref 22
John 18:37-38 ref 134
John 2 ref 304
John 20:1, 19 ref 289
John 20:27-29 quote 181
John 20:28 ref 58
John 3 ref 67, 144
John 3:14 ref 226
John 3:16 ref 15, 77, 247
John 3:34 quote 199
John 4:23-24 quote 252
John 4:31-34 quote 19
John 4:34 ref 39
John 5 ref 185
John 5:37-38 quote 51
John 5:37-38 ref 51
John 5:39-47 quote 52
John 5:43 ref 58
John 5:46-47 quote 40
John 6:35 ref 19
John 6:46 ref 50, 51
John 6:50-58 ref 250
John 6:53-58 quote 18
John 6:53-58 ref 1
John 6:56 ref 22, 226
John 6:63 quote 18
John 6:66 ref 25
John 7:16-18 quote 283
John 7:18 ref 283
John 7:19 ref 217

John 7:22 ref	289
John 7:24 quote	279
John 7:24 ref	43, 233
John 8 ref	175
John 8:1-11 ref	183
John 8:28 ref	226
John 8:31 ref	22, 226
John 8:31-32	134
John 8:43 ref	225
John 8:43, 12:47 ref	18
John 8:47 quote	225
John 9:13-16 ref	289
John 9:1-7 ref	255
John 9:31 quote	254
Jonah 3:8, 9 ref	78
Joshua 13:22 ref	106
Joshua 24:15 ref	67
Joshua 5:12-14 ref	52
Joshua 7 ref	25
Joshua 7:1 ref	37
Joshua at 8:33-35 ref	92
Jude 19 ref	313
Jude 5 quote	53
Judges 11:29 ref	99
Judges 13 ref	51
Judges 13:25 ref	99
Judges 14:6, 19 ref	99
Judges 15:14 ref	99
Judges 2:19 ref	102
Judges 3:10 ref	99
Judges 6 ref	51
Judges 6:34 ref	99
Lamentations 3:37–39 quote	62
Leviticus 10 ref	25
Leviticus 10:10 ref	298
Leviticus 11 ref	12, 221, 278, 293
Leviticus 11:12 ref	278
Leviticus 11:47 ref	298
Leviticus 12 ref	297
Leviticus 14 ref	303
Leviticus 14:9 ref	124
Leviticus 15 ref	124, 297
Leviticus 15:3 ref	124
Leviticus 18 ref	227
Leviticus 18:19 ref	299
Leviticus 18:22 ref	193, 299
Leviticus 18:23 ref	299
Leviticus 18:24-28 quote	202
Leviticus 18:7 ref	123
Leviticus 18:7-18 ref	299
Leviticus 18:8 ref	189
Leviticus 19:13 ref	124
Leviticus 19:15-18 quote	277
Leviticus 19:15-18 ref	184
Leviticus 19:15-19 ref	185
Leviticus 19:18 quote	178
Leviticus 19:18 ref	157
Leviticus 19:34 quote	159
Leviticus 19:9-10 ref	294
Leviticus 20 ref	278
Leviticus 20:11 ref	123
Leviticus 20:18 ref	299
Leviticus 20:21 ref	278
Leviticus 20:22-23 quote	202
Leviticus 23 ref	12, 241, 288, 290
Leviticus 23:15-22 ref	291
Leviticus 23:2 ref	288
Leviticus 23:3 ref	288
Leviticus 24:10 ref	91
Leviticus 24:19 ref	184
Leviticus 24:22 quote	159
Leviticus 24:22 ref	179
Leviticus 25:25 ref	49
Leviticus 5:7	169
Leviticus 7 ref	168, 278
Leviticus 7:21 ref	192
Leviticus 7:26 ref	123
Leviticus. 3:17 ref	123
Luke 1:33 ref	129
Luke 1:4 quote	140
Luke 1:5-25 ref	170
Luke 1:71-79 quote	67
Luke 10 ref	162
Luke 10:22 ref	51, 58
Luke 10:25-28 ref	39
Luke 10:25-29 ref	183
Luke 11:16 ref	179
Luke 11:20 ref	97
Luke 11:29 ref	179
Luke 11:42 ref	39
Luke 12:10 quote	69
Luke 12:11 ref	259
Luke 12:41 ref	294
Luke 13:10-17 ref	289
Luke 13:28 ref	70
Luke 14:1-6 ref	289
Luke 14:26 ref	77
Luke 14:27-28 quote	44

Luke 16:10 quote	220
Luke 16:10 ref	41
Luke 16:13 quote	57
Luke 16:17 ref	223
Luke 16:31 ref	225
Luke 17:10 quote	64
Luke 17:33 ref	42
Luke 18 ref	162
Luke 18:18-22 ref	39
Luke 18:29-30 ref	42
Luke 19 ref	79
Luke 2:21 ref	296
Luke 22 ref	12
Luke 22:19 ref	151
Luke 22:20 ref	150
Luke 22:8, 15 ref	190
Luke 23:43 ref	303
Luke 23:45 ref	112
Luke 23:46 ref	58
Luke 24:1 ref	289
Luke 3:3 ref	298
Luke 3:8 ref	78
Luke 4:14-21 ref	171
Luke 4:18 ref	116
Luke 4:6 ref	53
Luke 4:8 quote	252
Luke 5:37 ref	110
Luke 6 ref	185
Luke 6, 13, 14 ref	185
Luke 6:37 quote	279
Luke 6:37 ref	279
Luke 6:37–38 quote	2
Luke 6:38 ref	16
Luke 6:43–45 quote	232
Luke 7 ref	64
Luke 7:31-35 quote	180
Luke 7:32 ref	180
Luke 8:21 ref.	18
Luke 9:24 ref	42
Luke 9:62 ref	42
Malachi 2:13-16 quote	182
Malachi 2:15 quote	241
Malachi 2:15-17 ref	40
Malachi 2:16 ref	178
Malachi 2:1-9 ref	134
Malachi 2:6 ref	134
Malachi 3:10 quote	269
Malachi 3:13-15 quote	216
Malachi 3:5	157
Malachi 3:5 ref	243
Malachi 3:6 ref	53
Malachi 4:4-6 quote	314
Mark 1:4 ref	298
Mark 10 ref	162
Mark 10:17-19 ref	39
Mark 10:2 ref	181
Mark 10:2-12 ref	189
Mark 12:15 ref	182
Mark 12:28-33 quote	157
Mark 13:11 ref	259
Mark 14:12 ref	190
Mark 15:38 ref	112
Mark 16:2, 9 ref	289
Mark 2 ref	185
Mark 2:22 ref	110
Mark 2:27 ref	289
Mark 3 ref	185
Mark 3:28-30 quote	69
Mark 4:24 ref	2, 16
Mark 6:1-11 ref	289
Mark 6:26 ref	78
Mark 7 ref	64, 185
Mark 7:18-19 ref	221
Mark 7:19 ref	221
Mark 7:26 ref	310
Mark 7:5-9 ref	101
Mark 7:8, 9, 13 ref	289
Mark 8:11 ref	179
Mark 8:18 ref	22
Mark 8:18 ref.	18
Mark 8:35 ref	42
Mark 9:33-48 ref	42
Mark 9:40 quote	25, 252
Mark 9:47-48 quote	66
Matthew 1:23 ref	160
Matthew 10:16 ref	106
Matthew 10:19-20 quote	259
Matthew 10:28 quote	61
Matthew 10:34 ref	42
Matthew 10:39 ref	42
Matthew 11:12 ref	217
Matthew 11:16 ref	180
Matthew 11:20, 21 ref	78
Matthew 11:25-30 ref	206
Matthew 11:29, 30 ref	185
Matthew 12 ref	185

Matthew 12:1 ref	289
Matthew 12:39 ref	179
Matthew 12:48-50 ref	89
Matthew 12:50 ref	58
Matthew 13 ref	20, 80, 98
Matthew 13:13 ref	225
Matthew 13:13 ref	18
Matthew 13:24-30 ref	112
Matthew 13:33 ref	206
Matthew 13:42 ref	70
Matthew 13:44 ref	162
Matthew 13:44–46 quote	39
Matthew 13:44-46 ref	42
Matthew 13:45-46 ref	162
Matthew 13:50 ref	70
Matthew 13:52 ref	127
Matthew 13:54	134
Matthew 15 ref	64, 185
Matthew 15:20 ref	222
Matthew 15:21-28 ref	309
Matthew 15:2-6 ref	101
Matthew 15:3, 6 ref	289
Matthew 15:7-9 ref	102
Matthew 15:9 ref	134
Matthew 16:1 ref	179
Matthew 16:13-20 ref	115
Matthew 16:18 quote	95
Matthew 16:18 ref	83
Matthew 16:19 ref	50
Matthew 16:25 ref	42
Matthew 16:4 ref	179
Matthew 17 ref	51
Matthew 17:7 ref	190
Matthew 18 ref	189, 233
Matthew 18:15-20 ref	40
Matthew 19:16, 17 ref	134
Matthew 19:3 ref	181
Matthew 19:9 ref	177
Matthew 21:13 ref	93
Matthew 22:13 ref	70
Matthew 22:15-22 ref	182
Matthew 22:19 ref	182
Matthew 22:34-40 ref	183
Matthew 22:36-40 ref	21
Matthew 22:41-46 quote	50
Matthew 23 ref	86, 107, 111
Matthew 23:13 quote	5
Matthew 23:1-3 quote	272
Matthew 23:13 ref	108, 112
Matthew 23:15 ref	116
Matthew 23:2 ref	112
Matthew 23:23 quote	275
Matthew 23:23 ref	39, 41
Matthew 23:25, 26 ref	21
Matthew 23:28 ref	307
Matthew 23:29-36 ref	109
Matthew 23:37-39 ref	47
Matthew 24:12 quote	15
Matthew 24:12 ref	33
Matthew 24:22 ref	90
Matthew 24:24 quote	115
Matthew 24:35 ref	134
Matthew 24:51 ref	70
Matthew 25:30 ref	70
Matthew 25:32-33 ref	68
Matthew 25:41 ref	66
Matthew 26:39 quote	41
Matthew 27:51 ref	112
Matthew 28:1 ref	289
Matthew 28:18 ref	53
Matthew 28:19, 20 ref	11
Matthew 28:19-20 quote	202
Matthew 28:19-20 ref	228
Matthew 28:20 ref	39, 134
Matthew 3:16-17 ref	51
Matthew 3:2 ref	78
Matthew 3:7-12 ref	98
Matthew 3:8 ref	78
Matthew 4:10 quote	267
Matthew 4:11 ref	268
Matthew 4:16 ref	220
Matthew 4:17 ref	78
Matthew 4:23 ref	89, 134
Matthew 4:4 quote	267
Matthew 4:4 ref	21, 39, 138
Matthew 4:7 quote	267
Matthew 4:9 ref	270
Matthew 5 ref	176
Matthew 5:17 ref	176
Matthew 5:17-19 ref	39
Matthew 5:18 ref	209, 273
Matthew 5:18-19 quote	273
Matthew 5:21-26 ref	177
Matthew 5:27-32 ref	178
Matthew 5:31-32 ref	177
Matthew 5:33-37 ref	178
Matthew 5:37 ref	300
Matthew 5:43-48 ref	178

Matthew 5:48 quote	206
Matthew 5:6 ref	19
Matthew 6 ref	176
Matthew 6:15 ref	77
Matthew 6:19-24 ref	294
Matthew 6:33 ref	19, 26
Matthew 6:7 ref	232, 253
Matthew 6:9 ref	58
Matthew 7 ref	176
Matthew 7:12 quote	178
Matthew 7:15 ref	106
Matthew 7:15-23 ref	116
Matthew 7:2 ref	2, 16
Matthew 7:21, 22 ref	20
Matthew 7:22-24 quote	181
Matthew 7:24-29 ref	71
Matthew 7:28, 29 ref	134
Matthew 7:3-5 ref	279
Matthew 8 ref	64
Matthew 8:12 ref	70
Matthew 9:14 -17 ref	110
Matthew 9:35 ref	134
Matthew. 7:13–14 quote	284
Micah 3:8 ref	99
Micah 6:8 quote	233
Micah 6:8 ref	157
Micah 7:18-19 quote	96
Nehemiah 10:31 ref	288
Nehemiah 13:15-22 ref	288
Nehemiah 9 ref	102
Nehemiah 9:16-29 ref	102
Numbers 11:17 ref	277
Numbers 11:17, 25, 26, 29 ref	99
Numbers 14 ref	25, 281
Numbers 14:18 ref	55
Numbers 15:15-16 quote	159
Numbers 15:15-16, 29 ref	179
Numbers 15:32-36 ref	281
Numbers 15:37-38 ref	293
Numbers 16 ref	25, 97, 281
Numbers 16:30 ref	215
Numbers 19 ref	298
Numbers 21 ref	128
Numbers 22 ref	51, 128, 259
Numbers 22-24 ref	106
Numbers 24:2 ref	99
Numbers 25:1-3 ref	92
Numbers 27:18 ref	99
Numbers 29:12-35 ref	169
Numbers 3:12, 13, 16-18 ref	124
Numbers 30 ref	300
Numbers 32:11-12 ref	91
Numbers 35 ref	123
Numbers 35:30 ref	184
Numbers 35:33 ref	123
Numbers 6:2-3 quote	305
Numbers 8:4 ref	165
Numbers 8:7 ref	124
Obadiah 12-14 ref	101
Obadiah 21 ref	58
Philemon 18 ref	79
Philippians 1:15-18 quote	112
Philippians 2:12 ref	23, 71
Philippians 2:12-13 quote	214
Philippians 2:2 ref	118
Philippians 3 ref	190
Philippians 3:19 ref	57
Philippians 3:5 ref	190
Philippians 3:5-6 quote	205
Philippians 3:5-6 ref	205
Philippians 4:13 quote	78, 206
Philippians 4:8 ref	308
Proverbs 1:2,3,7,8 ref	134
Proverbs 1:8 ref	134
Proverbs 15:29 quote	254
Proverbs 16:6 quote	168
Proverbs 23:23 ref	134
Proverbs 28:4 quote	110
Proverbs 29:18 quote	249
Proverbs 3:1 ref	134
Proverbs 3:11-12 quote	306
Proverbs 30:5-6 quote	264
Proverbs 4:1,2 ref	134
Proverbs 4:2 ref	134
Proverbs 5:12 ref	134
Proverbs 6:20-23	134
Proverbs 6:23 ref	134
Proverbs 7:2 ref	134
Proverbs 8:10 ref	134
Proverbs 8:32-36 ref	134
Psalm 105:8 ref	129
Psalm 111:10 quote	249
Psalm 112:10 ref	70
Psalm 119 ref	243
Psalm 119:105 ref	134
Psalm 119:130 quote	259

Psalm 119:41 ref	41
Psalm 119:43, 44, 142, 160 ref	134
Psalm 122 ref	100
Psalm 13:5 ref	41
Psalm 138:2 ref	134
Psalm 14:1-3 ref	177
Psalm 15 ref	157
Psalm 18:25-27 ref	134
Psalm 2:9 ref	61
Psalm 23 ref	243
Psalm 23:4 ref	61, 306
Psalm 24:3-4, 101 ref	157
Psalm 26:4 AV ref	111
Psalm 26:4 ref	111
Psalm 31:16 ref	41
Psalm 32:8-9 quote	16
Psalm 33:11 quote	120
Psalm 33:4 ref	134
Psalm 34:16 quote	65
Psalm 34:7 ref	51
Psalm 35:16 ref	70
Psalm 37:12 ref	70
Psalm 40:10 ref	41
Psalm 45:6	129
Psalm 48:10 ref	50
Psalm 52:8 ref	90
Psalm 53:1-3 ref	177
Psalm 73:1 quote	90
Psalm 78:1 ref	134
Psalm 78:8 ref	102
Psalm 85:7 ref	41
Psalm 95:7-11 ref	70
Revelation 1:4 ref	47
Revelation 1:6 ref	91, 118, 170
Revelation 10:9 ref	18
Revelation 11:19 ref	165
Revelation 12:10 ref	209
Revelation 12:11 ref	147
Revelation 13:16-17 ref	239
Revelation 14:15-18 ref	165
Revelation 14:9, 11 ref	239
Revelation 15:5-8 ref	165
Revelation 16:9, 11 ref	70
Revelation 18:2 ref	298
Revelation 19:14-16, 21 ref	61
Revelation 19:15 ref	97
Revelation 19:17 ref	90
Revelation 2 ref	109
Revelation 2:14 ref	60, 106, 109
Revelation 2:14-16 quote	106
Revelation 2:20 ref	60, 109
Revelation 2:22-23 ref	255
Revelation 2:24 ref	109
Revelation 2:25 ref	109
Revelation 2:6, 15 ref	109
Revelation 2:9 ref	109
Revelation 21:23 ref	50, 134
Revelation 21:5 ref	133
Revelation 21:8 quote	66
Revelation 21:8 ref	97
Revelation 22:15 ref	97
Revelation 22:18, 19 ref	203
Revelation 22:18-19 quote	264
Revelation 22:5 ref	134
Revelation 3 ref	109
Revelation 3:1 ref	31, 47
Revelation 3:1–3 quote	36
Revelation 3:14-22 ref	31
Revelation 3:15-16 quote	59
Revelation 3:19 ref	43
Revelation 3:20 ref	22
Revelation 3:3 ref	109
Revelation 3:4 ref	109
Revelation 3:9 ref	86, 109
Revelation 4:5 ref	47
Revelation 5:10 ref	91, 118, 170
Revelation 6:15-17 ref	61
Revelation 6:9-11 ref	87
Revelation 7:15 ref	165
Revelation 9:20-21 quote	70
Romans 1 ref	299
Romans 1:1-4 quote	130
Romans 1:17 ref	206
Romans 1:18-20 quote	122
Romans 1:18-21 quote	237
Romans 10 ref	13
Romans 10:1-11 ref	206
Romans 10:12 ref	71
Romans 10:16 ref	162
Romans 10:4 quote	234
Romans 10:4 ref	239
Romans 11 ref	90
Romans 11:16 ref	104
Romans 11:17-18 quote	98
Romans 11:2-5 quote	96
Romans 11:5 ref	90
Romans 11:7 ref	90
Romans 12:1-2 quote	231

Romans 12:1-2 ref	252
Romans 12:5 ref	90
Romans 12:7 ref	134
Romans 13:1-2 ref	182
Romans 13:8-14 ref	255
Romans 14 ref	196
Romans 14:1 quote	191
Romans 14:10 ref	112
Romans 14:11 ref	20
Romans 14:12 ref	164
Romans 15:12 ref	104
Romans 15:4 quote	314
Romans 15:4 ref	134
Romans 2 ref	190
Romans 2:12-15 ref	121
Romans 2:12-16 quote	193
Romans 2:14-16 ref	17
Romans 2:23-29 quote	191
Romans 2:28-29 quote	102
Romans 2:29 ref	190, 238, 245
Romans 2:4 ref	76, 150
Romans 2:6-8 ref	14
Romans 3 ref	211
Romans 3:10-18 ref	177
Romans 3:19-20 quote	213
Romans 3:20 ref	206
Romans 3:28 quote	213
Romans 4 ref	190
Romans 4:12, 16 ref	72
Romans 4:15 quote	125
Romans 4:16 quote	130
Romans 4:16 ref	136
Romans 4:4 ref	212
Romans 5:13 quote	125
Romans 5:20 ref	13
Romans 5:8 ref	72, 75
Romans 6:10 ref	172
Romans 6:1-2 quote	216
Romans 6:14 ref	213
Romans 6:14, 15 ref	23
Romans 6:15-18 quote	224
Romans 6:16 quote	164
Romans 6:17-18 quote	252
Romans 6:19 quote	77
Romans 6:19 ref	240
Romans 6:5-7 quote	224
Romans 6:6 ref	264
Romans 7 ref	13
Romans 7:12 quote	211
Romans 7:12 ref	213
Romans 7:14 quote	211
Romans 7:14 ref	106, 135, 208, 213
Romans 7:4-6 ref	21
Romans 8:15-17 quote	67
Romans 8:19-22 ref	50
Romans 8:2 ref	106
Romans 8:28 quote	216
Romans 8:28 ref	307
Romans 8:29-30 ref	163
Romans 8:33-34 quote	170
Romans 8:34 ref	50
Romans 8:6-8 quote	149
Romans 9 ref	128
Romans 9:17 ref	96
Romans 9:23-24 quote	94
Romans 9:25-29 quote	96
Romans 9:27 ref	90
Romans 9:28, 31, 32 ref	134
Romans 9:4-5 quote	101
Romans 9:6-8 quote	90
Romans 9:9 ref	38
Romans 9-11 ref	9, 97, 153
Titus 1:15-16 quote	299
Titus 2:11–14 ref	23
Titus 2:11-15 quote	69, 314
Titus 2:13 ref	50
Zechariah 14:16-19 ref	173, 292
Zechariah 2:7-8 ref	153
Zechariah 2:8 quote	100
Zechariah 6:11-15 ref	172
Zechariah 7:12 ref	99, 134
Zechariah 7:8-13 ref	157
Zechariah 7:8-14 ref	102
Zephaniah 2:3 quote	249
Zephaniah 3:1-7 ref	134
Zephaniah 3:17; ref	41
Zephaniah 3:4 ref	42

www.ingramcontent.com/pod-product-compliance
Lightning Source LLC
Chambersburg PA
CBHW071153300426
44113CB00009B/1189